When You're Expecting Twins, Triplets, or Quads

HarperResource

An Imprint of HarperCollins*Publishers*

When You're Expecting Twins, Triplets, or Quads

PROVEN GUIDELINES FOR A HEALTHY MULTIPLE PREGNANCY

Revised Edition

Barbara Luke, Sc.D., M.P.H., R.D.,
and Tamara Eberlein

First edition published by QuillResource as *When You're Expecting Twins, Triplets, or Quads: A Complete Resource* in 1999

WHEN YOU'RE EXPECTING TWINS, TRIPLETS, OR QUADS, REVISED EDITION. Copyright © 1999, 2004 by Dr. Barbara Luke and Tamara Eberlein. All rights reserved. Printed in the United States of America. No part of this book may be used or reproduced in any manner whatsoever without written permission except in the case of brief quotations embodied in critical articles and reviews. For information, address HarperCollins Publishers Inc., 10 East 53rd Street, New York, NY 10022.

HarperCollins books may be purchased for educational, business, or sales promotional use. For information, please write: Special Markets Department, HarperCollins Publishers Inc., 10 East 53rd Street, New York, NY 10022.

Designed by Jennifer Ann Daddio

Printed on acid-free paper

Library of Congress Cataloging-in-Publication Data

Luke, Barbara.
    When you're expecting twins, triplets, or quads: proven guidelines for a healthy multiple pregnancy / Barbara Luke and Tamara Eberlein.—revised ed.
        p.   cm.
    Includes bibliographical references and index.
    ISBN 0-06-054268-3 (alk. paper)
    1. Multiple pregnancy.   2. Multiple birth.   3. Twins.   4. Triplets.
5. Quadruplets.   6. Child development.   I. Eberlein, Tamara.
II. Title.

RG567.L84   2004
618.2'5—dc21   2003047168

05 06 07 08 WBC/RRD 10 9 8 7 6 5 4

To the next generation of children in our family—
my son, Peter Martin Wissel,
my sister's children,
Nathaniel Lane Pearson and Alisa Christine Pearson,
and my brother's children,
Megan Rand Luke and Julia Ann Luke
—BARBARA LUKE

For my twins,
James and Samantha Garvey,
and my singleton, Jack
—TAMARA EBERLEIN

Contents

Acknowledgments

We would like to thank the following individuals for their help in the development of this book.

At the University of Michigan Health Systems: Suzanne Wanty, M.S.N., R.N., Family Nurse Practitioner, for her dedication, expertise, and creativity in helping to establish the Multiples Clinic at the University of Michigan. Clark Nugent, M.D., for his careful reading of and thoughtful comments on the entire manuscript, and for his support in making the Multiples Clinic a success. Elaine Anderson, P.T., M.P.H., physical therapist and research associate at the University of Michigan, the developmental specialist who evaluated all of our twins and triplets in our follow-up study, and who developed the exercises recommended in this book. Mary Ann Zettelmeier, M.S.N., M.S., R.N., Clinical Nurse Specialist in Perinatal Nursing, for her review of and suggestions on the labor and delivery section of this book. Eileen J. Wright, M.S.N., R.N., Clinical Nurse Specialist in Neonatal Nursing, for her help on the section about the neonatal intensive care unit. Timothy R. B. Johnson, M.D., chairman of the Department of Obstetrics and Gynecology, for his support. The obstetricians and midwives who have referred patients to the Multiples Clinic. And all the families who invited us into their lives by participating in the Multiples Clinic and follow-up.

At the University Consortium on Multiple Births: Frank R. Witter, M.D., at the Department of Gynecology and Obstetrics at Johns Hopkins University in Baltimore, Maryland; Roger B. Newman, M.D., at the Department of Obstetrics and Gynecology at the Medical University of South Carolina in Charleston; and Mary Jo O'Sullivan, M.D., at the Department of Obstetrics and Gynecology, Jackson Memorial Hospital, University of Miami, Florida, for their commitment to improving the outcomes of multiple-gestation pregnancies. Many of the recommendations in this book are based upon our collaborative research.

At the Rush–Presbyterian–St. Luke's Medical Center: Hal Bigger, M.D., for his review of and advice regarding the neonatal and newborn sections of this book, and for his help in obtaining newborn footprints; and the nursing staff in the neonatal intensive care unit for their assistance with the footprints.

At the Phoenix Perinatal Associates: John Elliott, M.D., for his review of the section on the obstetrical care of women pregnant with triplets and quadruplets.

We also gratefully acknowledge the invaluable contributions of the many parents of multiples who freely shared their experiences and expertise in the course of lengthy interviews. Our thanks in particular go to Helen Armer, Marcy Bugajski, Karen Danke, Kelly Kassab, Judy Levy, Lisa McDonough, Amy Maly, Ruth Markowitz, Stacy Moore, Heather Nicholas, Anne Seifert, Ginny Seyler, and Elin Wackernagel-Slotten. We also appreciate the many readers who wrote to us, either by letter or via their reviews on www.amazon.com, to share their experiences.

A special thank-you goes to Tanya Leonello for her beautiful illustrations.

Introduction

BARBARA LUKE, SC.D., M.P.H., R.D.

What Is the University Consortium on Multiple Births?

Back in 1988, I began graduate studies toward my doctorate degree at Johns Hopkins University School of Hygiene and Public Health in Baltimore, Maryland. Years before, I had conducted a pilot study examining the relationship between maternal weight gain and twin birthweight—evaluating the effect of weight gained by specific weeks' gestation on twin birthweight. For my dissertation, I reviewed the medical records of all twin births at Johns Hopkins Hospital between 1979 and 1989, and found a strong relationship between twin birthweights and (1) how much a woman weighed before she became pregnant, and (2) how much weight she gained by 24 weeks' gestation, and overall. I also examined many other factors that influence this relationship: whether or not the woman smoked during her pregnancy; whether she became anemic; her height; her race and ethnic background; whether she had been pregnant before, and the outcomes of those prior pregnancies.

After earning my doctorate from Johns Hopkins University in 1991, I continued to do research on improving outcomes in twin pregnancies. I also expanded my interest to include triplets and quadruplets.

When I moved to the University of Michigan at Ann Arbor in 1995, I continued to work with obstetricians at Johns Hopkins, as well as those at the University of Miami and the Medical University of South Carolina. Although the number of multiple pregnancies has increased greatly over the past 20 years, no single center has enough data to conduct research alone—so we pool our data. This alliance is known as the University Consortium on Multiple Births.

In recent years, other centers have joined us, including the University of Texas Medical Branch at Galveston, the University of Pennsylvania, the University of Kansas, Columbia University, and Mount Sinai School of Medicine. Every year we present our research on multiple pregnancies at the Society for Maternal-Fetal Medicine, the scientific society of high-risk obstetricians.

For six years, I ran a clinic for women pregnant with multiples at the University of Michigan. The goal: to improve outcomes for women pregnant with multiples by providing special prenatal care, patient education, risk screening, and intensive nutrition therapy. This is the clinic we refer to as the Multiples Clinic throughout the book, and many of the mothers quoted have participated in this program. In 2002, I moved to the University of Miami in Florida, where I continue to conduct research on improving outcomes in multiple pregnancy, as well as teach.

The advice in this book is designed to allow readers to reap the same rewards—including easier pregnancies and healthier babies—as Multiples Clinics' patients do.

Chapter 1

Your Unique Pregnancy

TAMARA: As I lay flat on the examining table, the radiology technician smeared my belly with greasy jelly, then turned the screen toward me. I was about to catch my first glimpse of the baby that had been growing inside me for 18 weeks.

But as she slid the probe across my abdomen, she began to frown. Pushing the screen to one side to block my view, she fiddled with the knobs. Then she stepped into the hall to summon a doctor. Together, they manipulated the dials of the ultrasound machine, whispering and pointing.

Trying to squelch a sudden rush of fear, I choked out the words: "What is it? Is something wrong with my baby?"

The doctor turned the screen to face me again and said, "Well, here's what we've got. This is a leg, and an arm, and this is the head. And now, over here, we see a foot, and a back, and *another* head—twins! And they look just fine."

If you too have joined the ranks of expectant mothers of multiples—twins, triplets, even quadruplets or more—congratulations! You're now in a special group whose membership is swelling more and more each year. Between 1975 and 2000, twin births rose by 100 percent. During that same period, the birthrate of "supertwins" or "higher-order multiples" (meaning three or more babies born together) surged a whopping 587 percent.

You've probably got a thousand questions and concerns about your pregnancy, but chances are, you've had trouble finding the answers you need. "As soon as I found out that I was going to have twins, I read everything I could find on the subject. Yet most pregnancy books have only a page or two about multiples, and the books devoted to twins focus on taking care of the babies after they're born," says Judy Levy, mother of twin girls and an older daughter.

Or perhaps you succeeded in finding some material on multiple pregnancy but were put off by its gloom-and-doom tone. "Everything I read about having twins seemed so frightening, as if the writers were saying, 'You will definitely have all sorts of problems—and your babies will too.' I couldn't bear to read that scary stuff," says Stacy Moore, mother of twin boys. "What I really needed was some sensible advice on the specific steps I could take to avoid complications and give my babies the best possible start in life. And I found it—at a special clinic for expectant mothers of multiples, where I learned that many problems associated with multiple births are preventable. I did everything they told me to do, and my whole pregnancy went very smoothly. My twins were born big and healthy at full term, weighing 6 lb., 11 oz., and 6 lb., 1 oz."

DR. LUKE: Here's where I come in. As a professor of obstetrics and gynecology at the University of Michigan Medical School in Ann Arbor, and a researcher and nutritionist, I founded the clinic that Stacy Moore attended, and directed it for six years. This is the Multiples Clinic we refer to throughout the book, and many of the mothers quoted participated in this program.

I'm now a professor at the University of Miami School of Medicine in Miami, Florida, where I'm working with experts from renowned universities across the country, as the University Consortium on Multiple Births.

Our goal is to improve pregnancy outcomes—in other words, to help our patients have the healthiest pregnancies and the healthiest babies. To achieve that, we provide special prenatal care, including patient education, risk screening, and intensive nutrition therapy.

The Multiples Clinic program works. Our clinical success proves it. Compared to the average mother of multiples, women who follow our guidelines experience significantly fewer complications before the birth of their children. For instance:

- Our expectant mothers develop fewer infections.
- They have less trouble with high blood pressure and preeclampsia.
- The moms in our program have a lower incidence of preterm premature rupture of the membranes.
- Our patients are hospitalized for preterm labor less frequently, and they spend fewer days in the hospital if they are admitted.

For infants born to our moms, the results are even more impressive:

- Triplets born to mothers in our program *weigh 35 percent more at birth*, on average, than triplets typically do. That's very significant, given that the average birthweight for triplets nationwide is just half that of the average singleton.
- Our twins are generally born *20 percent heavier* than the average twins delivered at the same gestational age.
- Two out of three of our newborns weigh more than 5½ pounds at birth, and one out of four is born weighing more than 6 pounds. These birthweight figures, which are significantly better than the average for infants of multiple-gestation pregnancies, prove that you can break the "rule" that says twins are always born small.
- Sixty percent of our mothers of twins *deliver at 36 weeks or later,* compared to only about 40 percent of twin moms nationwide.
- Our babies are *healthier at birth*, regardless of when they are born, because they have grown well right from the start of the pregnancy.
- Infants born to patients in our program *go home sooner* than the average multiple-birth baby, spending only half as much time in the hospital. (Their hospital bills are only half the average too!)

What's more, the benefits are long-term. Follow-up studies of children born to mothers in our program reveal that, at age three, our children have significant advantages:

- Children from our program are less likely to have delays in mental development.
- Delays in motor development are also less common than in nonprogram children.
- Our youngsters grow better.
- Hospitalizations are not as frequent among program children.

To describe the University Consortium on Multiple Births' clinical program in complete detail, I've teamed up with Tamara Eberlein, a professional writer and mother of twins. Our first edition of *When You're Expecting Twins, Triplets, or Quads*, published in 1999, garnered accolades from readers and health care professionals alike (and an Outstanding Book of the Year Award from the American Society of Journalists and Authors!). In this revised edition, we provide additional advice based on the very latest scientific studies; expanded coverage on a variety of topics, from nutrition to new medical treatments; and an all-new, all-original recipe section.

The guidelines in this book are not based on opinion or speculation, but rather on years of research involving thousands of twin, triplet, and quadruplet pregnancies. Follow our advice, and you and your babies should reap the same rewards our clinic patients do.

The Information You Need

"I'd had a typical, routine pregnancy with my first child a year and a half earlier," says Judy Levy. "So when I learned I was carrying twins, I figured it would be just like a regular pregnancy, only more so. But it turned out to be more challenging than just 'more so.'"

Why shouldn't a woman who's expecting twins or supertwins just follow the same standard advice given to a woman pregnant with one baby (a singleton)? Because when you're carrying multiples, your pregnancy requirements go beyond what is standard.

You have specific medical requirements that must be considered in choosing health care providers. You have special nutritional needs. You have distinct concerns about physical exertion and workday demands. You face a higher risk of medical complications, and your babies face a higher risk of prematurity and other health problems. Psychologically, your pregnancy presents extraordinary joys as well as extraordinary challenges. Circumstances surrounding your labor, delivery, and recovery may be more complex. And your babies' experiences after birth may be markedly different from those of most singletons.

In fact, information geared toward the average pregnant woman could, for you, be insufficient or misleading—or even harmful. That's because your pregnancy is unique. It's more exciting and more rewarding in the end (when your arms are very full of your bundles of joy), but it is also more demanding.

This note of caution must be sounded not only when triplets or quadruplets are on the way, but also in the case of twins. "With all the supertwins being born now, our society has become blasé about twins," explains Amy Maly, mother of identical twin girls. "We've been programmed to think that it's no big deal to be expecting 'just two.' But as someone who's been there, I can attest to the fact that a twin pregnancy can be tricky. It pays to be careful."

TAMARA: I want to tell you my story, not to scare you with what can go wrong, but to motivate you to do everything in your power to ensure that your pregnancy goes well. And you do have a lot of power! You'll be making dozens of decisions daily that can affect your unborn babies. Armed with the appropriate information, you will make wise choices.

I did not.

When I learned I was expecting twins, I was elated—but also unnerved. What did I know about having twins? So I bought every book I could find on the subject and read with interest the many volumes devoted to the intricacies of taking care of twins: what to name them, how to feed them, whether to dress them in matching outfits.

Yet I was disappointed to find little in-depth information on the pregnancy itself. The material that did cover gestation seemed to say that a can-do mind-set was the key to having healthy multiples. Readers were urged to "make a double effort to stay in shape," to regard with skepticism the "inflated reports" of complications in multiple pregnancies, and to be wary of obstetricians who might impose "unnecessary restrictions" on activities.

Thus persuaded that a happy outcome was practically a given, I felt pleased by my own doctor's upbeat, unbossy, laissez-faire attitude. There were no special nutritional recommendations, even after I lost 16 pounds in my second trimester during a two-week bout of food poisoning. There was no insistence that I cut back at the office, despite my 11-hour workdays. There were no detailed instructions on how to recognize the warning signs of trouble early enough to avert disaster—and so I assumed there would *be* no disaster.

I was wrong. Nine weeks before my due date, my water broke and my twins were born. My 3-pound son was too weak to suck or cry; his 2-pound sister couldn't even breathe. What followed was a nightmarish blur of respirators and incubators, brain hemorrhages and faltering heartbeats, fear and guilt and regret.

Too late, I wondered if the advice I'd read had been misguided. Too late, I searched the medical literature for information on preventing problems in multiple pregnancies. Too late, I asked my doctor to clarify his description of the warning signs of preterm labor, and I realized I'd had those vague symptoms for weeks.

Thank goodness, my babies beat the odds. A month after their birth, with all their medical woes behind them and their weight at 4½ pounds, my twins came home. To see them today—perfectly healthy, normal, school-age kids—no one would guess what a rough start they had. But I will never forget.

So when Dr. Luke invited me to co-author this book, I jumped at the chance. I wanted to write the book I wish I'd been able to read when I was pregnant—a book that could help other mothers-to-be of multiples give their babies a better beginning than my own twins had.

DR. LUKE: For more than 30 years, I've counseled thousands of pregnant women and have helped generations of children to begin their lives healthy and strong.

In this book, you'll get the benefit of these years of experience, with sensible guidelines geared specifically toward expectant mothers of twins and supertwins. You'll learn about the common risks and how to avoid them. You'll understand the need to educate not only yourself but also your partner, your boss, your friends, maybe even your doctor. You'll get the information and support needed to guide you through this extra-special experience of being pregnant with multiples.

You'll also meet some of the mothers from our clinical program, as well as other mothers of multiples from around the country, including readers of the first edition of *When You're Expecting Twins, Triplets, or Quads* who wrote to us about their experiences. You'll hear from women who sailed through their multiple pregnancy with a minimum of discomfort or inconvenience, and women who had to sacrifice much for the sake of their babies. Women who began their pregnancy with a good understanding of nutrition, and women who renounced lifelong poor food habits so that their unborn babies might thrive. Women who conceived multiples the first time they tried to get pregnant, and women who endured years of infertility treatments before finally conceiving. Women who were warned against even trying to go forward with a multiple pregnancy, yet succeeded in giving birth to robust twins, triplets, or quads.

Their successes can help you as well, even if you never visit our clinic. As Judy Levy said to me shortly after her twins were born (Micah Marie weighed an impressive 7 lb. and Kayla a sturdy 6 lb., 4 oz.), "The appointments at the Multiples Clinic gave me a lot of vital information and welcome emotional support. Most of what I learned, though, a woman could also learn from a book—if such a book existed."

Now such a book does exist—and it's better than ever. We've already helped tens of thousands of babies to be born bigger and healthier, as one reader attests: "I believe that following the advice in this book enabled me to carry my twins to 40 weeks, and to give birth to a 7 lb., 7 oz., boy and a 7 lb., 1 oz., girl—almost 15 pounds of baby! This book gave me the knowledge and information I did not get anywhere else, including the doctor's office."

With this revised edition, you'll benefit from more than 100 new pages of information, advice, and how-to tips, targeted specifically toward women like you. I also invite you to visit my Web site, www.drbarbaraluke.com, for personalized nutrition counseling, either as a one-time evaluation or throughout your pregnancy.

Conception: A Miracle Multiplied

"I had always been fascinated with the science of conception. It seemed like an utter miracle. Once I learned that I was carrying twins, I imagined over and over the amazing moment when *two lives* began inside of me. Just thinking about it filled me with wonder, with love, and with a fierce determination to protect these babies who were coming into being," says Lydia Greenwood, mother of boy/girl twins.

Like Lydia, you can put to good purpose your awe at the miracle of a multiple conception. The more clearly you understand the biological changes occurring inside you, the easier it will be to dedicate the next months to nurturing your unborn babies. Start by reviewing the basics of how babies are conceived.

Every month during a woman's childbearing years (from menarche to menopause), her ovaries release a mature egg. This process is called ovulation. The egg travels down the fallopian tubes, where fertilization (also known as conception) occurs if the egg unites with the father's sperm. During fertilization, the genetic material, or chromosomes, from both mother and father combine. Then the fertilized egg begins to divide. Within a week after fertilization, this dividing egg, which is now called a zygote, embeds itself in the lining of the uterus.

The dividing egg, bathed in fluid, begins to separate into outer and inner layers. The outer layer grows to form the major portion of the placenta, the vascular organ that will provide nutrients to the new life. The inner layer becomes the embryo, which develops into the baby itself. By the second week of life, the embryo is firmly implanted in the endometrium (lining of the uterus) and is surrounded by tissues rich in carbohydrates.

The conception and development of multiples is similar to that of a singleton baby, but with a few essential differences. Of primary importance is twin type—in other words, whether the multiples are identical or fraternal.

THE BIG QUESTION: IDENTICAL OR FRATERNAL?

"It amazes me how often people ask if my boy/girl twins are identical," says Lydia Greenwood. "True, they share the same height, weight, blond hair, and blue-green eyes. But isn't it obvious that they differ dramatically in their, uh, plumbing?"

Many people are unaware of the differences in twin types. Yet knowing your children's twin type can help you better understand their developmental differences. And in the event that one child suffers from a disease with a strong genetic link, twin type helps you assess the risk to the other multiples—because fraternals are far less likely than identicals to share the same disease. Not to mention that you, your children, and every curious passerby will want to know the answer to the question "Are they identical or fraternal?"

Identical twins begin the same way as a singleton, with one egg and one sperm. But the zygote divides an extra time, producing two separate and identical zygotes. If one zygote then divides yet again, identical triplets will form. An additional division will result in identical quadruplets (though these are exceedingly rare). Identical twins or supertwins are also called monozygotic (MZ), indicating that they developed from a single zygote.

The timing of this additional division determines the structure of the fetal membranes—the inner membrane, or amnion; the outer membrane, or chorion; and the placenta:

- When the split happens within three days of conception, while the original zygote is still traveling down the fallopian tube, these identical twins will have two separate placentas, two chorions, and two amnions. This is a diamniotic, dichorionic twin pregnancy.
- When the extra division of the zygote occurs four to seven days after conception, the twins will have separate amnions but will share one chorion, and their placentas will be fused. This is termed a diamniotic, monochorionic twin pregnancy.
- If the split occurs after the eighth day following conception, the identical twins will share the same placenta, chorion, and amnion. This is described as a monoamniotic, monochorionic twin pregnancy.
- For identical triplets, the structure of the fetal membranes varies. Sometimes all three have separate amnions, chorions, and placentas, referred to as triamniotic and trichorionic. In other cases, two babies share membranes, while the third has separate membranes. Very rarely, all three share the same placenta, chorion, and amnion.

Approximately one-third of all twin pairs are identical. Because identical twins share 100 percent of their genes, they are always of the same sex and have the same basic physical features, such as hair color and eye color. Some pairs are mirror-image—one is right-handed, the other left-handed; their hair whorls are reversed; they may have matching birthmarks on opposite sides of their bodies. Though identicals can vary significantly in size at birth if one twin received a disproportionate share of nourishment *in utero* (while growing inside the uterus), adult height usually differs by less than two inches. Identicals typically have very similar IQs and often share many personality characteristics.

Fraternal twins result when the mother produces two eggs instead of one in the normal monthly cycle, and the eggs are fertilized by separate sperm. Fraternal triplets form from three eggs and three separate sperm; fraternal quads form from four eggs and four sperm. These fertilized eggs travel independently through the fallopian tubes and each embeds in the lining of the uterus. Fraternal twins always have separate placentas, chorions, and amnions, although if they embed close to each other, their placentas may fuse. Fraternal twins are called dizygotic (DZ), meaning that they developed from two separate zygotes.

About two-thirds of all twins are fraternal. Half of these pairs are boy/girl, one-fourth are girl/girl, and one-fourth are boy/boy. Sharing, on average, 50 percent of their genes, fraternal twins are no more alike genetically than are nontwin siblings. That's why fraternal twins should not be expected to have the same appearance, personality, intelligence level, or rate of growth and development, any more than singleton brothers and sisters would.

Unfortunately, there are no official national data on twin type among higher-order multiples. One survey of families with triplets, however, suggests that only about 6 percent of triplet sets are identical. The majority are composed either of three fraternal siblings or of an identical pair plus one fraternal sibling.

Even before your babies are born, you may be eager to know their twin type. For some parents, the answer is available early on. Prenatal tests such as chorionic villus sampling and amniocentesis can determine twin type by the second trimester. Usually, ultrasound early in pregnancy provides the answer. For instance, if the ultrasound screen reveals that only one chorion is shared by both babies, the twins are identical. And in the case of boy/girl twins, gender is indisputable evidence that the babies are fraternal.

TAMARA: Before each ultrasound, my husband and I reminded the radiologist not to tell us the babies' sexes. We didn't want to miss that thrilling moment at the delivery when the doctor would say, "This one is a girl!" or, "This one is a boy!"

But one time he slipped and told us our twins were definitely fraternal. When I asked how he knew, he hemmed and hawed, then gave some vague answer about seeing two placentas. I said, "But isn't it possible for identical twins to have two separate placentas if the

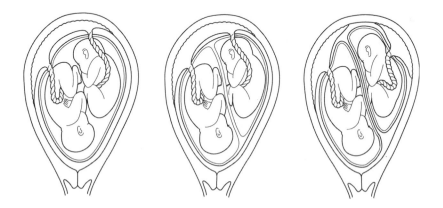

Left: *Monoamniotic, monochorionic twin pregnancy.* Center: *Monochorionic, diamniotic twin pregnancy.* Right: *Diamniotic, dichorionic twin pregnancy.*

zygote splits soon after conception?" He gave me a guilty look and then said, "Well, I'm pretty sure they are fraternal." Later I realized that the only way he could be certain was if the twins were a boy and a girl. Of course, that's what they turned out to be.

In other cases, parents may have to wait for the babies to be born in order to learn their twin type, even if they would prefer to know ahead of time. "We were curious to know if the twins were fraternal or identical, but it was a hard question to answer during the pregnancy. On the ultrasounds, no one could quite tell if the girls had two separate placental sacs or just one," explains Amy Maly. "We finally got our answer at delivery, when the doctor examined the placenta and determined that there was just a single sac—meaning our girls are identical."

Even after the birth, the question of twin type may remain unanswered if the doctor does not carefully examine the placenta. In that case, time may tell. Two bald baby boys with bluish eyes may leave you wondering about twin type—but only until one sprouts a crop of dark curls and his eyes deepen to brown, while his twin's hair grows in straight and blond and his eyes stay light.

In some situations, though, even time does not reveal the answer. Some fraternals bear such a strong family resemblance that they're mistaken for identicals; some identicals differ enough in size or behavioral style that they're assumed to be fraternal. "When my twin girls were born, the placenta somehow got 'lost' on the way to the lab where it was supposed to be analyzed," says Elin Wackernagel-Slotten. "We figured we would get our answer once the girls grew past the infancy stage, but it hasn't worked out that way. They have the same hair color, eye color, height, even the same birthmark on their necks. But their faces are different enough that most people can tell them apart after about 10 minutes. We think they're identical, but we're not completely sure—even though the girls are teenagers now."

If the passage of time leaves you wondering still, consider getting a definitive answer to the twin-type question by asking your pediatrician to order a comparative examination of your twins' blood types. Two dozen red blood cell characteristics are examined. If differences are detected, the twins are fraternal; if all blood groups match, the twins are almost certainly identical. This test can cost several hundred dollars.

A less expensive and newer alternative is a genetic test available via mail order from Affiliated Genetics, Inc. It includes tiny nylon brushes used to collect samples of cells from the inside of each child's cheek. You mail the samples to a lab, where technicians compare specific sites in the cells' DNA that are known to vary greatly among individuals. The DNA of fraternal multiples will show many differences, whereas the DNA of identicals will match completely. Results take one to two weeks. (To order a kit, call Affiliated Genetics at 800–362–5559, or order online at www.affiliatedgenetics.com. The cost is $120 plus $10 handling for twins; add $60 for each additional multiple.)

Who's Having Multiples?

The natural incidence of twins is one in 89 births. Yet by the year 2001 (the most recent year for which statistics are available), the National Center for Health Statistics reported that the birthrate of twins in the United States had skyrocketed to one in 33. At the same time, the birthrate for higher-order multiples surged upward from its 1975 rate of one in 2,950 to its 2001 rate of one in 539. (Of these, triplet births account for one in 584; quadruplet births account for one in 8,036; and births of quintuplets or more account for one in 47,364.)

What has caused this explosive rise in multiple births? And just who is giving birth to all these triplets, quadruplets, and more? To answer these questions, several factors must be considered.

Some women are naturally prone to producing more than one egg during ovulation and are therefore more likely to give birth to fraternal twins or supertwins. This tendency runs in families, and you can inherit the trait through either your mother's or your father's side of the family.

Your male partner and his family history have *no influence* on your chances of conceiving fraternal multiples. That makes sense, given that it is the woman's ovulation pattern alone that sets the stage for this type of twinning. In other words, it doesn't matter one bit how many pairs of fraternal twins are perched on your husband's family tree. (Most people are unaware of this fact, as you'll realize long before you are asked for the hundredth time, "Which side of the family do twins run on, yours or your husband's?")

A factor influencing the rising rate of multiple births is the tendency for women today to have children later in life than previous generations did. Between the years 1975 and 2000, among women age 30 and older, the proportion of all births more than doubled (from 17 percent to 36 percent), while the proportion of women giving birth for the first time increased nearly fivefold (from 5 percent to 24 percent). That is significant because biologically an older woman is more prone to conceiving multiples. For instance, a woman who is 35 to 40 years old is *three times* more likely to give birth to fraternal twins than a woman between the ages of 20 and 25. This effect may be compounded when a woman waits until her thirties to marry, because twins are more often conceived in the first months after marriage—perhaps owing to more frequent sex! Widespread use of oral contraceptives plays a part too, since a woman's chances of having twins double if she conceives in the first month after discontinuing birth-control pills.

Race is another issue in determining who has multiples—or at least who has fraternal multiples. Whereas monozygotic twinning is completely random, and the MZ rates worldwide are remarkably constant at about three to four per 1,000 live births, the dizygotic twinning rate varies. In the United States, the rate of multiple births differs considerably between ethnic and racial groups. The rate for twin births (per 1,000 live births) is highest for African Americans at

32.3, followed by Caucasians at 31.3, Japanese at 25.8, Chinese at 23.3, Native Americans at 21.7, Hispanics at 20.2, Hawaiians at 19.7, and Filipinos at 18.1.

The primary cause of the current rise in multiple births, however, has been the use of modern infertility treatments, also known as assisted reproductive technologies (ART). An estimated one out of 10 American women of childbearing age has some type of fertility problem, and the treatments used to overcome these conditions vastly increase the odds of a multiple pregnancy. For instance, 20 percent of women who conceive while taking an ovulation-stimulating drug such as Pergonal have multiples, as do 10 percent of those who get pregnant using Clomid or a similar medication.

The more complicated fertility-enhancing techniques now in use can increase the chances of a multiple pregnancy by as much as 25 to 40 percent. Technologies such as in vitro fertilization (IVF), gamete intrafallopian transfer (GIFT), and zygote intrafallopian transfer (ZIFT) all essentially transfer a number of eggs at various stages of development into the fallopian tubes or the uterus, in the hope that at least one will continue to develop. Sometimes no fertilized eggs grow, sometimes one, and sometimes more than one.

Today, one-third of twins, more than three-fourths of triplets, and nearly all quadruplets and other higher-order multiples are the products of infertility treatments. The majority of multiples conceived through ART are fraternal, because they form from separate eggs that have been fertilized by separate sperm. However, because eggs fertilized through ART also seem to have an increased tendency to divide that one extra time, an infertility patient who becomes pregnant is more likely than the average woman to give birth to identical twins. Fortunately, a number of recent studies have demonstrated that twins conceived through ART are no more likely to have problems than twins who were conceived spontaneously.

DR. LUKE: In our Multiples Clinic, it sometimes seems that nearly every patient we're currently treating has conceived her multiples through infertility treatments. Then a few months later it might happen that most of the moms we're seeing have conceived their multiples spontaneously.

The proportion of multiples conceived through ART compared to those conceived spontaneously varies greatly around the country, as shown by the statistics from the University Consortium on Multiple Births. In the University of Miami program, only about 6 percent of twins are the result of infertility treatments, and 94 percent are spontaneous. At Johns Hopkins University and the Medical University of South Carolina, about 12 to 15 percent of twin pregnancies are from ART, and the other 85 to 88 percent are spontaneous. In comparison, at the University of Michigan, about 37 percent of twin pregnancies are due to ART, and only about 63 percent are spontaneous.

When it comes to triplets and quadruplets, however, the figures are quite different. Regardless of the area of the country, 90 to nearly 100 percent are the result of infertility treatments.

Getting the News: How and When Multiples Are Diagnosed

One of the earliest clues that a woman is carrying more than a single baby is that she's experiencing nausea and vomiting. Though it may seem like small consolation at the time, morning sickness can be a good sign. As the placenta or placentas begin to grow, they become the source of the hormones that help to maintain the pregnancy. Only about one-third of mothers with singleton babies experience nausea, compared to one-half or more of mothers-to-be of multiples. This is believed to be related to the larger placental mass and the greater amount of hormones being produced.

Another hint that multiples may be present is when a woman's uterus is larger than expected for a particular stage of pregnancy. With twins, this is often evident by the 14th week of pregnancy. With supertwins, the larger-than-average uterus is frequently noted even earlier.

DR. LUKE: The first day she came to our Multiples Clinic, Stacy Moore told me, "My obstetrician said my belly was bigger than one would normally see at 17 weeks. Thinking that we might have miscalculated my due date, she scheduled an ultrasound. That's when we saw *two* heads."

How much larger is the uterus of a woman carrying multiples? For the sake of comparison, imagine that four women are lined up in a row, and you are looking at them in profile. Each is 24 weeks pregnant.

1. For the expectant mother of a singleton, her growing uterus has lifted up from her pelvis and has created a mound that rises about as high as her navel. In other words, her pregnancy has only recently begun to "show." Her uterus is the size of a ball about 20 inches around (imagine a football with its pointy ends cut off).
2. The twin mom is larger—the size you'd expect to see at 32 weeks if she were carrying just one baby. Her uterus, the size of a basketball, is about 30 inches around.
3. The triplet mother looks like she's 36 weeks into a singleton pregnancy. Her uterus is the size of a smallish beach ball, about 33 inches around.
4. And the woman expecting quadruplets is as large as a singleton mom would be at 40 weeks. As big as an average beach ball, her uterus is about 36 inches around—in other words, full-term size.

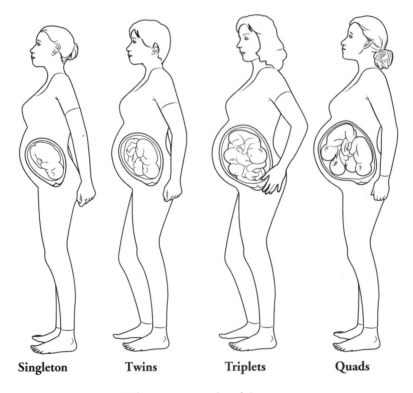

Singleton   **Twins**   **Triplets**   **Quads**

Sideways view at 24 weeks' gestation

Another indication that can be noticed as early as 10 to 12 weeks into the pregnancy is the sound of two hearts beating. Using a sensitive device called a Doppler that amplifies sound, an obstetrician can hear a baby's heartbeat, which is easily distinguished from the mother's because it is much more rapid. Twins are suspected when the doctor hears two distinct rapid heartbeats. Often, though, this clue is overlooked until some later test reveals the truth. Amy Maly chuckles. "It was fortunate I was lying down during that first ultrasound when the radiologist asked me, 'Did your obstetrician hear two heartbeats? Because I see two babies.'"

Multiples also may be suspected when a woman feels more fetal movement than she did with a previous pregnancy. This alone is not conclusive evidence of a multiple pregnancy, however. A woman already familiar with the feeling of a baby moving inside her is generally more sensitive to fetal movement. She may notice those first kicks earlier in a second pregnancy—perhaps by the 14th week rather than the average of 18 to 22 weeks—even if there is only one baby inside. Or the baby may simply be more active than his older sibling was.

Some women receive their first hint that multiples may be present when they get the results of their alpha-fetoprotein (AFP) test. This test, generally performed 15 to 18 weeks into the pregnancy, measures the level of a protein produced by the growing fetus that is present in the amniotic fluid and, in smaller amounts, in the mother's blood. A high AFP suggests several possibilities: that the pregnancy is more advanced than had been believed; that the baby has a serious medical problem such as spina bifida (a defect of the spinal column); or that there's more than one normal fetus growing. To determine the specific reason for the high AFP reading, the doctor will order additional diagnostic tests, such as amniocentesis or ultrasound. (For more on prenatal testing, see Chapter 2.)

These days, the majority of multiple pregnancies are diagnosed through ultrasound, a technology that uses sound waves to project a picture of a fetus onto a monitor screen. Ultrasound can detect the baby's heartbeat, estimate gestational age, track fetal growth, reveal gender, detect certain birth defects, and confirm the presence of multiples.

Because ultrasound can be done at almost any point in a pregnancy, some mothers learn early on that their pregnancy is something beyond the ordinary. "I had my first ultrasound at eight weeks," says Judy Levy. "The doctor looked at the monitor, then held up two fingers. I said, 'Oh, you mean V for victory? The baby seems fine?' He replied, 'No, I mean two—there are *two babies*.' My legs started shaking."

Yet even ultrasound can sometimes miss the diagnosis if one multiple is "hiding" behind a wombmate. "Early in my pregnancy, I had spotted a bit, so at eight weeks my doctor did an ultrasound. She saw one perfectly healthy fetus, and said everything looked good. Two months later, though, I started feeling terrible—very tired, vomiting all the time. I figured I had the flu, but the doctor decided to order another ultrasound just to make sure my baby was okay. We were all looking at the screen when suddenly this expression of shock came over the doctor's face. She stared at me and said, 'Now you have *twins* in here!' We're still not sure why no one saw the second baby on that earlier ultrasound," recalls Marcy Bugajski, mother of fraternal twin boys.

How Your Unborn Babies Grow

"I had a ritual I did weekly throughout my pregnancy," says Lydia Greenwood. "Every Sunday evening, I sat down with a wonderful book called *A Child Is Born* by Lennart Nilsson. It shows the most amazing photographs of babies at various stages of prenatal development, from the earliest embryonic days onward, and explains when each part of the body develops. I loved to picture my own little twins snuggled up together inside me, and to track all the miraculous changes they would be going through in the coming week."

You may experience a similar satisfaction in tracking your babies' development, in one form or another, as they grow week by week. This understanding can help you to feel closer emotionally to your unborn babies. And it can make the restrictions that go along with a multiple pregnancy—the guidelines on what and when to eat, the limits on physical activity and work hours, for instance—seem far less onerous and easier to follow.

But first you need to understand something. Because the exact date of conception usually is not known (except in the case of infertility treatments), a pregnancy is dated from the first day of a woman's last menstrual period—which typically occurs *two weeks before* the actual moment of conception. In other words, when your doctor says you're 12 weeks pregnant, your babies have in fact been growing inside you for about 10 weeks.

Early Pregnancy: The Embryonic Period

The first two months of life are known as the embryonic period. This is the most critical time in all of human development, because it is when the body's essential internal and external structures begin to form. Anything that disrupts normal development at this stage could lead to malformations and birth defects or even pregnancy loss. That's why any woman who is trying to conceive or believes she may have just become pregnant should take extra care to avoid exposure to potentially harmful influences, such as viruses, radiation, medications, and alcohol. (For more on such dangers, see Chapters 4 and 6.)

Miscarriage is also most common during this stage of development, usually due to some genetic or physiologic problem. Sometimes the loss of the embryo occurs so early that the woman does not even realize she was pregnant; she may simply believe her menstrual period was a few days late that month.

In a normal, healthy pregnancy, however, the embryo or embryos continue to develop in predictable ways. Here's what is happening to your unborn multiples as they grow week by week. (Remember that these weeks are calculated from the date of your last menstrual period, about two weeks before actual conception.)

Week 1: Your monthly menstruation begins. Pregnancy is calculated from day one of your period (referred to as the LMP, or last menstrual period).

Week 2: After your menstrual period ends, the endometrium, or lining of the uterus, begins to build up again in preparation for a possible pregnancy. Ovulation, or the release of a mature egg from the ovary, takes place during this time. Conception occurs if the mature egg is fertilized by the father's sperm as it travels through the fallopian tube to the uterus.

Week 3: The week-old fertilized egg or eggs embed in your endometrium, which has reached its greatest thickness and maximum richness in blood supply and nutrients.

Week 4: The placenta or placentas have grown deeper into the endometrium. As the mother's blood supply bathes the outside of the placentas and the unborn babies' circulation flows within the placentas, nutrients are passed to the babies and their waste products are carried away.

Week 5: The organs and tissues of the growing embryos are evolving, particularly the spinal cord and nervous system and the heart and circulatory system. Once their blood supply has been established, the embryos are no longer dependent on the meager supply of nutrients from the eggs, and growth can begin in earnest. By the end of this week, each baby's umbilical cord—the vital link to the placenta—has formed.

Week 6: By now, the early stages of heart formation are complete and each baby's heart has begun to beat! Soon the embryos will start to produce their own blood. Meanwhile, the limbs are forming. By the 26th day after conception, your babies have the beginnings of arms. By day 28, budding legs are visible.

Weeks 7 and 8: Rapid cellular growth during this time causes a significant event to occur—a "folding" of the developing embryos, who now assume a more tubular C-shaped curvature. The eyes develop and become pigmented. Fingers and outer ears start to take shape and soon after, the early beginnings of toes become apparent.

Weeks 9 and 10: The fingers, toes, and outer ears become more developed. By the close of the 10th week—the end of the embryonic period—all major organs have been formed. A space called the amniotic cavity, which had formed between the embryo and the inner lining of the placenta, has gradually filled with fluid to become the amniotic sac, or bag of waters. The developing embryos float in their sacs as they grow, cushioned from shocks from the outside environment and kept at an even temperature.

If you could peer inside yourself and see your babies' faces, you would notice clearly recognizable eyes, eyelids, noses, mouths, and ears. You would also see that each baby has a well-developed head, neck, arms, and legs, with clearly defined fingers and toes. In other words, each of your babies now has an unquestionably human appearance!

DR. LUKE: Throughout the embryonic period—in fact, throughout all of growth and development before birth—the upper portions of the body mature earlier than the lower portions. In other words, your babies' heads, hearts, arms, and hands develop more quickly than their legs, feet, and urinary and reproductive systems.

It's interesting to note that, after birth, this rule still applies. I see this again and again when patients who have delivered return to the Multiples Clinic to show off their children. The babies can raise their heads long before they can sit up; they are able to push up on their hands and arms long before they learn to stand.

Growth of Your Embryos

Days After Conception	Length of Embryo (inches)	Main External Characteristics
22	0.06–.08	Embryos are still straight.
26	0.12–.14	Embryos have become C-shaped. Arms appear as small swellings. Eyes begin to develop.
28	0.16–.20	Hands begin to form. Legs appear as small swellings. The lens of the eye starts to develop.
33	0.32–.40	Fingers are forming; wrists and elbows become apparent. Feet begin to develop. Eyes and nostrils are clearly defined.
35	0.48–.56	Ears begin to form. Eyes become pigmented.
40	0.84–.88	Fingers are formed. Eyelids are clearly visible. Toes begin to be defined.
45	1.00–1.08	The external ear becomes apparent. Toes are short and stubby. Fingers become elongated.
48	1.12–1.20	Fingers and toes are clearly defined. The head, trunk, and limbs have a distinctly human appearance.

Table 1.1

LATER PREGNANCY: THE FETAL PERIOD

The fetal period includes the last month of the first trimester, plus the entire second and third trimesters. Although it is also a period of rapid growth, the fetal period is different from the embryonic period in that no *new* structures are being formed; development is mainly in size. For this reason, the unborn babies are less susceptible to harm caused by external factors such as X-rays, drugs, and viruses—though, of course, they still can be adversely affected.

Although it was previously believed that fetuses could obtain all their essential nutrients from the mother's bloodstream, it is now known that many factors affect their growth and their ultimate size and health at birth. Genetics plays a large part, as do the mother's weight prior to conception and her pattern of weight gain during pregnancy.

Here's how your multiples grow and develop, month to month, during the fetal period:

Month 3: Your babies are becoming even more human in appearance as the eyes move from the sides of the head to the front of the face, and the outer ears develop further. The brain has been growing rapidly, so that the head accounts for about half of each baby's "sitting length," or crown-rump length. Arms and legs grow to reach their relative length in proportion to the rest of the body, although the development of the lower limbs still lags behind that of the upper body. By the end of this month, the external genitals are clearly developed.

Months 4 and 5: The length of each fetus is increasing rapidly, so that by the end of this period the fetuses have grown to half of what will be their length at birth (provided they are born close to full term). Lower-body development is beginning to catch up to the upper body; by now, each baby's head is only about one-third of his crown-rump length. Hair and eyebrows are now visible. Most exciting, the babies' kicks are strong enough for you to feel them!

Months 6 and 7: Your multiples have red, wrinkly skin. Their respiratory and nervous systems are developing quickly, yet are still too immature to function adequately outside the womb.

Months 8 and 9: Your babies' heads now account for only one-fourth of their sitting length. Overall, their bodies are growing more rounded as they accumulate the fat they need to cope with life after birth.

Average Fetal Growth

Weeks	Head Circumference		Abdominal Circumference		Femur Length	
	(Inches)	(Millimeters)	(Inches)	(Millimeters)	(Inches)	(Millimeters)
12	3	78	2.5	64	0.4	9.5
16	5	126	4.5	115	0.8	22
20	7	178	6.25	158	1.3	34
22	8	198	7	175	1.5	38
24	9	223	8	200	1.75	45
26	10	248	8.75	223	1.9	49
28	11	272	9.75	246	2.1	53
30	11.5	285	10	256	2.2	56
32	12	303	11	283	2.4	62
34	12.5	312	12	302	2.5	64
36	13	327	12.75	322	2.7	69
38	13.5	331	13.25	336	2.8	70
40	14	347	14.25	366	3	75

Table 1.2

The growth of multiples basically parallels that of a singleton, but with several important differences. One of these differences works to your babies' advantage—multiples generally develop slightly faster than singletons do. For example, the average triplets are more mature at 30 weeks than is the typical 30-week singleton. Multiples' lungs, in particular, tend to be ready sooner to deal with the challenges of the world outside the womb.

But in another important way, multiples are at a developmental disadvantage. Whereas an unborn singleton's weight climbs until 40 weeks' gestation before slowing down, in multiples this *slowing-down of the growth rate occurs much earlier*—typically after 34 weeks for twins, 30 weeks for triplets, and 26 to 27 weeks for quadruplets. As a result, multiples tend to be born at a lighter birthweight compared to that of a singleton born at the same gestational age. This compounds the problems caused by the fact that multiples are also more likely to be born prematurely. (This issue is discussed in more detail later in this chapter and in Chapters 6 and 9.)

Certain multiples are at particular risk for low birthweight:

- Identical twins or supertwins—monozygotic siblings tend to be lighter than fraternals.
- Girls—the hormone testosterone generally gives boys a boost in terms of weight.
- Infants born to short and/or lightweight mothers—such children have a genetic propensity toward smaller size.
- Higher-order multiples—the more babies are sharing space in a single uterus, the smaller each is likely to be. The average birthweight for twins, for example, is 5 lb., 3 oz. For triplets, the typical birthweight is 3 lb., 11 oz. Quadruplets are born weighing an average of just 2 lb., 13 oz.

Fortunately, there is a lot you can do to minimize the effects of these risk factors. Those specific steps are the focus of this book and are described in detail in subsequent chapters.

DR. LUKE: You'll notice that, in many instances, my guidelines differ depending on how many babies you're expecting. That's because the demands of a triplet pregnancy are not the same as those of a twin pregnancy; the demands of a quadruplet pregnancy are not the same as those of a triplet pregnancy.

Our readers understand this. One writes, "This is the only book I found that was of any use to a mother pregnant with triplets. All the other prenatal books for multiples mostly deal with twins, and as an afterthought, an extra baby or two were thrown into the text, it seemed. I had no complications during my pregnancy, and I went to 35 weeks. I delivered my triplets weighing 5 lb., 10 oz.; 6 lb., 2 oz.; and 5 lb., 10 oz. I am sure a lot had to do with the 'baby growing' methods of Dr. Luke." Another says, "This is the only book I read

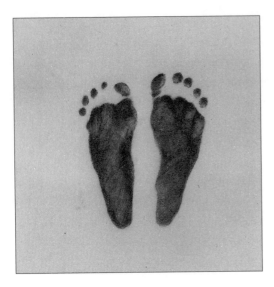

22 weeks

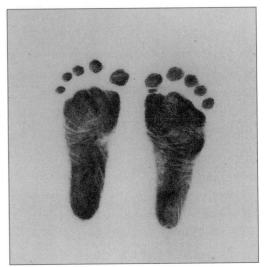

24 weeks

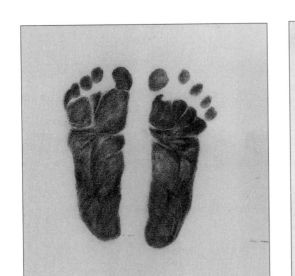

26 weeks

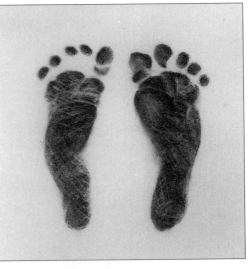

28 weeks

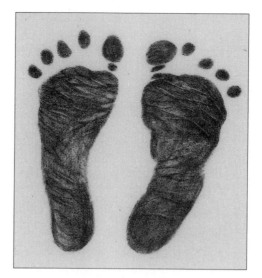

30 weeks

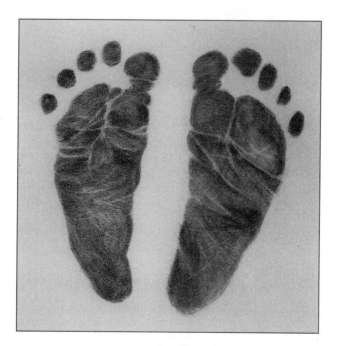

34 weeks

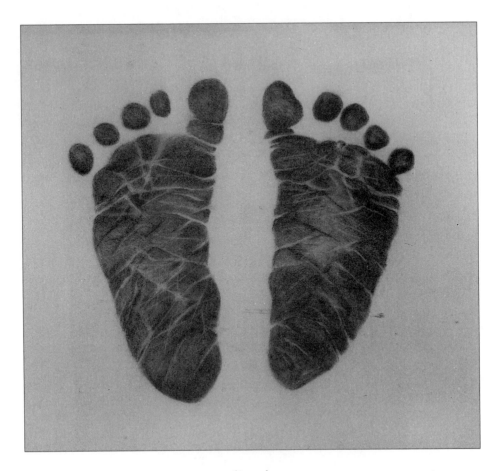

40 weeks

that reaches out to would-be mothers of quadruplets. It empowers pregnant women to give their babies the best possible start in life. I recently delivered four healthy baby boys!"

I've found that women in our Multiples Clinic are much better able to follow our daily guidelines on diet, rest, and physical activity once we translate the data on fetal growth into terms they can easily understand. For instance, a woman may be tempted to skip breakfast or work overtime. But when she has a graphic illustration of the difference in size between babies born prematurely and those born closer to full term, she is more motivated to take positive, preventive action for her children's sake.

One of the most helpful tools we've developed is a chart that compares actual footprints of babies born at various gestational ages, from 22 weeks all the way up to 40 weeks. As Amy Maly said to me, "The footprints of the preemies were so tiny. They were scary—but inspiring too. Every time I thought, 'Ugh, I can't eat another thing,' or, 'I'm supposed to stay in bed, but maybe it wouldn't hurt to do a little housecleaning,' I'd look at those footprints and feel renewed determination to do whatever was best for my babies." We've reproduced these footprints here, in the hope that you will find inspiration in them too.

Countdown to Due Date

TAMARA: Looking back, I hate to admit how naive I was about my due date. My twins were conceived in late September, which meant the due date was June 22. I had read that the average twin pregnancy is three weeks shorter than a singleton pregnancy, so I assumed my babies would be born around the beginning of June.

What I failed to appreciate was that an average is only that—*an average*. It is not a guarantee, not a given, not a promise set in stone.

I didn't even come close to carrying for the "typical" 37 weeks. My babies were born at 31 weeks and spent more than a month in the neonatal intensive care unit, struggling to make up for the growth and development they had missed by departing too early from the protective environment of the womb.

That is not to say your due date is meaningless, of course. In fact, it's a vital piece of information for you and your entire health care team. It's important to know what it means and how it is calculated.

In a singleton pregnancy, birth typically occurs about 280 days after the first day of the woman's last menstrual period (or about 266 days after conception). This is equal to 40 weeks, 10 lunar months, or approximately 9 calendar months. But this 40-week rule does not apply to multiple pregnancies, for several reasons:

- As stated earlier, the growth rate for multiples typically begins to slow down earlier than it does for singletons. And the more babies there are, the sooner growth slows. Although the reasons are not completely clear, there is evidence that when babies are growing poorly, the body senses that the uterine environment is not a healthy one and may trigger premature labor.
- Multiples generally are more mature developmentally than are singletons of the same gestational age, and they are therefore ready to be born two to three weeks sooner. Though the physiology of this is not well understood, it may be that the

stress of sharing the womb with one or more siblings triggers some built-in safety mechanism that accelerates development. While this added maturity does not *cause* multiples to be born sooner, it does help to prepare them for life outside the womb.

- With twins and supertwins, the placentas tend to age more quickly and therefore begin to function less efficiently. This factor may contribute directly or indirectly to a shorter gestation.
- The uterus can only stretch so far. The combined weight of several babies, several placentas, and a whole lot of amniotic fluid eventually signals to the body that it's time for labor to start, no matter how much longer the calendar says the pregnancy should continue. By the time she reaches 32 weeks, the uterus of a woman carrying twins is already as large as that of a singleton mom at the full 40 weeks. For the mother of triplets, the uterus is stretched to full-term size by 28 weeks. And with quadruplets on board, a woman's uterus reaches full-term size as early as 24 weeks.

Anne Seifert, mother of quadruplets, knows from personal experience how these factors can combine to limit the length of a multiple pregnancy. "My obstetrician originally said we would aim for me to carry the quads to 34 weeks," says Anne. "But by week 24, my uterus was already stretched beyond the size a singleton's mother would be at full term. We both realized there was no way I'd be able to make it to 34 weeks. It was all I could do to get to 31."

If a due date based on 40 weeks' gestation is not realistic for mothers-to-be of multiples, when *should* you expect to deliver? Here are the averages:

- Twins are typically born at 35 to 36 weeks' gestation.
- Triplets, on average, arrive at 32 weeks.
- Quadruplet pregnancies generally last about 30 weeks.

Keep in mind, though, that these figures are *averages*. Your pregnancy may run a little longer than is typical—or labor may begin sooner than average. Consider these statistics:

- Ten percent of singletons are born before 37 weeks; 2 percent are born before 32 weeks.
- Fifty-seven percent of twins arrive prior to 37 weeks; 12 percent arrive prior to 32 weeks.
- Ninety-two percent of triplets are delivered before 37 weeks; 37 percent are delivered before 32 weeks.

- Ninety-eight percent of quadruplets are born before 37 weeks; 65 percent are born before 32 weeks.

Your own obstetrical history plays a part too. If you've already given birth at least once, you're at an advantage during your multiple pregnancy. The latest research, from 2002, reveals the following:

- Your risk of delivering twins prior to 35 weeks' gestation is only half that of a woman for whom a twin pregnancy is her first.
- Your risk of delivering triplets prior to 30 weeks' gestation is only one-fourth that of a woman for whom a triplet pregnancy is her first. Also, if your previous single-ton pregnancy lasted at least 37 weeks, your triplets are likely to grow faster and be born heavier than triplets born to a first-time mother.

Another factor to consider is your age. Surprisingly, although younger women tend to do better during singleton pregnancies, older moms-to-be of multiples may have an advantage over younger ones. For instance:

- Women age 30 or older are significantly more likely to carry their twins for at least 35 weeks than are younger women.
- Triplets born to mothers age 40 and over tend to be among the healthiest. This may be due in part to higher socioeconomic status and earlier prenatal care.

So think of your due date as a goal, not a given. Focus on getting as close as possible to full term by carefully following your doctor's instructions as well as the guidelines in this book, and don't feel discouraged even if problems arise.

If that seems like an overwhelming challenge at times, try to think positively and proactively. It's understandable if you feel upset as you read about potential problems in twin or supertwin pregnancies, but remember that your emotions are running high right now. The hormonal fluctuations of pregnancy can cause frequent mood swings—particularly so when you're carrying multiples. Remind yourself too that knowledge equals power. The more you know about your unique pregnancy, the more you can do to ensure an excellent outcome.

As one twin mom says, "I bought this book shortly after my multiples were diagnosed because I didn't want advice on whether to give the babies rhyming names or let them sleep in the same crib—I wanted guidance on how to get through my high-risk pregnancy with as few complications as possible, so that I would be able to go home with two healthy babies. This book does an excellent job of educating you about potential problems and, more importantly, listing concrete and doable things that will maximize your chances of avoiding these problem areas."

Don't get discouraged even if complications do develop. "I had a worrisome pregnancy. I experienced some bleeding, my cervix was weak, and I was having constant contractions from 18 weeks onward. Preterm labor was a serious threat, and I had to stay on bedrest for four and a half months!" recalls Heather Nicholas, mother of boy/girl twins. "But I ended up carrying those babies to 38½ weeks. At birth, Madeleine weighed 7 lb., 3 oz., and Benjamin weighed 6 lb., 15 oz.—so both were heavier than the average *singleton* at that gestational age."

You may experience various complications, as Heather did—or you may sail through your pregnancy with a minimum of trouble. But no matter what, remember that your actions can have a strongly positive influence on the health and well-being of *all* your babies.

Chapter 2

The Best Medical Care for Expectant Mothers of Multiples

Ginny Seyler was not the type of woman to take chances. She had conceived easily the first month she and her husband, David, had tried to start a family, but that pregnancy had ended in miscarriage. Then followed nearly four years of infertility. Finally, thanks to Clomid, Ginny conceived again—but severe bleeding at seven weeks threatened to end this pregnancy as well.

The fertility specialist who was treating Ginny immediately scheduled an ultrasound. "I expected to be told that I was miscarrying again. Instead, on the screen we saw a healthy baby growing. Then we saw another healthy baby, and we were thrilled! But when the doctor saw a *third* baby, our excitement turned to shock. I have a master's degree in maternal-child health, so I knew more than the average person about the challenges a triplet pregnancy presents," Ginny explains. "I realized that, this very day, I would have to begin a quest for the best obstetrician I could find."

Ginny was right on target. A multiple pregnancy carries a greater potential for problems than does a singleton pregnancy. The most important step you can take to minimize risk is to select a doctor experienced enough to anticipate these potential problems, detect them early, and treat them in the best way possible. A general practitioner, family doctor, midwife, or even a regular obstetrician generally will not have the extra training and years of experience required to provide the most advanced and appropriate care for an expectant mother of multiples. You need a maternal-fetal medicine specialist—an obstetrician who has received extensive special-ized training and put it to use in the management of high-risk pregnancies.

DR. LUKE: If you're expecting supertwins, like Ginny, you're probably already convinced of the need for specialized care. But if you're carrying twins, you may think a specialist is unnecessary.

Think again. Because twin pregnancies are fairly common, not all doctors recognize the unique needs of women who are carrying "just two." Too often it is the patient and her babies who pay the price for that overly casual attitude. For instance, one doctor who had recently delivered stillborn twins was heard to say defensively, "Why would anyone think I should have referred that patient to a special-risk obstetrical clinic? Just because it was a twin pregnancy didn't mean it was high-risk." The tragic outcome, though, proved him wrong.

The truth is that *all* multiple pregnancies involve some increased risk, as reported in many studies from researchers around the country, including our research group, the University Consortium on Multiple Births. Anyone who tells you otherwise is misinformed.

This is not to say that you necessarily will have difficulties during this pregnancy. You may experience no complications whatsoever. Still, it's smart to be prepared. Think of a medical specialist as an insurance policy—you hope you never need to make a claim, but if tough times do arise, you'll be happy to have that policy in place. One reader reports, "It was because of Dr. Luke's advice that I put myself into a perinatologist group's care. Because of their proactive approach when I began to show signs of preterm labor, my twins arrived at 31 weeks instead of 26 weeks, as they were threatening to do."

As Judy Levy said to me during one of her prenatal visits to the University of Michigan Multiples Clinic, "I appreciate that my obstetrician never treats me like I'm 'sick' or implies that I will definitely have problems just because I'm expecting twins. Yet it's a relief to know that, because he specializes in high-risk pregnancies, he's well qualified to deal with any complications that might develop. I would feel much more anxious if I didn't have him on my team."

Assembling Your Health Care Team

Finding a qualified maternal-fetal medicine specialist is not hard—if you know where to look. Here's how to start your search:

- Ask for a referral from your gynecologist, family doctor, or fertility specialist.
- Contact the obstetrics department of the best hospital in your area and ask for names of high-risk obstetricians affiliated with that facility.

- Contact the American College of Obstetricians and Gynecologists: 409 12th Street, SW, PO Box 96920, Washington, DC 20090-6920. Telephone 800–673–8444; Web site www.acog.org. ACOG can provide a list of maternal-fetal medicine specialists in your area.
- To confirm the credentials of any doctor you're considering, call the American Board of Medical Specialties' toll-free hotline at 866–ASK–ABMS, or check their Web site at www.abms.org. You can find out if a particular doctor is a board-certified specialist, the year he or she became certified, and when recertification is due.

When you call to make your first prenatal appointment, be sure to specify that yours is a multiple pregnancy. You want to be seen promptly, so don't accept any lengthy delays. "When I phoned the high-risk obstetrician who had been recommended to me, the receptionist said that the doctor had no time available for another six weeks. I said, 'Oh please, this is *quadruplets!*' She gave me an appointment for the following week," says Anne Seifert.

If there are several qualified specialists in your area, try to check out each one personally before making your selection. Even a five-minute visit or phone call can help you assess which doctor's style suits you best. Does he or she seem like the type of physician who establishes a personal relationship with each patient—or the type who's too busy to give you the extra time you may need?

"I picked my obstetrician because he was the director of women's health at a top hospital. But I learned that credentials aren't everything," says one mother of twins. "You need someone who makes you feel comfortable, someone who listens to you. Yet my doctor had his hand on the doorknob at every appointment. I felt too rushed to ask all my questions, and too flustered by his obvious impatience to remember his hurried answers."

Contrast this woman's experience with that of Karen Danke, mother of fraternal twin boys. Says Karen, "My obstetrician went way beyond the call of duty. During the eight weeks I was on hospitalized bedrest, he came to visit me every day—even when I didn't need to be examined—just to keep my spirits up. We chatted about vacations, college, all kinds of things. He even lent me CDs from his home collection. And he literally dried my tears when I got discouraged."

IF YOU ALREADY HAVE A DOCTOR—BUT HE'S NOT A SPECIALIST
Often a woman does not learn that she is carrying multiples until well into the second trimester. By that time, she has already been someone's patient for several months. The big question then is whether to switch to a high-risk specialist or stick with the current doctor.

This can be a tough decision. You may feel embarrassed at the thought of saying to a physician, "I'm going elsewhere for my prenatal care." But don't let that stop you from doing what is best for you and your babies—especially if you have not been 100 percent thrilled with your care so far.

"I'd been warned against switching obstetricians in the middle of a pregnancy because it was important that a doctor have time to really get to know the patient. That's why I stuck with my original doctor even after I learned I was expecting twins, though he did not specialize in multiple gestation," says Meredith Alcott, mother of identical twin girls. "In hindsight, though, I do wish I had changed to a specialist. I received the standard care you'd expect during a singleton pregnancy—but what I needed went beyond standard. For instance, my obstetrician gave only perfunctory answers to my questions about diet and other special needs of a twin pregnancy. And he never saw me more than once a month, even after I developed complications."

Recognize too that even if your regular obstetrician can offer quality care for a twin or supertwin pregnancy, other health care providers in her practice may not be as capable. "My own doctor was terrific. But the disadvantage in not going to a specialist was that the rest of her office staff wasn't as up-to-speed on multiple pregnancy as they might have been," explains Benita Moreno, mother of fraternal twin boys. "The nurses, for instance, were supposed to advise me on what to eat, help me learn to recognize contractions, teach me about warning signs to watch for, and so on. But they weren't helpful at all. They even made critical remarks about how heavy I was getting, though both my doctor and my nutritionist had urged me to gain weight quickly!"

Switching doctors under circumstances similar to Meredith's or Benita's should not cause you more than a few moments of discomfort. But it is admittedly much more difficult to leave your current physician if you already have a close, trusting relationship with her—and particularly if she has cared for you during a previous pregnancy.

DR. LUKE: We all see many health professionals over the years—general practitioners for sore throats and earaches, dentists for chipped teeth and annual cleanings, perhaps an orthopedist or physical therapist for back problems. But for most women, our obstetrician holds a special place in our hearts. He was the one who gave us the news that we were expecting, saw us through bouts of nausea and vomiting, and told us we looked radiant when we were eight months pregnant and felt elephantine. He was there with words of encouragement when labor was painful and we wanted to give up. And it was our obstetrician who, with patience and skill, brought our precious children into the world.

It's natural you would feel reluctant to defect from the doctor you trust by turning your care over to an unknown doctor, even though you know it's advisable to see a specialist. In this case, there is another option: the team approach.

Ask your general obstetrician, family practitioner, or midwife to work together with your maternal-fetal medicine specialist now that you're carrying multiples. If your pregnancy is going well, they may agree that you can continue to see your old health care provider during the early months, then transfer your care to the specialist. Just be sure to make the switch by your 18th week. Most complications develop after 20 to 24 weeks, so you would want to be established in your specialist's care by then. And, of course, the specialist should be in charge of all the additional monitoring that occurs during the last months, and of the delivery of your babies.

The team tactic worked well for Judy Levy. "I used our family doctor during my first pregnancy and was very pleased with my obstetric care, so I had planned to use her again the second time I got pregnant. I had already scheduled my first prenatal checkup with her when, a few weeks before the appointment, an ultrasound showed twins. After much consideration, I decided to take advantage of the extra measure of care a specialist could provide, yet I still wanted my family doctor to be involved," Judy explains. "And she did stay involved. For instance, at 28 weeks, I scheduled a consultation with her to discuss the pros and cons of attempting a vaginal birth after a cesarean. And I continued to see her for all nonpregnancy-related problems, like a bad case of bronchitis. My family doctor was very supportive of this cooperative approach. She even came to my delivery to cheer me on! And now that the twins are born, she's their family physician too."

HOSPITAL OPTIONS

TAMARA: I never gave much thought, during my twin pregnancy, to the hospital where I'd be delivering. My obstetrician had told me the name and location of the hospital with which he was affiliated, and I had accepted that without question. Oh sure, I made certain I knew how to get there without getting lost. I even timed the drive from my home to the hospital—19 minutes—many months before my due date, in anticipation of the exciting journey that would occur once I went into labor. But it didn't cross my mind to research the hospital's facilities for mothers or for newborns.

So when my water broke unexpectedly only 31 weeks into my pregnancy, and my doctor ordered me to rush to the hospital at 2 A.M., I had not the slightest idea of what to expect. As I gave birth to my tiny twins just two hours later, the staff of the small community hospital responded capably and kindly—yet clearly they were not equipped to take care of premature newborns. As soon as my son and daughter were stable enough to be moved, ambulances whisked them to a major medical center 30 miles away.

Left behind at the little community hospital, I did not get to see or touch or hold my precious babies until I was discharged two days later. Those were the longest, loneliest, scariest days of my life.

It is difficult under any circumstances to learn that your newborns have medical problems. But you'll be even more upset if you are forced to be separated from them. To ensure that this doesn't happen, you need some basic information about hospitals.

Hospital nurseries are divided into three categories, according to the level of care they can provide to newborns. Here's how it breaks down:

- *Level I:* Most hospitals in the country are classified at this level. These facilities can manage routine, uncomplicated labors and deliveries and care for healthy, full-term newborns. They can also handle mild complications an infant may develop, such as jaundice.
- *Level II:* These hospitals have the staff and equipment to take care of many complications that newborn multiples may experience if born prematurely, including mild to moderate respiratory distress syndrome and the need for gavage feeding (feeding through a tube inserted through the nose and into the stomach).
- *Level III:* Typically found in large cities and/or affiliated with universities, these facilities are equipped to care for the sickest and smallest babies. Along with a regular nursery for well newborns and a special-care nursery for infants with mild to moderate medical problems, these hospitals include a full neonatal intensive care unit, or NICU (sometimes pronounced "nick-you"). Staff includes full-time neonatologists (pediatricians who specialize in the care of newborns), as well as pediatric neurologists, surgeons, and developmental experts.

In light of the fact that newborn multiples are at risk for needing special medical care, the best way to guarantee that you and your babies remain in the same hospital after delivery is to give birth at a Level III facility. This is not as complicated as it sounds, because most maternal-fetal medicine specialists are affiliated with such hospitals. If you've already found a physician qualified to manage your multiple pregnancy, chances are that he or she has admitting privileges at the type of hospital you need.

If you haven't yet found a doctor, call your area hospitals and ask what level nursery they have. Once you identify the closest Level III facility, ask for a referral to a maternal-fetal specialist on their staff. "I chose my hospital *before* I chose my obstetrician," says Karen Danke. "I knew this facility had a great reputation, especially for its NICU. I wanted to make sure that if my twins needed extra care after birth, they would already be in the hospital best qualified to help them." Your babies may never need such care—many multiples do not—but it's important that it be available, just in case.

Not only your babies but you too can benefit from this. That's because hospitals with Level III nurseries also generally have the most advanced facilities for treating problems that might develop during the course of a high-risk pregnancy, or after delivery.

Once you have chosen an obstetrician and a hospital, it's a good idea to take a tour. Usually run by the nursing staff in obstetrics, a hospital tour gives you an opportunity to ask questions, see the actual labor and delivery rooms, and perhaps visit the NICU. Familiarizing yourself with the facilities under relaxed, calm conditions will help you to feel less anxious should you need to be admitted during the pregnancy, as well as allow you to approach labor and delivery with more confidence.

Nurses: The Heart and Soul of Health Care

An integral part of every aspect of medicine, from prevention to acute care, is the nursing staff. During the course of your pregnancy, you'll meet many nurses. Some work in your doctor's office or clinic. Others care for you during labor and delivery, and during your recovery from childbirth. The nursing staff is also a vital component of your babies' hospital health care team. Many of these professionals, such as nurse practitioners, clinical specialists, and midwives, have received additional specialized training and are qualified to perform a variety of duties that were previously done only by doctors.

Take advantage of the knowledge and skills of the nurses you encounter. They can educate you and your partner on what to expect during this important time in your life, teach you how to watch for danger signs, and translate confusing data into practical and usable information. Equally important, nurses provide the warm, caring, emotional support that is so comforting during a potentially complicated pregnancy.

A Vital Team Member: Your Dietitian

When you're expecting a team of babies, you need a *team* of health care providers. That team is led, of course, by your obstetrician. But it should also include a registered dietitian.

Prenatal nutrition—what you eat when you're pregnant—has long been recognized as a critical factor in your health and the health of your unborn babies. For more than 30 years, the American College of Obstetricians and Gynecologists (a professional organization for medical doctors who specialize in women's reproductive health care) has recommended that nutrition assessment and dietary counseling be a part of prenatal care. Since most medical doctors have little training in nutrition, your best bet is to ask your physician for a referral to someone who specializes in this field.

A registered dietitian (or RD) is the type of health care professional best equipped to evaluate your diet. She or he can make sure you're getting the right varieties of foods, in the right quantities, to promote optimal growth and development of your unborn babies. Your dietitian can also offer advice for the postpartum period to ensure success in breast-feeding and to help you regain your figure after delivery.

"Having access to the nutrition counseling offered by the Multiples Clinic was a real advantage," says Helen Armer, mother of triplets. "My babies were all a good size when they were born—one weighed almost 6 pounds, and the others were close to 5 pounds. I don't think that would have happened without Dr. Luke's nutrition program."

Not just any nutritionist will do, however. Many lack the additional training and experience needed to counsel mothers-to-be of multiples. "I made an appointment with a dietitian, but as it turned out, she was used to taking care of heart patients. She didn't know much about obstetrical patients, and she knew even less about the nutritional demands of unborn triplets," Ginny Seyler laments.

DR. LUKE: It is unfortunately true that it's often tough to find a dietitian who has much experience with multiples. Look for someone who specializes in obstetrics; she will be most familiar with the nutritional demands of pregnancy and can properly adjust upward the requirements for certain nutrients, depending on how many babies you're carrying. As Judy Levy says, "For me, having the benefit of a nutritionist who was knowledgeable about multiple pregnancy was a real plus. She gave me the kind of specific menu-planning advice and concrete details one doesn't typically get from an obstetrician. And she was seeing me more often too—once a week, compared to only once a month for the obstetrician."

For a referral to a qualified professional in your area, call the Nutrition Hotline of the American Dietetic Association (ADA) at 800–366–1655, ext. 5000. This service will provide the names and phone numbers of up to three dietitians in your area. Ask for members who belong to the ADA specialty subgroup called the Women's Health and Reproductive Nutrition Dietetic Practice Group. ADA also has a Web site at www.eatright.org. Click on the "Find a Dietitian" icon.

I also invite you to get personalized nutrition advice directly from me on my Web site, www.drbarbaraluke.com.

The Doctor—Patient Partnership

You and your obstetrician are partners for this very unique period in your life. That partnership involves rights and responsibilities for both of you, as outlined in the American College of Obstetricians and Gynecologists' book on prenatal care *Planning Your Pregnancy and Birth* (3rd edition, 2000).

You have a right to:

- Quality care without discrimination
- Privacy
- Know the professional status of your health care providers and their fees
- Advice about your diagnosis, treatment, options, and the expected outcome
- Active involvement in decisions about your care
- Refuse treatment
- Agree or refuse to participate in any research that affects your care

You have a responsibility to:

- Provide accurate and complete health information
- Let your doctor know whether you understand the medical procedures and what you are expected to do

PREPARING FOR YOUR FIRST PRENATAL VISIT

The more your obstetrician knows about you and your pregnancy, the better prepared she will be to detect and treat any potential health problems. Yet it's not always easy to remember every detail when you're sitting in a doctor's office.

The Prenatal Care Questionnaire below can help. Spend some time filling in the answers before your first prenatal visit. This overall picture of your medical history and current health can help your obstetrician plan the prenatal care that's right for you and your unborn babies.

Also call any other physicians you have used—your family doctor, gynecologist, previous obstetrician, fertility specialist (if applicable)—and request that your medical records be forwarded to your new obstetrician as soon as possible. Be sure to provide your obstetrician with complete information regarding any prior pregnancies, whether or not they resulted in a birth. This is particularly important if any of your pregnancies ended three or more weeks before your due date, or if any of your children weighed less than 5½ pounds at birth. Studies show that there is a strong tendency to repeat the birthweight and gestational age at birth of previous pregnancies—and these risk factors are greatly compounded now that you're expecting multiples.

You'll want to talk to your female relatives about their childbearing experiences, because genetics may play an important role in the course and outcome of your pregnancy. For example, there is evidence that the risk of prematurity may be carried through the maternal side of the family tree. Ask your mother, sisters, and maternal aunts if their pregnancies ended earlier than expected, and take note of their babies' birthweights. Find out if anyone experienced complications such as heavy bleeding with delivery. Also be sure to inform your doctor of any genetic disease in your family or your husband's family. Forewarned with this knowledge, your obstetrician can take extra precautions to reduce the risks associated with such a family history.

Finally, promise yourself to be completely honest with your obstetrician about any sensitive issues such as sexually transmitted diseases or alcohol and drug use. Remember, it can be very dangerous to your unborn babies if you fail to disclose that you have herpes, for example, or that you are tempted to drink even though you're pregnant.

Prenatal Care Questionnaire:
Information You Should Provide to Your Doctor

Family Health History

Your ethnic background _____

Your partner's ethnic background_____

Inherited genetic disorders _____

Any previous children born with a birth defect _____

Medical and Surgical History

Current medications taken _____

Past medications taken _____

Allergies and allergic reactions _____

Current medical conditions _____

Past medical conditions _____

Prior surgeries _____

Exposure to infectious diseases _____

Menstrual History

Age at your first menstrual period _____

Date of your last menstrual period _____

History of use of birth-control pills _____

Other methods of contraception _____

Lifestyle Habits

Type and place of employment _____

Alcohol use _____

Cigarette use _____

Recreational drug use _____

Exposure to toxic substances _____

Past Pregnancies

Miscarriages or induced abortions _____

Length of gestation of any previous pregnancies _____

Complications before delivery _____

Length of labor _____

Method of delivery (vaginal or cesarean) _____

Complications after delivery _____

Newborn's birthweight _____

Newborn's medical condition _____

PRENATAL CHECKUP PRIMER

What's the major difference in prenatal care for an expectant mother of multiples? You will have more frequent checkups with your obstetrician than a woman pregnant with just one baby. Though the precise schedule of prenatal appointments varies according to the doctor and the patient's needs, here is a typical checkup routine:

Frequency of Prenatal Checkups

Weeks of Pregnancy	Mother of Singleton	Mother of Multiples
0–24 weeks	Monthly	Monthly
24–28 weeks	Monthly	Every other week
28–32 weeks	Every other week	Every other week
32–36 weeks	Every other week	Weekly
36 weeks–delivery	Weekly	Weekly

Table 2.1

It is vital that you not skip any of your appointments with the obstetrician. Babies born to mothers who do not receive adequate prenatal care tend to do much worse than those whose mothers were closely followed by medical professionals. "I realized that the best way to give my triplets a good chance of being born healthy was to keep all my prenatal appointments and follow every single instruction from my obstetrician and from the Multiples Clinic," explains Helen Armer, who carried her triplets to an impressive 36 weeks.

Because the laboratory tests and medical history you provide at your first prenatal checkup will establish your personal database for this entire pregnancy, it is typically a long visit. Allow plenty of time.

Subsequent visits are much shorter. These usually involve the following:

- Measuring the growth of the uterus
- Estimating the babies' sizes, positions, and relative growth
- Listening to the babies' heart rates
- Monitoring your blood pressure
- Recording your weight and calculating your weight gain
- Testing your urine

- Performing additional tests and evaluations, depending on how many weeks pregnant you are
- Reviewing any symptoms you may be experiencing
- Answering your questions

This last point is an essential aspect of quality prenatal care, so prepare for it in advance. "I arrived at each appointment with a list of questions and a notepad for recording the doctor's answers," says Judy Levy. "I think this made the doctor take my concerns more seriously. He spent a lot of time with me, and even photocopied articles from medical journals for me, because he knew I wasn't going to stop asking questions until I had the information I wanted." (Use the Prenatal Care Fact Sheet below as a guide to questions you should ask and to have a permanent record of your doctor's answers.)

If you have trouble asserting yourself, bring your partner along for moral support. "My doctor always seemed to be in a hurry, so I was intimidated about taking up his time with a lot of questions," says Meredith Alcott. "Luckily my husband is more outspoken than I am. He came with me to every appointment and told the obstetrician, 'We have a list of questions here, and we're not leaving until they're all answered.'"

What if you have a question that seems too important to save for your next checkup? Don't hesitate to call your doctor—day or night—with any pressing concerns. "At first, I said to myself, 'Oh, I shouldn't bother the doctor.' But then I realized that protecting my unborn babies was a lot more important than letting my doctor eat his dinner uninterrupted!" says one mother of twins.

Prenatal Care Fact Sheet:
Information Your Doctor Should Provide to You

Office Procedures

The type of care given in the office or clinic _____

Necessary laboratory tests _____

Schedule of routine examinations _____

Basic Pregnancy Information

Your due date _____

The expected course of the pregnancy _____

Nonemergency symptoms to report at your next checkup _____

Emergency Action Plan

Signs and symptoms to report to the doctor immediately _____

How to recognize contractions _____

What to do if you feel contractions _____

What to do if bleeding occurs _____

What to do if fluid trickles from your vagina _____

What to do if fluid gushes from your vagina _____

Labor Plan

Plans for hospital admission _____

Circumstances under which vaginal delivery will be attempted _____

Circumstances under which cesarean delivery will be performed _____

Analgesic and anesthetic options for labor _____

Recommended educational literature _____

Referral to childbirth preparation class _____

Referral to infant care classes _____

Referral to local support group for parents of multiples _____

Referral to tours of labor and delivery ward, newborn nursery, NICU _____

Prenatal Tests for Moms-to-Be of Multiples

"This may sound weird, but I enjoyed all my prenatal tests—even the 'yucky' ones that required drawing blood or drinking overly sweet, syrupy stuff," says Lydia Greenwood, mother of boy/girl twins. "Each time the results showed that my babies were growing well and that my own health was holding firm, I felt a surge of confidence in my ability to cope with a multiple pregnancy."

Do you, like Lydia, appreciate the chance to learn more about your unborn babies through the many prenatal testing technologies available today? If so, good—because you're likely to face a considerable amount of testing. Women carrying multiples generally undergo more types of these tests, and with greater frequency, than do mothers of singletons.

Knowing what to expect can make the process easier. As one reader explains, "I felt less out of control, because all of the tests and procedures are explained in this book. Being informed helped me settle down." Here's what you should know about prenatal tests:

PELVIC EXAMINATIONS
During the first prenatal visit, the obstetrician performs a pelvic examination by placing several gloved fingers inside your vagina in order to feel your cervix and other internal organs. This allows her to estimate how many weeks pregnant you are and to check for any cervical or structural problems. She also takes a Pap smear by using a small brush or swab to scrape a few cells

from your cervix. These are examined under a microscope to detect any abnormal cervical changes.

The pelvic examination is generally not repeated until after the 24th week of pregnancy. However, if you are experiencing symptoms of preterm labor, such as uterine contractions, pelvic pressure, or vaginal discharge, your obstetrician may do a pelvic exam in order to check for changes in the cervix.

URINE TESTS

At each prenatal visit, your urine is tested for the presence of ketones (by-products of fat breakdown), which indicate that your diet does not include sufficient carbohydrates and/or calories. Urine is also tested for protein, which may be a sign of kidney disease or preeclampsia (a serious pregnancy complication related to blood pressure). If you experience pain or other urinary symptoms, urine is analyzed for bacteria; if an infection is found, you are treated with antibiotics.

BLOOD TESTS

To check for iron-deficiency anemia, or low iron in the blood, the doctor draws blood and evaluates your hemoglobin (the oxygen-carrying, iron-containing component of red blood cells) and hematocrit (the percentage of red blood cells in the blood). Because the drain on your iron stores is greater when you're carrying more than one baby—and because adequate iron is so important to your babies' growth as well as your own health—you're checked more frequently for anemia than is a singleton mom. If you are anemic, you can increase your iron stores by eating iron-rich foods (see Chapters 3 and 4).

Your blood is also evaluated for the Rh factor. If your blood is Rh negative and your partner is Rh positive, this can potentially cause problems for your unborn babies, particularly if this is not your first pregnancy. To prevent you from making antibodies against your babies, your obstetrician may give you injections of a drug called Rho-Gam, at about 28 weeks' gestation and/or immediately after delivery.

Blood is also tested for hepatitis B, syphilis, and HIV antibodies, because these infections can be passed on to your unborn babies and cause serious harm. These blood tests may also be repeated later in pregnancy, if necessary.

ALPHA-FETOPROTEIN TEST

Alpha-fetoprotein (AFP) is a type of protein produced only by an unborn baby or its yolk sac. The test for alpha-fetoprotein, which is performed 15 to 18 weeks into the pregnancy, involves analyzing the level of this protein in the mother's blood.

High levels of AFP may indicate that a woman is carrying more than one baby—or that the twins she'd been told to expect are in fact supertwins! Elevated AFP can also mean that the pregnancy is further along than previously estimated, or it may suggest that the unborn baby has a neural tube defect such as spina bifida. A low AFP measure indicates an increased possibility of Down syndrome or other chromosomal problem, though these results are not as reliable in a multiple pregnancy.

AFP is only a screening test, not a diagnostic procedure. Abnormal results indicate the need for further testing, such as ultrasound or amniocentesis.

ULTRASOUND EXAMINATIONS

One of the wonders of modern medicine, ultrasound allows doctors to safely peek inside the womb without disturbing the pregnancy. This technology uses sound waves to create a picture of your unborn babies, the fluid surrounding them, the membranes separating them (if present), and the placenta or placentas. It is performed either by inserting a lubricated probe into the vagina or by moving a lubricated transducer back and forth across the abdomen. The probe or transducer records the echoes of sound waves bouncing off the babies, then projects the resulting images onto a video screen.

By measuring the various images, your doctor can more accurately determine your due date, gauge each baby's growth and development, and identify potential problems. (Ultrasound is also used as a guide for amniocentesis and chorionic villus sampling, described later in this chapter; it greatly reduces the risk of these procedures.)

For a woman pregnant with a singleton, ultrasound examinations are typically performed only once or twice—around the 18th week of pregnancy and perhaps again at 32 to 36 weeks. As the mother-to-be of multiples, however, you can expect to have five or more ultrasounds.

If you were an infertility patient, you may have your first ultrasound examination within the first eight weeks of your pregnancy, in order to determine the number of fetuses present. An early ultrasound also may be ordered when a woman experiences vaginal bleeding or when the doctor wants to evaluate the status of the pregnancy.

At around 18 weeks, your doctor performs what is called a structural ultrasound. This involves a very thorough evaluation of the internal and external organs of each baby as well as the structure of the placenta or placentas. At this point, the children's gender and twin type can often be detected.

Beginning at about 24 weeks, moms of multiples generally have an ultrasound every three to four weeks. Your doctor wants to monitor the growth of each baby, check the volume of amniotic fluid, and assess the location and functioning of the placenta or placentas.

Many parents find that these glimpses into the world inside the womb enhance the emotional bond they feel to their unborn babies. "My husband and I looked forward to our monthly ultrasounds. When we saw over time how both boys were keeping right up with the average growth rate for *singletons*, we felt really encouraged. That did a lot to make up for the aches and inconveniences of pregnancy," says twin mom Stacy Moore.

Sometimes, however, the findings are upsetting. "When an ultrasound showed that my twins had cysts on their heads, right away we were referred to a genetic counselor. The cysts turned out to be nothing serious, and in fact they disappeared on their own—but in the meantime, my husband and I were going nuts with worry," says one mother of twins. If you have any questions about your ultrasounds, don't hesitate to ask your doctor for clarification.

One exciting new development is the use of vaginal ultrasound to estimate the length of the cervix. Because the cervix shortens and softens as labor approaches, this measurement helps to predict which women are likely to deliver prematurely. For example, a study from 2001 found that a cervical length of less than 20 millimeters at 23 weeks occurred in only 8 percent of twin pregnancies, but accounted for 40 percent of cases in which twins were born before 33 weeks. Having this information about cervical length will help your doctor assess your risk for preterm labor and, if necessary, take appropriate steps to prevent your babies from being born early.

FETAL FIBRONECTIN TEST

Fetal fibronectin is a protein produced during pregnancy that functions as a biological glue, attaching the fetal sac to the uterine lining. During the first half of pregnancy (up to about 22 weeks' gestation), it is normal for fetal fibronectin to be found in a woman's vaginal secretions. In most cases, after 22 weeks, this protein is no longer present until a few weeks before labor. When fetal fibronectin is detected after 22 weeks, it indicates a possible increased risk of preterm delivery.

If your doctor recommends this test, she will use a cotton swab (similar to that used for a Pap smear) to collect samples of your vaginal secretions. A lab then analyzes the sample, preferably within 24 hours. If results are negative, you can feel reassured that the risk of preterm delivery is currently low. A positive result, while less reliable, allows your doctor to take preventive measures to delay labor for as long as possible.

Amniocentesis

This procedure has been used for nearly 40 years. It is routinely recommended for women 35 and older, when the risks of age-related pregnancy problems increase significantly. Amniocentesis is also advised when there is a family history of chromosomal abnormalities, or when a previous child was born with Down syndrome or a neural tube defect.

Here's how the test works: As the fetuses grow, cells from their bodies are discarded into the amniotic fluid. During amniocentesis, fluid containing these discarded cells is retrieved so that the genetic material they contain can be evaluated.

The procedure is guided by ultrasound. After cleaning your skin with antiseptic, the obstetrician inserts a long, very thin needle through your abdomen and into your uterus, then withdraws some of the amniotic fluid from each baby's amniotic sac. (In a small minority of cases, amniocentesis triggers an infection, premature labor, or even loss of the pregnancy. Most women, though, experience only slight cramping.) The fluid is sent to a laboratory, where the cells are grown and then examined for chromosomal abnormalities. The babies' gender is also determined, should you care to have this information. Test results are usually available within two weeks.

Amniocentesis is generally performed between the 15th and 20th weeks of pregnancy. Prior to 15 weeks, the complication rate is higher; after 20 weeks, it is much more difficult to perform a therapeutic abortion should the parents decide to end the pregnancy based on the test results. The procedure does carry a small risk of fetal loss. In singleton pregnancies, amniocentesis causes the loss of the fetus in about 0.6 percent of cases. In twin pregnancies, the rate of fetal loss is 2.7 percent.

Amniocentesis also may be performed toward the end of a pregnancy in the event of premature labor, because the results help to determine if the babies' lungs are mature enough to function. Late amniocentesis can also reveal various medical problems that may make it advisable to deliver the babies early because they would do better outside the womb.

Chorionic Villus Sampling

Chorionic villi are tiny projections from the chorion, a membrane that eventually becomes part of the placenta closest to the baby. Because villi contain a baby's genetic material, a sampling can be tested for a wide variety of congenital conditions.

The procedure is similar to amniocentesis. Guided by ultrasound, the obstetrician inserts a long, thin needle into the uterus, either through the abdomen or through the vagina and cervix, to collect a sampling of villi from each fetus. (There is a small risk of miscarriage, but most women experience only slight bleeding or none at all.)

A distinct advantage of CVS over amniocentesis is that it can be done earlier in the pregnancy, between the 10th and 12th weeks. Test results are ready within two weeks. If the results are abnormal, parents have the option of terminating the pregnancy during the first trimester, when therapeutic abortion is safest. This earlier diagnosis also allows parents greater privacy, since family and friends may not yet even be aware of the pregnancy.

The disadvantage is that, compared to amniocentesis, CVS carries about double the risk of miscarriage. Furthermore, because CVS is a newer technique, it is not available in all areas of the country.

GLUCOSE TOLERANCE TEST

Between the 24th and 28th weeks, you are tested for gestational diabetes. First you are given a special high-carbohydrate beverage to drink; one hour later, blood is drawn and its sugar content measured. If your blood glucose level is high during this screening test, you are scheduled for an oral glucose tolerance test (OGTT). This test is administered over a period of three hours. First you fast overnight. Then blood is drawn and analyzed. Next you drink the special high-carbohydrate beverage, and then have your blood drawn again after one, two, and three hours. If the results show two or more high levels of blood glucose, you may be given a special diet or placed on insulin until the end of your pregnancy.

The incidence of gestational diabetes is two to three times higher among women pregnant with multiples. This is in large part related to the hormonal actions of the placenta on carbohydrate metabolism during the second half of pregnancy. These actions are greater in a twin or supertwin pregnancy because of the larger size or greater number of placentas present. For this reason, some physicians recommend screening expectant mothers of multiples for gestational diabetes early in pregnancy, then repeating the tests again later.

NONSTRESS TEST

Many women carrying a singleton never undergo a nonstress test. But as a mother-to-be of multiples, you are more likely to have this test, which is done during the third trimester. Frequency and timing depend primarily on your babies' twin type and the presence of complications. Here's a typical schedule:

- Monoamniotic, monochorionic twins (one placenta, no separating membrane): twice weekly beginning as early as the 28th week.
- Diamniotic, monochorionic twins (one placenta, a single-thickness membrane): weekly beginning at 30 to 32 weeks.

- Diamniotic, dichorionic twins (two separate placentas, or two fused placentas with a double separating membrane): weekly beginning at 34 weeks.
- If the estimated weight of one or more of your unborn babies is below the 10th percentile, the nonstress test may be performed earlier and/or more frequently.
- With triplets or quadruplets, the test is usually done more often, depending on fetal growth and other clinical factors.

The purpose of the nonstress test is to evaluate your unborn babies' heartbeats and movements, as well as the frequency of uterine contractions, using external fetal monitors. If the heart rate of one or more babies does not react to movement, or if a baby does not move at all, or if other abnormalities are noted, fetal distress may be present.

BIOPHYSICAL PROFILE

This profile includes an assessment of your unborn babies' heart rates, breathing patterns, body movements, muscle tone, and amount of surrounding amniotic fluid. The heart rates are measured using the nonstress test, and ultrasound is used to determine the other measurements. Each of these measures is given a score and totaled. A score of 8 to 10 is normal. If any baby scores lower than 8, your doctor will probably repeat the test the next day. The complete evaluation takes about half an hour.

DOPPLER FLOW STUDIES

Doppler is a form of ultrasound that converts sound waves into signals. These studies evaluate the quality of blood flow through the umbilical cords of your unborn babies. The test is recommended toward the end of the pregnancy if growth has slowed down for one or more of your babies.

A TEST TO AVOID: THE X-RAY

X-rays are not a part of the normal battery of prenatal tests. The ionizing radiation used in X-rays can harm your unborn babies. Postpone elective X-rays (such as those routinely taken during a dental checkup) until after delivery. If you do need the procedure—because you've broken a bone, for instance—be sure to tell the doctor that you're pregnant. She will then take extra precautions to protect your babies, such as placing a lead shield over your abdomen.

Childbirth Preparation Classes

TAMARA: I was so excited about being pregnant that I started phoning around to find a childbirth preparation class almost as soon as I had passed my first trimester. The course I liked best, though, wasn't scheduled to begin until my seventh month. I figured that was fine—I would have plenty of time to finish the classes before the babies were born.

That's not how it worked out, of course. My twins ended up being born the night before my first class was supposed to meet. For me, childbirth preparation training consisted of the labor and delivery nurse commanding, "Breathe like this. Now blow like this. Good. Keep it up." Needless to say, I had never felt so *unprepared* in my life.

Childbirth classes are designed to help first-time parents get ready, physically and mentally, for the rigors of labor and delivery. The most common methods (Lamaze, Bradley, and Grantly Dick-Read) all center on the premise that much of the pain felt during childbirth stems from fear and tension. Although the specific techniques vary, the courses share the goal of relieving discomfort through knowledge, relaxation techniques, and emotional support. Instructors can also help you evaluate your labor options and prepare a birth plan (for instance, positions you'd like to try and people you'd like to be present). Provided you discuss these preferences with your obstetrician well ahead of time, chances are she'll try to accommodate them if possible.

Even if you've given birth before, consider taking a refresher course. The classroom environment offers an opportunity to practice the breathing and relaxation exercises and to receive updated information on any hospital policies that might have changed since your last delivery. It's also a forum for meeting new friends who, like you, are about to expand their families.

For the most rewarding experience, shop around for a class designed for expectant parents of multiples. "My instructor had never dealt with a twin pregnancy before. She had little input on how my labor and delivery might be different from a singleton mother's. But still, it was worthwhile. The breathing techniques didn't help me much, but the focusing and relaxing strategies were useful," Stacy Moore says. Be sure your course includes information and advice on cesarean sections, since about half of all twins and nearly all triplets and quadruplets are delivered this way.

For more information, contact the following organizations:

- American Academy of Husband-Coached Childbirth (aka the Bradley Method): PO Box 5524, Sherman Oaks, CA 91413-5224. Telephone 800–4–A–BIRTH; Web site www.bradleybirth.com.

- Lamaze International (aka American Society for Psychoprophylaxis in Obstetrics): 2025 M Street NW, Suite 800, Washington, DC 20036-3309. Telephone 800–368–4404; Web site www.lamaze.org.
- International Childbirth Education Association: PO Box 20048, Minneapolis, MN 55420. Telephone 952–854–8660; Web site www.icea.org.

Keep in mind that it's wise to schedule the class for your second trimester in case you end up delivering early, as many mothers of multiples do. If you need to go on bedrest—another common occurrence in multiple pregnancies—consider hiring an instructor to come to your home for private lessons. Not only will you feel more prepared for childbirth, but the tedium of bedrest will be alleviated by the companionship and sense of purpose such instruction can provide.

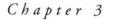

Chapter 3

Weight-Gain Goals
and Nutrition Know-How

Feeling like your life is not completely under your control right now? No wonder. Starting from the day you get the big news that not just one but two or more babies are on the way, your pregnancy is prone to *surprises*. Your delivery date is harder to predict. It's possible you'll have to stop working sooner than you'd anticipated. You may need to go on bedrest unexpectedly. If you're normally a careful planner or a take-charge type, it's disconcerting to feel suddenly that you are no longer directing the action.

But there's one aspect of this surprise-filled pregnancy over which you do have *total control:* your diet. That's terrific, because nutrition is one of the most important factors affecting you and your unborn babies.

This isn't mere speculation. Decades of research, involving thousands of twin and super-twin pregnancies, support this statement: What you put in your mouth in the coming months will determine, to a significant extent, the size and health status of your babies at birth—and beyond. Consider this:

- Babies who are well nourished *in utero* have significantly higher birthweights and are healthier at birth than less well-nourished babies born at the same gestational age.
- Good intrauterine growth may reduce the likelihood of premature birth. Evidence suggests that some survival mechanism detects when babies are not growing well in the womb and may trigger labor. (For instance, twins whose rate of growth during pregnancy is among the lowest 10 percent are five times more likely to be born

before 33 weeks. Triplets whose rate of growth during pregnancy is among the lowest 25 percent are likely to be born five weeks earlier than average, whereas triplets whose growth is among the highest 25 percent are likely to be born nearly three weeks later than average.)

- Even if they are born prematurely, babies who have been properly nourished in the womb have *fewer illnesses* and recover from them more quickly than do infants whose mothers had inadequate diets.

- Because the prenatal period involves the most rapid growth of the entire life cycle, optimal nutrition now provides your babies with the best blueprint for a healthy childhood. And that, in turn, gives them a running start on being healthy adults.

Each of your unborn babies has the same genetic potential as any other unborn baby—the potential to weigh 6, 7, even 8 pounds or more at birth. For multiples, certain factors can limit the realization of that potential: the length of your pregnancy, the amount of space available inside your womb, your level of physical activity. The proper diet helps to minimize the negative influences of those factors, so that each of your babies can come as close as possible to reaching his or her genetic potential for a healthy birthweight.

So don't think of the special nutritional demands of multiple pregnancy as a burden. Instead, see them as a means of empowerment. When you decide to make every bite count, your babies reap the benefits. "The nutrition program at the University of Michigan Multiples Clinic gave me an element of control over my pregnancy and increased my confidence in my ability to carry my twins to term," says Stacy Moore, mother of fraternal twin boys. "I firmly believe that my careful attention to diet was the major reason why my twins had such healthy birthweights—Steven was 6 lb., 11 oz., and Brandon was 6 lb., 1 oz."

DR. LUKE: I tell moms-to-be that pregnancy has a lot in common with gardening. You can't just throw seeds into soil, neglect to feed or water them, and still expect blue-ribbon roses. You have to nurture and nourish your potential showstoppers. So it's only logical that nutrition would play an important role in pregnancy.

Multiples are not automatically born small. There are lots of 6- and 7-pound twins out there to prove it. In fact, I recently encountered a pair of twins whose birthweights were 8 lb., 2 oz., and a whopping 11 pounds! The moms who deliver the largest and healthiest multiples are in general the ones who are diligent about meeting their prenatal dietary goals: gaining the right amount of weight, at the right time, by eating the right foods.

Every time I walk into the newborn nursery or NICU, the nurses say that they can immediately tell which infants were born to mothers from our clinic, and which were not—

because our babies are usually bigger. Our statistics prove it: Triplets born to our Multiples Clinic patients weigh 35 percent more at birth, on average, than triplets typically do. And our twins are generally born 20 percent heavier than the average twins delivered at the same gestational age.

Your multiples can benefit from our nutrition program too. It's simple:

- Follow the weight-gain and dietary guidelines in this chapter and Chapter 4.
- Make use of the highly nutritious recipes at the back of the book.
- Personalized nutrition counseling is just a click away, when you visit my Web site, www.drbarbaraluke.com.
- For even more in-depth information on nutrition during pregnancy, as well as throughout your babies' childhood, consult another of our books, *Program Your Baby's Health: The Pregnancy Diet for Your Child's Lifelong Well-Being.*

What's Your Weight-Gain Target?

TAMARA: When an ultrasound unexpectedly revealed that I was carrying twins, my obstetrician gave me a big bearhug and his heartiest congratulations. What he didn't give me was any particular advice related to my new status as an expectant mother of multiples.

Finally I asked him if I needed to change my diet or increase the weight-gain goal he'd given me at the beginning of my pregnancy. He replied, "Oh, just keep on eating what you've been eating. And maybe you should plan to gain an extra 5 pounds, just to be safe. Let's aim for a total of about 30 pounds instead of 25." I followed that advice to the letter, putting on precisely 30 pounds.

But it wasn't enough. Staring at my 3 lb., 6 oz., son and my 2 lb., 5 oz., daughter as they lay in their isolettes in the NICU, I realized it wasn't *nearly* enough.

Unfortunately, many expectant mothers of multiples receive little or no nutrition advice. Those who are given a diet to follow may discover that it's the same diet prescribed for all the pregnant patients in a doctor's practice—most of whom are of course expecting singletons. Doctors who have limited experience with multiple pregnancy are not always aware of the increased nutritional needs of women like you.

"The other physicians in my obstetrician's practice were not as knowledgeable about multiple pregnancy as she was," says Benita Moreno, mother of fraternal twin boys. "One time when my own doctor was out of town, I had to see one of her associates. Because I'm plump to begin with and had gained another 5 pounds that month, this doctor belittled me for eating too much! When I told my dietitian what had happened, she was appalled and said, 'No one should *ever* tell a pregnant mother of multiples not to gain weight.'"

Such misinformation stems from the fact that most research on weight gain during pregnancy has focused on singletons—because in the past, multiple births were rare. But now the data on twins, triplets, and quadruplets are beginning to add up. And not surprisingly, prenatal weight gain seems to be even more important when a woman is pregnant with multiples. In a singleton pregnancy, a woman can gain anywhere from 20 to 60 pounds and still have a 7-pound baby born at full term. But with multiples, a much narrower range of weight gain is associated with a good outcome.

Stated simply: You probably need to *gain more* than you imagined—and certainly more than your friends expecting singletons have been counseled to gain. You also need to put on those pounds *more quickly* than a singleton mom does. The more babies you're carrying, the less time you have to gain the needed weight, because the shorter your pregnancy probably will be. (Remember, you're very unlikely to go a full 40 weeks.) Based on extensive research on multiple pregnancies, here's what is recommended:

Weight-Gain Guidelines for Moms-to-Be of Multiples

If You're Expecting . . .	Your Total Weight-Gain Goal Is . . .
Twins	40–56 lb. (for a normal-weight woman)
Triplets	58–75 lb.
Quadruplets	70–80 lb.

Table 3.1

DR. LUKE: The number of babies you're carrying is the most important factor in determining your weight-gain goal, but it's not the only one. Your prepregnancy weight is a vital consideration too.

The thinner you were before you conceived, the more you need to gain now. That's because if you are underweight, the first pounds you put on will go primarily to correcting your own weight deficit, rather than to promoting the growth of the babies inside you. You should therefore aim to gain the amount it would take to bring you within the normal weight range for your height and body build (as outlined in Table 3.2 below), *plus* the amount recommended for the number of babies you're expecting. My co-author Tamara, for example, would have been well advised to aim for a weight gain of 50 to 66 pounds, given that she began her twin pregnancy about 10 pounds underweight.

What if you were overweight when you conceived? Sometimes heavy women look at pregnancy as an opportunity to slim down. Overweight patients have said to me, "I know I'll lose weight automatically when the babies are born. So if I can just maintain my current weight during the pregnancy, in nine months I'll be 25 pounds thinner." This faulty reasoning is "penny-wise and pound-foolish." The mom's body may be in better shape after delivery, but what shape will the babies' bodies be in? To keep your babies growing well, you *must* gain a reasonable amount of weight from eating the right foods. An overweight woman who is carrying twins can get by with gaining somewhat less than we normally recommend for twin pregnancies. (See page 64 for specific guidelines.) However, if you're expecting supertwins, you should stick with our recommendations, even if you were overweight when you conceived.

Prepregnancy Weight-for-Height and Body Frame Size (Pounds / Inches)

Height	Small Frame			Medium Frame			Large Frame		
	Under-weight	Normal Weight	Over-weight	Under-weight	Normal Weight	Over-weight	Under-weight	Normal Weight	Over-weight
57"	94	104	125	100	112	134	109	122	146
58"	95	105	126	102	114	137	112	124	149
59"	96	107	128	105	117	140	114	127	152

(continued)

Height	Small Frame			Medium Frame			Large Frame		
	Under-weight	Normal Weight	Over-weight	Under-weight	Normal Weight	Over-weight	Under-weight	Normal Weight	Over-weight
60"	98	109	131	107	119	143	116	129	155
61"	101	112	134	110	122	146	118	132	158
62"	104	115	138	113	125	150	122	136	163
63"	106	118	142	115	128	154	126	140	168
64"	109	121	145	118	131	157	128	143	172
65"	112	124	149	120	134	161	132	147	176
66"	114	127	152	123	137	164	135	150	180
67"	117	130	156	126	140	168	138	154	185
68"	120	133	160	129	143	172	141	157	188
69"	122	136	163	131	146	175	144	160	192
70"	125	139	167	134	149	179	146	163	196
71"	128	142	170	137	152	182	149	166	199
72"	131	145	174	140	155	186	152	169	203

Note: Underweight means 10 percent or more below normal weight-for-height and frame size. Overweight means 20 percent or more above normal weight-for-height and frame size.

Table 3.2

In setting a weight-gain goal, expectant mothers of multiples also need to consider several additional factors:

- Is this your *first pregnancy*? For women who have not given birth before, the uterus has not yet been stretched. Higher weight gain will help to ensure better fetal growth. Try to gain an additional 5 to 7 pounds as quickly as possible.
- Was your pregnancy the result of *infertility treatments*? If so, you should aim to gain an additional 4 to 6 pounds during the first half of your pregnancy. Though the exact reason is not known, evidence suggests that this extra weight can reduce the risk of miscarriage in pregnancies resulting from assisted reproductive technologies.
- Are you a *smoker*, or did you recently quit smoking? In the blood and other tissues, smokers tend to have lower levels of many essential nutrients. Smokers in general are also thinner. If you're still smoking, you've never had a better reason to stop. If you quit when you became pregnant, good for you! But remember that your body needs time to replenish those nutrients that cigarettes siphoned off. Be particularly careful to eat a balanced diet, and plan on gaining an additional 5 to 7 pounds.

Your Weight-Gain Pattern: Why It Matters So Much

Pregnant women are often told that there's no need to gain a lot of weight early on, because the baby is so small that it doesn't yet require much in terms of calories. But current research has demonstrated that just the opposite is true. There are a number of reasons why it is vital for mothers-to-be of multiples to put on a significant number of pounds in the first one-half to two-thirds of their pregnancy:

- Your weight gain up to 28 weeks has the greatest influence on the babies' rate of growth. Recent research on twin pregnancies has shown that the amount you gain *before* 28 weeks' gestation significantly influences your babies' growth rates both before and *after* 28 weeks—and all the way up to their delivery date. With triplets and quadruplets, the weight you gain before 24 weeks has the greatest effect on your babies' rate of growth, while weight gained after 24 weeks has less effect on growth rate. (For instance, triplets whose moms gain at least 36 pounds by week 24 generally are born nearly half a pound heavier than triplets whose moms did not hit this early weight-gain goal.) Therefore, your pattern of weight gain may actually be more important than your total weight gain.

- Certain hormonal changes of pregnancy are expressly intended to facilitate maternal weight gain long before the fetuses themselves gain any significant amount of weight. (That's why pregnant women feel so ravenous, often even before they realize they have conceived!) The purpose is to increase your body stores of fat and other nutrients during the first half of pregnancy, thereby providing a nutritional reserve for the second half of pregnancy, when diet alone can't keep pace with the nutritional demands of the fetuses. In other words, a significant portion of the weight you gain early on is needed to sustain your babies' growth later.
- It becomes harder to gain weight as your pregnancy progresses. The bigger your babies grow, the less room there is for your stomach to expand. As anyone who has given birth to a full-term singleton can attest, by the time a woman reaches 40 weeks, there's scarcely any room left for food. With multiples, that 40-week size arrives much sooner—at around 32 weeks for twins, 28 weeks for triplets, and 24 weeks for quads.
- You won't have a full nine months in which to gain, since multiples are almost always delivered before 40 weeks. The more babies you're carrying, the less time you'll have to put on the needed pounds.

To ensure that your weight-gain pattern is optimal, you'll want to set *three weight-gain goals*. The first target is the amount you need to gain by the 20th week of pregnancy; the second target is the amount you need to gain by the 28th week; and the third is the amount you need to gain between week 28 and your delivery date. Here are the recommended targets, along with the average length of pregnancy for the number of babies expected. (Singleton pregnancy is included for the sake of comparison.)

Optimal Weight-Gain Patterns During Pregnancy

Type of Pregnancy	Weight Gain by 20 Weeks	Weight Gain by 28 Weeks	Total Weight Gain	Average Length of Gestation
Singleton	12 lb.	20 lb.	25–35 lb.	40 weeks
Twins	25 lb.	38 lb.	40–56 lb.	36 weeks
Triplets	35 lb.	54 lb.	58–75 lb.	32 weeks
Quadruplets	45 lb.	65 lb.	70–80 lb.	30 weeks

Table 3.3

If you were underweight to begin with, or if you lost weight during the first trimester owing to morning sickness or other illness, you should make up that deficit early in your pregnancy. "I got a bad stomach virus shortly after conceiving my twins, and I lost 7 pounds. Since I'm slender to begin with, Dr. Luke was very concerned. She told me I had to gain 40 pounds by my 24th week of pregnancy," says Judy Levy, mother of fraternal twin girls.

Note: *Even if you were overweight* before becoming pregnant, if you're expecting supertwins, the recommended weight gain by 24 weeks remains the same—45 pounds for triplets, and 55 pounds for quadruplets.

Understanding BMI: The Body Mass Index

A healthy weight is more than just a number on the bathroom scale. It's a balance between your body's proportions of muscle and fat. The amount of body fat associated with good overall health ranges from 20 to 25 percent.

Body fat isn't easy to measure. The old caliper method, used by many health clubs, is not accurate. However, new scales that have recently come on the market do a fairly good job of measuring body fat as well as weight. One such product is the Taylor Body Fat Analyzer & Scale ($49.99).

Another option is to estimate your body fat using the body mass index, or BMI. To calculate your prepregnancy body mass index, locate your height in the far left column of Table 3.4, then move across that row to find your weight. At the top of your weight column is your body mass index. A BMI in the range of 20 to 24 is optimal; below 20 is underweight; above 24 is overweight; and above 29 is obese.

Determining Your Body Mass Index (BMI)

Body Mass Index

Height (inches)	17	18	19	20	21	22	23	24	25	26
				Body Weight (pounds)						
58	82	87	91	96	100	105	110	115	119	124
59	85	90	94	99	104	109	114	119	124	128
60	87	93	97	102	107	112	118	123	128	133
61	90	96	100	106	111	116	122	127	132	137
62	93	99	104	109	115	120	126	131	136	142
63	96	102	107	113	118	124	130	135	141	146
64	99	105	110	116	122	128	134	140	145	151
65	103	109	114	120	126	132	138	144	150	156
66	106	112	118	124	130	136	142	148	155	161
67	109	115	121	127	134	140	146	153	159	166
68	112	119	125	131	138	144	151	158	164	171
69	116	122	128	135	142	149	155	162	169	176
70	119	126	132	139	146	153	160	167	174	181
71	122	130	136	143	150	157	165	172	179	186
72	126	133	140	147	154	162	169	177	184	191
73	129	137	144	151	159	166	174	182	189	197
74	133	141	148	155	163	171	179	186	194	202
	Underweight			Normal Weight					Overweight	

Table 3.4

Body Mass Index

27	28	29	30	31	32	33	34	35
			Body Weight (pounds)					
129	134	138	143	149	154	159	163	168
133	138	143	148	154	159	164	169	174
138	143	148	153	159	165	170	175	180
143	148	153	158	165	170	175	181	186
147	153	158	164	170	176	181	187	192
152	158	163	169	176	181	187	193	198
157	163	169	174	181	187	193	199	205
162	168	174	180	187	193	199	205	211
167	173	179	186	193	199	205	212	218
172	178	185	191	199	205	212	218	224
177	184	190	197	205	211	218	225	231
182	189	196	203	211	218	224	231	238
188	195	202	207	217	224	231	238	245
193	200	208	215	223	230	238	245	252
199	206	213	221	230	237	244	252	259
204	212	219	227	236	244	251	259	266
210	218	225	233	243	250	258	266	274
			Obese					

Now that you know your prepregnancy BMI, use that number to check Table 3.5. This gives you a more detailed picture of exactly how much weight you need to gain, and when, in order to promote the healthiest possible growth for twins. (Boldface weights are for weeks 20, 28, and 38.)

Week-by-Week Weight-Gain Recommendations for Women Pregnant with Twins, Based on BMI

Weeks' Gestation	10	12	14	16	18	**20**	22	24	26	**28**	30	32	34	36	**38**
BMI <20.0															
Advised Gain (lb.)		1.25–1.75 lb./week					1.5–2.0 lb./week				1.25–1.5 lb./week				
Advised Range (lb.)															
Upper	18	21	25	29	32	**35**	39	43	47	**51**	54	57	60	63	**66**
Lower	13	15	18	21	23	**25**	28	31	34	**37**	40	42	45	47	**50**
BMI 20.0–24.9															
Advised Gain (lb.)		1.0–1.5 lb./week					1.25–2.0 lb./week				1.0 lb./week				
Advised Range (lb.)															
Upper	15	18	21	24	27	**30**	34	38	42	**46**	48	50	52	54	**56**
Lower	10	12	14	16	18	**20**	23	25	27	**30**	32	34	36	38	**40**
BMI 25.0–29.9															
Advised Gain (lb.)		1.0–1.25 lb./week					1.0–1.5 lb./week				1.0 lb./week				
Advised Range (lb.)															
Upper	13	15	18	20	23	**25**	28	31	34	**37**	39	41	43	45	**47**
Lower	10	12	14	16	18	**20**	22	24	26	**28**	30	32	34	36	**38**
BMI >29.9															
Advised Gain (lb.)		0.75–1.0 lb./week					1.0 lb./week				0.75 lb./week				
Advised Range (lb.)															
Upper	10	12	14	16	18	**20**	22	24	26	**28**	30	31	33	34	**36**
Lower	8	9	11	12	14	**15**	17	19	21	**23**	25	26	28	29	**31**

Table 3.5

Note that Table 3.5 refers to twin pregnancies. If you are expecting supertwins, your weight-gain goals are different. Table 3.6 gives the numbers for all women pregnant with triplets, no matter what your BMI; Table 3.7 is for all women expecting quadruplets.

Week-by-Week Weight-Gain Recommendations for Women Pregnant with Triplets

Weeks' Gestation	10	12	14	16	18	**20**	22	24	26	**28**	30	32	**34**
Advised Gain (lb.)	1.5–2.0 lb./week					2.0–2.5 lb./week							
Advised Range (lb.)													
Upper	20	24	28	32	36	**40**	45	50	55	**60**	65	70	**75**
Lower	15	18	21	24	27	**30**	34	38	42	**46**	50	54	**58**

Table 3.6

Week-by-Week Weight-Gain Recommendations for Women Pregnant with Quadruplets

Weeks' Gestation	10	12	14	16	18	**20**	22	24	26	**28**	30	**32**
Advised Gain (lb.)	2.0–2.5 lb./week					2.5 lb./week						
Advised Range (lb.)												
Upper	25	30	35	40	45	**50**	55	60	65	**70**	75	**80**
Lower	20	24	28	32	36	**40**	45	50	55	**60**	65	**70**

Table 3.7

DR. LUKE: Weight gain in the range of 100 pounds or more is the nagging fear of many mothers-to-be of multiples and their obstetricians. It's true that gains beyond a certain point no longer benefit a mom or her babies. But if you follow the specific guidelines outlined in this chapter and the next regarding portion sizes and food choices, you won't gain 100 pounds or come anywhere close to it. Our recommendations are based on a diet with balanced proportions of proteins, carbohydrates, and fats as well as lots of fluids. Wholesome, healthy foods will fill you up, make you feel energized, and keep your babies growing stronger every day.

On the other hand, a diet based on French fries and chocolate cake may enable you to gain 50 or 65 pounds—or much more—but you'll feel sluggish and run-down, and your babies won't grow very well. And you'll still be left with 20, 30, or 40 extra pounds to lose, months after you deliver. So go ahead and enjoy your cheeseburger, but go light on the fries. Treat yourself to an occasional candy bar, but only after you've finished your pork chops and green beans.

Following the food plan in this chapter and in Chapter 4 is the best way to promote optimal growth for your unborn babies, while assuring that you'll be able to regain your figure after delivery. You don't have to take my word for it. Consider what one reader has to say: "I'm 5 feet, 2 inches tall and had a prepregnancy weight of 120 pounds. I delivered healthy twins at 39 weeks, with weights of 7 lb., 1 oz., and 6 lb., 12 oz. I followed the diet and weight-gain recommendations from this book. At six weeks postdelivery, I'm only 10 pounds over my prepregnancy weight—which tells me that all the weight the book recommended I gain really *did* go toward supporting the healthy development of my babies."

A Better Way Than the Bathroom Scale to Plot Your Progress

The bathroom scale is not necessarily the best way to plot your weight-gain progress, because it does not really indicate how your babies are growing. That's why anthropometric measures may be used to evaluate the health and nutritional status of your pregnancy. For this, nutritionists measure body fat in three sites: the upper arm, midback (at the base of the shoulder blades), and midthigh. A simple way for you to periodically monitor these changes yourself is to use a tape measure to track your upper-arm circumference midway between elbow and shoulder, and your thigh midway between hipbone and knee.

Remember that pregnancy hormones cause you to put on pounds long before your babies gain any significant amount of weight. The fat your body stores during the first half of pregnancy serves as a nutritional reserve for the second half, when it's difficult to take in enough calories to meet your babies' metabolic demands for growth.

Most women find this a very interesting phenomenon to track, because weight gain (as measured by the bathroom scale) and your babies' growth (as measured by ultrasound) rapidly increase after about 28 weeks of pregnancy, while body fat (as measured at the upper arm and midthigh) remains the same or even decreases. Twin mom Judy Levy says, "It was interesting to see that my upper-arm measurement stayed at 10 inches from 28 weeks all the way to when I delivered at 37½ weeks, even though I gained 20 pounds during that time."

An additional measurement done at each prenatal visit is an assessment of your fundal height, or an estimate of the size of your uterus. While lying on your back, the doctor or nurse measures the distance from the top of your belly to your pubic bone. This provides an indirect measure of your babies' growth. For a singleton pregnancy, this figure (measured in centimeters) is typically about the same as the length of the pregnancy in weeks. For example, 26 weeks into her pregnancy, the average expectant mother of a singleton has a fundal height of 26 centimeters.

When you're pregnant with multiples, of course, your uterus grows much faster. But don't be alarmed if, after the 30th week or so, your obstetrician notes during one of your visits that the fundal height hasn't increased. Your babies may have changed positions, and you are probably "wider" that week than you were before—but the doctor doesn't measure width.

Use the chart on the following pages to keep track of your own measurements, your weight-gain progress, and the results of various tests:

Plotting Your Progress

DATE								
WEEK	**10**	**12**	**14**	**16**	**18**	**20**	**21**	**22**
Fundal height								
Cervical exam								
Blood pressure								
Upper-arm circumference								
Weight								
Net gain								
Hemoglobin								
Hematocrit								
Glucose (one-hour)								
Rho-Gam								
Urine culture								

ULTRASOUND DATE								
WEEK	**10**	**12**	**14**	**16**	**18**	**20**	**21**	**22**
50th percentile (grams)	35	58	93	146	223	331	399	478
50th percentile (ounces)	1.2	2	3.3	5.1	7.9	11.7	14	17
Baby A								
Baby B								
Baby C								
Baby D								

Plotting Your Progress

DATE

WEEK	23	24	25	26	27	28	29	30
Fundal height								
Cervical exam								
Blood pressure								
Upper-arm circumference								
Weight								
Net gain								
Hemoglobin								
Hematocrit								
Glucose (one-hour)								
Rho-Gam								
Urine culture								

ULTRASOUND DATE

WEEK	23	24	25	26	27	28	29	30
50th percentile (grams)	568	670	785	913	1,055	1,210	1,379	1,559
50th percentile (lb./oz.)	1 lb., 4 oz.	1 lb., 8 oz.	1 lb., 12 oz.	2 lb., 0 oz.	2 lb., 5 oz.	2 lb., 11 oz.	3 lb., 0 oz.	3 lb., 7 oz.
Baby A								
Baby B								
Baby C								
Baby D								

(continued)

Plotting Your Progress

DATE

WEEK	31	32	33	34	35	36	37	38
Fundal height								
Cervical exam								
Blood pressure								
Upper-arm circumference								
Weight								
Net gain								
Hemoglobin								
Hematocrit								
Glucose (one-hour)								
Rho-Gam								
Urine culture								

ULTRASOUND DATE

WEEK	31	32	33	34	35	36	37	38
50th percentile (grams)	1,751	1,953	2,162	2,377	2,595	2,813	3,028	3,236
50th percentile (lb./oz.)	3 lb., 14 oz.	4 lb., 5 oz.	4 lb., 12 oz.	5 lb., 4 oz.	5 lb., 11 oz.	6 lb., 3 oz.	6 lb., 11 oz.	7 lb., 2 oz.
Baby A								
Baby B								
Baby C								
Baby D								

Table 3.8

Need-to-Know Nutrition

Knowing how much weight to gain and when to gain it in order to maximize your babies' growth is step 1. Step 2 is learning when and what to eat. Yet it can be very difficult to find practical advice that can transform dietary guidelines from a confusing array of grams and milligrams into a workable, day-to-day eating plan. As one mother of triplets says, "I loved my obstetrician, but I admit he didn't give me much in the way of specific suggestions on how often or how much to eat, or even on which foods would be most beneficial."

Yet planning your prenatal diet doesn't need to be complicated. Follow this simple rule: *Eat three meals a day, plus two to three substantial snacks.* Most women find a workable schedule to be breakfast, midmorning snack, lunch, midafternoon snack, dinner, and bedtime snack. Understand too that a snack does *not* mean carrots and celery sticks. It means something substantial, a mini-meal—cereal and milk with bananas, a tuna fish sandwich, a frozen dinner like macaroni and cheese, or a jumbo muffin with a large glass of milk.

If this sounds like you should be eating almost all the time, you are right! And here's why: The central issue is blood glucose control, which means maintaining an appropriate blood sugar level. Your unborn babies' nervous systems need a constant supply of glucose in order to develop properly. When you skip meals or go too long without a snack, your blood sugar level drops and your babies are deprived of the glucose they need. Fasting is particularly dangerous because it leads to extremely low blood sugar, or hypoglycemia, which can trigger preterm labor.

Fortunately, eating so often won't be as hard as you think, because being pregnant with multiples makes you feel much hungrier than usual. "Before I even realized I was pregnant, and long before I knew it was twins, I couldn't understand why I was suddenly so famished all the time. For instance, I was stopping at Burger King every afternoon, though I'd never done that before. I guess my body knew that my babies needed the extra food, even if my brain hadn't yet gotten the message," says Stacy Moore.

Don't wait for hunger to signal that it's time to fuel up, though. To take in enough calories to support a multiple pregnancy, you need to *eat at least every two to three hours.* "I knew I couldn't rely on hunger pangs to tell me when to sit down to a meal or snack. When you're supposed to eat every two hours, you never get much chance to feel hungry. Instead, I just watched the clock," says Helen Armer, mother of triplets. "I was very disciplined about doing exactly what the Multiples Clinic staff had told me to do, so I never ever missed a meal or snack." Helen's dedication paid off: At birth, her largest baby weighed 5 lb., 13 oz., and even the smallest weighed a respectable 4 lb., 11 oz. Compared to the national average for triplets of just 3 lb., 11 oz., the Armer trio were downright hefty.

If you're someone for whom additional weight gain is recommended (you're underweight, you're a former smoker, etc.), you need to eat even more often. For instance, Judy Levy, whose prepregnancy weight was a mere 105 pounds, was advised to eat every 90 minutes. "I'd look at the clock and say, 'Oops, I haven't eaten anything in an hour and a half. Time to nourish those twins,'" says Judy.

Eating frequently also keeps you feeling your best. Stacy Moore explains, "I knew that if I felt woozy, it meant my blood sugar had dropped because I had gone too long without food. I learned to keep some crackers with me at all times, in case I became lightheaded."

Conscientiously following this eating schedule will help to ensure that your babies are well grown at birth, even if they arrive early. As one reader reports, "My identical twin girls were born healthy at 36 weeks. It is because of the diet that Dr. Luke recommends in this book that the pediatrician exclaimed excitedly during their first exam, 'They're so strong. They're behaving like full-term newborns!'"

DR. LUKE: The metabolic and hormonal changes that occur with pregnancy are all geared toward creating and maintaining the environment most favorable for fetal growth and development. These changes include an increased requirement for all nutrients. But the need for certain nutrients is far greater than the need for others.

That's why the National Academy of Sciences' Food and Nutrition Board publishes recommended dietary allowances (RDAs) for pregnant women, setting a standard for how much of each specific nutrient an expectant mother should take in each day. These RDAs, however, are geared toward women pregnant with singletons. No guidelines have yet been established for women pregnant with twins, triplets, or quadruplets. So how can you know how much of each nutrient you need to nourish your unborn babies?

In our clinic, we advise moms-to-be of twins to increase their intake of each nutrient by 50 to 100 percent over the RDAs for a singleton pregnancy. Women carrying triplets and quads need to boost their nutrient intake even more. Table 3.9 lists my own educated estimates of the nutritional requirements for women pregnant with multiples. Until more extensive research can provide us with better answers, these figures are your best bet.

Estimated Nutrient Requirements
for Expectant Mothers of Multiples

Nutrient	Dietary Sources	Nonpregnant	Singleton Pregnancy	Twin Pregnancy	Triplet Pregnancy	Quadruplet Pregnancy
Calories	Proteins, fats, and carbohydrates	2,200 kcal	2,500 kcal	3,500 kcal	4,000 kcal	4,500 kcal
Protein (20%)	Meats, seafood, poultry, dairy products	110 g	126 g	176 g	200 g	225 g
Carbohydrate (40%)	Breads, cereals, pasta, dairy, fruits	220 g	248 g	350 g	400 g	450 g
Fat (40%)	Dairy products, nuts, oils	98 g	112 g	155 g	178 g	200 g

Table 3.9

What's So Important About These Nutrients?

It's wise to keep a detailed record of what you eat for a week and to review it with your dietitian. Says Anne Seifert, mother of quadruplets: "Dr. Luke had me keep a log of every bite I ate. Then she analyzed it to make sure I was getting enough of everything I needed, particularly protein and fat."

Protein and fat? That's right. Although many people, in general, should cut down on high-fat fare and mega-portions of meat, this advice is not targeted toward expectant mothers of multiples. One reader explains it well: "While pregnancy is a very limited time in *your* life, it is a time of literal life-and-death importance to the *babies* you are carrying. No, a diet comparatively high in protein and fat is not healthy for most people—but for a limited time period and for a specific purpose, you will survive it. The point is to give your body the nutrients it needs to build all those babies."

To motivate yourself to achieve the right balance of protein, carbohydrate, and fat, it helps to understand how each contributes to the well-being of your unborn babies.

Proteins are the body's basic building blocks.

Proteins are made up of amino acids, structural units that are essential for building and repairing tissue as well as forming blood, bones, and the brain. Amino acids are also vital components of enzymes, hormones, and antibodies (part of the immune system). Once you are pregnant, you need extra protein in order to build the placentas; to allow for increases in breast and uterine tissue and in blood volume; and, of course, to promote the babies' growth.

Some of the amino acids in protein cannot be made by the body. These are called the essential amino acids, and they must be included in the diet. For this reason, the quality of the protein you eat during pregnancy is important. Protein foods that contain all essential amino acids—called complete proteins—include meat, fish, poultry, eggs, and dairy products.

Fats promote proper nerve development and help prevent pregnancy complications.

Fat provides a carrier for the fat-soluble vitamins A and D and plays a critical role in nerve development and tissue growth. In fact, fat is an integral part of nearly every cell in your babies' bodies.

As with protein, some of the structural components of fat—called the essential fatty acids—cannot be manufactured by the body and must be supplied from food. Good sources include all seafood and fish, egg yolks, and oils such as flaxseed, canola, and olive. During pregnancy, a higher intake of essential fatty acids such as omega-3 provides many benefits:

- It significantly lessens the mother's risk of developing preeclampsia, a serious complication of pregnancy characterized by a rapid rise in blood pressure (see Chapter 6).
- Omega-3 helps to reduce the risk of preterm delivery, perhaps by inhibiting the synthesis of prostaglandin, a substance that initiates labor.
- This essential fatty acid promotes the development of your unborn babies' nervous systems and vision.
- Evidence suggests that babies born to mothers who got plenty of omega-3 have a reduced risk of developing high blood pressure in the future.

Carbohydrates provide energy.

Every living creature needs an energy source. Carbohydrates provide the primary energy source for adults—and the *only* energy source that can be used for unborn babies' developing nervous systems. Carbohydrates come in two forms: simple and complex. Simple carbohydrates are found in fruits, honey, milk, and refined sugar. Complex carbohydrates include potatoes, corn, wheat, and rice.

Adequate intake of carbohydrates also helps prevent two common problems of pregnancy. The first is constipation. Fiber, a nondigestible form of carbohydrate, absorbs water as it passes through the digestive system and aids in proper bowel function. High-fiber foods include breads and cereals made from bran or whole grain, and raw fruits and vegetables.

The second problem, which afflicts expectant mothers of multiples even more often than it does other pregnant women, is hypoglycemia, or a sudden drop in blood sugar. Symptoms include shakiness, dizziness, fatigue, irritability, and mood swings. Carbohydrates help to maintain a regular blood sugar level, especially when eaten in combination with protein foods—for instance, crackers with peanut butter or cheese, cereal and milk, or prosciutto with melon.

DR. LUKE: In Table 3.9 on page 73, you'll notice that the proportion of calories you should get from protein, fat, and carbohydrates remains the same, no matter how many babies you're carrying. But the required calorie counts increase with each additional baby.

Rather than thinking of the daily diet in terms of these percentages, however, most of our patients find it easier to talk about the basic food groups. That's why I've translated the requirements to create the menu guidelines in Table 3.10, which lists the appropriate number of servings per day from each food group. These guidelines also reflect a pregnant woman's need to increase her intake of calcium, iron, and other tissue-building nutrients, depending on the number of babies she's expecting.

Recommended Servings per Day from the Food Groups

Food Group	Serving Size	Nonpregnant	Singleton	Twins	Triplets	Quadruplets

Dairy	8 oz. (1 cup) milk
	8 oz. (1 cup)
	  cottage cheese*
	8 oz. (1 cup)
	  ice cream
	1 oz. (1 slice)
	  hard cheese
		4	6	8	10	12

Vegetables	½ cup cooked or 1 cup fresh	4	4	4	5	6
Fruits	½ cup or 1 fresh	4	4	7	8	8
Grains, breads	1 oz., 1 cup cooked, or 1 slice	8	8	10	12	12
Fats, oils, and nuts	1 tsp. oil 1 tsp. butter 1 oz. nuts	4	5	6	7	8
Eggs	1 fresh	—	1	2	2	2
Meat, fish, poultry	3 oz.	2	2	3	3	4

*Calcium-fortified brands

Table 3.10

The Food Groups Demystified

"It seemed like a nuisance at first to keep track of the food groups. I'd lose count by mid-afternoon—was I up to four servings of grains and five of dairy, or was it five grains and four dairy?" admits Lydia Greenwood, mother of boy/girl twins. "But then my dietitian filled me in on how each type of food was helping the babies inside me. Suddenly it was a source of satisfaction to tally up my day's intake and make sure the scores came out right." To share that sense of motivation, here is what you need to know:

What Dairy Does for You and Your Babies

Dairy products are your diet's richest source of calcium, which is needed to build your babies' bones and teeth. Dairy foods also contain other important vitamins and minerals, and are a good source of complete proteins. Except for their lack of iron, dairy products are considered by many nutritionists to be the perfect food.

It's not hard to get enough dairy if you get creative. "My dietitian told me to drink at least a quart of milk every day," says twin mom Judy Levy. "All that milk went down more easily once I started warming it up and stirring in some chocolate, vanilla, or honey. I actually looked forward to drinking a big thermos of flavored milk during my morning commute to work." For an added boost, try a calcium-fortified brand of milk such as Lactaid, which has 500 milligrams of calcium per glass.

Whole milk is best for expectant moms of multiples because it provides extra calories and fat. But if you don't like the taste, you do have other options. Judy admits, "I was used to drinking skim milk, so whole milk made me gag. Finally I realized that, in order to get the quantity of milk I needed, I had to switch back to skim. To make up for the lost fat, I ate a lot of premium ice cream."

Ice cream as an acceptable option for some of your daily dairy servings? Sure! "I would never have thought it was wise to have milkshakes every night if Dr. Luke hadn't told me to. But those really helped me put on the weight I needed, while providing a calcium boost too," reports Heather Nicholas, mother of boy/girl twins.

Dairy foods also make excellent bedtime snacks. Because they are digested slowly, they can prevent hunger-induced awakenings in the middle of the night. Good options include a grilled-cheese sandwich, cereal with milk, and any favorite ice cream treat. Place a small carton of milk in a cooler next to your bed in case you do wake up hungry. The amino acids that milk contains help you fall asleep again quickly.

Facts About Fruits and Vegetables

Produce has lots of fiber, which aids digestion and helps prevent irregularity. Fruits and vegetables also have a high water content, which keeps you hydrated. And they are excellent sources of water-soluble vitamins, such as folic acid and vitamins A and C.

When it comes to produce, color is the key to nutrient density—the deeper the color, the more nourishing the food. For example, romaine and red-leaf lettuce have more nutrients than iceberg; carrots and broccoli have more than cauliflower. So fill your shopping cart with the darkest, brightest fruits and vegetables you can find. Create a colorful salad every day, using a variety of dark green lettuces, purple cabbage, tomatoes, red and green peppers, and other veggies.

Just be careful not to overdo produce at the expense of protein. Says Judy Levy, "I love fruits and vegetables, but overdosing on them made me uncomfortably full. If I ate too big a salad, I couldn't find room for my meat."

Going with the Grain

Cereal, bread, pasta, rice, and other grain products are rich in fiber as well as the B vitamins that are essential to good health. And because they are fortified, they help to ensure that you get the nutrients you need. For instance, fortified grain products are good sources of folic acid, or folate, which helps prevent neural tube defects such as spina bifida and also may reduce the risk of miscarriage.

Ginny Seyler, mother of triplets, says, "During my pregnancy, I ate a bowl of whole-grain cereal first thing each morning. It made me feel like the day's diet was getting off to a good start." Grain products have the added advantage of being portable, versatile, and inexpensive.

Fats and Oils: Heroes, not Villains, During Pregnancy

When you don't take in enough calories from carbohydrates, the body must get its energy from fat—either from the foods you eat or from the fat stored on your hips and other areas of the body. This is a problem, because one of the by-products of the breakdown of fat, called ketones, can be toxic to your unborn babies. So even though you're probably used to thinking of fat as bad, during a multiple pregnancy you need to readjust your viewpoint.

"During my first pregnancy, I would have felt like I was polluting my body and my baby if I ate cheeseburgers or milkshakes. But for the second pregnancy, when I was carrying twins, I needed the extra calories and fat," says Judy Levy.

Don't be surprised, though, if other people fail to understand this. Meredith Alcott, mother of identical twin girls, recalls, "Even after we realized I was carrying twins, my obstetrician told me to stick to a low-fat diet. But my dietitian had other ideas. She said, 'Forget low-fat for now! Go get yourself some Ben & Jerry's ice cream.'"

THE EXCELLENCE OF EGGS

Eggs contain a wide variety of nutrients, but it is their protein that's especially beneficial. The type of protein in egg whites is of the highest biologic value, because it provides all the essential amino acids in sufficient amounts. In fact, egg-white protein is used as the standard against which all other proteins are judged. Furthermore, egg yolks are a rich source of iron, calcium, magnesium, and phosphorus.

For maximum nutrition, try the new eggs that are enriched with vitamin E and omega-3 fatty acids, marketed under brand names such as Eggland's Best, Wilcox Farms, Golden-Premium, and The Golden Hen. These eggs come from chickens whose feed is fortified with vitamin E, flaxseed, and fish oils. Compared to regular eggs, these enriched eggs contain two to six times the amount of omega-3 fatty acids and vitamin E.

THE MANY BENEFITS OF MEATS, POULTRY, AND SEAFOOD

Many of the essential nutrients needed in larger quantities during a multiple pregnancy are supplied by meats, fish, and poultry. Of these, the most highly recommended are the red meats—beef, liver, and pork. (Although pork is advertised as "the other white meat," nutritionally it is more similar to red meat than to poultry.) Red meats are excellent sources of the complete protein that's vital to your babies' growth. They are also rich in iron, which protects against anemia and its complications. That's why you should aim to eat red meat twice a day.

Most women aren't accustomed to eating anywhere near that much red meat, so the adjustment can be challenging at first. "I was used to mainly meatless meals, so it was tough to find high-protein foods that both my stomach and my taste buds could tolerate. Slabs of meat just made me gag," says Judy Levy. "But through trial and error, I discovered some good strategies. For instance, pasta-and-protein combinations let me get the meat down. My favorites were lasagna with ground beef, spaghetti with meatballs, Hamburger Helper, and eggs with ham on an English muffin."

It also helps to increase your intake of red meat gradually. "I had always eaten low-fat foods and hardly ever ate red meat. But in my second trimester, I became anemic and was told to start eating meat several times a day. That night, my dad came over and grilled a London broil. I felt awful for two days afterwards! My stomach ached, and it seemed as though the food was stuck in there forever," says Heather Nicholas. "My dietitian explained that people who haven't eaten meat in a long time lack the enzymes necessary to digest the additional fat. As my body adjusted, I felt a lot better."

In addition to the red meat, include some other form of protein—chicken, turkey, cheese, yogurt, milk, eggs, or peanut butter—with every meal or snack. Not only does this promote optimal development for your babies, but it also stabilizes your blood sugar so you can feel your best. One note of caution: Do be careful to avoid uncooked and undercooked meats, poultry, fish, and eggs. These can be a source of parasites or bacterial food poisoning.

Are you a vegetarian? See Chapter 4 for more information about following a vegetarian diet during a multiple pregnancy.

DR. LUKE: Some of our patients at the Multiples Clinic get tired of hearing about weight gain and nutrition and what they should eat. One woman even ribbed me, in a not so gentle way, for being adamant about the importance of diet. But she did stick with the program, and her babies were born big and healthy. A few days after she delivered, she came to me and said, "One of my twins had to spend just a few hours in the NICU. When I was there, I looked around and saw all these babies who were so much smaller than my daughter. Finally I understood why you kept on my case about eating right. Thanks for being my nutrition advocate."

Putting what you've learned into practice requires more than the right attitude, I realize. That's why this revised edition of our book includes a new chapter packed with all the practical advice you'll need to stick with a healthy eating plan. Turn to Chapter 4 for trimester-by-trimester menu suggestions, smart eating strategies for all situations, new ways to manage morning sickness, and more.

Chapter 4

Putting Your Food Plan into Action

DR. LUKE: I've often heard moms-to-be of multiples say, "I understand how much weight I should gain and how often I should eat. But exactly *what* should I be eating? How can I plan my daily menus? What recipes will help my babies get the nutrients they need? It all seems so complicated."

To answer those questions as simply and completely as possible, we've included lots of additional information about nutrition in this revised edition of *When You're Expecting Twins, Triplets, or Quads*. For instance, our easy-to-follow advice on food choices now includes:

- 25 Food All-Stars that make nutritious eating easy
- 50 original recipes, each designed for maximum nutrition as well as great taste
- 100 specific menu suggestions for meals and snacks, organized trimester-by-trimester and targeted to maximize your babies' development during each stage of pregnancy
- Information for women who follow a vegetarian diet
- Strategies for making smart food choices in all kinds of situations—at home, at the office, and on the road
- Updated recommendations, based on the very latest studies, for the specific vitamins and minerals that are most beneficial during a multiple pregnancy
- New ways to manage morning sickness, and how to stay motivated about eating right

Superstar Foods

The simplest way to get many of the nutrients you and your unborn babies need, starting today, is to eat more of the "Top 25 Food All-Stars." Foods earn a spot on this list based on three criteria: high nutrient content, flavor, and versatility as an ingredient in recipes. Table 4.1 lists the winners, along with the benefits of each:

Top 25 Food All-Stars

Food Group	Food	Nutritional Attributes
Dairy	Yogurt	Easily digested, high-quality protein; type of carbohydrate that promotes stable blood sugar; strengthens immune system. Provides calcium; magnesium; phosphorus; riboflavin; vitamins B_{12} and D; zinc.
	Milk	High-quality protein; type of carbohydrate that promotes stable blood sugar. Provides calcium; iodine; magnesium; phosphorus; potassium; vitamins A, B_{12}, and D; riboflavin.
	Cheese	High-quality protein. Provides calcium.
Eggs	Eggs	High-quality protein. Provide biotin; chromium; phosphorus; vitamins A, B_6, and D; zinc.
Fish and shellfish	Coldwater fish	High-quality protein. Provide biotin; calcium; niacin; omega-3 essential fatty acids; riboflavin; vitamins A and B_{12}.
	Shellfish	High-quality protein; low-fat. Provide calcium; copper; iodine; manganese; vitamin D.

Food Group	Food	Nutritional Attributes
Fruits	Apples	Fiber; type of carbohydrate that promotes stable blood sugar. Provide chromium.
	Avocados	Fiber. Provide copper; magnesium; potassium; pyridoxine; vitamins A, B, and E.
	Cherries	Type of carbohydrate that promotes stable blood sugar. Provide vitamins A and C.
	Oranges	Fiber; type of carbohydrate that promotes stable blood sugar. Provide folic acid; vitamins A and C.
Grains and cereals	Barley, bulgur, oatmeal	Protein; fiber; type of carbohydrate that promotes stable blood sugar. Provide iron; magnesium; manganese; selenium; zinc.
	Wheat germ	Protein; fiber; low-fat. Provides folic acid; magnesium; phosphorus; thiamin; vitamin E; zinc.
Nuts	Cashews, peanuts, walnuts	Protein; fiber. Provide biotin; copper; magnesium; manganese; pyridoxine; zinc.
Vegetables	Asparagus	Fiber. Provides copper; folic acid; magnesium; potassium; riboflavin; thiamin; vitamins A, C, and E.
	Broccoli	Fiber. Provides calcium; chromium; folic acid; magnesium; manganese; riboflavin; vitamins A, C, and K.
	Cabbage	Fiber. Provides folic acid; riboflavin; vitamins A, C, and K.

(continued)

Food Group	Food	Nutritional Attributes
Vegetables	Pumpkin	Fiber. Provides chromium; vitamins A and C.
	Spinach	Provides calcium; chromium; folic acid; iron; magnesium; manganese; potassium; riboflavin; vitamins A, C, and K.
	Sweet potatoes, yams	Fiber; type of carbohydrate that promotes stable blood sugar. Provide chromium; vitamin A.
	Tomatoes	Provide carotenoids (especially lycopene and lutein); vitamins A and C.

Table 4.1

RECIPES YOU (AND YOUR BABIES) WILL LOVE

Take a look at the Best Recipes for Moms-to-Be of Multiples, beginning on page 307. All of these recipes include one or more (in some cases, as many as five) of the Top 25 Food All-Stars. For easy reference, check the All-Star Rating at the bottom of each recipe to see how many All-Stars it offers.

Many of the common Food All-Stars—eggs, milk, vegetables, meat—are ingredients readily found in most cookbook recipes. Other All-Stars—pumpkin, legumes, nuts, tofu—appear less frequently in typical cookbooks. That's why so many of the original recipes included in this book contain these often-overlooked nutritional powerhouses.

You'll also want to take note of each recipe's Blue-Ribbon Rating. This indicates the number of nutrients the recipe provides, per serving, at a level of 20 percent or more of the recommended dietary allowance for pregnancy. Some recipes earn as many as 15 ribbons!

Menus for Moms-to-be of Multiples

From Chapter 3, you know about the importance of the various food groups. From Table 3.10 on page 76, you learned how many servings from each group to eat each day, based on the number of babies you're expecting. Now all you need are some specific menu suggestions to help you plan ahead.

The following Master List of Menu Suggestions includes 100 nutritious and flavorful menu items; recipes for 50 of these are at the back of this book. Let this list be an inspiration as you plan your weekly menus and prepare your shopping lists. (Note: An asterisk indicates that the item is included in the recipe section, which begins on page 307. For other suggested menu items, consult your favorite cookbook.)

Master List of Menu Suggestions

BEEF ENTRÉES
Beef and Barley Soup
Beef Brisket
*Beef Stew
Beef Tacos
Beef Teriyaki
Cheeseburgers
Corned Beef and Cabbage
Hamburgers
London Broil
*Mini–Meat Loaves
Pepper Steak
Pot Roast
Sloppy Joes
Spaghetti and Meatballs
*Spicy Beef

PORK ENTRÉES
Baked Ham
*French Toast with Ham and Cheese
Grilled Ham and Cheese Sandwich
Grilled Pork Chops
*Ham and Pumpkin Quiche
Marinated Pork Tenderloin
*Pasta with Peas and Ham
*Pork and Cashew Bok Choy
Pork Roast
*Pork with Apple Stuffing

Quiche Lorraine
*Spicy Pork with Peanut Sauce
Sweet and Sour Pork

POULTRY ENTRÉES
*Cashew Chicken
*Chicken and Dumplings
*Chicken and Sweet Potatoes
*Chicken and Wild Rice Casserole
*Chicken-Barley Soup
Chicken Cordon Bleu
Chicken Pot Pie
Chicken Salad
*Golden Chicken Salad
*Greek Lemon Chicken
Grilled Chicken
*Pasta with Chicken and Peanut Sauce
Roasted Chicken
Roasted Turkey
*Seasoned Baked Chicken
Turkey Burgers
Turkey Meat Loaf

SEAFOOD ENTRÉES
*Citrus Salmon
Grilled Salmon
*Linguine with Clams and Dried Tomatoes
Manhattan Clam Chowder

New England Clam Chowder
*Salmon Burgers
*Shrimp and Scallop Grill
Shrimp Egg Foo Yung
Tuna Casserole
Tuna Salad

VEGETARIAN ENTRÉES
*Asparagus Quiche
*Autumn Pancakes
Baked Manicotti
Cheese Lasagna
Deviled Eggs with Toast
Egg Burritos
Extra-Cheese Pizza
French Toast with Applesauce
*Ginger Stir-Fry
*Greek Spinach and Cheese Pie
Grilled Cheese and Tomatoes
*Lentil Soup
*Mediterranean Sauté
*Oatmeal-Walnut Pancakes
Oatmeal with Dried Cherries
*Pasta with Green Sauce
*Powerhouse Granola
*Pumpkin Waffles
*Ratatouille
*Salsa Frittata
Scrambled Eggs and Raisin Toast

*Spinach and Pumpkin Casserole
*Vegetarian Lasagna
*Vegetarian Stroganoff
*Wild Rice Omelet

SIDE DISHES AND SNACKS
Apple Slices and Peanut Butter
Baked Apples with Cheddar Cheese
*Chickpea Salad
Cottage Cheese and Fruit
Fruit Salad with Cheese and Crackers
*Harvest Muffins
Oatmeal-Walnut Cookies with Yogurt
Pear, Walnut, and Cheese Salad
*Pumpkin Custard
*Pumpkin-Fruit Muffins
*Pumpkin Loaf
*Sunrise Bread Pudding
*Tabbouleh
Vanilla Yogurt with Walnuts and Wheat Germ
*Weekend Hash Browns
Whole-Wheat Toast with Peanut Butter
*Yogurt Guacamole

SMOOTHIES
*Basic Fruit Smoothie
*Basic Vegetable Smoothie
*Ginger Smoothie

Take menu planning a step further by selecting dishes that best suit your stage of pregnancy. The menus that follow are specifically designed to satisfy the nutritional needs of your unborn babies (as well as your own body), depending on whether you're in your first, second, or third trimester.

First Trimester: Focus on Folic Acid and Other B Vitamins

The first trimester, also called the embryonic period, includes the time from conception to the 12th week of pregnancy. During these weeks, 70 percent of the nutrients you supply to your unborn babies is devoted to their brain growth and neurological development. An adequate intake of folic acid now helps to prevent neural tube defects such as spina bifida. All vital organs are also forming at this time, and folic acid promotes their proper growth. Good sources of folic acid (also called folate or vitamin B_9) include fortified rice, pasta, breads, cereals, and grains; poultry; lentils and beans; green leafy vegetables; avocados; oranges; and papayas.

With some creativity, you can easily up your intake of folic acid–rich foods. Tessa Walters, mother of fraternal twin boys, reports, "I wasn't big on fruits and veggies before I got pregnant, but I found some simple ways to increase my intake of folic acid. For instance, I doubled the beans in my chili recipe, added avocado to my tacos, and started topping my salads with diced peppers and chickpeas."

The other B-vitamins are important during the first trimester because they too are involved in the formation and growth of all tissues. B-vitamins are known as water-soluble vitamins because they are not stored in the body for very long. That means you must eat a steady supply to promote your babies' optimal growth.

Below are the B-vitamins you need, and the foods that provide them:

- Thiamin (B_1): beans, enriched whole grains, fish, nuts, peas, pork, soy
- Riboflavin (B_2): dairy foods, green leafy vegetables, legumes, meat, nuts
- Niacin (B_3): dairy foods, eggs, fortified cereals, meat, poultry, shellfish
- Pantothenic acid (B_5): mushrooms, peanuts, salmon, whole grains
- Pyridoxine (B_6): bananas, eggs, fish, legumes, meat, nuts, poultry, yams
- Biotin (B_7): barley, corn, egg yolks, fortified cereals, milk, peanuts, soybeans, walnuts
- Cobalamin (B_{12}): fish, fortified cereals and breads, grains, meat, nuts, poultry

Remember too that the placentas are developing rapidly during this time. As the vital middleman between mother and baby, the placenta delivers nutrients from your bloodstream and carries away the waste products. Any factors that interfere with placental growth now will adversely affect your babies' growth later in the pregnancy. To help the placentas develop properly, be sure to get plenty of protein and foods rich in iron.

Use the following menus to help plan your daily diet. This way, you'll get the nutrients your unborn babies need most right now. (An asterisk indicates that the recipe is included at the back of this book.)

Menu Suggestions for the First Trimester

BREAKFAST
*Asparagus Quiche
*Powerhouse Granola
*Pumpkin-Fruit Muffins
Scrambled Eggs and Raisin Toast
Whole-Wheat Pancakes

LUNCH OR DINNER
*Cashew Chicken
*Chicken-Barley Soup
*Ginger Stir-Fry
*Golden Chicken Salad
*Linguine with Clams and
    Dried Tomatoes

*Pasta with Chicken and Peanut Sauce
*Pork and Cashew Bok Choy
*Pork with Apple Stuffing
*Spicy Beef
*Spicy Pork with Peanut Sauce

SNACKS
Baked Apples with Cheddar Cheese
*Basic Fruit Smoothie
*Basic Vegetable Smoothie
*Ginger Smoothie
Pear, Walnut, and Cheese Salad
*Sunrise Bread Pudding

SECOND TRIMESTER: FOCUS ON IRON AND FIBER

The second trimester is defined as the fourth, fifth, and sixth months of pregnancy. Your babies have now "graduated" from embryo to fetus status. The main difference between the embryonic and fetal periods is that now, in the fetal period, no new structures are being formed. Your babies' growth is mainly in size. Yet proper nutrition—supplied through your diet, of course—is still a powerfully positive force in their development.

An adequate intake of iron is very important during this middle trimester. Because you are carrying multiples, your blood volume has increased by 100 percent or more over your non-pregnant levels. Red blood cells, which carry oxygen throughout the body, have increased by 50 to 60 percent. If the level of iron in your red blood cells falls too low, iron-deficiency anemia develops. Symptoms include fatigue, lightheadedness, pallor, and shortness of breath. Untreated, anemia can adversely affect the growth of your babies, and also increase your own risk for complications both during and after the birth.

Are iron supplements the answer? Probably not. Many women find that iron pills exacerbate nausea and may also lead to constipation. Furthermore, it takes more than iron to build your blood; it also takes protein, vitamin B_{12}, and other nutrients. That's why it's far better to rely on foods rich in heme iron—lean red meats, pork, fish, poultry, and eggs—with additional iron coming from enriched or fortified grains and breads, nuts, beans and lentils, spinach, dried fruits, and wheat germ.

Fiber is also important now. During the second trimester, your gastrointestinal system slows down to absorb more nutrients from the foods you eat. This can lead to constipation. Fiber-rich foods help to keep you regular. Best bets include fruits such as oranges, apples, raisins, and pears, and vegetables such as beans, broccoli, tomatoes, and potatoes.

Though the fatigue of early pregnancy has probably passed, there may be times when you need a quick pick-me-up. If you find yourself dragging, select a snack in the 250-calorie range that provides an immediate energy boost to sustain you until your next big meal. Here are suggestions that fit the bill:

- Spread a small banana with peanut butter.
- Top yogurt with a sprinkling of crunchy granola.
- Make a trail mix of nuts, raisins, and sweetened coconut.
- Eat low-fat cottage cheese with high-fiber crackers and grapes.
- Melt low-fat cheese on top of fresh apple or pear slices.

Find more snack suggestions, as well as midpregnancy mealtime menu ideas, in the following list. (Items marked with an asterisk are included in the recipe section at the back of this book.)

Menu Suggestions for the Second Trimester

BREAKFAST
Egg Burritos
*Harvest Muffins
*Pumpkin Loaf
Scrambled Eggs and Raisin Toast
*Wild Rice Omelet

*Mediterranean Sauté
*Pasta with Green Sauce
*Seasoned Baked Chicken
*Shrimp and Scallop Grill
*Vegetarian Stroganoff
*Wild Rice Omelet

LUNCH OR DINNER
Beef Brisket
*Beef Stew
*Chicken and Sweet Potatoes
Corned Beef and Cabbage
*Greek Lemon Chicken
*Greek Spinach and Cheese Pie
*Lentil Soup

SNACKS
*Basic Fruit Smoothie
*Basic Vegetable Smoothie
*Chickpea Salad
*Ratatouille
*Tabbouleh
*Yogurt Guacamole

The third trimester includes the seventh, eighth, and ninth months of pregnancy. During this time, your babies' bones and teeth require a steady supply of calcium. Although this mineral has been important right from the beginning of your pregnancy, it is even more critical now. If your diet does not contain adequate amounts, calcium is mobilized from your own bones in order to meet the needs of your babies. If this occurs, your ultimate risk for osteoporosis increases significantly. The older you are, the more problematic this becomes, since you have fewer years to rebuild bone density before the onset of menopause weakens your bones further. Calcium is also an important element in the prevention of preeclampsia.

Dairy foods such as milk, cheese, and yogurt are excellent sources of calcium. Boost your calcium intake further by eating sardines and salmon with bones, eggs, tofu, spinach, beans, peanuts, and potatoes. Also try these tips:

- Substitute nonfat evaporated milk or calcium-fortified milk for regular milk in recipes, doubling the calcium content.
- Mix plain yogurt with dried onion soup mix to create a tasty, calcium-rich dip for vegetables.
- Try fruit-flavored yogurt on top of pancakes.
- Bake quiche for breakfast or lunch.
- Have pudding or custard for a midmorning snack.
- Choose calcium-fortified orange juice rather than regular juice.
- Go for creamy, milk-based soups rather than broth-based varieties.

The third trimester is also when you have a particular need for the omega-3 fatty acids. Here's why:

- Omega-3s are critical to your babies' vision and neurological systems, which are developing most rapidly during this period.
- Through a biochemical mechanism, omega-3 fatty acids block the formation of factors that can lead to premature labor.
- They may also protect your own brainpower. During pregnancy, the mother's blood level of omega-3 fatty acids drops by almost two-thirds, as compared to her prepregnancy level—probably as a result of the growing babies' need for this vital nutrient. Recent studies show that the expectant mother's brain shrinks by about 3 percent during the last trimester. This may explain the memory loss that has long been associated with pregnancy, and may be linked to postpartum depression as well.

But don't count on supplements to give you the essential fatty acids you need. A typical capsule of fish oil contains only about 0.3 gram of omega-3, compared to 5 grams in a 7-ounce serving of Pacific salmon, 4.2 grams in Atlantic herring, 4.1 grams in canned anchovies, 3.4 grams in canned salmon, and 3 grams in canned tuna. Aim for at least two servings per week of fish (preferably farm-raised, to avoid the risk of mercury contamination).

Not a fan of fish? Flaxseed oil is an excellent source of omega-3. You'll also benefit from using flaxseed, olive, or canola oil when cooking, rather than butter, margarine, or other vegetable oils. Another option is to try the new eggs that are enriched with omega-3 fatty acids and vitamin E.

Aim to get 1,000 milligrams of omega-3 fatty acids per day. How?

- Have tuna salad for lunch. A 3-ounce serving of tuna provides 1.2 grams of omega-3.
- Choose a coldwater fish such as salmon or mackerel for dinner.
- Make a snack of shrimp cocktail.
- Order anchovies on your pizza.
- Use canola or flaxseed oil in your salad dressing.
- Use olive oil instead of margarine on your bread.
- Sauté poultry and vegetables in canola or safflower oil rather than butter.

By this stage of pregnancy, resting is far more important than cooking. Use the following easy menu suggestions to keep your meals and snacks simple yet satisfying. (An asterisk means the recipe appears at the back of this book.)

Menu Suggestions for the Third Trimester

BREAKFAST
*Autumn Pancakes
Blueberry Muffins
*French Toast with Ham and Cheese
*Oatmeal-Walnut Pancakes
*Weekend Hash Browns

LUNCH OR DINNER
*Asparagus Quiche
*Chicken and Dumplings

*Chicken and Wild Rice Casserole
Grilled Pork Chops
Grilled Salmon
*Ham and Pumpkin Quiche
Manhattan Clam Chowder
*Pasta with Peas and Ham
*Salmon Burgers
*Salsa Frittata
*Spinach and Pumpkin Casserole
Tuna Salad

SNACKS
*Basic Fruit Smoothie
*Basic Vegetable Smoothie
Cottage Cheese and Fruit

*Golden Chicken Salad
*Pumpkin Custard
Vanilla Yogurt with Walnuts and
    Wheat Germ

Hopefully, you're feeling confident by now that you can nourish your unborn babies quite well by following the food plan in this book. Sure, there's a lot to learn—but the rewards are well worth it. As one reader reports, "Though I found some of the dietary guidelines challenging, they helped me to understand the needs of my developing twins, as well as to set goals for myself. After hitting 38 weeks, I delivered very healthy 7 lb., 5 oz., and 7 lb., 3 oz., boy/girl twins. Not bad for someone 5 feet 1 inch tall."

Guidelines for Vegetarians

DR. LUKE: Normally, a vegetarian diet can be very healthful if you are knowledgeable about nutrition, conscientious about getting enough protein, and careful to combine foods properly to ensure that you get all the essential amino acids. Remember, though, that a multiple pregnancy places extra demands on your body, including a greatly increased need for calories and protein. Satisfying these demands can make a significant difference in the size and health of your babies at birth. I believe these nutritional needs can be met most easily and reliably through a diet that includes animal-based proteins, particularly red meat.

However, if you are strongly committed to vegetarianism and are willing to monitor your food intake carefully, the following section can help you satisfy your own and your babies' nutritional needs. Be sure to check out the many vegetarian recipes at the back of this book. I've designed each one for maximum nutrition (and great taste).

There are several different types of vegetarian diets. As shown in Table 4.2, some vegetarian diets are far more restrictive than others.

Types of Vegetarian Diets

Vegan	Eliminates all animal products, including eggs and cheese, concentrating solely on vegetables, legumes, fruits, and grains
Macrobiotic	Emphasizes cooked foods, especially whole grains, with moderate amounts of vegetables and beans, minimal amounts of fruits, little if any dairy foods or eggs, and occasional small servings of mild white fish
Lacto-vegetarian	Includes dairy products along with vegetables, fruits, and grains, but eliminates eggs
Ovo-vegetarian	Includes eggs along with vegetables, fruits, and grains, but eliminates dairy products
Lacto-ovo vegetarian	Includes dairy products and eggs along with vegetables, fruits, and grains

Table 4.2

Protein is critical to a healthy pregnancy because it provides the body's basic building blocks. In fact, protein is the single most vital nutrient for your babies' growth. That's why the focus of this section is on a lacto-ovo vegetarian diet, which includes both eggs and dairy products. Omitting these vital components makes it extremely difficult to meet the nutritional demands of a multiple pregnancy (or even a singleton pregnancy).

If you currently follow a vegan, macrobiotic, or other more restrictive diet, it is extremely important that you add eggs and dairy to your diet starting today. In fact, every meal or snack you eat should include milk, cheese, or yogurt. Eat plenty of eggs too. Egg whites contain the highest-quality protein, while egg yolks are an excellent source of iron.

The chief components of protein are 20 amino acids that are needed for protein synthesis. Of these acids, 10 are considered nonessential because the body can synthesize them. However, the remaining 10 cannot be formed by the body and must be supplied from food. These 10 are termed essential amino acids.

The Amino Acids

Nonessential Amino Acids	Essential Amino Acids
Alanine	Arginine
Asparagine	Histidine
Aspartic acid	Isoleucine
Cysteine	Leucine
Glutamic acid	Lysine
Glutamine	Methionine
Glycine	Phenylalanine
Proline	Threonine
Serine	Tryptophan
Tyrosine	Valine

Table 4.3

Foods that provide all of the essential amino acids include milk, yogurt, cheese, and eggs (as well as beef, poultry, and fish). Many other foods contain protein, but are missing one or more of the essential amino acids, or provide them only in very small amounts.

In planning your pregnancy diet, consult the two tables below. They will help you identify the foods that can best provide the essential amino acids. Table 4.4 compares the amino acid content (in grams) of a typical-size serving for each type of food—for instance,

8 ounces of milk versus 3.5 ounces of fish versus 1 ounce of cheese. The boldface numbers in each column represent the six foods with the highest content of each of the essential amino acids.

For the sake of comparison, these foods can be ranked according to the number of boldface figures each food merits, per serving. (Remember, a boldface figure indicates that the food is one of the top six providers of a given amino acid.) Awarding one point for each figure, here's how these foods stack up:

- Beef, chicken, and fish: 10 points
- Eggs: 10 points
- Cottage cheese: 9 points
- Yogurt: 8 points
- Milk: 1 point
- Peanut butter: 1 point
- Lentils: 1 point

Some vegetarian readers may be more accustomed to analyzing food choices in terms of equal amounts of food, rather than by the typical serving sizes used in Table 4.4. For that reason, Table 4.5 provides a comparison of the amino acid content of various protein-rich foods, based on equal weight—in this case, 100 grams, or about 3.5 ounces. Again, the boldface numbers in each column represent the six foods with the highest content (per 100 grams) of each of the essential amino acids.

The foods can also be compared according to the number of boldface figures each earns, per 100 grams. Awarding one point for each boldface figure, here's how they rank:

- Beef, chicken, and fish: 10 points
- Cheese: 10 points
- Peanut butter: 9 points
- Cottage cheese: 7 points
- Eggs: 4 points

Essential Amino Acid Content (in Grams) of Protein-Rich Foods, per Serving

Food	Serving Size	Arginine	Histidine	Isoleucine	Leucine	Lysine	Methionine
Beef	3.5 oz.	**1.87**	**1.01**	**1.33**	**2.34**	**2.46**	**0.76**
Chicken	3.5 oz.	**1.71**	**0.80**	**1.36**	**1.99**	**2.22**	**0.73**
Fish	3.5 oz.	**1.48**	**0.73**	**1.14**	**2.00**	**2.27**	**0.73**
Cheese	1 oz.	0.27	0.25	0.44	0.68	0.59	0.19
Peanut butter	2 tbsp.	**0.97**	0.20	0.28	0.52	0.29	0.10
Cottage cheese	3.5 oz.	0.57	**0.42**	**0.73**	**1.28**	**1.01**	**0.38**
Eggs	2 jumbo (130 g)	**0.98**	**0.38**	**0.88**	**1.38**	**1.16**	**0.50**
Lentils	3.5 oz.	**0.70**	0.25	0.39	0.65	0.63	0.08
Yogurt	8 oz.	0.42	**0.35**	**0.77**	**1.41**	**1.26**	**0.41**
Tofu	3.5 oz.	0.44	0.19	0.32	0.50	0.43	0.08
Bread	2 slices (60 g)	0.18	0.10	0.20	0.34	0.14	0.08
Milk	8 oz.	0.29	0.22	0.49	0.79	0.64	0.20

Table 4.4

Phenylalanine	Threonine	Tryptophan	Valine	Calories (kcal)	Protein (g)	Carbohydrate (g)	Fat (g)
1.16	**1.29**	**0.33**	**1.44**	222	29.6	0	10.7
1.06	**1.13**	**0.31**	**1.33**	239	27.3	0	13.6
0.96	**1.08**	**0.28**	**1.27**	113	24.7	0	0.9
0.37	0.25	0.09	0.47	114	7.1	0	9.4
0.42	0.28	0.08	0.34	190	8.1	6.2	16.3
0.67	**0.55**	**0.14**	**0.77**	103	12.5	2.7	4.5
0.86	**0.78**	**0.20**	**1.00**	194	16.2	0	13.0
0.45	0.32	0.08	0.45	116	9.0	20.0	0.5
0.77	**0.58**	0.08	**1.16**	137	14.0	18.8	0.4
0.32	0.27	0.10	0.33	68	6.6	2.0	3.7
0.24	0.14	0.06	0.22	160	5.0	30.0	2.2
0.39	0.36	**0.11**	0.54	149	8.0	11.4	8.2

Essential Amino Acid Content (in Grams) of Protein-Rich Foods, per 100 Grams (3.5 Ounces)

Food	Arginine	Histidine	Isoleucine	Leucine	Lysine	Methionine	Phenylalanine
Beef	**1.87**	**1.01**	**1.33**	**2.34**	**2.46**	**0.76**	**1.16**
Chicken	**1.71**	**0.80**	**1.36**	**1.99**	**2.22**	**0.73**	**1.06**
Fish	**1.48**	**0.73**	**1.14**	**2.0**	**2.27**	**0.73**	**0.96**
Cheese	**0.94**	**0.87**	**1.55**	**2.39**	**2.07**	**0.65**	**1.31**
Peanut butter	**3.01**	**0.64**	**0.89**	**1.64**	**0.90**	0.31	**1.31**
Cottage cheese	0.57	**0.42**	**0.73**	**1.28**	**1.01**	**0.38**	**0.67**
Eggs	**0.75**	0.30	0.68	1.06	0.89	**0.39**	0.66
Lentils	0.70	0.25	0.39	0.65	0.63	0.08	0.45
Yogurt	0.17	0.14	0.31	0.58	0.51	0.17	0.31
Tofu	0.44	0.19	0.32	0.50	0.43	0.08	0.32
Bread	0.32	0.18	0.32	0.58	0.22	0.14	0.40
Milk	0.12	0.09	0.20	0.32	0.26	0.08	0.16

Table 4.5

Threonine	Tryptophan	Valine	Calories (kcal)	Protein (g)	Carbohydrate (g)	Fat (g)
1.29	**0.33**	**1.44**	222	29.6	0	10.7
1.13	**0.31**	**1.33**	239	27.3	0	13.6
1.08	**0.28**	**1.27**	113	24.7	0	0.9
0.89	**0.32**	**1.66**	403	25.0	1.3	33.0
0.86	**0.25**	**1.06**	593	25.2	19.3	51.0
0.55	0.14	**0.77**	103	12.5	2.7	4.5
0.60	**0.15**	0.76	149	12.4	1	10
0.32	0.08	0.45	116	9.0	20.0	0.5
0.24	0.03	0.47	56	5.7	7.7	0.2
0.27	0.10	0.33	68	6.6	2.0	3.7
0.24	0.10	0.36	267	8.2	50.0	3.6
0.15	0.05	0.22	257	31.0	0.58	0.51

In selecting your meals and snacks, remember the basic rule about combining grains either with dairy products or with legumes. This pairing of foods assures that you are getting enough of all the amino acids at each meal or snack—both the essential and the nonessential—and that your intake of protein is sufficient. Good combinations include:

- Cereal with milk
- Macaroni and cheese
- Peanut butter with whole-grain bread
- Rice with beans

For more ideas, refer to the recipes at the back of the book. You'll find 16 vegetarian entrées, plus a dozen side dishes, snacks, and smoothies.

Eat-Smart Strategies for Every Situation

You are much more likely to eat the right foods, in the right quantities, at the right times, if you plan ahead. To keep the foods you need at hand, wherever you are, try these tactics:

Stock your cupboards, refrigerator, and freezer with the basics.

"Right after our first appointment with Dr. Luke, my husband, Curt, went to the store and loaded up on meats, multigrain breads and cereals, canned and frozen vegetables, and premium ice cream. He also shopped regularly for fresh produce and dairy products to make sure the cupboard was never bare," says Amy Maly, mother of identical twin girls.

If you have a large freezer, take a tip from Anne Seifert: "My husband had a meat delivery service stock our freezer with steaks, chops, chicken, and ground beef. It looked like a mountain of meat at first—but before the quads were born, I ate it all!"

Think takeout.

It's not always possible or practical to cook at home. Perhaps you and your partner both have busy schedules, or you've been put on bedrest, or you just don't feel like cooking. Yet that doesn't mean you can't eat well. Most grocery stores have a prepared-foods section, and delicatessens offer good-as-homemade lunch and dinner entrées and desserts.

"I happen to like chopped liver, so I bought it in bulk from the best deli in town and ate tons of it on crackers every night as a bedtime snack," says Judy Levy. "At birth, Micah Marie weighed 7 lb. and Kayla weighed 6 lb., 4 oz. I took one look at my chubby, healthy twins and thought, '*That* is where all that chopped liver went.'"

Don't shun fast foods.

You may be surprised to learn that fast-food restaurants, in addition to providing convenience and economy, can meet the dietary needs of expectant mothers of multiples quite well. Most offer hot breakfasts that provide plenty of calories and protein, like egg-and-sausage on a biscuit. The hot sandwiches—cheeseburger, fish fillet, chicken patty on a bun—are also good sources of protein and fat. Many also offer extras like baked potato bars, corn on the cob, and hot chili. Look for a salad bar to round out the meal.

One reader took this advice to heart, with excellent results. She writes, "Thanks to Dr. Luke's advice, I had my cheeseburgers and milkshakes and cheesecake along with my fruits, lean meats, fish, and vegetables. I had it all without guilt, since I had learned that I was doing the right thing for my babies. This helped me bring my two 6-pound babies home with me three days after they were born."

Practice on-the-job snacking savvy.

Remember, when you are pregnant with multiples, you should be eating *at least five times a day*—more often if you were slender before this pregnancy, or if you're expecting triplets or quads. This includes workdays. Because your schedule at work is likely to be less predictable than when you are at home, it's wise to bring food to the office.

Stock your desk with nonperishables like crackers, cookies, peanut butter, instant oatmeal, cup-of-soup mixes, canned puddings, and single-serving containers of applesauce. "Granola bars and dried apricots were convenient workday snacks. Snickers bars were great too—lots of calories, protein, and fat, and yummy to boot," says Heather Nicholas.

If you have access to a refrigerator at work, bring in yogurt, cottage cheese, milk, and sandwiches. There's a microwave? A frozen prepared entrée can make a hearty, healthy lunch when paired with fruit or vegetables. Judy Levy says, "My favorite was Stouffer's macaroni and cheese. The 20-ounce size has 680 calories, 26 grams of protein, and 600 milligrams of calcium."

You may want to explain your dietary needs to your supervisor or co-workers, but don't let their raised eyebrows keep you from eating whatever and whenever you should. "During business meetings, my boss would lose track of time and forget to break for lunch. I'd be *starving*, yet the conversation would go on and on," says Judy Levy. "Finally I had to throw politeness to the wind. I'd pack my pockets and purse with snacks—crackers, bananas, yogurt—and just dip in and eat whenever I got hungry. My boss would laugh and say to our clients, 'Don't mind her; she's expecting twins.' But he never got the hint that I needed real food."

Eat right, on the road and in the air.

If your work involves travel, whether around town or around the world, it's important to plan ahead for your diet. Keep beverages and snacks in your car, just in case you are running late or get caught in traffic. Stacy Moore says, "Since I sell advertising to car dealerships, I do most of my work from my car. To make sure I'd have plenty of food on hand during the workday, I packed a cooler with sandwiches, cheese, yogurt, and fruit, and ate between visits to clients."

When traveling by plane, you may not always know when or even if you'll be served a meal. Pack your carry-on bag with easy-to-eat snacks like peanut-butter crackers, mini-cheeses, and apples. The dry air of an airliner's pressurized cabin contributes to dehydration, so also bring along plenty of bottled water and juice boxes. Staying hydrated minimizes uterine contractions, which can lead to preterm labor. It also prevents the uncomfortable swelling that can result from sitting still too long, because all those fluids force you to get up and walk down the aisle to the bathroom.

Once you arrive at your destination, follow this strategy from Helen Armer: "Early in my triplet pregnancy, I had to travel on business several times a month. As soon as I got to the city where I was staying, I'd rent a car, find a grocery store, and buy whatever I needed to eat while at the hotel."

Additional tactics to try: Each morning, have a healthy and filling breakfast sent up by room service. If you are joining a client for lunch or dinner at a restaurant, order an appetizer, salad, soup, and entrée.

Managing Morning Sickness

"Morning sickness? What morning sickness? I never felt sick to my stomach at all during my twin pregnancy," says Amy Maly. And you may not either.

But sorry to say, many expectant mothers of multiples do experience nausea and vomiting—and the more babies you're expecting, the worse it's likely to be. That's because these symptoms are triggered by pregnancy hormones, which of course are present in much higher amounts when you're expecting more than one baby. In this regard, that queasy feeling is a positive sign: It indicates that the placenta or placentas are growing and producing sufficient hormones for the pregnancy to continue.

Morning sickness is in fact an inaccurate name. "I felt nauseous almost all the time. For me, it was morning-noon-and-night sickness," says Marcy Bugajski, mother of fraternal twin boys. "It's hard to work up an appetite when you're constantly vomiting."

Finding successful ways to cope with queasiness is important, not only because you want to feel better, but also because you need to eat (and keep it down) if your babies are to thrive. Fortunately, there are new strategies as well as time-honored techniques for overcoming morning sickness. Use trial and error to find the ones that are most effective for you.

- The newest thinking in the treatment of nausea and vomiting is the "salty-and-sweet" approach. Try eating some pretzels and lemonade, or some potato chips and cola. Though these foods are not very nutritious, they are often easier to keep down—and that's important during this difficult stage of pregnancy. Says Judy Levy, "This tactic really worked for me. The combination of lemonade and potato chips eased my nausea pretty quickly. Once I was feeling better, I could go on to eat healthier foods the rest of the day."

- Going too long without eating or drinking causes your blood sugar to drop, which in turn can trigger nausea. So eat frequently—at least every two hours. In your purse or briefcase, carry portable snacks such as peanut-butter crackers and a juice box.

- It's a myth that eating only fruit will ease morning sickness. Though fruit triggers a rapid rise in blood sugar that makes you feel better for a short while, pretty soon your blood sugar falls again, leaving you even more nauseous than before. To keep blood sugar on a more even keel, be sure to eat some protein along with a carbohydrate snack.

- Be aware that foods you normally enjoy may be completely unappealing to you now. "I had always loved sweets, but during my quadruplet pregnancy, they made me sick. Yet here was the one time I needed such high-calorie foods!" says Anne Seifert. "Fortunately, I found that fruit pies and ice cream didn't upset my stomach the way candy or chocolate did."

- Some women find that dairy products stay down most easily. When nausea strikes, reach for some milk, yogurt, cottage cheese, or ice cream, or a milkshake.

- If you tend to vomit even when your stomach is empty, try sucking on a Popsicle. "I ate a lot of Popsicles for breakfast," says Karen Danke, mother of fraternal twin boys. "Vomiting up a Popsicle was a lot less unpleasant than having the dry heaves."

- If mornings are your worst time, set your alarm for 2 A.M. (unless you can already count on a full bladder to awaken you in the middle of the night). Get up and have a bowl of cereal with milk, then go back to bed. When you wake up in the morning, your blood sugar won't be as low as it otherwise would have been. For many women, this reduces early-morning nausea.

- If you can't stand the thought of getting out of bed at night (after all, you'll be doing that often enough after the babies are born), keep a pack of dry crackers on your nightstand. Munch a few as soon as you wake up in the morning, even before climbing out from under the covers. Or ask your partner to provide a few bites of breakfast in bed. Karen Danke says, "It helped to have my husband bring me some dry toast to eat before I even tried to get up."

- Keep a "queasiness diary." For a few days, write down the foods you eat and try to find a pattern to your nausea. You may notice, for example, that eating fried foods sends you running for the bathroom. Skip the French fries in favor of a more nutritious and digestible baked potato.
- In your diary, also make note of any smells that upset your stomach, then take steps to avoid these. Common offenders include cigarette smoke, perfume, coffee, and fish. "The odor of my cat's canned food never failed to make me throw up," says Karen Danke. If you feel nauseous while preparing a meal, it could be that cooking smells are setting you off. The fix: Get takeout or have your partner handle the cooking.
- Some moms-to-be find that sipping ginger tea settles the stomach. Try this recipe: Peel and finely dice a knuckle-size piece of fresh ginger. Place in a mug and fill with boiling water; steep for five to eight minutes. Add brown sugar to taste.
- Whip up a Ginger Smoothie, included in the recipe section of this book (Appendix A). It is specifically designed to ease nausea, and it tastes delicious.
- You'd rather swallow a pill than sip tea or smoothies? A study published in 2001 found that, in dosages of one gram per day, capsules containing ginger significantly reduced nausea and vomiting in pregnancy.
- Dress for comfort. Clothing that's too snug around the waist or neck can trigger the gag reflex. Skip the turtlenecks and buttoned-up collars in favor of crewnecks and V-necks. Hit the stores for loose-fitting maternity skirts and slacks, rather than squeezing into your prepregnancy wardrobe. Wear belts around the hips rather than the waist. Switch from briefs to bikini underpants.
- Try acupressure. Look in pharmacies or health food stores for a pair of antinausea wristbands called Sea-Bands (typically advertised as a remedy for motion sickness). Each elasticized band has a plastic button that presses on the acupressure point on the wrist purported to ease queasiness.

None of these strategies relieves your morning sickness? Don't cajole yourself into "putting up and shutting up." Instead, call your obstetrician right away if:

- You haven't been able to keep any food or water down for 24 hours or more
- Your mouth, eyes, and skin feel dry
- You are becoming increasingly weak and fatigued
- Your ability to think clearly and to concentrate is decreasing

These are signs of serious dehydration. You may need to be admitted to the hospital to receive fluids, nutrients, and medications intravenously. In fact, about 42,000 pregnant women in the United States are hospitalized every year for severe nausea and vomiting, also called hyperemesis gravidarum. The treatment you receive in the hospital should help you feel better fast—and that's exactly what your unborn babies need most.

Rest assured, though, that for most expectant mothers of multiples, symptoms subside by the end of the first trimester. Says Karen Danke, "The most encouraging thing I can say about morning sickness is that it does eventually come to an end. Hang in there! And in the meantime, try all the tips anyone offers for easing the nausea. You never know what might work for you."

Nutritional Supplements: Turbo-Boosters for Your Diet

TAMARA: During the 18th week of my twin pregnancy, after lunching at a restaurant with some co-workers, I wound up in the hospital with salmonella food poisoning. After nearly two weeks of nonstop vomiting and diarrhea, I had lost 16 pounds—everything I'd gained during my pregnancy, and then some. My already slender frame became spindly and my face looked almost skeletal.

As soon as I felt better, I worked hard to put the weight back on. But for the twins growing inside me, the lost ground was never regained. At birth, they were "small for gestational age," or "SGA"—the term doctors use to describe babies who are born weighing less than expected for the amount of time spent in the womb. And because my babies were born nine weeks early, their SGA status compounded the problems associated with their prematurity.

DR. LUKE: I wish I'd known Tamara when she was pregnant, because I'd have recommended that she immediately add nutritional supplements to her daily diet. Any woman who loses weight while carrying multiples—whether from the nausea and vomiting of severe morning sickness, the flu, food poisoning, or any other illness—can benefit from these special products. I also strongly recommend nutritional supplements for pregnant women who are underweight, for ex-smokers (whose nutritional status is often compromised), and for anyone expecting three or more babies.

Nutritional supplements are specially formulated foods, available in beverage and pudding form. They are nutritionally balanced, calorically concentrated, and easy to digest. Taken between meals and before bed, they can be a key factor in helping you achieve the early, rapid weight gain you need.

There are three basic types of nutritional supplements. Here's how they compare to a glass of whole milk:

- Regular supplements: These provide one-third to two-thirds more calories than does the same-size serving of milk. They also contain 50 percent more protein, and three times the carbohydrate. Two or three servings a day boost your caloric intake by 400 to 750 calories.
- High-calorie or high-protein supplements: This type supplies about twice as much protein and four times as much carbohydrate as a glass of whole milk. These supplements also contain double the calories, so two or three servings daily can add 500 to 1,000 calories to your diet. These are often your best choice, because they're available in a wide range of flavors, which keeps your taste buds from getting bored, and because you can buy them in most supermarkets and drugstores.
- High-calorie and high-protein supplements: These are the "big guns" because, ounce for ounce, they pack the biggest nutritional punch. They're the most useful for improving your nutritional status as quickly as possible, and with the smallest quantity of food. Compared to a glass of whole milk, these supplements provide more than three times as many calories, two to three times as much protein and fat, and more than four times the carbohydrate. Two to three servings per day add 900 to 1,400 calories to your diet. In addition, they provide as much as 60 grams of high-quality protein—the equivalent of 20 ounces of steak! Although they cost about the same as high-calorie or high-protein supplements, they are not as readily available in local stores, and they come in only one flavor (vanilla). Ask your pharmacist to order them for you. Check with your health insurer too, since these special supplements may be covered under your plan if your obstetrician writes you a prescription.

All these types of nutritional supplements are also available directly from manufacturers. If you order by phone using a credit card, the products are delivered directly to your door. For maximum economy and convenience, buy several cans in your local store to see if you like the taste, then order them in quantity from these manufacturers:

- Mead Johnson & Company: PO Box 3204, Evansville, IN 47731-3204. Telephone 800–247–7893; e-mail askmeadjohnson@bms.com; Web site www.meadjohnson.com.

- Ross Products/Abbott Laboratories: 625 Cleveland Avenue, Columbus, OH 43215-1724. Telephone 800–986–8510; Web site www.ross.com.
- Sandoz Nutrition (available through McKesson Corp.): Telephone 800–446–6380; Web site www.mckesson.com.

Nutritional supplements are not for everyone. They are so sweet and rich that, for some women, they can trigger nausea, depress the appetite, or lead to diarrhea. Triplet mom Helen Armer says, "Each day for several weeks, I drank two or three cans of the nutritional supplements. But they gave me diarrhea, so Dr. Luke decided they were doing me more harm than good. I wasn't sorry to stop—I didn't care much for the taste."

For many moms-to-be of multiples, though, these high-powered dietary products are a boon. "I drank two cans of supplements daily from my ninth week of pregnancy until the day I delivered my quads. Because they are really thick, like sweetened condensed milk, I thought they tasted best when served ice-cold or diluted with water. For variety, I mixed in chocolate powder or blended in some fresh fruit," says Anne Seifert. "Especially considering the trouble I had eating much food in the final weeks, I think these drinks helped my babies to be born bigger than they otherwise would have been. I only wish I had learned about them sooner, so I could have been using them right from the start of my pregnancy."

Comparison of Nutritional Supplements

Supplement Type and Name	Nutrients per Serving (8 oz.)				Flavors
	Calories	Protein (g)	Carb. (g)	Fat (g)	
Whole Milk	150	8	12	8	Plain
Regular Supplements					
Sweet Success	200	11	38	3	Vanilla, chocolate, strawberry, strawberry-banana
Instant Breakfast	200	12	31	3	Vanilla, chocolate
Boost	240	10	40	4	Vanilla, chocolate
Sustacal	240	14.5	33	5.5	Vanilla, chocolate, strawberry, eggnog

(continued)

Supplement Type and Name	Nutrients per Serving (8 oz.)				Flavors
	Calories	Protein (g)	Carb. (g)	Fat (g)	
Ensure	250	8.8	40	6.1	Vanilla, chocolate
ReSource	250	9	34	9	Vanilla, chocolate, strawberry
ReSource Fruit Beverage	180	9	36	0	Fruit-flavored

High-Calorie or High-Protein Supplements

Sustacal Pudding	240	6.8	32	9.5	Vanilla, chocolate, butterscotch
Ensure Pudding	250	6.8	34	9.7	Vanilla, chocolate, butterscotch, tapioca
Sustacal Plus	360	14.4	45	13.6	Vanilla, chocolate, strawberry, eggnog
Ensure Plus	355	13	47.3	12.6	Vanilla, chocolate, strawberry
Ensure Plus HN	355	14.8	47.3	11.8	Vanilla, chocolate
ReSource Plus	360	13	47	13	Vanilla, chocolate

High-Calorie and High-Protein Supplements

Deliver 2.0	470	17.7	47	24	Vanilla
TwoCal HN	475	19.8	51.4	21.5	Vanilla

Table 4.6

Do You Need Vitamin or Mineral Pills?

With all the good food you're getting by following the dietary recommendations in this book, you're going a long way toward fulfilling your own nutritional needs as well as those of your babies. Yet some supplements are still recommended.

Many pregnant women are told to take prenatal multivitamins. However, there are several problems with these.

- They can suppress your appetite, so you take in fewer of the calories your babies need.
- Because they often contain too high a level of many nutrients, prenatal vitamins may make you feel nauseous, further affecting your ability to eat needed foods.
- These supplements often trigger constipation.
- Prenatal formulas also may include minerals, thereby interfering with your body's ability to absorb all the vitamins in the pills.

A better bet is to take a multivitamin that contains only vitamins, not minerals, and that does not exceed the RDA levels for nonpregnant women. Be sure the brand you select does have folic acid, since your body is better able to absorb this nutrient from supplements than from food. Many such brands are available, including Spring Valley Essential and One-a-Day Essentials. Take one pill daily during your first trimester. After that, nausea generally abates, so you can double the dose.

Certain additional supplements are strongly recommended, and should be included in your daily routine as soon as you know you are pregnant with multiples. The first is an over-the-counter pill that combines calcium, magnesium, and zinc. These supplements serve several functions:

- Calcium has been linked to blood pressure. Studies suggest that it may be helpful in reducing hypertension and its complications. It also helps to relieve heartburn, a common discomfort of pregnancy.
- Magnesium lowers your risk for premature labor by keeping the uterus from contracting. It is also helpful against heartburn. In addition, magnesium may protect your babies' developing nervous systems—so that even if they are born early, their problems may be less severe.
- Zinc is vital for the development of your babies' nervous systems. It also lowers the chances of infection and preterm premature rupture of membranes.

Look for brands that contain, per tablet, 333 milligrams of calcium carbonate, 133 milligrams of magnesium oxide, and 5 milligrams of zinc sulfate. (One brand to try is Nature Made.) Take three tablets, three times a day, for a total of nine.

You should also take two additional vitamin supplements:

- Vitamin C, an antioxidant, has recently been shown to be very effective in reducing the risk of preeclampsia. The recommended dosage is 1,000 milligrams daily.

- Vitamin E, another antioxidant, also helps to prevent preeclampsia. Take 400 IU each day.

Think it's a hassle to take so many pills each day? "It was sort of a pain," admits Stacy Moore. "But I found that I was less likely to forget if I took them along with my meals. Having food in my belly also eliminated the queasiness and unpleasant aftertaste the pills could sometimes trigger if taken on an empty stomach." Table 4.7 provides a ready reference of your daily supplement schedule.

Suggested Daily Dosage of Supplements

Dosage per Tablet	First Trimester	Second Trimester	Third Trimester
Multivitamins at nonpregnant RDA level	1 tablet	2 tablets	2 tablets
Calcium/magnesium/ zinc at 333 mg/ 133 mg/5 mg	9 tablets	9 tablets	9 tablets
Vitamin C at 1,000 mg	1 tablet	1 tablet	1 tablet
Vitamin E at 400 IU	1 tablet	1 tablet	1 tablet

Table 4.7

Drink Water, Water Everywhere

Water is vital for every living creature. But when you're expecting multiples, it's particularly essential—for you and your babies. Here's why:

- Dehydration can trigger uterine contractions, which in turn can lead to premature birth. "Anytime I slacked off on my water intake, I got dehydrated and started having contractions—sometimes as many as 12 an hour!" says quad mom Anne Seifert.

- The hormonal changes that occur during pregnancy make you more prone to urinary-tract infections, which also can trigger premature labor. Drinking plenty of water guards against this potential complication.
- During pregnancy, your metabolism revs up. In the first trimester, before your blood volume increases, an adequate intake of fluids helps to dissipate some of this additional body heat.
- Pregnancy hormones can leave you constipated. Drinking water improves regularity.
- Staying hydrated reduces your susceptibility to headaches, dry skin, and complexion problems.

How much should you be drinking? Aim for at least *eight 16-ounce glasses* of water every day. Although taking in this much water every day may seem like a formidable task, with some forethought it can be integrated into your daily routine as easily as any other healthy habit.

"To keep track of my water intake and make sure I was getting enough, I developed a system," says triplet mom Ginny Seyler. "Each night, I filled up three Tupperware jugs with Brita-filtered tap water and put them in the refrigerator. The following day, I made sure I finished one entire jug every few hours—for instance, one by lunchtime, the second by late afternoon, and the last one before bedtime."

For maximum convenience, plan to have water within easy reach at all times. Helen Armer, another mother of triplets, says, "At work, I kept a bottle of water on my desk constantly. After I went on bedrest, there was always a jug of water on the nightstand." In your car, keep a jumbo thermos of water and a travel mug (to reduce spills), or a cooler stocked with bottled water.

Experiment and you'll soon figure out which way water tastes best to you. Stacy Moore explains, "I like my water cold, so each night I froze several sports bottles full of water. That way they stayed refreshingly icy all through the next day while I was driving around in my car for work." Lydia Greenwood, mother of boy/girl twins, had the opposite preference. "Ice water gave me stomach cramps. I preferred liter-size bottles of spring water served at room temperature." For other women, a touch of flavor helps. "Getting all that water down was easier if I added a lemon slice or splash of fruit juice to it," suggests twin mom Marcy Bugajski.

There is one downside: "Drinking so much water every day made me have to go to the bathroom every 15 minutes," Marcy moans. "I learned to finish it all by dinnertime so that I'd have a chance to urinate it all out before I went to sleep."

You can use those bathroom breaks as a means of double-checking your hydration level. "Dr. Luke told me to monitor myself. If I wasn't urinating at least once every two hours, or if my urine wasn't almost colorless, it meant I needed to drink more water," explains Judy Levy.

Understand that this prescription for fluids means mostly H_2O. Other beverages, if consumed in excess, have disadvantages:

- Milk is low in iron, and filling up on too much may decrease your appetite for iron-rich foods like beef and pork. A quart or two of milk per day is great for providing calcium and protein, but don't overdo it.
- Fruit juices can cause wide swings in your blood sugar levels. Limit juice to no more than a quart a day.
- Soda pop, club soda, and other carbonated beverages may make your stomach uncomfortably bloated, leaving little room for the food you and your babies need.
- Coffee and many types of tea contain caffeine, which can lead to unstable blood sugar levels as well as irritability, nervousness, and fatigue. They also act as a diuretic and thereby contribute to dehydration, which can in turn trigger contractions. What's more, caffeine can interfere with the absorption of minerals, particularly calcium. Your best bet is to limit coffee and tea to no more than one or two cups daily, preferably decaffeinated.

So stick to water. You'll soon develop a taste for it, if you haven't already. To inspire you, here is one reader's success story: "My nurse said I was one of the most hydrated people she had ever seen. I told her that Dr. Luke's book said to drink, drink, drink as much water as possible—and I did. The nurse said it was probably a factor in having such a lengthy twin pregnancy. My girls were 7 lb., 6 oz., and 6 lb., 11 oz. They left the hospital with me after three days."

Another bonus? Keeping up the water habit after you deliver will help you get your figure back more quickly.

Ingestibles Your Babies Want You to Avoid

Along with all the things you should be eating and drinking, there are several things you should *not* be ingesting while pregnant:

ORAL MEDICATIONS

Before you became pregnant, you probably didn't think twice about popping two aspirin for a headache or taking antibiotics when you had an infection. But now that you're expecting, you must be mindful of the medications you take. That's not to say you have to suffer stoically through whatever symptoms might develop. Some over-the-counter drugs are generally considered safe during pregnancy. These include:

- Acetaminophen (Tylenol) for headache and other pain
- Vaginal creams that contain clotrimazole (Gyne-Lotrimin) or miconazole (Monistat 7, Monistat 3) for yeast infections

Other drugs, both over-the-counter and prescription, can have serious negative effects on your babies' growth and development. Aspirin, for example, may cause bleeding problems. The common antibiotic tetracycline can permanently stain your children's teeth and may slow bone growth. The acne drug Accutane can cause major birth defects, as can some tranquilizers and psoriasis medications.

For safety's sake, be sure that each one of your health care providers—not just your obstetrician, but also allergist, internist, dentist, physical therapist, etc.—knows that you are pregnant. That information is crucial in determining whether or not the benefits outweigh the risks in prescribing any particular medication.

Also, review with your doctors the list of every medication you normally take, whether occasionally or regularly, prescription or over-the-counter. If you have a chronic condition such as allergies, your doctor may switch you from one type of medication to another type that is safer during pregnancy. Do not, however, suddenly stop taking important medications, such as those for asthma or seizures, without your doctor's approval.

ALCOHOL

Many women report that they develop an aversion to alcoholic beverages during pregnancy, even if they had enjoyed an occasional drink before conceiving. This is no mere coincidence. It is nature's way of protecting unborn babies. "Normally I enjoy a glass of wine with dinner, but once I got pregnant, alcohol didn't appeal to me at all. The smell, the taste, the very mention of it, turned me off," says Lydia Greenwood, mother of boy/girl twins.

The fact is, alcohol is poison to your unborn babies, for several reasons:

- Alcohol can alter levels of at least seven vital nutrients. These nutritional deficits contribute to the increase in birth defects. For instance, drinking during pregnancy more than doubles the risk of having a baby with cleft lip.

- The amniotic fluid surrounding the fetuses acts as a reservoir for alcohol. Because the babies lack the necessary enzymes to metabolize alcohol, they are exposed to it long after your body has cleared it from your own blood supply.
- Alcohol interferes with protein synthesis, a critical process in your babies' development. Potential consequences for your unborn babies include stunted growth, birth defects, and mental retardation. In the United States, alcohol use during pregnancy is the major cause of mental retardation and learning and behavioral problems.
- Alcohol also may be directly toxic to the placenta, causing the unborn babies to suffer a special kind of malnutrition.

The effects of alcohol are dose-related, meaning that the more a woman drinks, the more profoundly damaged her babies are likely to be. Women who are chronic alcohol abusers (defined as drinking six or more drinks per day) throughout pregnancy have a 30 to 40 percent chance of delivering a baby with fetal alcohol syndrome (FAS). In the United States, FAS affects approximately 5,000 babies per year—that's one in every 700 births. More than 80 percent of children with FAS suffer the following:

- Delayed growth, both before and after birth
- Mental retardation
- Poor coordination
- Attention deficit disorder with hyperactivity (ADHD)
- Malformations of the face

Additionally, 20 to 50 percent of FAS children have these problems:

- Birth defects of various kinds
- Cardiac problems
- Impaired vision
- Hearing loss

Even when a woman's alcohol consumption is significantly less than this, her babies are still at risk. Nearly 50,000 babies in the United States—that's one in 70 babies—are born each year with a condition called fetal alcohol effects. This condition is characterized by some, but not all, of the birth defects associated with FAS.

How about moderate drinking? As little as three drinks per week can more than double your babies' risk for being born weighing less than 5½ pounds. This greatly compounds the potential problems, given that multiples are already at higher risk for low birthweight.

The message is clear: When you are pregnant, total abstinence is the only prudent course. There is no safe amount of alcohol that you can have during pregnancy.

Did you have a few drinks before you realized you were expecting? Don't panic—they're not likely to have done your babies harm. But if you continue to use alcohol now, you are endangering all your babies. The wisest course of action is to stop drinking immediately. If you find that you cannot stop, tell your doctor at once. You have a medical problem, and medical treatment is available.

Cigarettes

Smoking is one of the worst habits you can possibly have when you're pregnant. You already know all the hazardous long-term effects cigarettes can have on your own body, such as cancer, heart disease, and emphysema. But you may not be aware of the harm it can do in the relatively short period of time you are pregnant—with very serious consequences for your children's health.

With each cigarette, you expose your unborn multiples to thousands of toxic substances. Your body must then divert some of its stores of vitamins to detoxify these substances, thereby reducing the amount of essential nutrients available for fetal growth. One of these toxic substances is carbon monoxide, which binds to hemoglobin and lowers the amount of oxygen in your blood. This is turn reduces the oxygen to the placenta, the vital middleman in your babies' growth and development. The result is an increase in placental infarcts, or areas where the placental tissue dies due to lack of oxygen. Consider these facts:

- Miscarriages occur significantly more frequently among smokers.
- Your babies are already at risk for preterm birth by virtue of being multiples. If their prenatal environment is polluted, the danger rises even higher. For instance, even if you smoke fewer than 10 cigarettes a day, you increase your risk of delivering your twins before 37 weeks' gestation by 30 percent; 10 or more cigarettes daily boosts that risk by 40 percent. Delivering your twins before 35 weeks is three times as probable if you smoke. Delivering extremely prematurely, before 33 weeks, is four times more likely for smokers.
- Low birthweight is also an inherent hazard for twins and supertwins. Maternal smoking doubles twins' risk of being born weighing less than 5½ pounds, and increases *more than sevenfold* their risk of weighing less than 3½ pounds at birth.

- Mental retardation occurs 60 percent more often among children whose mothers smoked during pregnancy. The more you smoke, the greater the risk.
- Cleft lip is nearly 80 percent more common among babies born to smokers.
- Neural tube defects such as spina bifida occur more often among children exposed to cigarette smoke before birth. In part, this may be due to the fact that cigarettes deplete the mother's stores of folic acid.
- A serious digestive disorder called pyloric stenosis occurs twice as often in infants born to smokers. The condition causes projectile vomiting, and requires surgical correction.
- Children whose mothers smoked during pregnancy have a threefold increased risk of experiencing problems with motor control, attention, and perception.

Even after delivery, your smoking—or smoking by anyone in your household—can present serious hazards to the health of your babies. Here is why:

- Sudden infant death syndrome (SIDS) occurs significantly more often among infants exposed to secondhand smoke.
- Children of smokers are more prone to respiratory illnesses, including asthma, bronchitis, and colds.

Don't fool yourself: There is no "safe" level of smoking. Even the lightest smokers—those who have only one to five cigarettes per day—are 56 percent more likely than nonsmokers to have babies with low birthweights.

Approximately 12 percent of pregnant women smoke. If you are among them, today is the day to stop. Studies have shown the nicotine patch to be useful during pregnancy. Discuss this safer alternative with your doctor. Also, consider joining a support group, either a local face-to-face group or an on-line option such as www.Quitnet.com. Because such groups provide encouragement and moral support, plus practical advice on handling cravings, they are often the key to success.

Stay Motivated

Many moms find it inspirational to have a graphic illustration of how their babies grow as the weeks of pregnancy pass. So imagine for a moment your babies' heads. What size are they now? What size will they be next month? What size will they be the first time you hold your newborns in your arms? Provided they are properly nourished, here's what you can expect:

- At 12 weeks into the pregnancy, your babies' heads are each about the size of a grape.
- At 16 weeks, the size of an apricot.
- At 20 weeks, the size of an egg.
- At 24 weeks, the size of a tangerine.
- At 28 weeks, the size of a lemon.
- At 32 weeks, the size of a large orange.
- At 36 weeks, the size of a grapefruit.
- At 40 weeks, the size of a small cantaloupe.

Given the proper guidance about diet, most expectant mothers of multiples are happy for the opportunity to have such a direct and positive influence on their pregnancy. Stacy Moore states it simply and eloquently when she says, "I was told that the bigger my twins were at birth, the more likely it was I'd be able to bring them home with me when I left the hospital. So I ate and ate and ate. And guess what? My boys did come home with me, just three days after their birth. For me, that was the ultimate goal—and the ultimate reward."

Chapter 5

Your Body:
How to Look Good, Feel Great,
Work Smart, and Play It Safe

When you're expecting multiples, you're likely to experience the physical changes of pregnancy sooner and more intensely than do women carrying a singleton. There are two main reasons for this. The first is hormonal: During a multiple pregnancy, your body produces much higher levels of the various pregnancy hormones, including estrogen and progesterone.

The second reason has to do with sheer size—your belly will grow far larger than that of a woman pregnant with just one baby. Consider these comparisons:

- With twins, your uterus is the same size as that of a singleton mom who is 6 to 8 weeks further along in her pregnancy.
- With triplets, your uterus is the same size as that of a singleton mom who is 10 to 12 weeks further along in her pregnancy.
- With quadruplets, your uterus is the same size as that of a singleton mom who is 14 to 16 weeks further along in her pregnancy.

Some of the changes in your body are delightful, you will discover. Others can cause discomfort, so you'll want to find safe and effective ways to minimize the symptoms. Most important, certain physical changes that accompany a multiple pregnancy require significant—but temporary—modifications in your lifestyle. Be disciplined about following the guidelines in this chapter, and you'll be taking important steps toward safeguarding your own health and that of your unborn babies.

Beauty and the Belly

You're expecting your figure to be transformed, of course. But did you know that your hair and skin might look different too? A revved-up circulation and those pregnancy hormones (which for you are present in such abundance) are responsible. "My hair got very thick and luxurious. It was enormous! I loved that," says Stacy Moore, mother of fraternal twin boys. Indeed, it's common during pregnancy for your mane to thicken noticeably and to grow more quickly. Enjoy it while it lasts! Soon after delivery, it will return to normal as you shed those extra strands.

What about coloring your hair? In the past, doctors thought hair dye might potentially be harmful to fetuses. Today, though, it is believed to be safe because so little dye is absorbed through the skin. So if you yearn for a new hue for your tresses, go ahead.

Certain changes are also taking place in your skin, many of which you'll welcome. "The whole time I was expecting, my complexion was peaches-and-cream—soft, rosy, clear, with no pimples. Maybe it was the glow of pregnancy times two," says Lydia Greenwood, mother of boy/girl twins.

Other skin conditions brought on by hormonal changes are, however, less pleasing. Some women develop a brownish discoloration around their eyes and over their noses, called chloasma, or the "mask of pregnancy." Also commonly making an appearance is a brownish line, the linea nigra, that runs from the center of the abdomen to the top of the pubic bone. You may suddenly notice that the palms of your hands and perhaps the soles of your feet are red and itchy. On your legs, little spider veins may surface. There's not a lot you can do about these skin conditions other than to apply moisturizer, if it makes you feel better, and to take heart in knowing that they generally disappear shortly after delivery.

What about stretch marks—those reddish, slightly indented striations that often spring up on the tummies of pregnant women? It's the luck of the draw. Some mothers-to-be of multiples don't get stretch marks, even after gaining 60 pounds or more. This trait tends to run in families, so ask your own mother how she fared to get a hint of what might be in store for you.

Don't be too surprised or dismayed if stretch marks do develop, however. The phenomenon is common enough among mothers of multiples that it has a special name: twin skin. Stacy Moore confides, "At about six months, bright red stretch marks sprouted all over my belly. They faded to silver after the boys were born, yet still I'm left with 'twin skin.' Bikinis are a thing of the past, I guess. But I try to look at those marks as a badge of motherhood."

What to Wear When Expecting a Pair (or More)

DR. LUKE: The problem with most maternity clothes, our patients at the Multiples Clinic report, is that they aren't roomy enough where room is needed most—in the tummy. Garments that fit well in the shoulders and sleeves are too snug around the middle. If you buy clothes in larger sizes, so that they fit comfortably in the waist area, you're swimming in them everywhere else.

I'm waiting for some enterprising mother of multiples to design her own line of maternity clothing for expectant moms of twins and supertwins. She'll make a fortune. But until that happens, you may want to raid your husband's closet. Many of the moms in our program "borrow" their husbands' clothing, particularly the oversized sweaters, sweatshirts, T-shirts, and jogging pants.

Amy Maly agrees. "By the time I took a leave from work, the only clothes that fit were my husband's oversized T-shirts, so I wore those around the house all day," she says. Couple that T-shirt with a pair of maternity leggings, and you've got an outfit that fits the bill for grocery shopping or running errands.

For more formal occasions, you'll need something dressier. When you shop, keep in mind that women expecting multiples often feel overheated. For maximum comfort, choose garments made of breathable fabrics in styles that offer extra roominess in the belly—a denim jumper, a cotton tent dress, a jersey cat suit.

Unless you're sure you'll need it, hold off on buying a maternity coat. "Even though it was winter, I was so warm all the time that I could just wear my regular coat, leaving it unbuttoned," explains Judy Levy, mother of fraternal twin girls and an older daughter.

And do plan on needing a maternity wardrobe much sooner than the mother of a singleton might. "When I was pregnant with my firstborn, I was five and a half months along before I started to wear maternity clothes. With the twins, though, I had to break out the maternity wardrobe at eight weeks," laughs Judy Levy. "Because I'm normally petite, all my old maternity clothes were size small. I grew out of most of them halfway through the twin pregnancy and had to buy a whole new maternity wardrobe in much larger sizes."

Considering that your feet must now bear a lot more weight than they're accustomed to, it's no surprise that they may ache. Choose shoes that provide good support, nonskid soles, and extra cushioning. "I stuck primarily to sneakers. They were the most comfortable, and with those deep treads and rubber soles, I didn't have to worry about slipping," says Stacy Moore.

You may need to buy a few pairs of shoes in a larger size than you normally wear. During pregnancy, the hormones that loosen up your pelvis in anticipation of delivery also loosen the ligaments around your other joints, including those in the feet. Coupled with a tendency for the lower extremities to swell during pregnancy, it's no wonder that your regular shoes may feel too snug.

As for high heels, leave them in the closet until after delivery. Your center of balance shifts forward during pregnancy, and even more so with multiples, making you less steady on your feet and more prone to twisting an ankle or tripping on an uneven sidewalk. Any heel higher than two inches leaves you at risk for a fall, and the consequences can be severe—bleeding early in pregnancy, or contractions and preterm labor later on.

Common Discomforts of Pregnancy . . . Multiplied

With all those babies inside, your extra-large tummy can lead to some extra aches and pains. Here's how to ease those uncomfortable physical symptoms:

BACKACHES

With each passing month, the curve in your lower back becomes more exaggerated due to the increasing weight of your belly. This triggers back pain, particularly in the lower (lumbar) region.

- Limit standing to no more than two hours at a time early in pregnancy, and to a maximum of an hour at a time later. If you have been diagnosed with cervical changes, feel uterine contractions, or have had a bout of preterm labor, limit on-your-feet time even more strictly. When you must stand, place one foot on a low stool; every few minutes, switch around and elevate the other foot.
- When you sit, choose a chair with a straight back, armrests, and a firm cushion; elevate your legs on a footstool. To protect your back as you rise to a standing position, lean forward and push from the hips, keeping your back and neck straight.
- Check your mattress for firmness. If it seems overly soft, have someone place a board between the mattress and box spring. Then take advantage of every opportunity to get horizontal. "For back pain, what helped me the most was rest," says twin mom Judy Levy. When it's time to get up, start from a side-lying position and gently push yourself up sideways.
- A gentle massage relieves backache and other pains. Marcy Bugajski, mother of fraternal twin boys, says, "My husband, Dave, often gave me a back rub while I lay on

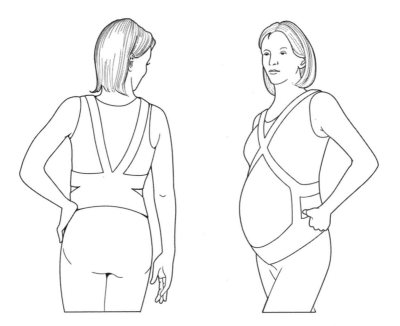

Prenatal Cradle *supportive maternity garment*

my side. That was heaven! And if I woke up with leg cramps in the middle of the night, he'd gently straighten my legs, flex my feet, and rub my calves till the ache went away." You might also look for a professional masseuse with experience in providing massage for pregnant women. She should use a special chair that allows you to lean forward with full-body support and a perfectly aligned spine, or an arrangement of pillows that offers support in a side-lying position. Call local spas and ask if they have special programs for pregnant women, or get a recommendation from your health care professional.

- Warm water soothes tired muscles, but it can be risky to climb in and out of the tub when a multiple pregnancy diminishes your sense of balance. Invest in a shower stool so you can sit in your shower stall and enjoy the pulsating water on your neck and back.

- The typical stance of a pregnant woman—with fingers clasped under her belly—provides support for your growing uterus. But it's hard to carry groceries, open doors, work at a keyboard, or wash the dishes with your hands holding up your belly. A more practical solution is the Prenatal Cradle, a harnesslike maternity garment that supports your abdomen while helping to keep your shoulders back and posture erect. Anne Seifert, the mother of quadruplets, explains, "The Prenatal Cradle has straps that go over your shoulders and crisscross on your back, and a band that winds around your middle and hooks down under your belly. It does look funny—the first time my husband saw me wearing it, he said, 'What in the world is that contraption?'—but it really does keep pressure off your back and bladder. Is it worth the price? You bet." (To order, contact Prenatal Cradle: PO Box 443, Hamburg, MI 48139. Telephone 800–607–3572; e-mail prenatalcradle@ prenatalcradle.com; Web site www.prenatalcradle.com.)

- Like your belly, your breasts are growing too, and the increased weight up top also contributes to backache. A good bra eases discomfort by providing proper support. If you're full-figured, wear a bra to bed at night too.

- A safe and soothing home remedy for backache is a glass of warm milk with a spoonful of honey mixed in. Before taking anything stronger, such as Extra-Strength Tylenol, get the go-ahead from your obstetrician.

SIDE ACHES

With many multiple pregnancies, growth in the height of the uterus slows down toward the end of the pregnancy, and the babies begin to spread out. Your doctor doesn't measure this sideways growth the way she measures fundal height, but the increased width will be obvious to you. For one thing, your maternity clothes suddenly feel snug. What's more, this rapid growth causes the ligaments that suspend your uterus within your pelvis (like a bony basket) to stretch. This can cause discomfort—a dull ache at times, or perhaps a sharp pain—along your side. It's likely to be more pronounced if you've never been pregnant before. To ease the sensation, try taking a warm shower or lying down with some pillows supporting the weight of your belly.

SWELLING

A common complaint for all pregnant women is swelling, particularly in the legs and ankles. In large part, this is caused by the fact that the growing uterus blocks the return of blood to the heart—an effect compounded in a multiple pregnancy because the uterus is so much bigger.

The best remedy for swelling is "down time"—meaning time spent lying down on your side. A prone position improves circulation to your kidneys and allows excess fluid to be eliminated. Your heart will not have to work as hard either, so you'll feel better all around. Want proof? Measure your ankles before and after a nap, or in the morning and again in the evening on a day when you didn't take your naps, and note the significant difference in the amount of swelling you experience.

Swelling can also cause pressure on nerves, particularly in your arms and legs. Some pregnant women develop carpal tunnel syndrome, a painful disorder caused by compression of the nerves and ligaments of the wrists. This will subside after delivery, but in the meantime, wrist splints may help ease the discomfort.

Another cause of swelling is dietary. Every gram of carbohydrate holds two grams of water (hence the philosophy of carbohydrate-loading practiced by many runners before a big race). To minimize excess fluid, cut back on your carbohydrate consumption at dinner. For instance, eat a steak and a big salad, but pass on the rice or potatoes, and see how your hands and feet feel in the morning.

HEARTBURN

During pregnancy, heartburn is caused primarily by a reflux of acid secretions from the stomach into the lower part of the esophagus. This occurs for two reasons. First, your growing uterus pushes aside the stomach and intestines, and this crowding triggers reflux. Second, the hormones of pregnancy cause changes in the gastrointestinal tract, including a slowing-down of digestion and elimination. This is nature's way of allowing you to absorb more nutrients from the foods you eat—but it also contributes to heartburn.

With a singleton pregnancy, symptoms typically begin at about 31 to 34 weeks. But because the uterus grows faster and hormone levels are higher with a multiple pregnancy, heartburn occurs sooner and can be much more severe, depending in part on the position of the babies. With a twin pregnancy, heartburn may begin around weeks 23 to 28; with triplets, by weeks 19 to 24; and with quadruplets, by weeks 16 to 21. "I had excruciating heartburn, particularly after week 26. I think that was the worst part of the whole pregnancy," says quad mom Anne Seifert.

While you may be tempted to try an over-the-counter remedy such as Tums, Mylanta, or Maalox, you're better off with the calcium/magnesium/zinc supplements recommended in Chapters 3 and 4. These provide needed nutrients while doubling as effective therapy for heartburn, with fewer side effects such as gas or diarrhea. If symptoms are so severe that you can't sleep or get comfortable, ask your doctor about prescription medication. Says Anne, "Oral medicine helped for a while, but toward the end, the only thing that relieved the discomfort was IV medication."

FULL BLADDER

Has the bathroom suddenly become the most popular room in your house? Blame your frequent need to urinate on the same two factors that contribute to heartburn: a growing uterus and elevated hormones.

The bigger your babies get, and the more of them you're carrying, the more pressure your uterus exerts on your bladder. This sensation can be particularly strong if the fetus closest to your cervix is positioned deep in your pelvis.

Hormonal changes of pregnancy also come into play. The amniotic fluid around the fetuses is changed many times a day to eliminate their urine and discarded cells. Your kidneys and bladder must therefore do double duty now, to expel not only your own wastes but also those of your unborn babies. With a multiple pregnancy, there is more amniotic fluid to process and higher levels of hormones acting on the kidneys. The result: a near-constant need to urinate.

This can be a real problem when you don't have easy access to a bathroom. "My drive to work takes about an hour. By the time I arrived each morning, I'd have to urinate so badly! Sometimes I couldn't imagine how I'd make it to my office building, which was two blocks away from the parking lot," says twin mom Judy Levy. To avoid that bursting-bladder sensation, scope out your commuting route and find a restaurant or service station midway where you can stop to use the bathroom facilities. Whenever you enter a building where you'll be for some time, ask for directions to a rest room—so you'll know where to go when you need to go.

The urge to urinate may also wake you in the middle of the night. Don't attempt to resolve this by cutting back on your intake of water. Remember, you need to drink eight 16-ounce glasses of water daily (as discussed in Chapters 3 and 4) in order to stay hydrated, avoid constipation, and reduce the risk of urinary-tract infection. But do take in your fluid before 8 P.M. so that most of it has time to pass through before you go to bed. Are those nightly bathroom visits continuing despite this strategy? Here's how Judy Levy looks at it: "I woke up to urinate at least three times a night. I kept telling myself it was good practice because, once the twins were born, I'd need to get up for all those nighttime feedings."

If you're expecting supertwins, the bladder problem can seriously interfere with sleep toward the end of your pregnancy. Helen Armer, mother of triplets, explains: "By week 30, sleeping for more than two hours at a stretch was almost impossible because my bladder would wake me up. So all day and all night, I'd nap briefly, get up to use the bathroom, then read awhile or watch a video with my preschooler before dozing off again for another hour or two." There's little more you can do to improve the situation at this point other than to feel glad that your delivery date is getting closer with each passing day.

Some women experience slight incontinence during pregnancy, leaking a little urine with every sneeze or laugh. If you share this problem, you might want to wear an absorbent pad. Also try Kegel exercises, which strengthen the muscles around the urethra (the outside opening of the urinary tract). Here's how: Contract or squeeze the muscles you normally use to halt the flow of urine; hold for 10 seconds; release; repeat 10 to 20 times. Do three complete sets of these exercises daily, and in a short time, you will see significant improvement in your ability to hold your urine. If the problem persists, consult your doctor.

Using the bathroom may also present a problem you hadn't anticipated: joint pain. Judy Levy explains: "Every time I went to the bathroom and had to squat down to reach the toilet seat, my knees ached. I wish I had thought to rent one of those toilet seats for the handicapped, which have handrails and a higher seat. That would make life easier for an expectant mother of multiples."

SHORTNESS OF BREATH

Like your other internal organs, your lungs are crowded by your growing uterus. The rib cage widens to adapt, but not enough to compensate fully for the reduced lung volume as pregnancy progresses. That means you won't be able to breathe as deeply as you normally do—so you won't be able to do things that require full, deep breaths, such as walking up a flight of stairs or running for a bus. Even carrying on a conversation may leave you winded.

Unfortunately, there is not much you can do about this other than to avoid activities that leave you short of breath. If you're uncomfortable even when lying down, try a semiseated position instead. "Gradually it became harder and harder to breathe in bed. The triplets took up so much space inside me that there was little room left for my lungs!" says Helen Armer. "It helped to stay propped up with lots of pillows instead of reclining all the way."

OVERHEATING

Pregnant women are like portable heaters: They're hot all the time, regardless of the season or thermostat reading. This is largely due to the high metabolism of the unborn baby—or babies, in the case of a multiple pregnancy—and the amount of heat these rapidly growing children generate.

To help dissipate the extra heat, the mother's blood volume increases—by about 50 percent for a singleton pregnancy, by nearly 100 percent for twins, and even more for triplets or quads. One sign of this increase is when you feel your heart beating faster and stronger, and perhaps hear the blood pounding in your ears. Even with the increased blood volume, however, you're likely to find yourself perspiring while others around you are shivering. "I got overheated much more easily during the twin pregnancy than in my previous singleton pregnancy. I had to sleep on top of the covers, even when my partner was huddled beneath several blankets trying to stay warm," says Judy Levy.

To minimize discomfort, dress in layers so you can peel off some clothes when overheated.

Keep a jug of ice water handy at all times. To avoid arguments over the bedroom thermostat setting, try an electric blanket with dual controls.

SLEEP DISCOMFORTS

When you are pregnant with two or more babies, it is absolutely critical for your physical and emotional well-being that you get enough rest. During the first three months, as your body adjusts to pregnancy, you may feel unusually tired, owing to rising hormones. By the second trimester, most women feel more energetic. But as your pregnancy progresses into the third trimester, you tire quickly. Ironically, it's at this point that the high metabolism of your growing babies, as well as their constant drain on your own metabolism, may be giving you the most trouble with sleeping.

A primary problem is finding a comfortable position for sleep. You can't lie on your stomach for obvious reasons. You shouldn't lie on your back because the weight of the fetuses presses on blood vessels supplying the uterus, causing your blood pressure to increase and possibly triggering contractions.

That leaves one option: lying on your side. Yet some women may be unaccustomed to that position. "I had always slept on my back, so switching to a side-lying position made my hips ache. The best way to relieve the pain was to have someone give me a good knuckle massage on the backs of my hips," says Lydia Greenwood, mother of boy/girl twins.

The right arrangement of pillows maximizes comfort. A wedge-shaped cushion, for example, tucks in right under your tummy to provide support where it's needed most. Place another pillow between your knees, to keep the weight of your belly from pulling you too far forward and straining your back muscles. If you tend to roll onto your back while you sleep, use pillows behind your shoulders and buttocks to keep you on your side. Or simplify matters with this strategy from twin mom Stacy Moore: "I bought a wonderful head-to-toe pillow that was stuffed with feathers, so it molded to my body everywhere. It made lying on my side much more comfortable. In fact, it was the best investment I made during my entire pregnancy."

Rolling from side to side may also be difficult—increasingly so with each passing week and with each additional baby you're expecting. Twin mom Judy Levy says, "By the third trimester, rolling over in bed was impossible. I couldn't stand to have the weight of my huge belly on top of me even for a moment—and it took a lot longer than a moment to roll all the way over. To change from lying on my left side to my right, I had to get up, walk around the bed, and climb back in on the other side of the bed. Of course, this would wake up my partner. We ended up sleeping in separate beds for the last few months. I needed space to be uncomfortable in." If you too end up temporarily evicting your mate, don't feel guilty. Expectant moms of multiples need

Suggested position for getting comfortable

to spread out when they sleep—and counting all those babies, there are already a lot of people sharing your bed.

Surprisingly, quad mom Anne Seifert had less trouble with sleep discomfort than did many mothers of twins or even triplets. The credit, she says, goes to her waterbed. "It was wonderfully comfortable when I was pregnant. Waterbeds provide excellent support and don't cause any painful pressure points. You definitely need the motionless kind, though, because otherwise the waves bounce you around too much."

What About Sex?

Sleep isn't the only bedroom activity that tends to change during pregnancy. Chances are, you've got some questions and concerns about sex too.

In most normal singleton pregnancies, couples can continue to have intercourse until the woman goes into labor or her membranes break. But with a multiple pregnancy, there's a greater chance that your doctor will tell you to limit or avoid sexual activity. This is particularly likely if you've had more than one miscarriage or if you've experienced any complications such as an incompetent cervix, placenta previa, infection, bleeding, leaking of amniotic fluid, uterine contractions, or a history of preterm labor. Why is sex considered risky in such cases? Because both a woman's orgasm and the prostaglandins in semen can trigger uterine contractions.

Be sure to talk to your doctor about sex, and follow whatever instructions she may give you.

If pain, bleeding, or loss of fluid from the vagina occurs during or after lovemaking, contact your health professional immediately.

Your doctor has given sex a green light? You may find that lovemaking is more satisfying and exciting than ever, owing to the higher levels of hormones, increased sensitivity of the breasts and genital area, and freedom from any concerns about contraception.

For some women, though, libido takes a nosedive during pregnancy. In the first trimester, nausea may interfere with desire. By the third trimester, your big belly and aching back may make it tough just to get comfortable in bed, much less get amorous. "My sister adored sex while she was pregnant. She even had intercourse just hours before labor began! But with two babies inside me, I felt clumsy, achy, and exhausted," says Lydia Greenwood. The more babies you're expecting, the earlier that "too big for comfort" feeling is likely to kick in.

Not all the loss of libido stems from physical factors. Emotions come into play too. For instance, some women feel so baby-focused during pregnancy that having sex simply doesn't cross their minds very often. "My doctor never prohibited sex, but I admit that while I was pregnant, it was the last thing on my mind. This was tough on my husband, because sex is usually the first thing on his mind, all day, every day," says Miriam Silverstein, mother of fraternal twin boys. "As I headed into my 38th week, though, I was eager for this pregnancy to be over. I had read that sex could bring on labor, so I started jumping on my husband every night. It wasn't really the sex I wanted—I was just eager to meet my babies. And he knew it!"

Other expectant mothers of multiples may feel strange about their growing bodies. "I've always taken pride in my slender, sexy figure. But once I was pregnant with twins, my bigger body seemed unfamiliar. It's not that I felt unattractive—I just didn't feel like myself," Lydia Greenwood admits. You may also be concerned about how your husband views your very pregnant body. Be honest about your concerns, and he's likely to reassure you that he finds you more appealingly feminine than ever. "Ed told me again and again that he thought my big belly was beautiful. That helped me to feel more alluring," says Lydia.

Fear for the babies can also interfere with sexual desire. "Early on, the obstetrician had told us that it was okay to have sex whenever and however we wanted. But when an ultrasound done midway through the pregnancy showed that our babies might have a physical abnormality, we were too afraid to do anything that might hurt the babies," explains one mother of twins. "Within a month it was determined that the twins were going to be fine, and bedroom activity immediately picked up again."

With your doctor's okay, try these tips for enhancing sex during pregnancy:

- Experiment with positions. "Because I wasn't able to lie on my back, my husband and I were inspired to find some new and interesting positions for sex," Miriam Silverstein confides. Side-lying and woman-on-top positions are best, as they do not place undue pressure on your abdomen.

- Don't play the martyr. Tell your partner what feels good and what doesn't.
- If you don't feel like having intercourse, or if your doctor has cautioned against it, explore other ways of sharing sensual pleasure. Give each other a massage, take a shower together, or read a sexy novel aloud.

Physical Activity: What's Safe, What's Not

TAMARA: During my twin pregnancy, I was a gal-on-the-go—attending a daily prenatal exercise class, working late most evenings, renovating my kitchen, planning a last romantic getaway with my husband. Maybe it's because I was in New York City, where everyone rushes to do as much as possible, as quickly as possible. Maybe it's because I'd read a book that urged expectant mothers of twins to "make a double effort to stay in shape" and to challenge any doctor who tried to impose "unnecessary restrictions" on activities. Maybe it's because I'm a type A person by nature.

Whatever my reasons, they were not good ones. Looking back, I realize my body was sending me signals about the need to slow down. Such as? The lightheaded sensation that came over me when I went to the gym during lunch hour instead of relaxing with a nutritious meal. The intense vaginal pressure I felt—as if the babies inside me were "falling out"—when I hurried to catch the last train home. The throbbing in my back and rhythmic tightening in my abdomen as I installed new linoleum in my kitchen. The utter exhaustion that overcame me on vacation as my husband and I walked around Key West.

My motto was "Everybody's uncomfortable when they're pregnant, so just do what needs to be done without whining." Not a bad philosophy—except that my interpretation of what needed to be done was 180 degrees off the mark. My body was not telling me to be stoic and strong; it was telling me to rest, relax, and limit my activities.

DR. LUKE: All pregnant women must be more cautious when it comes to physical activity—the day-to-day kind like climbing stairs and carrying groceries as well as recreational choices like running or bicycling. But as a mother-to-be of multiples, you need to be especially careful because you're challenging your body to do something extraordinary.

Physical exertion, particularly when it involves the large muscles of the back or legs, shunts blood away from your uterus. This in turn can trigger preterm contractions through the actions of the stress hormones called catecholamines. The effect: an increased risk of having your pregnancy cut short by days, weeks, or even months. That means if your babies are to have the time they need to grow and get strong, you need to slow down.

It's not always easy to alter the pace of your life. You've got a lot going on, and you hate to neglect any of it. When you see your friends who are pregnant with singletons carrying on pretty much as they normally do, you're tempted to behave likewise. "When I was pregnant with my first daughter, I didn't cut back on my activity at all. I was a full-time law student, worked part-time, and went to the gym regularly too," says Judy Levy. "During my twin pregnancy, though, I really had to take it easy. Dr. Luke was like a mother hen, nagging me to cut back on my activities. But that was good, because I needed the extra prodding."

Do you need extra prodding too? It's at your fingertips, as one reader of the first edition of this book reports: "This book, more than anything else I read, made me realize that I wasn't just pregnant, but responsible for the future of two other human beings. I credit following the advice in this book for the health and size of my twins." Here are the specific guidelines to follow:

Get as much rest—lying down—as possible.

Studies show a strong connection between fatigue and preterm labor. Lying down, on the other hand, decreases the catecholamines that can trigger uterine contractions. A prone position also improves circulation to the kidneys, thus helping to eliminate excess fluids.

Blood flow to your babies is better when you're horizontal, and better for you too, since your body doesn't have to work against gravity to pump blood back to your heart. Judy Levy says, "I felt woozy several times a day during the second half of the pregnancy. At first I tried to push through it and just keep on doing whatever I was doing. But then Dr. Luke explained, 'What you're experiencing is called "circulatory stress." When you feel like you're going to pass out, it means your brain isn't getting enough oxygen. That means your babies aren't getting enough oxygen either.' Once I realized that, I started lying down at the first hint of dizziness."

Don't wait until you're exhausted to lie down. Instead, schedule horizontal time into your routine. Plan on a two-hour nap in the morning, another two-hour rest period in the afternoon, and a third nap after dinner. And don't let anyone tease you about being lazy. You're not "doing nothing." You're gestating—helping your babies grow bigger and stronger, and keeping yourself healthier too.

Don't stand when you can sit.

Women who stand for more than six hours at a time triple their risk of preterm birth, a national study of nurses found. When you stand, blood vessels outside the uterus get compressed against the pelvis. In an attempt to restore circulation, the uterus contracts. "Going into the sixth month, I started to feel a lot of vaginal pressure. That motivated me to look for creative ways to sit down more often," says Marcy Bugajski. For instance, set the ironing board to

More suggested positions for getting comfortable

its lowest position and pull up a chair. Place stools by the stove and sink. Stuck in a long line at the bank? Ask the person behind you to hold your spot while you go sit on a nearby bench until it's your turn with the teller.

Limit stair-climbing, stooping, and bending.

Strenuous activity that involves the large muscles of the back or legs is particularly likely to trigger contractions. To prevent this, organize household tasks to minimize trips up the stairs. On errands, take the elevator. Instead of stooping, sit on the floor to pick up clutter. And be sure to have someone else vacuum, mop, and scrub the tub. "Once we learned that vacuuming and other household chores could bring on contractions, my husband took over the housework. That was okay with me!" says Stacy Moore, mother of fraternal twin boys.

Avoid lifting and carrying.

Weight-bearing causes abdominal muscles to tighten, increasing pressure on the uterus and possibly setting off contractions. Don't lift anything heavy. In lifting even a lightweight object, keep your spine straight and bend your knees in order to protect your back. To maintain your balance, never lift anything from overhead or carry anything so large as to make your gait awkward. The alternatives? Use a rolling basket to transport clothes to the laundry room. Find a grocery store that delivers. Put your toddler in a stroller, not a backpack.

Keep air travel to a minimum.

Most airlines allow pregnant women to fly up to 36 weeks' gestation on domestic flights, and up to 35 weeks' on international flights. However, these guidelines pertain to uncomplicated singleton pregnancies, not to pregnancies in which there's an increased risk of premature labor. As an expectant mother of multiples, you'd be well advised to fly only prior to week 24, only if absolutely necessary, and only with your doctor's approval. After the 24th week, resign yourself to staying home.

If you must lift something, keep it close to your body and use your knees, not your back.

Why this restriction? Because long-distance travel can trigger contractions. Flying often involves standing in long lines, running for connections, carrying luggage, missing meals, sitting in one cramped position for extended periods of time, and experiencing changes in cabin pressure. The consequences include fatigue, hunger, dehydration, poor circulation, and stress, all of which increase the risk of preterm labor.

If you must fly, follow these recommendations:

- Allow sufficient time for checking in and making connections, so you won't have to rush.
- Have a companion or porter handle all luggage.
- If you're tired, don't be shy about requesting a wheelchair to get to and from your gate.
- Carry aboard plenty of snacks and lots of water, but avoid gas-producing foods and carbonated beverages that might increase in-flight discomfort.
- Wear support stockings to improve blood flow.
- Keep your seatbelt on continuously while in the air, since air turbulence cannot be predicted.

Get help caring for your older children.

"My daughter was only 18 months old when I got pregnant with the twins, which meant she was still in diapers. By my sixth month, I couldn't change her anymore. I wasn't supposed to lift anything heavy, so I couldn't place her on a changing table. If I sat on the floor to deal with the diaper, I could barely get back on my feet again. I also wasn't able to lift her into or out of her crib or car seat," recalls Judy Levy. "This meant that I simply could not be home alone with my toddler. Someone else had to be available to handle all the 'heavy work.'"

As Judy discovered, reducing daily physical activity can be especially challenging when you have an older child. The best solution is to make arrangements for others to help you with the physical care of your toddler or preschooler. Enroll her in day care, hire a caregiver to come to your house, or line up a network of friends to provide assistance whenever your partner is not at home. If you are new to your neighborhood, contact a local church or synagogue for help.

Another smart option is to contact a local club for parents of multiples. Join even before your babies are born, and you'll benefit greatly from the practical advice and moral support of women who've already been down the road you're traveling now. Options include:

- National Organization of Mothers of Twins Clubs (NOMOTC): PO Box 438, Thompsons Station, TN 37179-0438. Telephone 615–595–0936 or 877–540–2200; e-mail info@nomotc.org; Web site www.nomotc.org.
- Mothers of Supertwins (MOST): PO Box 951, Brentwood, NY 11717-0627. Telephone 631–859–1110; Web site www.mostonline.org.

Easy-Does-It Exercise

DR. LUKE: As a swimmer since my teens and now a runner, I can appreciate that many women today have made a firm commitment to fitness. That's why this revised edition of *When You're Expecting Twins, Triplets, or Quads* includes expanded coverage on working out safely during pregnancy. We've drawn on the expertise of physical therapist Elaine Anderson, P.T., M.P.H., a research associate in the Department of Obstetrics and Gynecology at the University of Michigan. In this section and in Chapter 6, you'll find exercises specifically designed for expectant mothers of multiples.

You've heard hundreds of times how essential exercise is to good health—and in general that's true. The American College of Obstetricians and Gynecologists (ACOG) recommends that pregnant women engage in regular, moderate physical activity in order to achieve a variety of health benefits, including a decreased risk of gestational diabetes. However, the issue isn't clear-cut. One study published in 2002 found that, even for low-risk women pregnant with singletons, exercise during pregnancy was associated with significantly longer labors, smaller babies, and a higher rate of infections among mothers.

When you're pregnant with multiples, heavy-duty workouts can do much more harm than good. As with other types of physical activity, intense or prolonged exercise drives blood toward muscles and away from your uterus. It also increases blood levels of catecholamines, the hormones that can trigger contractions. So if you weren't very physically active before this pregnancy, now is *not* the time to turn athletic. Even if you have been accustomed to regular workouts, you still must modify your routine significantly.

Meredith Alcott learned that lesson the hard way. "I had always worked out before I got pregnant, so I figured I could keep it up—especially since my obstetrician didn't say anything to me about cutting back on physical activity. I'd go to work, come home exhausted, nap for two hours, then get up and hit the StairMaster," says Meredith, mother of identical twin girls. "Afterward I'd be so tired that it was all I could do just to eat dinner before collapsing back in bed. At the time, I didn't realize I was overdoing it, though looking back, that seems obvious."

Are you expecting supertwins? No matter how fit you are, you should avoid vigorous exercise entirely. After all, carrying triplets or quads is enough of a workout in itself! Starting the day her multiples are diagnosed, a woman pregnant with three or more babies should limit exercise to occasional short walks and slow, relaxed swimming.

What if you're expecting "only" twins? Provided you have no pregnancy complications or other risk factors for preterm labor, exercise within the following limits is generally safe:

- Get your doctor's go-ahead before doing any exercise program, even if it's a workout routine you've done for years.
- Do not overexert yourself. Warning signs such as perspiration, rapid heartbeat, breathlessness, or fatigue mean you need to slow down or stop.
- Scale back to a less intense type of workout. For example, walk instead of running; take a leisurely swim instead of doing race-the-clock laps; switch from step aerobics to a stretching class.
- Shorten your workouts. The 75-minute classes you used to take are too rigorous right now. Limit each exercise session to 30 to 45 minutes.
- Look for "gentle yoga" classes that focus on easy postures, breathing techniques, and deep relaxation. Save the more challenging ashtanga and "hot yoga" bikram classes until after your babies are born.
- Avoid maneuvers that require you to lie on your back. The weight of your uterus compresses major blood vessels, restricting circulation and possibly triggering contractions. If you're devoted to Pilates, stick to the seated exercises for now. You can resume those back rolls and bridges after the babies are born.
- Weight-training workouts should include absolutely *no heavy lifting*. Instead, maintain muscle strength safely by following the exercise routine called "Muscle-Tone Maintenance" in Chapter 6.
- Avoid activities that challenge balance, such as bicycling. An expanding uterus alters your center of gravity and leaves you more prone to falling. Love to cycle? Go for a leisurely spin on a stationary bike.
- Many fitness centers offer easy-does-it prenatal exercise classes. These can be a good option—but don't assume that a program is safe simply because it's marketed toward pregnant women. If the instructor urges participants to exceed the guidelines in this section, don't enroll.
- Dehydration can set off contractions, so drink plenty of fluids before, during, and after exercising.
- When the weather is hot or humid, exercise indoors only.

- Immediately halt your workout and call your doctor if you experience pain, dizziness, palpitations, or bleeding or leaking of fluids from the vagina.
- When you reach your 24th week of your twin pregnancy, cut your cardio-exercise routine to short walks and leisurely swimming only.

Is your prepregnancy workout partner teasing you about turning into a couch potato? She's misinformed. Share with her this reader's articulate words: "There is a perception, especially among younger, college-educated women, that any doctor who advises a pregnant mother to slow down and limit her physical activities is a neo-Victorian throwback who thinks pregnancy is a disease. As the first among my girlfriends to get pregnant, I heard a lot of this sort of talk. My (childless) workout buddy even tried to convince me to ignore my obstetrician's orders and exercise anyway! The fact remains that even for a healthy, fit woman, a multiple pregnancy carries higher risks for mother and babies than a singleton pregnancy does."

Remember, a few months away from the gym will not turn your muscles to mush. The body-building routine to follow now is the one that best builds your *babies'* bodies—in other words, rest and relaxation. You'll have plenty of time to regain your shape after the babies are born.

Words of Wisdom for Working Mothers-to-Be

TAMARA: For months, I'd been scheming how to get a plum job at a particular magazine I adored, establishing a new area of editorial coverage for women's health issues. Finally I managed to arrange an interview with the editor-in-chief, then completed a rigorous test of my skills. But after several weeks had passed with no word from her, I assumed the job had gone to someone else.

Suddenly I learned I was pregnant! All thoughts of pursuing a new position flew out of my head. Two days later, though, to my utter surprise, the editor invited me to lunch and offered me the job of my dreams. I looked at her dumbfounded. "I, um, I don't know what to say," I stammered. "I would love to work for you, but something has come up. . . ."

She peered at me intently for a moment, then opened her eyes wide and exclaimed, "You're pregnant!" I could only nod.

We spent the next half hour discussing whether I could set up the new department and build an inventory of ready-to-publish articles before going on maternity leave. I quickly outlined an ambitious plan, and the editor agreed to it. I was hired.

I worked hard and long. When an ultrasound done 18 weeks into my pregnancy unexpectedly revealed twins, I became doubly determined to succeed at the new job. Knowing that twins are typically born around 36 weeks instead of 40, I figured I'd have to cram an extra four weeks' worth of work into the next four months. So I worked faster and harder than ever—right up to the day when my water suddenly broke and my babies were born, nine weeks premature.

DR. LUKE: Approximately eight out of 10 women of childbearing age work outside the home, and each year, about 2.1 million of these women get pregnant. Those who work in physically and/or emotionally stressful jobs, studies show, are two to three times as likely to deliver prematurely. They are also more prone to pregnancy complications such as preeclampsia.

Most at risk are nurses, doctors, saleswomen, cleaning staff, assembly-line workers, and military personnel; people who work with chemicals or vibrating machines, or in a noisy, cold, or wet environment; anyone who works a rotating shift; any woman who puts in more than 45 hours per week; and women who retain responsibility for the majority of household chores, in addition to working outside the home (the infamous "second shift"). Mix any one or more of those risk factors with a multiple gestation, and you've got a potent recipe for trouble.

Does your work involve strenuous physical activity, exposure to hazardous substances, or high levels of stress? Are you experiencing any pregnancy complications? If so, speak to your doctor about taking an immediate leave of absence. Otherwise, an expectant mother of multiples can probably continue to work safely for several months by sticking to certain guidelines:

Rest during and after work.

In the course of an 8-hour shift, an expectant mother of multiples should lie down and rest at least twice, for a minimum of 20 to 30 minutes each time. Use a cot or sofa in the ladies' room, employees' lounge, a spare office, or your company's occupational health office, if possible. Or simply shut your office door, spread a thick blanket on the floor, and rest there. Twin mom Amy Maly suggests another option: "Since I live close to where I work, I was able to come home at lunchtime each day and lie down for an hour."

Make it an inviolable part of your weekday routine to rest again the minute you get home from work. Lie down for at least 30 to 40 minutes. What about dinner? Let your partner fix the meal or order takeout, so you don't have to stand in the kitchen and cook.

Reduce the physical demands of your job.

Extraneous physical activity can be avoided easily once you set your mind to the task. "To keep from overexerting myself, I made a conscious decision not to get up from my chair unless absolutely necessary," says Amy Maly, who works in the field of marketing. "Instead of walking to a co-worker's office to give her a message, I e-mailed everything. Whenever someone stopped by my desk, they would ask if I needed anything—photocopies, paperclips, a refill of my water carafe. People were always happy to help. It was amazing how much this conserved my energy."

Figure out how to arrange your office to keep everything within easy reach, so you don't have to get up from your chair. Then ask co-workers or maintenance personnel to do the heavy work in rearranging furniture as needed. Be sure to place a footstool beneath your desk, so you can elevate your feet.

If your job is inherently physically demanding, ask to be temporarily reassigned. "I'm an occupational therapist, so mine is not a sit-down type of job. At first, I wasn't sure how I would cope with the restrictions on physical activity that Dr. Luke suggested," says Heather Nicholas, mother of boy/girl twins. "My supervisor was very understanding, though. We agreed that whenever one of my patients needed to be lifted from the bed into a wheelchair, I would ask someone else to handle it. Any patient who required a lot of lifting was transferred to a different therapist. We even figured out ways that I could sit rather than stand while doing most of the therapy."

Cut back on work hours.

Limit yourself to no more than 4 to 6 hours of work in any given day, and to a maximum of 20 to 30 hours in a week. Set realistic goals for what you can achieve in that amount of time—and don't fool yourself into believing you can accomplish in 10 hours what normally takes 20 hours to do. If your supervisor sets impossible deadlines, renegotiate your duties. And say no to any suggestion that you should do the work from home. You're supposed to be resting and gestating, not dealing with the stress of running a satellite office from your basement.

If you're working a rotating shift, ask to be temporarily reassigned to more regular hours. Research shows that shift rotations are especially fatiguing, since the body must constantly adjust to different schedules of sleep and wakefulness.

Stress-proof your commute.

Leave home early enough to catch your ride without running. If the bus or train is crowded, ask a fellow commuter to give up his seat for you.

Going by car? Always remember to use your seatbelt and shoulder harness, fastening the lap strap below your abdomen. Stop the car and walk around awhile if your legs start to swell or cramp.

Judy Levy, an attorney, learned the importance of taking safety precautions. "My commute required an hour's drive each way. One morning in the 24th week of my twin pregnancy, as I was zooming down the middle of a 12-lane expressway, my tire blew out. I pulled over onto the center strip and sat there watching the 18-wheel trucks zoom by so fast that my car quivered. As I imagined myself trying to waddle across six lanes of high-speed traffic, I started to sob. Thank goodness I had a car phone and membership in an automobile association—two things no pregnant woman should be without. Help arrived about a half hour later, and pretty soon I was on my way again, shaken but unharmed. This experience woke me up to the fact that I couldn't just keep up with my normal life. I had to be careful in everything I did. Step one was to buy new tires!"

Leave the air travel to co-workers until after your babies are born.

As discussed earlier in this chapter, flying involves a number of risks for women pregnant with multiples. The fatigue, dehydration, poor circulation, and stress associated with long-distance travel can all trigger contractions. Yes, you may have to miss a business conference or skip the customary face-to-face contact with a faraway client. But those scenarios are infinitely preferable to finding yourself at an out-of-town hospital in preterm labor—or worse, giving birth before your babies are ready.

PLANNING AND NEGOTIATING A WORK LEAVE

TAMARA: At my 24-week prenatal checkup, my obstetrician casually suggested that I go on medical leave from work when I hit week 28. I was stunned. Most of my friends had worked right up to their due dates, and it had never crossed my mind that I might need to stop sooner.

"I just started that new job at the magazine, and I had planned to work until 36 weeks or so," I protested. "Are you sure I have to go on leave so soon?"

"Well, how about if we compromise on 32 weeks?" my easygoing doctor suggested. That seemed like a reasonable plan—until my twins shocked us both by being born at week 31.

DR. LUKE: When you're expecting multiples, you should *not* be expecting to work past your 28th week. In fact, we urge our patients at the Multiples Clinic to go on leave at 24 weeks, because that's when they need to begin resting for at least six hours each day. If a woman develops complications, or if she's expecting supertwins, it's likely she'll have to stop working even sooner. Quad mom Anne Seifert, for example, left her job as a dental hygienist at 16 weeks.

Whatever date your doctor gives you for beginning your leave of absence, don't argue or try to bargain for a later date! In most cases, your work can wait until you return, and if it can't wait, someone else can take care of it while you're out. But your unborn babies' needs cannot wait—and no one else can fulfill the all-important job of gestating your multiples.

Think of it this way: A year from now, will it really matter whether you sold nine extra widgets or landed one more client by working an extra two months? Probably not. But it's likely to matter a great deal whether your babies were born two months before they might have been, had you not gotten the rest you required.

It's wise to prepare yourself and your employer properly for your impending leave. This protects your rights as well as your professional reputation. Here's how to proceed:

Before you break the news, find out what you're entitled to under the law and company policy.

Many workers are covered under the federal Family and Medical Leave Act (FMLA) of 1993. This guarantees an employee the right to take up to 12 weeks of unpaid leave per year to care for a newborn, newly adopted baby, or seriously ill relative, or to recover from illness. (The physical limitations imposed by a multiple pregnancy qualify under this last category, provided your doctor submits a written statement to this effect to your employer.) During the leave time, the person's job or an equivalent one must be held for her, and health insurance provided through the employer must remain in effect. The law applies to companies with 50 or more employees within a 75-mile radius. To qualify, an employee must work more than 25 hours per week and have been on the job for a minimum of 12 months.

The Pregnancy Discrimination Act of 1978 requires employers with more than 15 employees to guarantee job security and paid leave to pregnant women if and to the same extent that they guarantee those benefits to workers with other medical conditions, such as broken legs or heart attacks. In other words, if your company gives male employees longer leaves for other health conditions, female employees may not be limited to 12 weeks for pregnancy- or childbirth-related health conditions. Likewise, if Joe in the next office got six months off for a sabbatical or midcareer training program, you should be able to command a similar deal.

Some states guarantee more generous maternity leaves than these federal laws do. For instance, Washington, DC, offers eligible employees up to 32 weeks off over two years. A number of states also have temporary disability insurance (TDI) laws that provide partial salary replacement for nonwork-related disabilities, including childbirth- and pregnancy-related conditions. The percentage of salary paid under TDI varies from state to state, as does the duration of the disability period allowed. To check on your state, call the regional office of the Department of Labor's Wage and Hour Division (listed in the "U.S. Government Offices" section of the phone book's blue pages).

Many companies offer their employees benefits that go beyond what's required by law. To avoid spilling the beans before you're ready, investigate your company's policy through an employee manual, an in-house on-line benefits file, or the human resources department's anonymous hotline. You might also contact the following organizations:

- The Women's Bureau at the Department of Labor: www.dol.gov/wb/welcome.html
- 9to5, National Association of Working Women: www.9to5.org
- Your state's labor department

Talk to your health professional about your work situation. She can prepare whatever documentation is necessary to help you obtain all the benefits to which you are entitled.

Make your announcement in the most professional way possible.

Conventional wisdom says not to announce a pregnancy until you're well into the second trimester, when the risk of miscarriage decreases. With multiples, though, you may want to break the news sooner. You will need to begin your leave much earlier in your pregnancy than the average mother of a singleton would, and you don't want your supervisor to feel that you've left her with inadequate time to prepare for your absence.

Be sure your boss is the first one in the office to learn the news. Keep your announcement professional in tone: "I'm pleased to announce that I'm expecting twins in mid-May." Don't sound apologetic ("Sorry to inconvenience you . . ."), pleading ("I need a favor . . ."), or overly personal ("I've been trying for years to get pregnant . . ."). Then present a plan for how your work could be covered in your absence. A clear-cut strategy sets a collaborative tone—so that when your boss learns that you'll need an extra-long maternity leave, she'll think, "This sounds doable," rather than, "Argh, we can't possibly cope."

Next, outline the schedule you anticipate: "My obstetrician has ordered me to begin my leave at 24 weeks, which will be February 15." Do prepare your supervisor for the possibility of an earlier departure: "Should complications with my pregnancy arise, my doctor may tell me to stop working sooner, perhaps without advance notice. I'll keep you apprised of any developments."

Karen Danke, mother of fraternal twin boys, says, "In hindsight, the best advice I can offer is to warn your boss ahead of time that you may need to stop working abruptly and go on immediate bedrest. That's what happened to me—but I wasn't prepared for it. I couldn't go into the office even for a day to tie up loose ends, so nobody knew what to do when all of a sudden I wasn't available. My boss and I both wish we had set up a contingency plan well ahead of time."

Note that under FMLA, you must give your employer 30 days' notice that you intend to take a leave—but only if your medical condition allows this advance notice. If you go into premature labor or have complications that require you to stop working immediately, you are not bound by this 30-day rule.

Be honest about your physical limitations and how they affect your job.

But don't make your "special needs" the central focus of every staff meeting or conversation around the water cooler. To maintain your professional image, refrain from complaining about morning sickness and swollen ankles. Use your home phone, not the office line, to research Lamaze classes. Maximize "face time" at the office by scheduling prenatal checkups well in advance, to claim those hard-to-get 8 A.M. or 6 P.M. appointments.

If you've proven yourself to be a valuable employee, chances are your boss and co-workers will be thrilled for you and happy to help in whatever way they can. "When I told my boss that I'd have to stop working almost immediately, he was wonderfully supportive," recalls Anne Seifert. "He said, 'I know all that you've been through to have children. You take as much time off as you need—now and after you deliver—and take care of yourself and those quadruplets. When you're ready to come back, your job will be here waiting for you.'"

DR. LUKE: Though you may at first be dismayed at the idea of leaving your job, even temporarily, look on the bright side. Without exception, our Multiples Clinic patients say that they feel much less stressed, and much more relaxed and well rested, once they go on hiatus from their jobs.

A few days after her leave began, for instance, one expectant mother of twins called me up and said, "That last week at the office, I was so exhausted and felt such intense vaginal pressure that I could hardly concentrate on work. Now that I don't have to set my alarm for 6 A.M., I can sleep late every morning. And it's great to be able to eat whenever I want, to read or relax all afternoon, and to take a nap when the mood strikes. Why in the world did I resist your suggestion to quit working even sooner? I'm infinitely more comfortable here at home—and I think my babies are too."

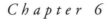

Chapter 6

Pregnancy Complications: How to Lower Your Risk

Here's good news: Many mothers-to-be of multiples sail through all three trimesters with no complications at all. "I didn't have any problems whatsoever with my twin pregnancy—not even morning sickness," says Stacy Moore, mother of fraternal twin boys.

Still, it's smart to be familiar with the warning signs of trouble. Even if you've had a perfect pregnancy up till now, a problem can arise at any point. And the earlier it's detected, the more likely it can be treated before serious consequences develop. Amy Maly, mother of identical twin girls, knows firsthand the importance of staying vigilant. "Everything was fine until my 31st week of pregnancy, when suddenly something just didn't feel right. There were no obvious symptoms—no pain, no bleeding—but I was suspicious enough that I called my doctor anyway. Thank goodness I did, because it turned out I was in preterm labor," says Amy. Prompt medical intervention halted the contractions and allowed Amy's pregnancy to continue for another five weeks. At that point, she developed preeclampsia—but by then, her twins were big enough to be born safely.

You also need to accept the possibility that you may develop a series of problems during the coming months, because multiple gestations involve a higher proportion of complications than do singleton pregnancies. Yet even in such cases, with the right medical treatment, the babies often can be born healthy and strong. Heather Nicholas, for example, had a very difficult pregnancy—vaginal bleeding, cervical complications, anemia, digestive problems, frequent contractions—and had to stay on strict bedrest for many months. Despite all that, she carried her twins to 38½ weeks, ultimately delivering a daughter who weighed 7 lb., 3 oz., and a son who weighed 6 lb., 15 oz.!

So as you read this chapter on pregnancy complications, try not to feel unduly alarmed. The goal is to familiarize yourself with the warning signs. That way, if trouble develops, you will recognize it and can alert your doctor immediately. Early detection and appropriate treatment are the best safeguards for your own health and that of your multiples.

As one reader of the first edition of this book explains, "My doctor later told me that over-all, I had one of the healthiest twin pregnancies she had ever seen—normal blood pressure, no anemia, very few preterm contractions, no bedrest, and two healthy babies who were dis-charged to go home with me. I think the crash course in high-risk obstetrics that I got from reading this book is one of the chief reasons why." Knowledge is power. You can use it to your advantage.

Signs to Watch for and Steps to Take

DR. LUKE: When patients from the Multiples Clinic call with a question, they some-times begin the conversation with an apology: "I'm so sorry to bother you with this trivial concern, because it's probably nothing." This stems from the fact that women tend to be stoic and self-sufficient, giving of themselves to others without taking time to meet or even take notice of their own needs.

This generosity of spirit is admirable in many areas of life. But when you're pregnant with twins, triplets, or quads, stoicism can be problematic. Right now, you need to give top priority to your own needs and those of your babies, so don't hesitate to bring up any con-cerns you may have. Good doctor-patient communication is a vital component of good medical care.

BLEEDING PROBLEMS
Early Vaginal Bleeding
Some women experience slight bleeding within the first week to 10 days after conception, when the fertilized egg or eggs implant in the lining of the uterus. This bleeding is perfectly normal. Yet because women who have conceived multiples are likely to experience heavier implantation bleeding than do mothers of singletons, you may initially mistake it for a menstrual period.

"I'd been trying to get pregnant for almost a year, with no success. So when I got my period in the middle of my sister's baby shower, I stayed in the bathroom crying for half an hour. I didn't realize until many weeks later that the bleeding I had thought to be a light four-day period was in fact caused by *twins* implanting in my uterus," says Lydia Greenwood, mother of boy/girl twins.

More serious is bleeding later in pregnancy, which may signal a miscarriage. With multiples, the risk of miscarriage before the 20th week of pregnancy is slightly higher than with a singleton. There is also the possibility that one or more fetuses could miscarry, while the remaining baby or babies would continue to grow and develop normally.

Incompetent Cervix

Another reason for bleeding early in pregnancy is an incompetent cervix, a condition in which the cervix spontaneously and painlessly opens early in pregnancy. This is believed to be the cause of many second-trimester miscarriages. An incompetent cervix may result from a genetic weakness of the cervix, or from trauma to the cervix during a previous delivery, abortion, or other medical procedure.

If detected early enough, the cervix may be sutured closed—a procedure called cerclage— and the pregnancy saved. "At 15 weeks, I started to bleed. It wasn't as heavy as a period, but it did last for two days. A vaginal ultrasound showed that my cervix was shortening," says twin mom Heather Nicholas. "My obstetrician said we could wait a week and see what happened, or we could put in a cerclage the next day. I opted for the cerclage, after which I had to go on bedrest for a week." Typically the cerclage is removed at about 37 weeks or just prior to delivery.

Rarely, the procedure may need to be repeated. Karen Danke, mother of fraternal twin boys, recalls: "My doctor put in a cerclage at 17 weeks. But at 21 weeks, the membranes started to bulge through the opening of my cervix. My obstetrician did a second cerclage, then had me spend the next 24 hours in a special 'incline bed' that kept my lower body elevated above my head. This was kind of uncomfortable, but it did keep pressure off my cervix. Fortunately, the second cerclage held."

Placental Problems

Complications involving the placenta or placentas are the most common causes of bleeding after the 20th week of pregnancy.

A condition called abruptio placenta occurs when the placenta partially detaches from the uterus before delivery. This results in moderate to heavy vaginal bleeding, and moderate to severe abdominal pain.

With a condition known as placenta previa, the placenta implants low in the uterus, partially or completely covering the cervix. This is more common in multiple gestations, owing to the increased number and/or size of the placentas present. As the cervix begins to open toward the end of the pregnancy, vaginal bleeding occurs.

What You Can Do

Immediately report any bleeding to your obstetrician. She will need to determine the cause of the bleeding and suggest appropriate treatment. Be prepared to go on bedrest if instructed to do so. (See "All About Bedrest" later in this chapter.)

IRON-DEFICIENCY ANEMIA

The majority of women pregnant with multiples eventually develop iron-deficiency anemia, a condition characterized by low levels of iron in the red blood cells that carry oxygen to the tissues. Your risk increases with each additional baby you're carrying, particularly if you had low or borderline iron reserves before becoming pregnant.

Symptoms include fatigue, lightheadedness, pallor, and shortness of breath. Admittedly, these signs are difficult to differentiate from the signs of pregnancy itself. "Toward the end of the pregnancy, my anemia was so bad that I felt tired all the time, even though all I was doing was lying in bed. It took every bit of my energy just to breathe," says Helen Armer, mother of triplets.

If untreated, anemia can adversely affect the babies' growth, as well as increase your own risk for complications both during pregnancy and after the birth. That's why your doctor will routinely test your hemoglobin and hematocrit (the iron-carrying components of your blood) several times during pregnancy—typically when you begin prenatal care, again at about 26 weeks, and again just before you deliver.

What You Can Do

To boost your iron stores, increase your intake of iron-rich foods, particularly red meats, liver, and liver pâté (see Chapters 3 and 4 for more details). Your physician also may recommend iron supplements. Judy Levy, mother of fraternal twin girls, says, "Despite all the liver and beef I was eating, I became anemic. My doctor told me to take blood-building medications that included iron along with vitamins B_6, B_{12}, and C, and were specially coated to minimize stomach irritation and maximize absorption. The supplements didn't completely fix the anemia, but they did keep it from getting worse."

GESTATIONAL DIABETES

This disorder is more common in women who are over age 30, are overweight, or have a family history of diabetes. Expectant mothers of multiples develop gestational diabetes two to three times more often than singleton moms do. This is thought to be due to the increased levels and effects of placental hormones.

Here's how it occurs: The body requires insulin, a hormone produced by the pancreas, to pull glucose into the cells for use as energy. By about the sixth month of pregnancy, the baby or babies are growing fast, so the mother must make extra insulin. Yet at the same time, she produces hormones that interfere with the action of insulin. When the insulin supply cannot keep up with the demand, the mother's blood sugar levels soar and she becomes temporarily diabetic. If gestational diabetes is not controlled, the babies may suffer from hypoglycemia (low blood sugar) and other metabolic problems immediately after birth.

Your urine should be tested for the presence of glucose at each prenatal checkup. In addition, all women are routinely screened for gestational diabetes at about 26 to 28 weeks of pregnancy—though you may be screened earlier and more frequently because you're expecting multiples. One hour after drinking a special beverage that contains 50 grams of glucose, your blood is drawn to determine your blood glucose level. If this reading is elevated, you undergo a second test in which blood is drawn hourly for three hours. If the results of this second test are also abnormal, gestational diabetes is diagnosed.

What You Can Do

Be alert for the warning signs of gestational diabetes—excessive thirst, increased frequency and volume of urination, constant fatigue, and recurrent vaginal yeast infections. Also find out whether any members of your extended family have diabetes or developed gestational diabetes during pregnancy.

If you are diagnosed with this disorder, your obstetrician may have two new members join your health care team: a physician and a dietitian who specialize in diabetes. You need to follow a special diet in which carbohydrates are evenly distributed throughout the day. In most cases, diet therapy is effective in controlling blood glucose levels. Some women, however, must receive insulin injections as well.

After delivery, gestational diabetes disappears. However, women who experienced this disorder during pregnancy have up to a 30 percent chance of developing type 2 diabetes later in life. After you deliver, make sure your doctor checks you for diabetes during each of your annual checkups.

INTRAUTERINE GROWTH RESTRICTION

Multiples don't always grow at the same rate *in utero*. One fetus may receive a disproportionate share of nutrients if the structure of the placenta or placentas favors this baby more than the others. A sibling who gets a smaller portion of nutrients winds up growing more slowly. This discrepancy is usually revealed through ultrasound and may be evident quite early in the pregnancy.

"The doctor discovered at about 24 weeks that one twin was growing much more slowly than the other was," recalls Marcy Bugajski, mother of fraternal twin boys. "That baby ended up being a lot smaller at birth—3 lb., 11 oz., compared to his brother's birthweight of 5 lb., 8 oz."

What You Can Do

If it's determined that one baby has begun to lag behind his siblings, your doctor will want to keep a close eye on the situation. You may be asked to come for additional checkups and ultrasounds. Careful attention to your diet, of course, becomes more crucial than ever.

At some point, it may become necessary to deliver all your multiples in order to give the smallest baby the best possible chance for a healthy outcome. "At 20 weeks, my ultrasound showed that all three of my babies were growing well. But by week 25, one baby's growth was about a week behind the others. Another ultrasound at 29 weeks showed that this baby had scarcely grown at all in the previous month," says Ginny Seyler, mother of triplets. "By 30 weeks, it was clear to my doctor that this child needed to be delivered, so I ended up having a cesarean section that day. We went through some rough weeks after their birth, but now all three babies are fine."

PREECLAMPSIA

This condition is characterized by a rapid rise in blood pressure, the presence of protein in the urine, sudden and extreme weight gain, and swelling of the hands and face from fluid retention. It typically occurs during the second half of pregnancy. The cause of preeclampsia is unknown, but it is more common among women who have preexisting high blood pressure. Preeclampsia occurs in about one out of 20 singleton pregnancies, but in nearly one in five multiple gestations. If you've previously delivered a baby at full term, your risk for developing preeclampsia during your multiple pregnancy is significantly reduced.

Bedrest is usually the recommended treatment. If your condition becomes severe, you will be admitted to the hospital and given medications to try to lower your blood pressure.

Because preeclampsia clears up after delivery, the ultimate "cure" is to give birth. However, the seriousness of the mother's condition must be balanced against the babies' readiness to face life outside the womb. "One Tuesday when I was getting close to 36 weeks, Dr. Luke called me to see how I was doing. I told her I felt puffy and my feet looked like blocks, and my legs were so swollen that they measured two full inches larger than normal. When Dr. Luke heard that, she said, 'I'm coming to get you right now. You're going to the hospital.' Sure enough, I had developed preeclampsia," recalls Amy Maly. "Because my blood pressure was so high, and because the doctor knew that both babies were already over 5 pounds, we decided not to postpone labor any longer. My identical twin girls were born early Thursday morning."

What You Can Do

Reduce your risk of developing this condition by upping your intake of certain nutrients:

- Omega-3, an essential fatty acid found in all seafood, fish oils, and flaxseed oil
- Vitamin C, an antioxidant available in citrus fruits and juices, kiwi, strawberries, red peppers, sweet potatoes, broccoli, and tomatoes
- Vitamin E, another antioxidant found in vegetable oils, nuts, seeds, wheat germ, mangoes, and asparagus

It's also vital to learn the warning signs of preeclampsia: swelling, particularly of the face; severe or constant headaches; abdominal pain in the upper right quadrant; blurred vision or "seeing spots"; and very rapid weight gain (a pound or more per day). This is particularly important if you began this pregnancy overweight, as excess pounds appear to increase a person's risk of preeclampsia.

Don't make the mistake of passing off these symptoms as normal discomforts of pregnancy. "I got so incredibly bloated that my weight jumped up 18 pounds in two weeks—but it was all due to water retention. Then I started seeing little silver spots in front of my eyes. Yet even though I'm a nurse, I didn't put two and two together," admits twin mom Marcy Bugajski. "I guess I tended to brush off the warnings. The doctors would talk about symptoms to watch for, but the words never really penetrated. You always think, 'This will never happen to me.' But I'm living proof that complications can develop even when you're sure they won't."

Preterm Labor: The Major Problem in Multiple Pregnancies

Of all the potential complications you might develop during a multiple gestation, preterm labor—characterized by the presence of regular uterine contractions and cervical changes that occur too early in a pregnancy—is probably the most common. It is also potentially the most dangerous for your babies because preterm labor can lead to preterm birth.

Approximately 10 percent of singletons, 50 percent of twins, 90 percent of triplets, and virtually all quadruplets are preterm or premature, meaning that they are born prior to 37 full weeks of pregnancy. Among infants born prematurely, nearly one in 10 does not live. In fact, preterm birth is the leading cause of neonatal death in this country. Preemies who do survive are at higher risk for a variety of medical problems, including hearing loss, vision problems, and developmental disabilities and delays. The earlier in pregnancy the babies are born, the more serious the consequences are likely to be.

CRITICAL TIME ZONES

Think of your multiple pregnancy as divided into six time zones, each with differing implications for babies born during that period. Here's how it breaks down:

Conception to week 20: Any pregnancy (singleton as well as multiple) involves some possibility of ending during this period. At this stage, pregnancy loss is called miscarriage.

Weeks 20 to 24—the border of viability: Most babies born in this time zone do not survive. Those who do must remain hospitalized for many months. Their chances of experiencing permanent adverse health effects are high.

Weeks 25 to 28—very early preterm for multiples: The odds of survival are better, but babies born during this period must still spend weeks or months in the NICU. They are at substantial risk for long-term medical consequences.

Weeks 29 to 32—early preterm for multiples: Many triplets and quadruplets are born during this time zone. Although the babies typically remain in the hospital for several weeks or more, depending on their medical condition, the outlook is generally good. If the mother received steroids to hasten the babies' lung development prior to delivery, the infants have a distinct advantage.

Weeks 33 to 35—preterm for multiples: Twins often are born during this time period. If they are well grown, they generally spend a week or two in the hospital and are unlikely to experience any long-term serious effects of their early birth.

Weeks 36 to 38—term for twins: This is the ideal time for twins to arrive. Babies born during this period, if well grown and healthy, tend to be as robust as the average newborn singleton. Usually they are able to leave the hospital soon after birth, at the same time the mother is discharged.

DR. LUKE: Using a football metaphor, we tell patients at the Multiples Clinic to think of each of these time zones as a potential touchdown. The goal is to make your pregnancy last all the way through whatever time zone you're in now, add another touchdown to your score, and then *stay in the game.* The more touchdowns you get before you deliver, the more likely you are to win big in the end—by taking a full team of healthy babies home with you when you are discharged from the hospital.

Remember that each of your multiples has the genetic potential to start his or her life as big and healthy as any singleton. Your babies didn't ask to be born with teammates, but since that's how they were drafted into the league, you want to do your best to make sure they aren't penalized for it.

Another way to view the health of babies at birth is to look at the length of their hospital stay and their hospital bill. Several years ago, I conducted a study with a neonatologist and an expert in finance. We wanted to determine which factor—being born prematurely, being a twin, or being a premature twin—had the greatest effect on the length of the hospital stay and the total cost of neonatal care, as measures of a newborn's medical condition. Surprisingly, we found that the most significant factor was premature birth, regardless of whether it had been a singleton pregnancy or a twin pregnancy.

This study used roughly the same time zones as outlined above. Table 6.1 shows how being born during each of these periods translated into average number of days spent in the hospital and average hospital bill.

Duration and Cost of Hospital Stay for Newborns

Weeks of Gestation	25 to 27	28 to 30	31 to 34	35 to 38	39 to 42
Days in hospital	71 days	39 days	12 days	4 days	3 days
Hospital bill*	$195,254	$91,343	$18,367	$4,308	$2,230

*Per infant, in 1991–92 dollars

Table 6.1

WARNING SIGNS OF PRETERM LABOR

TAMARA: It's all too easy not to recognize the often vague signs of premature labor, particularly if this is your first pregnancy. That's what happened to me.

Those frequent yet painless contractions that began around my 28th week I assumed to be the harmless Braxton-Hicks contractions I'd read about in pregnancy books. That pelvic pressure I experienced (particularly when tired) I interpreted as a normal discomfort of pregnancy. My persistent lower backache I attributed to the muscle strain that naturally went along with carrying twins.

Had I recognized these symptoms for what they really were—warnings that my babies would soon be born—I might have received medical attention in time to halt preterm labor. My babies might have had the benefits of an additional few days or even weeks to grow, before confronting the challenges of life outside the womb.

Please study the following list. Memorize the warning signs. And call your doctor, day or night, if you experience even a single symptom. It's far better to be told it's a false alarm than to ignore an alarm that's real.

- Contractions occurring at a rate of six or more per hour
- Rhythmic or persistent pelvic pressure
- Menstrual-like cramps, with or without diarrhea
- Sudden or persistent low backache
- Vaginal discharge, particularly discharge that has changed in color, consistency, or amount

DR. LUKE: To this list (which your obstetrician should discuss with you in detail), I want to add one more "symptom." If you have any intuition, premonition, or "funny feeling" that something just isn't right, let your doctor know without delay. Sometimes a vague impression is the only warning.

I'm reminded of the day a patient at the Multiples Clinic came in for a routine checkup at 30 weeks. She said, "I've been feeling kind of down lately—achy and depressed, nothing more. I wasn't even going to bother mentioning it, but my mother insisted I tell you." We did a pelvic exam and also monitored her contractions, and sure enough, she was experiencing preterm labor. We immediately took steps to stop the labor and succeeded in postponing delivery for an additional seven weeks. Yet if that woman hadn't mentioned the way she'd been feeling, her preterm labor would have progressed and her babies would have been born much sooner.

Her story is not at all unusual. Over and over, readers tell me of similar experiences. For instance, one woman writes, "My obstetrician gave me this book, and it undoubtedly saved my pregnancy. At 23 weeks, when I was feeling a subtle abdominal tightening, I turned to this book for information and learned that I was experiencing labor symptoms. Without this advice, I probably would have been too embarrassed to call my doctor or to go to the hospital so early in my pregnancy. I probably would have discounted my feelings as stress or indigestion. My preterm labor was stopped because this book helped me to identify the early signs and validated my feelings that something was not right."

How to Monitor for Uterine Contractions

Occasional contractions are a normal part of pregnancy. But excessive ones—more than five an hour—increase your risk of preterm labor. The longer the contractions continue, the stronger they become and the more difficult they are to stop.

That's why one of the most important things you can do during your multiple pregnancy is to monitor yourself for uterine contractions daily. There are three beneficial aspects to this:

- You learn what a contraction feels like
- You identify the activities that trigger contractions
- You realize when contractions are occurring too frequently

Recognizing contractions is easier if you've given birth before (although preterm contractions are *much less intense* than those you experienced during labor). If this is your first pregnancy, however, it may be tougher to distinguish the sensation of a uterine contraction.

Try this: Lie on your side and press your fingers gently over your abdomen. Normally your belly feels soft. But during a contraction, your uterus tightens painlessly for 20 seconds to two minutes and feels hard, like your biceps when you "make a muscle." You may also feel a heaviness or squeezing sensation in the abdomen, or an ache in the mid- to lower back, as the uterus tightens.

Next, build a session of uterine monitoring into your daily routine, beginning in your 20th week of pregnancy. It doesn't matter what time of day you monitor, but ideally you should do it for one hour each day. Again, lie on your side and use your fingertips to detect the abdominal tightening that signals a uterine contraction. Use a watch with a minute hand to time the duration of each contraction, then write down the exact time the sensation begins and when it subsides.

Also write down what you were doing before you lay down to monitor yourself. Were you cleaning the house? Standing in line at the bank? Carrying a toddler in from the car? Handling some crisis at work? Arguing with your mother over what to name the babies? Your notes help you identify the specific physical activities and emotional stresses that tend to trigger an increase in the number or frequency of contractions so you can take steps to avoid these in the future.

At the end of each hourlong monitoring session, look over your records to see how many contractions occurred and how far apart they were. Then follow these guidelines:

- If you had *fewer than four contractions* in an hour, you're doing well. Plan to monitor again tomorrow.
- If you had *four or five contractions* in an hour, but no other symptoms of preterm labor, drink several glasses of water to combat the dehydration that can bring on

contractions. Then lie on your side and monitor again for another 30 to 60 minutes. If the contractions have slowed, you can get up—but be sure to avoid any activities you suspect may have triggered the earlier contractions.

- If you have *six or more contractions* in an hour, call your doctor immediately. Be prepared to go to the hospital's labor and delivery unit for evaluation if instructed to do so.

Another way to detect contractions is with a device called a home uterine activity monitor (HUAM), which is generally used for two or more hourlong sessions daily. Around your waist (or what used to be your waist), you strap an electronic sensor designed to measure the frequency and intensity of uterine contractions. The data are recorded for one hour, then transmitted over telephone lines to a central office, where they are analyzed. Afterward, a nurse from the HUAM staff calls you to review the data and give appropriate instructions. Typically these instructions follow the same guidelines as outlined above for women who monitor themselves manually.

Patients themselves often appreciate the reassurance and feedback that HUAM provides, particularly under certain circumstances. For instance:

- Expectant mothers of multiples may find it difficult to distinguish between contractions and fetal movement. Ginny Seyler, mother of triplets, explains, "I went on HUAM at 18 weeks because I couldn't really feel my contractions or tell the difference between uterine activity and the babies' kicks. For that reason, monitoring was very reassuring. As long as the data showed I wasn't contracting more than four times an hour, I figured I was doing okay."
- Because the HUAM service operates 24 hours a day, it can be particularly useful when you're feeling contractions late at night and want reassurance or instructions as to the best course of action.
- HUAM provides a warning for when you are overexerting yourself. "One day at about 17 weeks, I went shopping for baby supplies with my mother. By the time I got home, I was utterly exhausted," recalls Anne Seifert, mother of quadruplets. "I strapped on the monitor for an hour, then sent in the data. Right away the HUAM nurse called me and said, 'What in the world have you been doing today? You had 14 contractions!' That was the first and last time I overdid it like that."
- Monitoring reinforces the fact that contractions really do subside when you stay hydrated and get adequate rest. Anne Seifert explains, "It's easy to fool yourself into thinking that there's no harm in cutting back on water intake, or skipping a nap in order to do the laundry. But with HUAM, the consequences were evident because

the next monitoring session would show I'd had a half-dozen contractions or more. Then the nurse would call and say, 'Lie down on your left side right now, drink 16 ounces of water, and monitor for another hour.' Sure enough, the second set of data would show that the contractions had subsided."

While many patients are convinced of the advantages of HUAM, scientific studies do not necessarily support the manufacturer's claims. HUAM users generally do arrive at the hospital earlier in labor, when more treatment options are available to forestall premature delivery—yet this advantage may be due to the daily contact with a supportive health care professional rather than to the device itself.

HUAM is available only with a doctor's prescription. Doctors themselves are divided on the usefulness of the device. Some support the use of HUAM during most high-risk pregnancies; others reserve it for triplet or quadruplet gestations only; and still others feel it is of little value. Likewise, not all health insurance companies cover the cost, which may go as high as $10,000 per pregnancy.

TAMARA: When my twins were a year old, I got pregnant again. Although this time I was carrying a singleton, my history of preterm birth meant that any subsequent pregnancy was automatically considered high-risk.

No longer unaware of the sensation or significance of early contractions, I was alarmed when I started to feel that familiar tightening in my abdomen as early as my 20th week. I immediately called my obstetrician, who suggested that HUAM could be useful in a case such as mine where preterm labor was clearly a risk. A few days later, the equipment arrived at my home, and I began monitoring twice daily.

From weeks 20 to 25, the data showed few contractions, which helped to alleviate the fear I felt about delivering early again. But by week 26, I was having five or six contractions each hour. The HUAM nurse alerted my doctor, who then placed me on modified bedrest as well as medication to calm the contractions. That worked—for a few weeks. When the number of contractions crept back up again, my doctor increased my medication and further restricted my activity. Again the contractions subsided, only to reappear several weeks later. Yet again, more medication and more time in bed brought the desired results.

Finally I reached my 37th week. My obstetrician said, "You can stop monitoring and go off the medication now. The baby's ready to be born anytime." Two days later, Jack arrived in the world—a healthy and robust baby who weighed 7½ pounds at birth.

I know that HUAM isn't for everyone, but I believe it helped me carry my younger son to term. If you're interested in trying this technology, talk to your obstetrician.

In-Hospital Treatment for Preterm Labor

If your doctor suspects preterm labor, she is likely to instruct you to go directly to the hospital's labor and delivery unit for evaluation. There, a monitor is placed around your abdomen to record the frequency and intensity of your uterine contractions. An internal examination determines whether you are experiencing cervical changes such as effacement (when the cervix thins out) or dilation (when the cervix begins to open). You then lie on your side and receive fluids, usually intravenously.

Unless there are major changes requiring immediate action, you are observed for several hours. During this period of observation, one of the following occurs:

- You have no cervical changes, and the contractions decrease or stop. You are likely to be sent home to rest and advised to monitor for other episodes of preterm contractions.
- You have no cervical changes, but the contractions continue. You may be given additional fluids and relaxation medication in an attempt to reduce the number of contractions. You may stay in the hospital a few more hours or even overnight until the contractions have subsided.
- You do have cervical changes and the contractions continue and become regular. If this occurs, your doctor may give you medications called tocolytics, which are designed to stop preterm labor.

The most commonly used tocolytics are magnesium sulfate, terbutaline (Brethine), indomethacin (Indocin), and nifedipine (Procardia). Typically, tocolytics are given intravenously or by injection to try to stop an episode of preterm labor. Once the acute episode has passed, tocolytic medications may be given in pill form, every two to four hours around the clock, in an attempt to keep preterm labor from starting again.

Tocolytics are not a cure-all. In many cases, they are ineffective, and they can have side effects. Their intensity depends on the amount and frequency of the dosage, and the type of medication given. Side effects may diminish over time. However, long-term use of tocolytics has been associated with the development of gestational diabetes, particularly when used in combination with steroids to help the babies' lungs mature.

Side Effects of Tocolytic Medications

	Terbutaline	Magnesium Sulfate
Heart rate	Increases by 10 to 30 beats per minute	—
Fluids	Tendency to hold extra fluids	—
Gastrointestinal system	Nausea, vomiting, constipation	Constipation, diarrhea
Blood vessels	Dilation of blood vessels resulting in feelings of warmth	—
Nervous system	Nervousness, trembling, trouble concentrating	Sleepiness, fatigue

Table 6.2

Amy Maly's experience with preterm labor is fairly typical. She tells her story: "I was 31 weeks pregnant with my twins. Suddenly my belly started to look really contorted—so tight that it seemed I could see the shapes of the babies right through the skin. It was confusing, because there wasn't any pain. But still, I figured something wasn't as it should be, so I called my doctor. I was told to drink a big glass of water and then come straight to the labor and delivery unit.

"At the hospital, an internal exam showed that my cervix had not dilated. Yet because I was having erratic contractions, I was admitted and given an IV of magnesium sulfate. The nurse explained that this smooth-muscle relaxant could help to halt my contractions. The 'mag sulfate,' as it's called, sapped my energy so severely that it was all I could do to blink! I couldn't even walk to the bathroom by myself. But it worked—the contractions stopped.

"After four days I was allowed to go home, but I had to take oral terbutaline and stay on strict bedrest. That lasted for five weeks. Thank goodness for my two wonderful sisters, who came in from out of state to take care of me."

Like Amy, many expectant mothers of multiples are able to return home once their preterm labor has been stopped. However, if oral tocolytics aren't enough to control your contractions, you need to stay in the hospital. Quad mom Anne Seifert describes her experience: "I was hospitalized from my 25th week until the end of the pregnancy. I received terbutaline injections via a computerized pump. The hospital staff taught me how to replace the vial of medication every three hours. I even learned how to change the site of the needle, which needed to be done every three days! At first, I couldn't believe they wanted me to take this thumbtack-like needle and poke it into my thigh, but I did it. It was easy to tell if the needle wasn't properly inserted, because pretty soon the contractions would begin."

If you are hospitalized for preterm labor, you're also likely to receive injections of betamethasone or dexamethasone, synthetic steroids that hasten the maturation of your unborn babies' lungs. This medication helps reduce the severity of prematurity-related respiratory problems. During the 1990s, some patients received multiple injections of these steroids over a period of many weeks. However, in 2000, both the National Institutes of Health and the American College of Obstetricians and Gynecologists began recommending only a single course of injections (two to four doses, 12 to 24 hours apart), to minimize side effects and maximize benefits. Steroids are generally given to patients at risk for preterm delivery, at some point between 24 and 34 weeks' gestation. Steroids are not given after 34 weeks unless there is evidence that the babies' lungs are immature.

Exciting new research offers hope of a simple yet effective way to reduce the risk of premature birth. In a recent study, pregnant women with a history of preterm birth were given weekly injections of a form of the hormone progesterone (called 17-alpha-hydroxyprogesterone caproate, or 17p), beginning at around 19 weeks' gestation. The results: Preterm deliveries were reduced by one-third among the women who received the hormones, as compared to women who received placebo injections. Although this study involved women pregnant with singletons, the treatment may also prove beneficial for women expecting multiples.

All About Bedrest

As you've probably noticed, many complications of pregnancy share a common treatment: bedrest. Staying horizontal can do lots of positive things for your pregnancy. For example, bedrest can:

- Reduce the strain on your heart
- Improve blood flow to your kidneys, which helps to eliminate excess fluids
- Increase circulation to the uterus, thus providing additional oxygen and nutrients to your unborn babies

- Minimize blood levels of catecholamines, the stress hormones that can trigger contractions
- Take pressure off your cervix
- Limit your physical activity, thereby reducing contractions
- Conserve your energy so that more of what you eat goes directly to promoting your babies' growth

DR. LUKE: There's no denying that it can be boring, frustrating, and inconvenient to stay in bed for days, weeks, or even months. But if your obstetrician puts you on bedrest, try to think of it as a positive force—something concrete you can do to benefit your babies. It's been said that attitude is nine-tenths of any job, and that's particularly true when it comes to bedrest. The first and most important step is to accept that this is the best therapy for the situation.

In our Multiples Clinic, we've tried to devise ways to show patients how big their unborn babies are at any given time, because it's hard to translate the fuzzy black-and-white images on an ultrasound screen into an accurate mind's-eye picture of real babies. We came up with the idea of making life-size dolls from paper measuring tapes, using the measurements—head circumference, abdominal circumference, and femur (thigh bone) length—from the patient's most recent ultrasound. When we sit these paper dolls on a pregnant woman's knee, suddenly she has a very strong sense of just how tiny babies born at 25 or 28 weeks really are—and how much her babies benefit, week to week, by staying snug in her womb.

This idea is taken one step further in the drawings below. The circles show an average baby's head circumference at various weeks of gestation. Imagine if your babies were born at your current stage of pregnancy, and you were cupping a little newborn's head in your hand. Then imagine your pregnancy continuing for another week, another two weeks, another two months—and see how much bigger your babies would be at birth.

Each day, each week that your babies spend growing stronger and healthier inside you is one less day, one less week they will have to spend in the hospital after their birth. Let these drawings inspire you to follow to the letter your doctor's instructions about bedrest.

In fact, thinking in these terms makes it easier to accept not only bedrest, but also any other inconveniences or restrictions your pregnancy may bring. Judy Levy put it eloquently: "It all came down to evaluating everything I did in terms of its potential effect on my unborn twins. Should I eat this hunk of steak, even though I had no appetite for yet another serving of meat? Yes, that would be good for the babies—so I ate it. Should I try to talk my doctor into letting

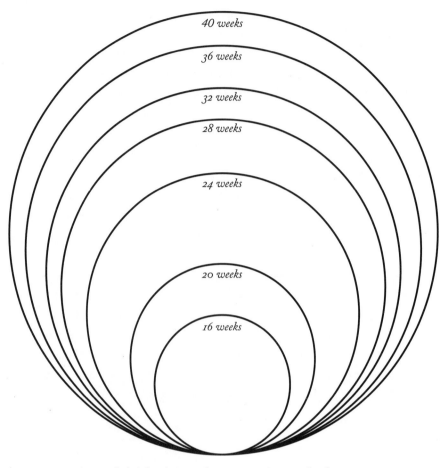

Average baby's head circumference at various weeks of gestation

me work an extra week? No, that might be bad for the babies—so I quit when he told me to. I did this even with little things like washing the dishes. Were the benefits of having a clean kitchen worth the risk of overexerting myself and perhaps triggering contractions? Of course not! When I looked at activities in that light, the answer was crystal clear."

Exactly What Is Meant by "Bedrest"?

There are three basic levels of bedrest. If your obstetrician orders you into bed, be sure to clarify exactly what she means.

"House Arrest," or Modified Bedrest

This is the least restrictive form of bedrest. Triplet mom Helen Armer explains, "I was told to stay in bed for two hours every morning and again every afternoon, as well as all evening and all night. This of course meant I could spend very little time away from home! I also had to strictly avoid any lifting, carrying, or housework, and to limit myself to one trip up and down the stairs daily."

In some cases, brief excursions out of the house are permitted, provided you take steps to avoid overexertion. Judy Levy recalls, "I hated the thought of missing out on all the fun of shopping for the twins' baby equipment. So with my doctor's permission and help, I got a handicapped parking sticker and a wheelchair, which allowed me to navigate through the stores. At first, I felt embarrassed. What if I was spotted by someone who knew I wasn't really disabled? But after the first time, I knew there was no other way I could handle any shopping without placing the babies at risk."

Your doctor cautions against such trips to the outside world? Then stay home. Violating your house arrest won't get you thrown in jail—but it may well bump you up to the next level of bedrest.

Strict Bedrest

This generally means you must spend almost all your time lying down. Heather Nicholas describes her experience: "At 19 weeks into my twin pregnancy, I started to feel lots of contractions. Because I'd already had a cerclage for an incompetent cervix, I immediately had to go on strict bedrest. I was allowed to shower once a day and to use the toilet as necessary. But that was it for the next four months, until I hit 36 weeks and the risk of preterm birth was past."

For many women on strict bedrest, a shower becomes the highlight of the day. "My daily shower made me feel so much more human," says twin mom Amy Maly. "For extra safety and comfort, my husband put a chair in the tub so I could sit down while I showered. He also asked me to shower only when he was home, in case I needed help." (Please note: Bathroom privileges do *not* include doing a load of laundry on your way to the bathroom.)

Hospital Bedrest

At some point in your pregnancy, complications may make it necessary for you to be admitted to the hospital. Depending on your situation, you may stay just overnight, or for several days, or for many weeks. Karen Danke says, "Because I had a history of preterm birth, my doctor was very concerned when, despite a cerclage, the membranes started to bulge through my cervix 21 weeks into my twin pregnancy. He put in a second cerclage, then had me on the strictest hospital bedrest. I was not even allowed to use the bathroom—it was bedpans and sponge baths only.

After a week, I was allowed to shower and use the toilet but still had to stay in the hospital for another seven weeks."

Day-to-Day Life: The View from the Bedroom

When you're spending the vast majority of your time in a horizontal position, you obviously have lots of practical concerns to address. First, you need to know how to get up safely. When you rise from bed after being prone a long time, you may feel lightheaded—and that could lead to a fall. To minimize the risk, follow these tips:

- Make sure your partner has cleared a path from bedroom to bathroom. He should remove all obstacles you might trip over, such as throw rugs, toys, and knickknacks.
- Never sit straight up from lying on your back. Instead, come first to a side-lying position, then slowly use your arms to push yourself up.
- Once you are sitting, remain seated in bed for a few minutes to allow any dizziness to subside.
- Slowly scoot out to the edge of the bed and push yourself up with your arms and legs.
- Once standing, keep your tummy tucked under and your chin tucked in, to maintain proper posture.
- Walk slowly and carefully to and from the bathroom.

Another immediate concern is how to manage meals while on bedrest. Remember that it is extremely important to meet all your nutritional needs. Start by writing out a very thorough grocery list and reviewing it with your husband, friend, or whoever will be handling your shopping. Next, figure out how you'll keep that good food accessible. Here are some tips from women who've met the challenge:

- "Each morning, my husband packed a cooler full of food for me and put it near the bed, so I could eat without getting up," says Heather Nicholas.
- "We got a mini-refrigerator and put it upstairs, so I'd always have plenty to eat," Ginny Seyler explains.
- A husband who's handy in the kitchen can make sure that each day gets off to a nutritious start and that each evening includes an appetizing and balanced dinner. Amy Maly recalls, "Each morning before he left for work, Curt cooked breakfast for me. And he always cooked a great dinner when he got home."

- Find a nearby friend or relative who can make a midday meal. "My dad often came by to fix my lunch," says Heather Nicholas.
- If you're on hospital bedrest, get your doctor's okay to bring in favorite foods from the outside. "I got pretty tired of the food from the hospital cafeteria, so it was hard to work up an appetite," admits Karen Danke. "To make sure I was getting the calories I needed, Dr. Luke brought me breakfast every morning—a McDonald's Egg McMuffin with bacon and cheese, hash browns, and orange juice. For snacks, my husband, Chris, brought my favorite Hostess fruit pies and big cartons of milk. And my family often delivered takeout dinners. All that went down a lot more easily than the institutional food."

You may need to arrange for professionals to handle certain tasks you are not able to manage from bed. For instance:

- A cleaning service can take over any household chores your husband doesn't have time for.
- Unless friends or relatives can manage the full-time care of your older children, a babysitter is a must. "Bedrest would have been impossible without my nanny," says Helen Armer. "Three-year-old Caroline was pretty cooperative about letting me rest, and we enjoyed watching videos, reading storybooks, and coloring together. But when she needed active play, it was vital to have the sitter on hand to take her bike-riding or to the playground. And, of course, the nanny gave Caroline her meals and baths."
- Medical services may be available through your hospital, so ask your obstetrician. Says Ginny Seyler, "The hospital runs a home-nursing program. Through this, I received visits from a childbirth educator and a lactation consultant, as well as visiting nurses who came to draw blood for lab tests."
- For personal needs—haircuts, massages—call local salons and day spas to ask if they provide at-home services.

BATTLING BOREDOM

Once you have the practical matters ironed out, you may confront another common concern that bedrest brings—boredom. Ginny Seyler admits, "It was devastating to switch from being on the go all day to suddenly being confined to bed with nothing to do. I missed my work, my exercise routine, my friends, everything." To combat boredom, consider these suggestions:

- Begin each day by changing out of your pajamas. You'll feel less like an invalid when wearing real clothes, even if just an oversized T-shirt and maternity leggings.
- Have someone put a television in your bedroom, and keep the remote on your night table. Subscribe to cable television, and tune in to mind-expanding programs to learn more about history, nature, and the arts. Also ask friends to suggest favorite videos and DVDs.
- Keep a big supply of paper and pens handy, or use a laptop computer. Then write—a pregnancy journal, a novel, a letter to a faraway friend, a business plan for that home-based company you've always dreamed of starting.
- Catch up on all the reading you've never had time to do. Go for variety— newspapers, magazines, professional journals, classics, romances, parenting books. Try books on audiotape too, for times when your eyes are tired.
- For a change of scenery, set up a second bedrest area in the spare bedroom or on the living room sofa. Spend mornings in one room, and afternoons in the other. If you're in the hospital, follow Karen Danke's suggestion: "When I needed a new venue, my husband took me for gurney rides around the hospital building and grounds."
- Try crossword puzzles, word searches, and other brain-teasers. Build a 3-D jigsaw puzzle.
- Do volunteer work over the phone. Raise funds for charity, chat with elderly shut-ins, or gather information for an environmental group. To get connected, contact a local church or synagogue, the American Red Cross, nearby community service agencies, or local public schools.
- Surf the Internet.
- Use an audio- or videotape program to develop a skill—learning a language, studying a cooking technique, or planning a garden.
- Earn continuing education credits. Says Anne Seifert, "I used my months on bedrest to take several correspondence courses I needed to maintain my professional accreditation. Having a home-study project made me feel like my time was well spent."
- Organize your old collections of coins, stamps, or seashells.
- Use catalogs or Web sites to shop for baby equipment and household items. Get a jump on birthday and holiday shopping too.

- If you have a talent for art, use this quiet time to sketch or paint. Need a model? Find inspiration in photographs. Create a masterpiece to hang in the nursery, or design your babies' birth announcement.
- Learn a craft or art like crocheting, knitting, crewelwork, or needlepoint. "I had never done crafts before, but I did enjoy cross-stitching some little baby bibs," Karen Danke says.
- Establish a daily routine for these various activities. That "what in the world should I do now?" feeling abates when you have a schedule and a sense of purpose.

Keep Your Spirits Up

Emotional support is vital for a woman on bedrest. As one reader of the first edition of this book reports, "My doctor put me on bedrest at 24 weeks. Because of this book, I know what to do to get support. That has really helped me emotionally, as I have dealt with family members who are less than supportive about all the extra care my husband and I are taking to make sure we get these babies here safely." To keep your spirits high, try these ideas:

- Contact with the outside world is vital, so set up standing phone dates with your husband, friends, relatives, and co-workers. "I loved that my husband called me two or three times each day, just to check on me and offer moral support," says Amy Maly.
- Join a support group for moms-to-be on bedrest, such as Sidelines High Risk Pregnancy Support: PO Box 1808, Laguna Beach, CA 92652. Telephone 888–447–475; e-mail sidelines@sidelines.org; Web site www.sidelines.org.
- Other support-group options: Ask your doctor or childbirth educator for names and telephone numbers of local women in your situation, and set up your own over-the-phone group. Says Karen Danke, "It was so helpful to be able to share my frustrations with other people who were in the same boat as I was. Some of the women Dr. Luke put me in touch with are still my good friends today." You're computer savvy? Start your own on-line support group.
- If you're in the hospital, chances are you'll find moral support right there in the obstetrics wing. "My six weeks on hospital bedrest went by surprisingly fast. I got to be friends with the other patients, and we all gave each other encouragement and support," says quad mom Anne Seifert. "The nursing staff was wonderfully compassionate too. They pampered me so much that I didn't have anything to whine about."

- Devise a countdown system. Karen Danke explains, "To make my hospital bedrest seem less interminable and more finite, Dr. Luke made me a huge wall calendar that I could see from across the room. It had 100 squares—one for each day from the time I began my bedrest until my 34th week, when it would be safe for me to go home—and special stickers for all the holidays. Each morning, Dr. Luke came to see me and we'd cross off the previous day. Those big red Xs helped me focus on how far I had come already, and how each day was taking my twins one step closer to a healthy start in life." That calendar is now in Karen's home—hanging on the wall of her baby boys' bedroom.

MUSCLE-TONE MAINTENANCE

Another excellent way to combat boredom and discouragement while staying in bed is to do some *very gentle* exercises. A bedrest workout also helps to alleviate stiffness in the joints, maintain muscle strength, prevent circulation problems, and promote regularity. The moves described here, specifically designed for pregnant women on bedrest, have been developed by Elaine Anderson, P.T., M.P.H., a physical therapist and research associate in the Department of Obstetrics and Gynecology at the University of Michigan.

Before you begin this exercise program, show your doctor the bedrest exercises in Tables 6.3 and 6.4, and have her check off those she feels will be beneficial for you. Ask her to fill in the appropriate number of repetitions (usually 12) for each movement, as well as the proper weight for dumbbells (typically 3 pounds), if using. Also ask if you should do the entire workout every day, or if you should alternate between the lower-body workout and the upper-body workout.

Whenever you exercise, observe these general guidelines:

- Drink a glass of water before and after your workout.
- Empty your bladder before exercising. A full bladder may stimulate contractions.
- Do *not* hold your breath. Inhale through your nose, then exhale through your mouth during the active part of the movement (i.e., exhale on the exertion). Breathe in again as you return to the starting position.
- All exercises should be performed smoothly and slowly, with no jerking. Your level of exertion should be low.
- Do not skip the stretching movements. Stretching promotes flexibility and helps prevent muscle soreness.

- If any exercise is uncomfortable, triggers contractions, or causes bleeding or an increase in vaginal discharge, immediately stop the workout and call your doctor without delay.

Lower-Body Bedrest Workout

Ankle Pumps

Position: Sitting or side-lying

Motion: Begin with legs straight. Flex foot to bring toes toward you as far as possible, then point toes away from you to make an arch. Switch to other leg.

Repetitions: _____

Ankle Circles

Position: Sitting or side-lying

Motion: Rotate foot in circles, first clockwise and then counterclockwise. (Only foot should move, not entire leg.) Switch to other leg.

Repetitions: _____

Buttocks Tightening

Position: Sitting or side-lying

Motion: Tighten the muscles in your buttocks; hold 5 to 10 seconds; relax.

Repetitions: _____

(continued)

Pelvic Tilt

Position: Semisitting (propped up with pillows)

Motion: Bend both knees up toward chest and place feet flat on bed. Tighten abdominal muscles while pressing lower back against the pillows to flatten the arch. Hold 5 to 10 seconds; relax.

Repetitions: _____

Inner Thigh Stretch

Position: Semisitting

Motion: Begin by doing a pelvic tilt (described above). While holding the tilt, let knees fall open to feel a stretch along inner thighs; then bring knees back together.

Repetitions: _____

Leg Rolls

Position: Semisitting

Motion: Straighten legs on bed, keeping feet shoulder width apart. Roll knees inward toward each other, then outward away from each other.

Repetitions: _____

Leg Slides

Position: Semisitting

Motion: Bend right knee toward chest and place right foot flat on bed. Straighten left leg, then slowly slide left heel toward you, bringing heel as close to buttocks as possible. Hold for a count of 3; slowly slide leg back out until straight. Repeat on opposite side.

Repetitions: _____

Inner/Outer Thigh Toner

Position: Semisitting

Motion: Keeping legs straight, slide right leg out to the right side until you feel a stretch; then slide leg back to the center. Repeat with left leg.

Repetitions: _____

Thigh Tightening

Position: Semisitting or side-lying

Motion: With legs straight, consciously tighten quadriceps muscle on top of right thigh. Hold for a count of 5; relax. Repeat with left leg.

Repetitions: _____

Leg Lifts

Position: Semisitting

Motion: Bend right knee toward chest and place right foot flat on bed. Straighten left leg, then raise it off bed 4 inches. Hold for a count of 3; lower leg. After finishing a complete set of repetitions, switch to other leg.

Repetitions: _____

Table 6.3

Upper-Body Bedrest Workout

Chin Tuck

Position: Sitting

Motion: Pull chin in toward chest; at the same time, lift back of the head up, elongating the neck. Done correctly, you should feel a stretch along the back of the neck and the upper back.

Repetitions: _____

Neck Side Bend

Position: Sitting

Motion: Keeping shoulders down, gently tilt head sideways to the right, as if trying to place right ear on right shoulder. Repeat on left side. (Do not tilt head backward.)

Repetitions: _____

Reverse Shoulder Circles

Position: Sitting

Motion: Raise both shoulders toward ears, then ease them toward the rear while squeezing shoulder blades together. Hold for a count of 3; relax.

Repetitions: _____

Front Arm Raises

Position: Sitting

Motion: Begin with arms at sides, elbows straight. Slowly raise both arms out in front of you, then overhead, reaching as high as possible. Hold for a count of 3; slowly lower back to starting position. (If using hand-held weights, you can alternate arms instead of doing both together.)

Repetitions: _____

Hand-held weights: _____ pounds

Side Arm Raises

Position: Sitting

Motion: Begin with arms at sides, elbows straight. Slowly raise both arms out to the side, lifting until arms are at shoulder level. Hold for a count of 3; slowly lower back to starting position. (If using hand-held weights, you can alternate arms instead of doing both together.)

Repetitions: _____

Hand-held weights: _____ pounds

Biceps Curl

Position: Sitting

Motion: Begin with arms at sides, elbows very slightly bent and pressed against your sides. With palms facing up, slowly bend elbows and raise hands toward shoulders. Tighten upper-arm muscles and hold for a count of 5; slowly straighten arms while lowering to the starting position. (If using hand-held weights, you can alternate arms instead of doing both together.)

Repetitions: _____

Hand-held weights: _____ pounds

Shoulder Stretch

Position: Sitting

Motion: Gently clasp hands behind head. Move elbows forward, toward each other; then move elbows backward, so they point out to the side. Squeeze shoulder blades together; hold for a count of 5; relax.

Repetitions: _____

Table 6.4

You may need to spend only a few days or a few weeks in bed before your doctor determines that a potential crisis has been averted and allows you to get up. In other cases, a woman must stay on bedrest until she delivers. If you complete your 36th week of pregnancy without going into labor, chances are you'll be released from bedrest. By that point, your multiples are big enough to be born safely, and no further attempts to forestall delivery are needed.

"After spending 20 weeks on bedrest, I was finally allowed out of bed at 36 weeks when the cerclage was removed. The doctor expected me to go into labor almost immediately, but nothing happened," says Heather Nicholas. "I was allowed to resume some activity, but I'd get winded just walking across the room. I was huge and uncomfortable, but I took a lot of satisfaction in knowing that I'd made it to the point where my babies would be delivered at a good birthweight. Two weeks later, they were born—with my son just an ounce shy of 7 pounds, and my daughter 3 ounces over. I was mighty proud when Dr. Luke said my multiples were about the same size as the average *singleton!*"

Selective Multifetal Reduction: A Difficult Decision

Eighty percent of all triplets, and nearly all quadruplets and other supertwins, are conceived through infertility treatments, also known as assisted reproductive technology (ART). In some cases, doctors prescribe medication that causes a woman to release more than one egg during a single cycle. In other cases, doctors transfer three or more fertilized eggs into a woman's uterus or fallopian tubes, in the hope that at least one will implant successfully. The purpose of such techniques is to boost the chances that the woman will get pregnant at all—yet the result is often a multiple gestation.

This occurs because, with ART, it is difficult to control the exact number of embryos that will begin to grow. The problem is that the more fetuses there are, the lower the chances that any of them will survive.

That's why the technique of selective multifetal reduction was devised. The rationale is straightforward: Eliminating one or more fetuses may improve the pregnancy outcome for those that remain. It is usually presented as an option to women carrying quadruplets or more, and it may be used in triplet pregnancies if requested. Typically the goal is to leave behind twins.

The procedure is done toward the end of the first trimester. The doctor passes a needle through the woman's abdomen (using ultrasound guidance) and injects potassium chloride into the fetal heart, which then stops beating. The fetal tissue is reabsorbed, and does not harm the remaining fetuses.

The advisability of reduction is not always clear-cut, however. The procedure does carry a risk of causing a miscarriage of all the fetuses. A recent, large study showed that the greater number of fetuses there are to begin with, the higher the risk of miscarrying all. For instance, when starting with three fetuses, the rate of full miscarriage from reduction is 4 percent; when starting with four fetuses, the rate is 7 percent; when starting with six, the rate is 15 percent. Also, reducing to triplets involves a higher risk of losing all the fetuses than does reducing to twins.

Further complicating the issue, doctors may offer conflicting opinions. "Because I had undergone fertility treatments, I knew it was a possibility that I would conceive multiples. So I wasn't all that shocked to find out several weeks into the pregnancy that there were three embryos. That's when my reproductive endocrinologist counseled me to strongly consider reducing to twins," says Hannah Rhodes. "Yet my obstetrician disagreed. He doesn't recommend reduction unless there are four or more fetuses because, he said, the outcome for triplets generally isn't much worse than for twins. I was prepared to do whatever the medical experts advised, but with two opposing opinions, I felt confused."

Ginny Seyler had a similar experience. "At seven weeks, my fertility doctor did an ultrasound. When she saw the second baby, my husband and I were thrilled. But when she saw the third, we got scared. Right away, the doctor started talking about selective reduction," Ginny recalls. "Yet when I later phoned a friend who is an obstetrician and asked if she recommended reducing from triplets to twins, she said, 'You can carry three. Go for it.'"

DR. LUKE: Complicating the issue is the absence of any national criteria for determining the advisability of selective reduction. That's why when a patient comes to the Multiples Clinic seeking guidance, we try to evaluate her individual situation with regard to a number of factors. Here's what we look at:

- The woman's height: Just as an individual who is six feet tall has a larger heart and greater lung capacity than someone who's five feet, a taller woman has a larger uterus and more room for her babies to grow before birth than does a shorter woman.
- Prepregnancy weight: A woman's weight before conception is an indirect measure of her nutrient reserves, which is an important consideration for fetal development. Being more than 10 percent below the ideal weight-for-height is associated with an increased risk for miscarriage, poor fetal growth, and premature birth (see Table 3.2 on pages 57–58). Conversely, women who prior to pregnancy were at a normal weight—or even as much as 20 percent above ideal weight—generally have more favorable pregnancy outcomes and are more likely to be able to carry supertwins.

- Lifestyle: Habits that can be harmful during any pregnancy—smoking, drinking, strenuous physical activity, and so on—are particularly dangerous during a supertwin gestation.
- Obstetric history: A woman who has given birth previously has an advantage. Because her uterus has already been stretched, she is likely to carry her supertwins about two weeks longer than a first-time mother will. On the other hand, a history of preterm labor or preterm birth would indicate that a subsequent supertwin pregnancy would be very high-risk.

When Hannah Rhodes came to the Multiples Clinic and asked about reduction, for example, we used these criteria to counsel her. She was 5 feet 6 inches tall—well above the minimum we hope for in a triplet pregnancy. Her preconception weight of 146 pounds was optimal, and she had been eating well and gaining appropriately from the very beginning of her pregnancy. She didn't smoke or drink alcohol. There were no preexisting health problems. She had a sedentary job and was willing to take a leave of absence whenever it should become advisable. Her health care team was excellent, she lived close to the hospital, and she was committed to following all instructions from her doctors. Best of all, Hannah had an excellent obstetric history: Her first pregnancy had gone to 42 weeks and resulted in a healthy 9 lb., 2 oz., baby. In short, there was every reason to believe she could handle a triplet pregnancy.

And she did, beautifully. When Hannah's babies were born at almost 36 weeks' gestation, the largest weighed nearly 6 pounds—a whopping size for a supertwin. Even the smallest weighed well over 4½ pounds, which is 25 percent heavier than the national average for triplets.

MAKING YOUR CHOICE

What if the odds of a successful supertwin pregnancy seem *not* to be in your favor? In some cases, reduction may be the prudent choice. "Because I was taking the fertility drug Pergonal, I had two multiple-gestation pregnancies. First I conceived quadruplets, and we reduced to twins. But in the second trimester, I lost both those babies," says Karen Danke. "A year later, I conceived again—quintuplets this time. Given that even a twin pregnancy had failed the first time, we knew there was no way I could ever carry quints. So again we opted to reduce, and this time, I was able to hang on to 34 weeks. We have healthy twin boys now, and we're thrilled to be parents at last."

In some cases, the toughest part of the selective reduction decision is not the analysis of the physical criteria that affect a woman's chances of carrying supertwins. Rather, it is the emotional element involved that requires the most serious soul-searching on the part of the pregnant woman and her partner.

"For years, we had longed to be parents, and we underwent a series of infertility treatments in our quest for children. Finally I conceived, only to be faced with this wrenching decision—to risk losing all my babies by continuing a quadruplet pregnancy, or to purposely sacrifice two so that the others might have a better chance to live," says Joni Quinn. "We knew we could love our quads no matter how disabled they might be. But it didn't seem fair to doom them all to living with severe handicaps—or worse, to dying at birth—when it was probably within our power to give two of them normal lives. It was the most difficult choice we ever had to make."

If you, like Joni, must struggle with a decision about selective reduction, seek help from a psychologist or social worker familiar with fertility issues. Don't rush; you have some time to make your choice, and there's a chance that nature may make it for you. "My husband and I were told that if we opted to reduce from quads to twins, the procedure would be done around the 10th week of pregnancy. We were also told that one or more of the fetuses might spontaneously miscarry before that," says Anne Seifert. "We decided that the best short-term policy was just to wait and see what would happen."

Should you ultimately choose reduction, don't let outsiders question or criticize your decision. One mother explains it this way: "I conceived quadruplets from taking Pergonal. After weeks of introspection, advice from doctors, and support from our families, my husband and I together decided to have the selective reduction. It was not easy, but we did what we felt was appropriate for us. I firmly believe it was the wisest choice, because even with 'just twins,' my pregnancy was very difficult—cervical problems, placenta previa, preeclampsia. After eight months, though, we finally became the parents of healthy twins. No one should criticize our choice unless they have walked a mile in our shoes."

If you do decide to reduce to twins, keep one point in mind: Your unborn babies are still at greater risk for slowed growth than other twins are. To promote optimal fetal growth after reduction, be vigilant about fulfilling your dietary needs and limiting physical activity.

What if you do opt to continue a supertwin pregnancy? Many couples say they find strength in turning the decision over to a higher power. "I spent 24 hours thinking of nothing except whether or not to do the selective reduction, then finally told my husband that this could not be an option for us," says Ginny Seyler. "I figured God had put these babies here for a purpose, and he would see us through this. Once the decision was made, I felt much more at peace."

For Anne Seifert, the wait-and-see approach brought her to 12 weeks—and still all the quads were growing fine. At that point, her decision came down to two simple questions. "Dr.

Luke asked me, 'Do you want four children? And if so, are you willing to drastically change your lifestyle for many months in order to help them be born as healthy as possible?' My answer to both questions was an emphatic *yes*! In the end, it was that simple." Anne ended up carrying her quads to 31 weeks. At birth, Andrew and Sarah weighed just over 2 pounds each; Lindsey and Mason topped 3 pounds. All four are doing fine.

Chapter 7

The Emotional Ups and Downs of Pregnancy ... Multiplied

From the time they were little girls, many women have fantasized about the perfect pregnancy. Most often the ideal includes a nine-month glow that leads to a healthy, full-term singleton, born vaginally with no complications (and minimal discomfort), successfully breast-fed, and discharged to go home right along with Mommy. With the diagnosis of a multiple pregnancy, however, each aspect of this cherished dream may be thrown into doubt. The ideal image is shaken up even more when a pregnancy complication or crisis arises—which of course happens more frequently when twins or supertwins are on the way.

So it's no wonder that these months before your multiples are born may prove to be one of the most emotionally charged periods you'll ever know. Understanding the typical psychological patterns of this time can help you cope in ways that are healthy both emotionally and physically.

Your Inner World: An Emotional Journey from Shock to Joy

DR. LUKE: Every patient I encounter in my work with the University Consortium on Multiple Births is in the midst of an emotional journey. It began the day she learned she was pregnant, but it intensified markedly the moment she was told that multiples were expected.

Because I follow patients for many months, from the diagnosis of twins or supertwins to the day of delivery and beyond, I've seen many women confront the myriad and mixed feelings that accompany this unique kind of pregnancy. From my observations, I've concluded that this psychological journey typically consists of five fairly predictable stages: shock, denial, anxiety/anger/depression, bargaining, and acceptance/adaptation. These are basically the same five stages first described by Dr. Elisabeth Kübler-Ross (herself a triplet) as the stages of grieving.

What does grief have to do with a happy event like a pregnancy?

The answer is that any major life event can trigger a series of emotions, and these emotions often follow a similar pattern. After all, when a significant change ushers in a new era in your life, no matter how excited you are about what's to come, you still experience some sense of loss over the "old life" being left behind. And few events are more profoundly life-altering than having a baby—except, of course, having several babies at once.

What's more, parents who have just been told that they're expecting multiples do in a sense "grieve" for the loss of the typical pregnancy and typical family they had imagined would be theirs. Ginny Seyler, mother of triplets, explains it this way: "It took me some time to come to terms with the fact that this was going to be a high-risk pregnancy and not the nice, normal, nine-month pregnancy I had always dreamed of. And because few people expect to have three children at once, I also had to get used to the idea that I would never have a 'normal' family. It was disturbing to realize that forevermore I'd be thought of as 'the person with the triplets.'"

Not everyone reacts in exactly the same way, of course. Some individuals may get stuck at one stage, while others may even skip a stage. And any new significant development or crisis in the pregnancy can spark the sequence anew, sending the parents-to-be back to Stage 1 to start over. Being familiar with these patterns can help you and your partner understand your emotions, ease your confusion, and inspire you to do whatever is in your babies' best interests.

Stage 1: Shock

Even when a couple has been trying to conceive, a positive pregnancy test can come as a shock. The sensation is then repeated, but more intensely, with the news that you're carrying twins, triplets, or quadruplets. This is particularly true when multiples are conceived spontaneously rather than through infertility treatments. "The possibility of having twins had never even crossed my mind, so I simply could not believe it at first when the doctor showed us two heads on the ultrasound. I was sure the image on the screen must be coming from someone else and not from me," says Stacy Moore, mother of fraternal twin boys.

The shock can be compounded if the entire pregnancy was a surprise, or if you had reason to believe that the pregnancy would be lost. "Midway through the first trimester, I had an episode of pretty severe bleeding. I went in for an ultrasound, expecting to be told that I was miscarrying my baby. Instead we learned that there were *three* babies. My husband and I were in complete shock—there's no other way to describe it," says Ginny Seyler.

The more babies you're carrying, the more of a jolt you're likely to feel—especially if you had nearly lost hope of ever getting pregnant at all. Sarah Turner shares her experience: "I had endured 13 years of infertility. I lost both my fallopian tubes after ectopic pregnancies, had many attempts at IVF, and had one triplet pregnancy that ended at seven weeks. Then we tried IVF using four donor eggs that had been fertilized by my husband's sperm. Twelve days later, I went to the lab for a blood test to check my blood hormone level. It showed that not only was I pregnant, but my hormone level was much higher than you'd expect in a singleton pregnancy. I was thrilled, because I figured it meant I was carrying twins. Then five weeks into the pregnancy, I had my first ultrasound. Everyone was in total shock when we discovered *four* babies."

It is also normal to experience renewed shock whenever a pregnancy crisis arises. A diagnosis of an incompetent cervix or preterm labor, or the detection of a birth defect, or the news that a cesarean delivery will be necessary, can spark a resurgence of that sense of shocked disbelief.

STAGE 2: DENIAL

The second stage of adjusting to a crisis involves temporarily blocking out reality. For some women, denial takes the form of a restrained or muted reaction to the multiple pregnancy. Triplet mom Hannah Rhodes explains, "Initially I was rather unresponsive to the news that I had conceived triplets. I told myself it was probable I'd lose one fetus, if not all three, and would never need to deal with the reality of having three babies at once. That feeling lasted for several weeks."

Even moms-to-be who readily embrace the news of an impending multiple birth can still experience denial as the pregnancy progresses, in that they may ignore any information that seems too alarming. Meredith Alcott, mother of identical twin girls, admits, "I started to read some books about twins, but they stressed all the things that could go wrong during the pregnancy. I was too freaked out to finish reading them. Instead, I tried to block any scary stuff from my mind."

Denial can also involve an automatic assumption that all the babies will be born big and healthy. "In whatever pregnancy books I read, I always skipped over the sections about the NICU. I just assumed all three of my triplets would be coming home from the hospital with me a few days after delivery. I was in total denial of the fact that most supertwins do need NICU care," says Ginny Seyler.

Because denial serves as a shock absorber, allowing a more gradual emotional adjustment to surprising news or a sudden crisis, it does have a useful purpose. But if the denial stage persists too long, it can interfere with expectant parents' judgment as to what might be best for their unborn babies.

TAMARA: I've come to believe that denial was a factor in my unrealistically optimistic attitude during my twin pregnancy, and that the stage had been set many years before. I was in kindergarten when my fascination with twins first took hold. Perhaps it was because my best friends, Penny and Paula, were twins, and my second-best friend had *two sets* of twin siblings. It seemed that everyone in the neighborhood was a twin, and I wanted to be one too.

My mother explained that she could not manufacture a twin for me out of thin air; if a person had not been born with a twin, the opportunity was forever lost. I settled on the next best thing: Someday, I vowed, I would have 12 children, and they would all be twins or triplets.

As I grew up, of course, I realized that the family I had imagined was possible only in fantasy. The more I learned about multiples, the more I realized how slim were my chances of ever having twins of my own. So when the radiologist told me he saw two babies on my ultrasound, I was overcome with a powerful sense that a miracle had occurred. Throwing my arms heavenward, laughing and crying at once, I sang out in jubilation, "Twins! I'm having twins! Oh, thank you, God!"

The radiologist was taken aback. "You're . . . you're happy about this?" he asked in a confused tone.

"Happy?" I replied. "I'm ecstatic! For years, I've dreamed of having twins, and now it's really going to happen. This is the most thrilling moment of my life!"

The doctor squinted at me skeptically. "Most women are pretty shaken up when they first get the news. I think you're the only one who has ever danced on the examining table. Well, hang on to that positive attitude. You're going to need it."

I took his advice too literally perhaps, and spent the next months in a state of high glee. I was certain that my dream was coming true at last and that nothing could possibly go wrong. In this state of euphoric denial, I mistakenly dismissed the warning signs of preterm labor as normal discomforts of pregnancy.

DR. LUKE: One effective way to help expectant parents move past denial is to make their unborn babies seem more real to them. Naming the children is a good first step. Health professionals refer to individual multiples as Baby A, Baby B, Baby C, Baby D, and so on, typically counting clockwise by position in the womb, with Baby A being the one closest to the cervix. But there's no reason you can't name your children long before you look into their eyes for the first time.

Joanie Stevens, mother of fraternal twin boys, explains: "I didn't want to find out the babies' genders before birth, so during the whole pregnancy I called them 'Peter-Louise' and 'Amy-Jamie.' It started as a joke, but as soon as I began using these names, I felt much closer to my unborn babies. They became real children to me, not merely a positive pregnancy test or a pair of fetuses."

You're not yet ready to settle on names that will stick after birth? An affectionate nickname can serve the same loving purpose.

A second boon to parents who are working through the denial stage is ultrasound. Years ago, before this technology was in common use, it was much more difficult for parents to conceptualize their unborn babies as real little people. They could see the mother's belly getting bigger, and they could listen to the babies' heartbeats, but still it was hard to image what their children looked like.

Today ultrasound is an integral part of prenatal care, particularly in multiple pregnancies, since it offers a means by which to monitor fetal growth and well-being. At the same time, it has the marvelous effect of demonstrating how each child is unique in temperament from the earliest stages of life. For the mother-to-be, it can be the single greatest motivator for keeping up positive health behaviors, like staying off her feet and eating well. For the father-to-be, it can bring the message home: "These are your children, your responsibility."

DR. LUKE: I remember one instance when we were looking at triplets on the ultrasound monitor, and the expectant mom said to her husband, "See how big they are getting, honey! Joshua is really the busy one, but I think Amanda is going to be the boss." I looked over toward her husband, whose color had drained from his face and who had backed up against the wall. Clearly, the experience of visiting their triplets via ultrasound was very different for each partner!

STAGE 3: ANXIETY/ANGER/DEPRESSION

Moving beyond the numbness of shock and denial, an expectant mother of multiples often finds herself flooded with emotion—especially anxiety. She experiences all the worries any pregnant woman may feel, only more so, because her pregnancy involves additional risks and she has concerns about several children rather than just one.

Judy Levy, who conceived fraternal twin girls when her older daughter was two years old, explains, "My twin pregnancy was such a different emotional experience compared to my first. Instead of sheer excitement and joy mixed with a bit of apprehension, the balance was reversed—with the heaviest emphasis being on the apprehension."

Worry is even more pronounced when pregnancy complications arise. "For the first few weeks after I was ordered onto bedrest, I was an emotional wreck. I was terrified every moment that I'd lose the triplets," recalls Ginny Seyler.

If you had problems in an earlier pregnancy, the sad memories can compound your present fear, making it difficult for you to take pleasure in this pregnancy or to plan for the babies' arrival. Karen Danke, mother of fraternal twin boys, explains: "My husband and I were scared the whole time, because we had previously lost twins at 21 weeks. This time, we were afraid to buy any baby clothes or furniture until we had passed the 30th week."

During this overwhelmed stage, it's common to feel like you are no longer in control of your own life. "First I had preterm labor, then weeks of bedrest, then preeclampsia. I'm the kind of person who likes to be in charge, but once all these complications developed, I felt helpless. Nothing seemed to be under my control—not my job, or my babies' health, or even my own body," says Benita Moreno, mother of fraternal twin boys. That feeling can trigger resentment. "Nothing was normal. I couldn't keep on with my regular life, nor could I enjoy this new experience of being pregnant. I felt cheated," Benita adds.

At that point, the guilt typically kicks in. One mother of twins explains it this way: "It was a chain of uncomfortable emotions. First I felt overwhelmed with worry about the babies. Then I felt angry about being forced to worry. Then I felt guilty for feeling angry, because anger seemed so unmaternal."

For other women, guilt arises from a sense (however undeserved) that they themselves are to blame for the high-risk status of their pregnancy. "I carried a real burden of guilt because I believed that by taking Clomid and conceiving triplets, I had put all my babies in danger," Ginny Seyler confides.

From self-blame to depression can be but a short hop. "I got really down for a while, feeling like I was a bad mother and I didn't deserve these sweet babies," admits one twin mom. "Fortunately, that let up after about a week, and I was able to let go of the guilt and develop a healthier, more productive attitude."

If you find yourself stuck in anxiety, anger, or guilt, it's important that you take steps to regain a sense of control—not only for your own sake, but also for your babies' sake. Why? Because emotional stress can trigger the same type of physiological reaction as can physical stress or overexertion. The body releases stress hormones called catecholamines, which can bring on uterine contractions. Fortunately, there are a number of ways to lower your stress level and brighten your outlook:

- Blame it on hormones. Pregnancy hormones can launch any woman on a mood-swing roller coaster. And since you've got higher levels of pregnancy hormones than does a singleton mom, your hormonal upheaval can deliver a double (or triple) whammy. Before sinking into "I'm rotten to feel this way" mode, realize that your mixed feelings are in part physiologically based. As your body adjusts physically, you'll regain your emotional equilibrium.

- Accept your anxieties, without obsessing about them. Instead of berating yourself for feeling worried, try to acknowledge that anxiety is simply part of your life for now. Judy Levy explains, "I called a friend who had recently delivered triplets after a series of pregnancy difficulties, and I asked her, 'When you were pregnant, how did you get rid of the anxiety?' She answered, 'I didn't. I *was* anxious, and there was no getting around that.' Somehow her words made me feel better. Once she had given me 'permission' to be nervous, I was better able to relax."

- Fight fear with information. Another key to coping with overwhelming emotions is to empower yourself through education. As you learn how to minimize risk by taking sensible steps to protect your own health and that of your babies, your sense of alarm diminishes. Your obstetrician and other health care providers are excellent sources of information, so talk candidly with them. Make lists of your questions, and bring them to each prenatal appointment. If you don't understand the answers, ask to have things explained again.

- Seek moral support. It's normal to feel ambivalent about having multiples, so share your emotions with someone who truly understands your negative feelings as well as your positive ones. The best candidate for that unique type of empathy: another mother of multiples. "What helped most in handling my fear and guilt was to connect with other moms-to-be of supertwins who were also on bedrest, and with women who had already given birth to multiples. We wrote letters, sent e-mail, and talked on the phone for hours. They gave me the information and support I needed, and helped me to feel less alone," Ginny Seyler says. "How did I find them? Through the Internet, Triplet Connection, and Mothers of Supertwins." (For information on these support groups, see Appendix B.)

Your obstetrician may also be able to provide emotional support. "One thing I loved about my doctor was how tuned in he was to the psychological challenges of a high-risk pregnancy," says Ginny Seyler. "For instance, by my third day on bedrest, I was despondent. I paged my obstetrician, and he spent 45 minutes on the phone with me—helping me face the reality that I might lose them, yet reassuring me that my chances of delivering three healthy babies were good. It was so important to know that he was there for me when I needed him."

If you should continue to feel very upset about the pregnancy for more than a few weeks, seek professional help in working through these feelings. While the support of a loving friend or dedicated obstetrician is important, sometimes a person needs the extra measure of insight and objectivity that a mental health professional can provide.

STAGE 4: BARGAINING

The bargaining stage of dealing with a pregnancy crisis represents an advance from the help-lessly overwhelmed emotions that preceded it, in that you now may feel a greater sense of calm and control over your situation. The problem is, if you push the bargaining too hard, your pregnancy may be jeopardized. Attempts at negotiation are most common among two cate-gories of expectant mothers of multiples: those who want to keep on working and do not understand the connection between long hours, stressful conditions, and preterm labor; and those on bedrest who feel frustrated by the lack of freedom and mobility.

"As an oncology nurse, I was working about 50 hours a week. Twenty weeks into my preg-nancy, I was advised to quit and go on modified bedrest, but I had just started a new job and didn't think I was eligible for a leave of absence. Besides, I felt sure I'd be able to take this preg-nancy to 37 weeks at least, and I wanted to work as long as possible. So I kept negotiating. 'What if I cut back my hours? What if I promise to elevate my feet whenever I'm at my desk? What if I lie down as soon as I get home from work?'" says Marcy Bugajski, mother of frater-nal twin boys.

"Then, in my 28th week, an internal exam of my cervix revealed that I was already fully effaced and slightly dilated. When she discovered that, Dr. Luke said, 'Marcy, you are off work and onto strict bedrest as of this moment.' But I replied, 'I can't just up and quit. I've got a job to do.' Dr. Luke looked at me sternly and said, 'If you don't get into bed right now and stay there, you are endangering your twins' lives.' Suddenly the message got through to me, and I felt really scared. I realized the job could go on without me, but these little babies could not. My priorities had to change—and fast."

DR. LUKE: Too often I've seen mothers-to-be of multiples bargain with their doctors, bend the rules, or insist on taking over major decisions about their care. "Why should I stop working now? I feel fine. How about if I continue for another six weeks? Okay, four weeks?" Or, "I can't stand being on bedrest. I'll just pop this load of laundry in, then run to the grocery store. I'll be back in half an hour, and no one will even know I was out." Or even, "I'm determined not to have a cesarean section. Doctor, promise me that you'll let me deliver vaginally."

It's understandable that patients want to be informed and involved. Particularly for women who by personality or profession are accustomed to wielding authority, it can be hard to let someone else take charge. But now that you're pregnant, you must hand over control to the people best qualified to make the decisions about your care: your obstetrician and other health care team members. Understand that the limitations they may place on your activities are not punishments, but precautions. Attempting to plea-bargain for a reduced sentence—to change strict bedrest to house arrest, for example—may only lead to deeper trouble.

Chapter 2 discussed the importance of choosing a highly qualified obstetrician to manage your multiple pregnancy. Now that you have chosen him, put your trust in him and let him do his job. Your doctor and the other members of your health care team have years and years of training and experience upon which to base their decisions, and the judgment needed to determine what is in your babies' best interests. Chances are you do not have this training—and even if you are a physician, you are not in a position to view your own case with the open-mindedness and objectivity that are required for optimal care.

Regardless of your role in the everyday world, your role for the next few months is as a patient. Do you chafe at the idea of "doing nothing" for your unborn babies? Do some of our recommendations—to rest, relax, relinquish responsibilities and activities—make an expectant mother's job seem annoyingly passive? Don't look at it that way. You're not doing nothing; you're *gestating*. Right now, for you, that's the most important job in the world. You're doing whatever it takes to allow your pregnancy to continue as long as possible, to help your babies develop as optimally as possible, and to keep yourself as healthy as possible.

So go ahead and ask for information and explanations; communicate your concerns and preferences. But don't argue with your doctor or try to cut a deal. Instead, let him guide your care. Take careful note of his advice, and that of any other member of your health care team, and follow it to the letter.

STAGE 5: ACCEPTANCE/ADAPTATION

The fifth and final stage of coming to terms with a pregnancy crisis involves finding ways to cope that are healthy for both mind and body. Acceptance means developing a new attitude—finding within yourself the willpower and maturity to see what needs to be done. Adaptation means translating your acceptance into appropriate actions—modifying your behavior to give your babies the best chance. Below, women who have achieved this share the secrets of their success:

- Figure out how to alleviate your frustrations without increasing your risk, Ginny Seyler urges. "One of the most aggravating aspects of bedrest was not being able to get our home ready for the triplets. Friends had given us tons of equipment and clothes, and I was dying to go down to the basement and sort through everything, but of course that wasn't allowed. Finally I found the perfect solution. I hired a teenager to come over, lug the stuff upstairs, unpack everything, organize it with me, and arrange it all according to my instructions. Not only was this an entertaining way to pass the long hours of bedrest, but it also helped me to feel more prepared for the babies' arrival."

- Focus on the ultimate reward, says Amy Maly, mother of identical twin girls. "Sure, I missed being able to just jump in the car and go wherever I wanted, whenever I wanted to. But I realized that this was hard and serious work, growing two babies at once. To keep on track, I concentrated on the incredible payback we were aiming for—a pair of healthy newborn twins."

- Find creative ways to motivate yourself, advises Helen Armer, mother of a triplet set that includes two boys and a girl. "Because I'm an engineer, I am used to working with graphs and numbers. I'm also very goal-oriented, and I was determined that all of my triplets would have healthy birthweights. I designed a chart to track fetal size and weight as estimated by monthly ultrasounds, and then extrapolated to calculate the babies' growth with each passing week. Whenever I needed a motivational boost to drink yet another quart of milk or stay in bed for that extra hour, I looked at my chart and got inspired."

- Cultivate cautious optimism, suggests Heather Nicholas, mother of boy/girl twins. "There is no need to have a gloomy outlook, because not all multiple pregnancies are complicated. Even if you do have problems, some aspects of your pregnancy will be perfect. For instance, I had a lot of difficulties, including a weak cervix, tons of contractions, and *20 weeks* on bedrest. But my delivery was a wonderful experience—painful of course, but beautiful too—and my babies were born huge and healthy."

- Look for the silver lining, Judy Levy advises. "If I hadn't conceived twins in my second pregnancy, I probably would have had only one more child. So despite the challenges of a difficult pregnancy, I really do feel multiply blessed because I'm finding that it's wonderful to have three children."

The World at Home: Your Man, Your Marriage, and Your Multiples

"This pregnancy wasn't the best timing, because my wife had just begun a new job. Benita and I had been talking about starting a family, but we hadn't planned to begin trying for at least a year. So when she conceived accidentally, it was quite a surprise for both of us. Then she went in for her first ultrasound at 16 weeks. As soon as she left the radiologist's office, she called me from the car phone and told me we were going to have twins. I was so freaked out that I had to leave work and come straight home. My stomach was in knots for a week," confesses Donald Moreno, father of fraternal twin boys.

Expectant fathers, just like expectant mothers, typically react with shock to the startling news that multiples are on the way. From there, they progress through essentially the same emotional stages described above as they come to terms with the implications of a high-risk pregnancy.

As the initial shock subsides, denial may set in. Telling himself that his own life won't change much until after the children are born, a husband may wrongly assume that for the duration of the pregnancy, it will be business as usual. That naiveté can set the stage for extreme dismay when his wife no longer joins him for a junk-food fest or scuba-diving expedition—or when complications force the mom-to-be onto bedrest and the dad must suddenly assume the role of caretaker for her and for the household.

If your partner is in a denial rut, he needs to learn more about the risks and precautions associated with a multiple pregnancy. One mother of twins reports, "My husband kept asking me to go to the gym with him as we always used to do. Then I convinced him to come with me to a prenatal checkup, where my obstetrician explained why it was so important for me to limit my activity. After that, my husband was much more understanding."

Moving on to the next stage, a man may experience the same level of overwhelming anxiety that his wife feels over a multiple pregnancy. Yet for him, the focus of worry may differ. Impending fatherhood is seen as a validation of his manhood, and as an outward sign of his role as provider and protector. Because twins or supertwins magnify these responsibilities, a husband may be doubly anxious about his ability to meet these challenges.

Fiscal concerns may come to the fore now. Ed Greenwood, father of boy/girl twins, explains, "I had been planning to leave a corporate job I found stifling and start my own business, but then I learned that Lydia was expecting twins. She encouraged me to follow my dream anyway, but I felt that with two babies to support, we would need the security of a steady paycheck. For a few weeks, it seemed that all I could think about was money."

Worries about the health of his wife and unborn babies can also overwhelm an expectant dad, triggering his protective instincts. If he takes his role as guardian to extremes—obsessively counting every calorie you eat, telling dinner guests it's your bedtime and hustling them out of the house if you so much as yawn—you may feel smothered. Try to appreciate the loving concern behind his actions, and encourage him to balance his instinct to protect with your need to be treated like a responsible adult.

Once that balance is achieved, chances are you'll enjoy being taken care of. "It was sweet to see how protective my husband became once I was pregnant with the twins," says Amy Maly. "He'd remind me to eat, get whatever I needed so I wouldn't overexert myself, and call me several times a day just to make sure I was okay. When I was on hospital bedrest, he even smuggled milkshakes into my room because I had complained about the hospital food."

Once he reaches the bargaining stage, your husband may be tempted to negotiate with the obstetrician on your behalf—"Come on, doctor, she really wants to work another few weeks, and I support her in that. Don't you think the leave of absence could be postponed a bit longer?" Or he may try bargaining with you, when his desires conflict with your own—"I know you're not up for a big vacation, honey, but a romantic weekend getaway could do us a lot of good." Your man is in bargaining mode? Gently remind him that it's vital to the babies' well-being that you adhere to your doctor's instructions and listen to your body's signals about the need for a low-key lifestyle right now.

There are several other important steps you can take to help your husband accept and adapt to a multiple pregnancy. To keep your marriage on track, consider these suggestions:

Make communication a top priority.

"I think husbands often keep their feelings hidden, because they want to be the great protectors for their wives. They try to be strong and macho, so as not to add to whatever worries the women may have," says twin mom Karen Danke. "But knowing the risks associated with a multiple pregnancy, it's too hard for a guy to handle all those emotions on his own. You've got to get him to open up and talk about his fears, or eventually the pressure inside him will build to the point where he just blows up."

Keep in mind too that while you and your husband are likely to pass through the same five emotional stages as you cope with a life crisis, you won't necessarily be at the same stage at the same time. In addition, your response at each stage may be different, making communication more difficult. Try to remain patient and supportive with one another as you talk things through.

Encourage his involvement in the pregnancy.

Conflict can also stem from the fact that men and women experience pregnancy very differently, physically and emotionally. No matter how focused on your husband you may have been previously, bodily changes now cause you to shift attention inward. You track your babies' every movement—you know when they're all asleep, when one has hiccups, and when they are jostling each other—and you are aware of them at every moment. Your most important world becomes the world within, and your introspective mood is a normal part of protecting and nurturing children.

Your husband, however, not having the constant physical reminders, can forget about the pregnancy for hours on end. Your single-minded focus on the babies can therefore make him feel left out of the loop. One father of triplets says plaintively, "My wife was so tuned in to what the babies were doing inside her belly—each kick, each hiccup—I felt like a fifth wheel." A man's sense of isolation is compounded when the outside world lavishes attention on the expectant mother of multiples and more or less ignores him.

To help your husband feel like he's a vital part of the action, encourage him to participate in the pregnancy as much as possible. Tell him when a baby is kicking, and place his hand on your belly so he can feel that miracle too. Let him assign silly or affectionate nicknames to each baby—"Pelican," "Kicky Feet," "Sweet Pea"—and then refer to the babies by those names. If he wants to play Mozart to your tummy to share his love of music with his progeny, go along with it. And bring him to your doctor appointments so that he can hear firsthand all the news of the pregnancy. "My husband came to every single one of my prenatal checkups, taking time off from work when necessary," says Stacy Moore. "It made us feel closer to each other and helped him feel closer to the twins. I let him know how happy his involvement and moral support made me."

Show your appreciation for all he does.

Given the physical limitations imposed by a multiple pregnancy, your husband will have to take over a number of responsibilities that you two used to share. The shopping, cooking, cleaning, gardening, and errand-running all fall on his shoulders for now, and he probably misses your contribution in those areas. Expressing your thanks helps him to handle these chores with good grace.

"I worried that my husband might feel unappreciated for all of the work he had to do taking care of me and our unborn babies," says twin mom Meredith Alcott. "So I told him, and often, that I recognized and appreciated his many efforts." Keeping it out in the open this way helps to alleviate any resentment that otherwise might fester. Tell your husband how proud you are of him for all he's doing to help your babies grow healthy and strong, and he'll feel proud too.

The Outside World: Where Everyone Wants a Piece of the Action

Stacy Moore loves to tell the story of how she first shared the news of her twin pregnancy with the outside world. "Our families knew we were scheduled for our first ultrasound that day, and we had invited people to come over in the evening and see the videotape of the baby that the radiologist had promised to make for us," Stacy explains. "Everyone was sitting in our living room—my mom, Tim's parents, his grandmother, his sister and her boyfriend. As I turned on the video, I said, 'Now watch carefully to see what the technician types.' Then on the screen appeared the letters, one by one: 'H-E-A-D-S.' Everyone said, 'Heads? Heads! Two heads! Oh, my God, it's twins!' Then they all started jumping up and down and hugging us. That was the most wonderful moment."

The world is fascinated by multiples, and as an expectant mother of multiples, you become an instant source of fascination to everyone around you. It's like being a movie star—the spotlight can be a thrill, but on occasion, it's an annoyance. You're likely to experience the positives as well as the negatives almost as soon as you break the news that multiples are on the way.

A FAMILY AFFAIR

You're probably noticing a shift in your relationship with your own parents and in-laws, particularly if this is your first pregnancy. Getting pregnant can be a rite of passage that makes you truly adult in their eyes, and your special status as the mother-to-be of multiples may lead the previous generation to treat you with new respect.

At the same time, though, your high-risk pregnancy may trigger a resurgence of protective parental instincts in them. As a result, they may bombard you with advice. "As soon as they learned I was expecting twins, both my mother and my mother-in-law started to tell me what to do all the time—stop driving, drink more milk, don't dye my hair. It was sweet in a way, because I knew they were thrilled about becoming grandparents. But sometimes it drove me crazy," admits Lydia Greenwood, mother of boy/girl twins.

You may feel resentful. "Back off! These are *my* babies." But everyone benefits if you can practice diplomacy, so keep these suggestions in mind:

- Grin and bear it, if you can. Your parents and in-laws want what's best for you and your multiples, and offering advice is their way of trying to help. Listen politely, but don't feel compelled to comply with every edict.

- Try not to get defensive. Your own subconscious concerns about your ability to cope with multiples may make you extra sensitive, even when no criticism is intended.
- If you feel you must speak up, say, "I know your advice is well meant. But please rest assured that I have an excellent health care team, and I need to follow *their* instructions." Then be generous about sharing less sensitive aspects of your pregnancy experience, such as your ideas for decorating the nursery. Parents are less pushy when they feel less shut out.

FRIENDS AND ACQUAINTANCES: THE HELPFUL AND THE NOT-SO-HELPFUL

Close pals, casual acquaintances, co-workers, and even complete strangers may all want to feel that they are a part of the excitement of your multiple pregnancy. Sometimes that can be a lot of fun. "I was one of the first among my friends to get pregnant, so to have it be twins cranked up the thrill factor for everyone. I really enjoyed all the extra attention and excitement that went along with being an expectant mother of multiples," says Stacy Moore.

That spotlight can be a boon, because people are more likely to lend a hand when they know that two or more babies are on the way. Judy Levy says, "Everyone was extra supportive because I was expecting twins. For instance, our neighbors threw a baby shower for me, even though this wasn't a first baby. It was nice to know people cared and wanted to help."

Unfortunately, not everyone offers "help" that is truly helpful. Due to the publicity that frequently surrounds multiple-birth babies born in sets of six or more, many people have become blasé about twins and even triplets. "I constantly heard remarks like, 'Oh, you're having twins? Well, just be glad it's not a half-dozen babies.' I didn't consider such comments to be particularly useful," says Judy Levy.

Even worse are the horror stories. "It seemed that every week there was another news show about the dangers of multiple births—complete with video footage of minuscule infants on respirators," says Judy. "But it was hardest to handle the personal stories people told me. For instance, a security guard mentioned that his twin brother had died at birth. Another woman revealed that she had lost a twin pregnancy at 24 weeks. Why would anyone think I needed to hear this?"

Judy coped by putting such "dire warnings" in perspective. "I reminded myself that my situation was different from theirs. For example, the security guard and his brother were born 50 years ago, and there have been many medical advances since then. The woman whose twins didn't make it had gained only 8 pounds during her pregnancy, whereas I had gained 40 pounds by my 24th week," Judy explains.

TAMARA: Just as people don't always know where to draw the line between helpful and hurtful remarks, they don't always recognize the difference between enthusiasm and intrusiveness. In our society, pregnant women are sometimes viewed as public property. And the more obviously pregnant you are, the more liberties people tend to take—touching your tummy, guessing at your weight, and asking the nosiest of questions.

I can't begin to count the number of times that casual acquaintances and even complete strangers asked, "Did you take fertility drugs?" or, "Will you be able to deliver vaginally?" or, "Do you plan to breast-feed?" I'm no prude, but I didn't feel particularly comfortable discussing my sex life, my vagina, or my breasts with people I scarcely knew!

At first, I'd give some vague answer, then try to change the subject. But after a number of embarrassing episodes, I came up with several stock phrases that helped to nip the nosiness in the bud. Here are a few of my favorite snappy responses to impertinent questions:

Did you take fertility drugs?
Why do you ask?
Will you be able to deliver vaginally?
We'll see when the time comes.
How can you even think about breast-feeding twins? You'll feel like a cow.
I'm having babies, not calves, and I'm looking forward to nursing.
Twins are double trouble.
No, they're twice as nice.
Do multiples run in your family?
I expect it won't be long before they run up and down the stairs and all around the house.
Pregnant with twins? Oh, you poor thing. The workload! I'm glad they're yours and not mine.
I'm glad they're mine too.

BODY-IMAGE BLUES

DR. LUKE: Another insensitive comment our patients too often hear, particularly if they are petite, is, "But you're so small, you can't possibly carry multiples!" I recall that one of the first women to attend our Multiples Clinic arrived at several appointments in tears. She felt discouraged because friends, neighbors, and even strangers in the supermarket frequently told her that she didn't look big enough to be pregnant with twins. Because her unborn babies were growing beautifully, we suggested that she respond by saying, "My multiples experts assure me that we're all doing just fine," but our encouragement was not enough to ease her distress.

Finally, two days before her due date, she walked into the Multiples Clinic radiant with joy. She was very large. As she stood sideways, nearly filling the doorframe, she said, "At last, everyone who sees me believes that I'm going to have twins!" Her babies ended up being two of the biggest multiples we've ever had in our program.

So if you find yourself feeling overly frightened by the insensitive remarks of every Tom, Dick, or Harriet, put your anxiety to good purpose. Use those comments as reminders to keep on your best behavior—to eat right, to get enough rest, to monitor yourself for contractions. If you do, chances are good that you will ultimately prove the naysayers wrong.

As aggravating as it is to be told that you're too small to carry multiples, to be teased about getting too big is even more hurtful—and potentially more harmful, if you let it affect your diet. Yet if you're following the recommendations to gain 40, 50, even 65 pounds or more (depending on your prepregnancy weight and the number of babies you're expecting), chances are that someone will say, "Lady, you are getting *fat.*" You need to disregard such comments if your babies are to thrive.

Admittedly, this is not always easy to do in our body-conscious society where slenderness is the ideal. You've probably been on a weight-watching vigil for much of your adult life, with the goal of taking off rather than putting on pounds. Slim women in particular may need to significantly alter their attitude about weight. "As an inveterate calorie-counter, I've always been proud of my size 4 figure, so it was a terrible shock to think of gaining 50 pounds," confesses Lydia Greenwood. "I knew my twins needed the nourishment, but I couldn't keep from feeling upset the day a co-worker teased, 'So much for miniskirts! You'll never be skinny again.' I had to keep reminding myself that when you're pregnant with twins, big is beautiful."

Women who are overweight prior to conceiving may confront a public unsympathetic to the need to gain additional weight during a multiple pregnancy. "When you're heavy to start with, there is such a stigma about eating. Even when you're expecting, you hear people whispering, 'Oh, my gosh, do you see how enormous she is getting?'" says Marcy Bugajski. "I even read a pregnancy guide that warned overweight women like me against gaining more than 25 pounds. Dr. Luke told me, 'Throw out that book! You can lose weight later. Right now, your babies need every mouthful.' Once I had 'permission' to gain, it was easier to ignore the snide remarks from uninformed outsiders."

While rude remarks from strangers may not be too hard to disregard, your partner's reaction may be more worrisome to you. Fortunately, most expectant fathers of multiples are very supportive. "My husband Curt made it his personal mission to be sure I was gaining enough weight. For instance, each morning he'd cook me two English muffins with eggs, cheese, and Canadian bacon—and he wouldn't leave for work until I'd eaten them both," says Amy Maly.

You may find it helpful if your obstetrician or dietitian explains to your partner the importance of adequate nutrition. Marcy Bugajski reports, "After Dr. Luke talked to my husband about the effect my diet would have on our unborn babies, he would constantly encourage me to eat. For instance, if I was too tired to get up and fix myself a snack, David would do it for me."

For additional moral support, a husband may even modify his own diet to more closely match your nutritional needs. "Fred knew that I wasn't happy about having to add a lot of red meat to my diet. So even though he didn't care for beef either, he started to cook it for dinner and eat it with me every night," says Heather Nicholas. "I appreciated that gesture. It made me feel like we were really in this together."

You're still feeling panicked as you see the scale climb toward 150, 175, or 200? Remind yourself that the extra pounds are temporary. Research has shown that if you return to your prepregnancy eating habits (provided you were eating well and wisely before you conceived), you will get back to your former weight within three to six months.

DR. LUKE: Keep in mind that this may be one of the most emotional times of your life. Because not all the news you receive during your multiple pregnancy is guaranteed to be good news, you need to stay aware of how you and your partner are coping with any crises.

In the course of these few months, you may have to deal with a barrage of physical and psychological issues. Although these trials may take a short-term toll, if you and your partner can stay on a healthy track, the long-term results will be great personal growth and a stronger partnership. Those are wonderful qualities to bring to your new role as parents of multiples.

Chapter 8

Giving Birth to All Those Babies

The countdown is near. You've been eating right, resting as much as possible, going to your pre-natal checkups, and visiting your unborn children via ultrasound to watch them grow bigger and stronger with each passing month. It won't be much longer now before your multiples are born—and that knowledge may leave you in a flutter of mixed emotions, from exhilarated anticipation to disquieting anxiety.

Delivery is undeniably easier when you're prepared, both mentally and physically. Child-birth classes (as discussed in Chapter 2) can provide valuable information and emotional sup-port, as well as training in specific exercises and techniques to use during labor. But because most of these courses are designed for expectant parents of singletons, you will want to study this chapter to ready yourself for the unique experience of giving birth to multiples.

Share the information with your husband too. Today most expectant dads are eager to par-ticipate in childbirth by offering comfort and coaching to their partners. This not only makes labor more manageable for the mother, but also enhances a father's emotional bond to his chil-dren. How can you make sure he doesn't miss the big event? Have your husband carry a pager, so you can reach him if you go into labor unexpectedly.

How to Recognize When Labor Has Begun

Although women have been giving birth since time immemorial, scientists still are not com-pletely sure what triggers labor. Various physical changes or signs occur in concert to prepare your body for childbirth, beginning several days or even weeks before you actually deliver. When you notice the following developments, you'll know that labor is not far off:

Lightening

Toward the end of pregnancy, a woman typically senses that the baby's head has settled deep into her pelvis. This event, known as lightening or "dropping," is evident owing to the lower position of the belly. The mother-to-be is now able to breathe more easily and eat more comfortably—but the tradeoff is additional pressure on the bladder and increased awkwardness while walking. Lightening is often a sign that delivery will occur within a few weeks, a few days, or even a few hours, as the pressure of the baby's head encourages the cervix to dilate.

As an expectant mother of multiples, however, you may have felt this deep-down pressure for many months if the baby closest to your cervix was already nestled in your pelvis, owing to the crowded conditions inside the uterus. If this is a new sensation for you, though, it indicates that delivery will probably occur soon.

Bloody Show

The next sign of impending labor is when the mucous plug—the blood-tinged, jellylike substance that has filled the opening of the cervix—is dislodged by changes in the cervix: dilation and effacement. Measurements of dilation—the opening up of the cervix—range from undilated or closed (0 centimeters) to fully dilated (10 centimeters). Effacement is the thinning that occurs before and during labor, ranging from no effacement to 100 percent.

Rupture of Membranes

Each of your babies has been growing inside a "bag of waters," or membranous sac. If this sac ruptures, you may feel fluid coming from your vagina, in anything from a slow trickle to a sudden gush. Although you may often hear comments like, "My water broke, so I knew that labor had begun," this will not necessarily be your experience. Some women, in fact, deliver their babies with the membranes intact. For others, the membranes rupture weeks or even months before delivery—a dangerous complication called preterm premature rupture of membranes (PPROM) that increases the risk of infection. For that reason, as soon as you realize or even suspect that your water has broken, it's vital to call your obstetrician and then go to the hospital immediately.

Stronger, More Frequent Uterine Contractions

Chances are that you've been feeling some contractions throughout your pregnancy. Called Braxton-Hicks contractions, these are normal. Yet they differ from true labor contractions in that they are irregular; they are brought on by fatigue, dehydration, or physical activity; and they disappear with rest and hydration. True labor contractions, on the other hand, occur at regular intervals of about five minutes or less, with each lasting about 30 to 60 seconds, and they continue regardless of what you do. Table 8.1 presents a comparison of true and false labor.

True Versus False Labor

Signs and Symptoms	False Labor	True Labor
Frequency of contractions	Irregular intervals	Regular intervals
Change in contractions	Disappear with rest	Continue despite rest
Location of contractions	Usually felt in the abdomen	Usually felt in the back and abdomen
Strength of contractions	Decrease in strength	Increase in strength
Effect of pain medicines	Pain is eliminated	Pain is less affected
Cervical changes	No change	Progressive effacement and dilation

Table 8.1

DR. LUKE: For women pregnant with one baby, the four signs of labor typically occur at term, or about 38 to 41 weeks of pregnancy. But as we tell our patients at the Multiples Clinic, with two or more babies labor usually comes much earlier. While the average singleton is born at 39.3 weeks, the average twins are born at 35.4 weeks, triplets at 32.1 weeks, and quadruplets 29.6 weeks.

The difficulty may be in recognizing symptoms of labor, particularly when they occur sooner than anticipated. Compounding this problem is that some women do not trust their own intuitive feeling that something is wrong and therefore fail to act on it. So remember, at whatever point in your pregnancy you experience any symptoms of labor, *call your physician.* He will most likely instruct you to get to the hospital for further evaluation.

TAMARA: If you're close to your due date, you probably won't have any qualms about calling your doctor at the very first indication of labor. But when labor begins well before the 37th week of pregnancy, the symptoms can be much milder and therefore more difficult to recognize. You may also be in a psychological state of denial: "It's way too early for the babies to be born, so these signs probably mean nothing at all. I'll just wait and see if they go away."

That's what happened to me. In my 31st week, asleep in bed at 1 A.M., I was awakened suddenly by a moist feeling between my legs. "Whoa, better go to the bathroom," I thought sleepily as I made my way toward the toilet. Lying down again, though, I gradually realized that there was still a slight, slow trickle. I had heard that when a woman's water broke, fluid could come gushing out, so I was skeptical that this tiny trickle could have the same significance. And I was reluctant to wake my doctor in the middle of the night just because my bladder was acting up.

After some time, I nudged my husband and told him what was happening. Groggily he murmured, "Based on my experience, I'd say everything is fine. We should both go back to sleep." And he did.

But his words brought me no comfort. "Based on his experience? *What* experience? *He* has never been pregnant before either." Finally, around 2:30 A.M., I called my obstetrician. "No contractions? Then you're probably just leaking a little amniotic fluid," he said reassuringly. "You may need to go on bedrest for a while. Meet me at the hospital, and we'll see what's going on."

Arriving at the labor and delivery unit, I said to the nurse on duty, "I guess I might be in labor." She chuckled and patted my arm, saying, "Honey, if you're not sure, you aren't." But as her fingers reached inside to check my cervix, her expression changed. "You're 9 centimeters dilated! Don't you feel any contractions?" Numbly I shook my head. The vague discomfort in my abdomen was nothing like what I had imagined labor to be. Moments later, my doctor entered the room. Labor had progressed too far to attempt to stop it now, he said. My babies were born about 45 minutes later, at 4 A.M.—just three hours after my water had broken.

If I had called my obstetrician as soon as I felt that first little leak of fluid, could anything have been done to delay my twins' birth for another few days or weeks? Perhaps not, given how quickly my cervix had dilated. But who knows? All that's certain is that with every moment of hesitation, opportunity had slipped away.

So please don't second-guess any symptoms you may have. Whether you're preterm or full term, when there is even the slightest suspicion that labor has begun, instantly alert your doctor.

What to Expect at the Hospital

When labor is suspected, your doctor instructs you to go to the labor and delivery unit of the hospital. There, you change into a hospital gown and a nurse takes your pulse, blood pressure, and temperature (your vital signs). The nurse or physician also performs a pelvic exam to determine if you are in labor and how far you have progressed.

Next, your contractions are monitored by a pressure gauge attached to a belt placed around your abdomen. Each baby's heartbeat is monitored by an ultrasound gauge, also attached to a belt. This is the same type of monitoring you may have received during the last few months or weeks of your pregnancy, referred to as nonstress testing or a biophysical profile (see Chapter 2). Also known as electronic fetal monitoring, these machines provide a record of the pattern of your contractions and your babies' heartbeats in response to the contractions, alerting the labor and delivery room staff to potential problems.

If your due date is still many weeks off, you are given fluids intravenously to combat dehydration and attempt to stop labor. Tocolytic medications can also be given through the IV line, as described in Chapter 6. Should it be determined that you are in labor but will not deliver for at least a day, and you are between 24 and 34 weeks' gestation, you may be given corticosteroid injections. These help your babies' lungs to mature more rapidly, thereby reducing the severity of certain complications of prematurity.

Throughout these procedures and those to follow, you are cared for by a team of nurses and other hospital staff. They work under the direction of your obstetrician, who checks on you periodically. If this is a teaching hospital, you may also be seen by physicians-in-training, known as residents.

WHEN LABOR IS INDUCED

Sometimes it's advisable to deliver the babies promptly, even though labor has not spontaneously begun. In such cases, labor must be induced. To achieve this, the doctor may rupture the membranes and/or administer a drug called Pitocin (a form of the hormone oxytocin) via IV to stimulate uterine contractions.

One reason for inducing labor is that after a certain point, a fetus becomes "postmature." As the aging placenta begins to function less efficiently, the uterine environment is no longer the healthiest place for the baby. If the pregnancy continues, the baby is more likely to experience complications. With singletons, this point is typically reached at 41 to 42 weeks. With multiples, this point comes earlier. For twins, the optimal time for delivery is 36 to 38 weeks. For triplets, the best time to be born is 34 to 36 weeks, depending on their weight and estimates of their lung maturity.

"At 38 weeks, my obstetrician said, 'Your twins are certainly big enough to be born safely now. We can induce labor tomorrow if you want, or we can wait a little longer,'" recalls Heather Nicholas, mother of boy/girl twins. "I was so huge and uncomfortable at that point, and so eager to meet my babies, that the decision was simple—induce!"

If it is determined that one or more of your multiples is in distress inside the womb—perhaps owing to infection or a problem with the placenta or umbilical cord—labor may be induced at that point, even if you haven't reached full term. "At almost 34 weeks, electronic fetal monitoring revealed that one baby's heart rate was fluctuating too much. My doctor told me this meant it was time to deliver. I was started on a Pitocin drip at noon, and shortly after 6 P.M., my babies were born," says Karen Danke, mother of fraternal twin boys.

In other cases, a problem with the mother's health may necessitate prompt delivery, such as when preeclampsia cannot be controlled with bedrest and medication. Marcy Bugajski says, "Because I developed preeclampsia, the doctor had to induce labor immediately, even though I was only at 34 weeks. I received IV magnesium to prevent seizures, as well as IV Pitocin to stimulate contractions. Still, nothing much happened until after the doctor broke my water. At that point, the contractions came quickly. My fraternal twin boys arrived five hours later."

OPTIONS FOR PAIN RELIEF

Long before you go into labor, you should familiarize yourself with the options for managing the discomforts of labor. Knowing ahead of time the pros and cons of the various medications will help you to feel calmer and more in control as your babies are born.

For some women, the relaxation techniques and breathing exercises learned in childbirth education classes are sufficient for coping with labor pains. "I told my doctor that I didn't want any pain medication unless it became absolutely necessary. In the end, I managed without it because I didn't feel the contractions that much. The only really painful part was a stabbing sensation in my leg, because one of the twins was hitting on a nerve," says Marcy Bugajski.

When additional relief is needed, two categories of medications can be used. The first type, called analgesia, lessens but does not eliminate pain. The second type, called anesthesia, produces numbness with or without a loss of consciousness. The most frequently used medications include the following:

Demerol

A systemic analgesia, this narcotic is administered via the IV line or by intramuscular injection. One mother of twins says, "I appreciated the way the Demerol took the edge off my pain and eased my anxiety. It helped me regain my composure and focus without taking away all sensation." Some women, however, dislike the drowsiness this medication can bring on. "I was sorry I'd had the Demerol because not only did it make me nauseous, but it left me groggy at a time when I wanted to be fully alert," says another mother of twins.

Epidural Block

This technique for administering analgesia is currently the most common method of pain management in labor. Medication is given via an epidural catheter (a small tube) inserted through a needle into the lumbar space below the spinal cord. While an epidural is very effective at minimizing labor pain, it can interfere with the mother's urge to push once the cervix is fully dilated. For that reason, the drug may be decreased or stopped as the time for delivery nears, allowing the mother to have full control over pushing. "I used no medication when I delivered my boy/girl twins. But two years later, when I gave birth to my singleton son, I asked for an epidural," says Lydia Greenwood. "Which would I recommend? Every woman has to make her own choice— but if I were doing it again, I'd opt for the epidural." An epidural is also commonly used for certain cesarean section deliveries, though for this a higher dosage of medication is given. A distinct advantage is that the mother can remain awake and alert during the birth of her babies.

Local Anesthesia

This type of medication is typically administered by injection at the opening of the vagina. It is given just before birth when the physician performs an episiotomy, a small incision that widens the vaginal opening to allow the babies to fit through more easily.

General Anesthesia

Because it produces unconsciousness, this category of medication is usually given only for certain cesarean deliveries or in the case of an emergency vaginal delivery. A potential danger of general anesthesia is that food or stomach acid may be aspirated into the patient's lungs. For that reason, it's wise to limit your intake to clear fluids as soon as you think labor has begun, in case you end up needing general anesthesia. Your doctor may also give you antacid medication to reduce the amount of acid in your stomach.

Although every effort is made to accommodate a patient's wishes regarding pain relief, other considerations come into play. Chief among these is the health of your babies. Most drugs can pass through the placentas and may slow the babies' heartbeats before birth. Pain medication taken by the mother also can affect the babies' ability to breathe after delivery, depending on the dosage and how soon before birth the drug was given.

Will You Deliver Vaginally?

Nearly every pregnant woman spends nine months wondering whether she'll deliver vaginally or by cesarean section (surgery that involves making an incision through the wall of the uterus). Often this question cannot be answered until the woman is actually in labor, when the course of events determines which method of delivery would be most appropriate.

An expectant mother of multiples, however, may have her answer long in advance of her delivery date. That's because most triplets and virtually all quadruplets are delivered by cesarean section, also called a C-section. The surgery is scheduled in advance, and the woman does not actually go into labor at all.

With twins, though, the matter is not as clear-cut. About half of twin pregnancies end in a vaginal delivery, and the other half are delivered by cesarean. Occasionally the first twin is born vaginally, but then complications arise—such as the baby's lowered heart rate or umbilical cord problems, or the mother's excessive bleeding—that necessitate delivering the second twin surgically.

The crucial factor in determining the method of delivery for twins is the babies' position in the uterus, particularly that of the infant closest to the cervix. If this baby is in a vertex position, meaning head down, your physician is likely to recommend that you try to deliver vaginally. However, if this baby is breech (feet first or buttocks first against the cervix) or transverse (sideways in the womb), you probably will be scheduled for a cesarean. Judy Levy says, "Before making the incision for the cesarean, my doctor did a final ultrasound right there in the operating room to see if the transverse twin might have turned at the last minute. If so, we would have tried for a vaginal delivery. But she hadn't, so we proceeded with the C-section."

In most cases, if the first twin is born vaginally, the second twin then moves down into position by the cervix and is also able to be born vaginally. When the second twin is breech or transverse, the obstetrician may try to maneuver this baby into a more favorable position by pressing her hands against the mother's abdomen. This technique, done with ultrasound guidance, is called external version.

If attempts to turn the baby do not succeed, the second twin may be born by cesarean—but not always. "Alex was closest to my cervix and head down, which meant there was no problem delivering him vaginally. But after he came out, there was all this extra space in my uterus, so Benjamin sprawled into a transverse position—and then we couldn't get him out," says Marcy Bugajski. "On the ultrasound screen, I could see the obstetrician's hand inside me, trying to turn the baby around. Finally she got hold of his ankles and pulled him out feet first. Those few minutes were not fun—but I was glad not to have a C-section on top of a vaginal delivery."

When it appears that a woman may possibly be able to deliver vaginally, but certain factors could ultimately require a cesarean, the obstetrician may opt for a trial of labor. In such a case, labor is allowed to progress under close watch, but the woman is also prepped for surgery. For instance, she may be placed in a delivery room equipped for surgery (called a double setup) and an epidural catheter may be inserted. If the trial of labor proceeds smoothly, the expectant mother can decide for herself whether or not to accept pain-relieving drugs, yet if a C-section becomes necessary, the anesthesiologist can immediately administer the required medication.

"To see if I could deliver vaginally, the obstetrician gave me Pitocin. Soon afterward, Dr. Luke came to visit me and said, 'Oh, I see you're doing a trial of labor.' I answered, 'This is no trial. These babies are coming out *today,* one way or another,'" says Heather Nicholas. "The whole time, I was lying on a hard, flat table in the operating room, with an epidural in place, in case the twins started to show any signs of distress. Fortunately, everything went fine, and my babies were born vaginally about nine hours later."

Another important consideration in determining the method of delivery is the mother's obstetrical history. Years ago, it was believed that once a woman had given birth by cesarean section, she had to deliver by cesarean for every pregnancy that followed. That's because the scar in the uterus—from the vertical type of incision commonly used in the past—was at risk for rupturing during a subsequent labor.

This practice has now changed. Today surgeons generally make a transverse (side-to-side) incision across the lower part of the uterus. This heals with a stronger scar and does not disrupt the muscular portion of the womb, so it is far less likely to cause problems in a future labor. Because a vaginal birth offers several advantages, including lower risk of infection, less bleeding, and quicker recovery, nowadays many women who previously had a C-section are offered the option of attempting to deliver vaginally. This is called a trial of labor after cesarean, or TOLAC. When successful, the delivery is referred to as a vaginal birth after cesarean, or VBAC (pronounced "vee-back").

If you had a C-section in the past, discuss your options with your obstetrician. (Keep in mind that the scar you see on your skin is not necessarily in the same position as the incision that was made in your uterus. Your medical records should indicate which type of uterine incision was used.) Provided there are no other factors indicating the need for a cesarean, an expectant mother of twins is almost as likely as a singleton mom to be permitted an attempt at VBAC.

Vaginal delivery involves three distinct stages of labor that last altogether about 12 to 14 hours, or somewhat longer for a first pregnancy. If you are having a scheduled cesarean delivery, you do not experience any of these stages because the surgery is performed before actual labor can begin. If you have a trial of labor but ultimately it's determined that you need a cesarean, you may proceed through part or all of the first stage, and possibly into the second, before a surgical delivery is performed. Here's what to expect during each stage:

First Stage

With each contraction, the normally thick cervix thins out and begins to dilate as it prepares to allow the first twin's head to pass from the uterus into the birth canal. A physician or nurse periodically places a few fingers inside your vagina to check the status of your cervix and, if necessary, to see whether your membranes have ruptured. This stage of labor is divided into three phases: early, active, and transition:

- During the early phase, contractions are mild, occurring at intervals of about 15 to 20 minutes, with each contraction lasting about 60 to 90 seconds. The cervix begins to dilate from 0 centimeters to about 5 centimeters.

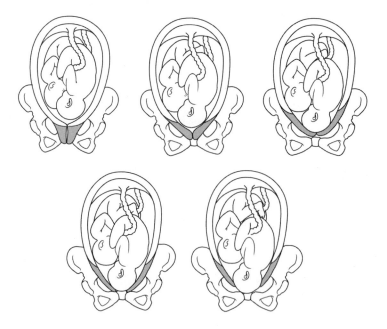

Dilation and effacement of the cervix during the first stage of labor

- As you enter the active phase, contractions become stronger and more frequent until they are about three minutes apart. Each contraction lasts an average of 45 seconds. Your membranes may rupture during this phase if they have not done so earlier. The cervix continues to dilate to about 8 centimeters.
- Transition, the end of the first stage of labor, is typically the most uncomfortable phase of childbirth. During this time, the cervix dilates from 8 to 10 centimeters. Contractions occur every two to three minutes, with each contraction lasting about 60 seconds.

DR. LUKE: Depending on the position of the twin closest to your cervix, the transition phase of labor may involve a backache that gets progressively worse. Some of our patients report feeling nauseated, chilled, and irritable. You're also likely to feel extremely tired. When I was in labor with my own son, I remember thinking, "I'm so exhausted, I don't know how I'm going to stay awake for the birth of this baby."

Many mothers laboring to deliver multiples find the physical and emotional sensations to be overpowering. You may completely lose track of time or even experience a kind of temporary amnesia. If you feel overwhelmed or panicked, rely on your husband or labor coach to help you cope.

Second Stage

Once the cervix has fully dilated, the head of the first twin can begin moving down into the birth canal. Your contractions may slow down, occurring every two to five minutes, with each one lasting about 60 to 90 seconds. The second stage can last more than an hour, so try to rest and relax between contractions.

You may have an urge to push or bear down with each contraction. This is a basic instinct, and for most women, the active participation feels gratifying. With an epidural analgesia, however, the urge to push may be delayed until the first twin's head has descended well into the birth canal.

As the first baby's head crowns (becomes visible at the opening of the vagina), you may feel great pressure and a burning sensation. This is due to the stretching of the perineum (the area between the vagina and the rectum). In a few moments, the stinging sensation abates as the pressure from the baby's head stretches the vaginal tissues, causing a natural numbing of the nerves. Your obstetrician also may perform an episiotomy—a surgical incision in the perineum to enlarge the vaginal opening—in an attempt to prevent injury to the perineum.

As the infant's head emerges, the physician checks to make sure the umbilical cord is not wound around the neck, wipes the baby's eyes, and removes any fluid from the nose and mouth. With the next contraction and a strong push from you, the first twin's shoulders are usually delivered, followed by the body. By convention, health care professionals refer to the firstborn twin as "Baby A."

In some cases, the second twin—"Baby B"—arrives just a minute or two later. "I pushed four times and out came Jacob. With the very next push, Zachary was born. It all happened so fast that the doctors didn't even have time to change their gloves between babies," Karen Danke recalls.

More commonly, however, the second twin follows after about 20 to 30 minutes, or even longer. During this interval, your health care team continues to monitor the unborn baby. Provided all is going well, they may encourage you to relax awhile before proceeding with the birth. Heather Nicholas says, "My first twin was born at 10:37 P.M. Then the doctor wanted me to rest, so the second twin wasn't born until 11:18. That was okay with me. I'd had an epidural, so although I could feel contractions, they weren't painful."

If the twins were in separate amniotic sacs, and the second twin's sac is intact, the doctor ruptures these membranes when it's time to get under way again. Take your cues for pushing from your body sensations, unless your health care team instructs you to do otherwise. If the second baby is in a breech position but your doctor determines that it is safe to try for a vaginal delivery, it is particularly important for you to push and to refrain from pushing as your doctor directs.

DR. LUKE: Patients at the Multiples Clinic are always relieved to hear that labor is generally no more painful with twins than with a singleton baby. You need to go through the first stage of labor, including transition, only once, even though you are giving birth to two babies.

While you do go through the second stage twice, this usually proceeds more rapidly with baby number two, particularly if she is smaller than the firstborn twin. And most of our patients who also have an older child tell us afterward that delivering multiples is no more uncomfortable than pushing out a singleton.

Third Stage

After both babies are born, you may continue to feel mild contractions as the placentas separate from the uterine wall and are delivered through the vagina. Usually the placentas are intact, but your doctor examines them carefully to see whether any small fragments may have remained inside you. If so, these are removed manually. Otherwise, the uterus would not be able to contract completely and bleeding would continue. You may also be given medication such as Pitocin to help the uterus stay firm and to further reduce bleeding. If you had an episiotomy or a tear in the perineum, it is repaired with stitches at this time.

After the hard work of labor, you may feel very hungry, shaky, or chilled. But the overriding sensation, provided all has gone well, is usually profound relief and a great sense of satisfaction.

Table 8.2 summarizes what is happening and how you may feel during each stage of labor.

Stages of Labor for Vaginal Birth of Twins

Stage of Labor	Contractions	Physical Changes	How You May Feel	What You Can Do
First Stage				
Early	Mild contractions, 15–20 minutes apart, lasting 60–90 seconds	Bloody show; cervix is 0–5 cm dilated	Relieved that labor has finally begun	Relax, sleep, practice relaxation techniques
Active	Stronger contractions, building to about 3 minutes apart, lasting about 45 seconds	Membranes may rupture; cervix is 5–8 cm dilated	Anxious, more tired; you may have a backache	Work with your labor coach; use your relaxation techniques; request pain relief if desired
Transition	Contractions are 2–3 minutes apart, lasting about 1 minute	Cervix finishes dilating to 10 cm	Nauseated, chilled, irritable, very tired; backache may worsen	Relax between contractions; pant or blow during contractions; do not push yet
Second Stage	2–5 minutes apart, lasting 60–90 seconds	First baby's head descends into the birth canal; first twin is born; then second baby descends and is born	Alert and in control	Push with your contractions
Third Stage	Contractions continue, but are less painful	Placentas separate from the uterine wall and are expelled	Exhilarated; perhaps shaky, hungry, chilled	Enjoy holding your newborns

Table 8.2

Important Information on Cesarean Sections

As they study their books on pregnancy, many expectant mothers skip over the chapters about cesarean sections. Attending childbirth classes, they tune out when the talk turns to surgical delivery. That's because most women dream of having a "normal, natural" childbirth experience that includes an uncomplicated vaginal delivery. And it's human nature to think, "Some people have problems, but *I* won't be one of them."

Yet the fact is that, as a mother-to-be of multiples, your chances of needing to deliver by cesarean are high. The current rate of C-section deliveries in the United States is 23 percent. But for multiples, the rate is much higher: About half of twins and nearly all supertwins are delivered surgically. Chances are that you will find greater satisfaction in giving birth if you make peace with the possibility of a cesarean before your delivery date arrives.

Why are so many multiples delivered by C-section? For supertwins, the answer is that it's not possible to adequately monitor all the babies during active labor. It would be exceedingly difficult to detect when a baby had developed a problem, or even to identify which baby was in distress. A vaginal delivery of higher-order multiples would also carry an unacceptably high risk of excessive bleeding or other complications for the mother.

With twins, a number of factors can affect the decision. Situations in which twins would typically be delivered by cesarean section include the following:

- Breech or transverse presentation of either twin, especially the one closest to the cervix
- Failure of one of the babies to descend into the birth canal
- A trial of labor that does not progress adequately, such as when the cervix does not dilate fully
- Placenta previa: one of the placentas is blocking the birth canal
- Abruptio placenta: a placenta separates from the uterine wall
- Fetal distress due to a tangled umbilical cord or other problem that prevents one of the babies from getting sufficient oxygen
- A health problem in the mother—such as severe infection, preeclampsia, or gestational diabetes—that would be aggravated by the stress of labor
- An active herpes infection in the mother, which could be passed on to the babies as they travel through the birth canal, with potentially life-threatening consequences

SCHEDULED VERSUS EMERGENCY C-SECTIONS

In some cases (such as with twins in transverse or breech presentation, or with supertwins), it is known well ahead of time that a cesarean will be performed. In that event, the surgery can be scheduled in advance. "By the 31st week of my quadruplet pregnancy, I was experiencing intense vaginal pressure, extreme nausea, and constant contractions despite the use of tocolytic medications. My body was clearly saying it couldn't take much more," says Anne Seifert. "My obstetrician told me, 'It's better to schedule the surgery for a time of day when the labor and delivery unit and the NICU will be fully staffed. We don't want to wait too long and have you go into labor at 1 A.M.' So we scheduled the cesarean for the following Friday morning."

In other cases, the expectant mother may be fully aware that she'll be having a C-section eventually, but a sudden complication necessitates emergency surgery. "At 30 weeks, I was admitted to the hospital because the doctor feared that the smallest baby was not doing well *in utero,*" says Ginny Seyler, mother of triplets. "An ultrasound revealed that blood flow to this baby was inadequate and his heart rate was not strong. Even though the other two babies would be better off staying inside me, this child clearly needed to come out. The doctors gave us 15 minutes to make a decision, and we opted to do the cesarean right away."

Sometimes a woman actually goes into labor and progresses up to a certain point before a vaginal delivery is finally ruled out. "My water broke at 8 P.M. the Friday of my 38th week, but I wasn't contracting. Pitocin did bring on contractions, yet still I didn't dilate. The doctor kept increasing the dosage of Pitocin, which made the contractions really hard—I remember one that lasted eight minutes! But my stubborn cervix stayed closed," says Stacy Moore, mother of fraternal twin boys. "Saturday night, my obstetrician suggested a C-section, but I asked to postpone it unless doing so would present a danger to the twins. The babies were fine, so we waited. By Sunday morning, though, I was still only 3 centimeters dilated. I hadn't slept or eaten in 36 hours. Dr. Luke came to see me, took my hand, and said, 'Stacy, you have put up a really good fight, but now it's time to see those babies.' I knew she was right, so we went ahead with the surgery. And guess what? The cesarean wasn't nearly as bad as I had feared."

Because a C-section is major abdominal surgery, it does involve some risks. For instance, any use of anesthesia can potentially cause adverse side effects. Any operation carries a risk of excess bleeding, blood clots, and infection. And uterine surgery leaves a scar that can weaken the womb and perhaps complicate a subsequent pregnancy. But because cesarean deliveries are performed so frequently in the United States and around the world, the risks associated with this type of surgery are minimal. When a cesarean delivery is clearly needed for the sake of the mother or the babies, the benefits certainly outweigh the risks.

What to Expect in the Operating Room

For a scheduled cesarean, you are admitted to the hospital the morning of the surgery or the day before, if you haven't already been admitted previously for observation or other treatment. "The morning of my scheduled C-section, my husband helped me to shower, massaged my feet with my favorite lotion, and got me into my hospital gown," says Anne Seifert. "Then we held hands as I was wheeled down to the operating room. I saw that it was room number 4—a good sign, I thought, when you're about to give birth to four babies."

First an IV line is put in to allow administration of fluids and medications. The anesthesiologist then inserts the catheter if you're having an epidural block. For an emergency delivery, general anesthesia may be used, in which case the mother is asleep for the entire operation. Your abdomen is washed with antiseptic solution or covered with an antiseptic-coated film. A cloth or paper drape is placed vertically above your chest to block your view of the surgical field.

One difference between a cesarean delivery of multiples versus a singleton is the number of people in or around the operating room. Along with your obstetrician and any doctors or nurses who will assist with the surgery, there is a team of neonatologists—one or more for each baby—as well as pediatric nurses. When supertwins are on the way, the room can get downright crowded. "There were about two dozen people in the operating room, including a camera crew from the University of Michigan, plus another two dozen people looking in from behind a huge window. Clearly, giving birth to quadruplets was not a private, intimate experience," Anne Seifert says, laughing. Most hospitals also allow your husband or other labor coach to remain in the operating room, usually seated by your head behind the screen that shields your view of the surgery.

The obstetrician makes an incision through the skin, then another incision into the uterus. Next, the amniotic fluid is suctioned off. Although you aren't able to see what's going on, if you're awake and alert, you can hear everything, and you may feel some tugging sensations. One mother of twins says, "There wasn't any discomfort, but I had the funniest sensation of being a bottle from which the doctor was attempting to extract two model ships."

If your partner peers over the drape, he can watch the babies being born. Ginny Seyler's husband did just that. "I thought the C-section would be a delicate procedure," says David Seyler. "But when I looked over the shield, it seemed like each minute the doctor was just sticking his hand inside my wife and pulling out another baby!"

Unlike a vaginal delivery, where the baby closest to the cervix is of course born first, there is no set birth order for delivering babies surgically. The obstetrician removes the babies from the uterus in whatever order seems most expedient. But again, the first to emerge is designated "Baby A," the second is "Baby B," the third is "Baby C," and so on.

Anne Seifert describes the scene at the birth of her quadruplets: "Making the incision took a while, because I had lots of scars and adhesions from previous surgeries. I know the doctor was pushing my belly all over, but I couldn't feel a thing. Then he reached in on the left side and pulled out Lindsey. I heard her cry loud and strong, and everyone said, 'Oh, what a big baby!' She *was* pretty big for a quadruplet born at 31 weeks—3 lb., 2 oz.

"Next to arrive was Mason, weighing 3 lb., 1 oz. It took the doctor a minute to get him out because he was up high, under my heart, and his foot was hooked around somebody's umbilical cord. He gave a good loud yell too. Then the doctor moved over to the right side of my uterus and lifted out Sarah. She was smaller—2 lb., 2 oz.—and her cry was softer. Finally it was time for Andrew, but the obstetrician couldn't seem to get him out. So a female doctor reached in with her smaller hands, and she was able to get hold of him. He was the littlest, at 2 lb., 1 oz., but he screamed the loudest.

"It was like tag teams. After a baby was born, a nurse would rush that infant over to a side door where a group of neonatologists was waiting. Then another baby would be pulled out of me, and he'd be whisked over to a neonatologist. The first baby was born at 11:10, and the last arrived at 11:14, so the whole thing happened amazingly fast."

After all your babies are delivered, the obstetrician removes the placentas and checks to make sure no fragments of placental tissue are left in the uterus. You are given Pitocin intravenously to make the uterus contract and halt the bleeding. The uterus and skin are then sutured closed. The entire operation takes about an hour, with the babies usually being born during the first 15 minutes.

Maximizing the Joy in a Cesarean Delivery

Some women are disappointed to wind up with a C-section. "When I had an emergency cesarean with my firstborn, I felt cheated out of an important maternal experience because I wasn't able to feel the actual moment of birth," Judy Levy explains. "With the twins, I was determined to feel more actively involved. So I talked ahead of time to another mother of multiples who'd had a C-section and asked her what she wished she had done differently. She gave me some great insights."

Here's what experienced moms of twins and supertwins recommend. Discuss these and any other preferences you might have with your obstetrician well before your delivery date. If all goes well, your doctor will probably be happy to take your wishes into consideration.

- Request that your obstetrician narrate the surgery as he goes along. Judy Levy says, "Hearing the doctor say, 'We're at the uterus now. Everything looks good. I can see both babies. Now I'm reaching in for this first child,' and so on, helped me to feel that I was aware of and participating in all that was going on."

- Ask to have the drape lowered for a moment after each baby is lifted from the uterus. "I wanted to get a good look at each little daughter the very moment she arrived in the world," says Judy Levy. "It was a thrill to think, 'This is my precious baby and she was *just born*.'"
- Though you probably won't be able to hold your multiples until after the surgery is over, it can be extremely satisfying to see your husband snuggling them. Stacy Moore says, "Right after the twins were born, the nurse showed them to me and then handed them to Tim. I cried with joy as I watched my husband hold our precious babies at last."
- Get permission for your partner to take pictures during the surgery. "My obstetrician told me, 'You have full media rights. Make a video if you want to.' So instead of sitting near my head, my partner was down at the other end of the operating table, with a camera," Judy explains. "These photos are such a treasure for me, because they let me connect to the actual moment of my twins' birth."
- Take pleasure and pride in your unique maternal experience. "When my older daughter was born, I worried that having a C-section somehow made me less of a mother," says Judy. "But with the twins, I didn't feel that way. I told myself, 'I am having *two* babies at once! What more could I possibly need in order to feel like a mother?' After all, I had done something not many mothers get to do—and it was truly miraculous."

Recovering from "Children-Birth"

Just as a multiple pregnancy is more challenging than a singleton pregnancy, so can the recovery period involve an increased chance of complications. Although most new mothers of twins and supertwins do not experience problems, you and your health care providers need to be on the lookout for warning signs and should take appropriate steps to minimize risk:

- A new mother of multiples may bleed more heavily after delivery because the uterus has been overstretched and because a greater portion of its surface area was covered by placental tissue. Alert the hospital staff if you are soaking the sanitary napkins or passing blood clots. The obstetrician may have to check for retained placental tissue or suture a missed tear.
- Heavier postpartum bleeding, coupled with the extra demands a multiple pregnancy placed on your iron reserves, can increase the likelihood of anemia. Symptoms

include dizziness, weakness, pallor, and shortness of breath. "The first day after the twins were born, just sitting on the side of the bed made me so dizzy that my ears were ringing. There was no way I could have stood up without passing out. By the following day, though, I felt much better," says Heather Nicholas. Do not attempt to get out of bed unassisted until your doctor gives you the go-ahead. To combat anemia, continue to eat an iron-rich diet as you did during pregnancy.

- Uterine cramps are common after delivery because the uterus is still contracting as it descends back into the pelvis. Your extra-large uterus must contract all the more to regain its former size, so you may experience stronger cramping than does the mother of a singleton. Over-the-counter analgesics such as ibuprofen can alleviate discomfort. (Don't be concerned if you notice that cramps are strongest while breast-feeding. It is normal for the babies' suckling to trigger the release of oxytocin, the hormone that stimulates uterine contractions.)

- More problematic than uterine cramping is when the postpartum uterus does *not* contract normally. This is more common after a multiple birth because the uterus has been overstretched, and there is a greater likelihood that placental fragments remained in the womb. A nurse or doctor periodically palpates your abdomen to see if the uterus is firm. If not, you are examined again for retained placental tissue or injury to the uterus and perhaps given additional oxytocin. You may also be encouraged to periodically massage your abdomen and to breast-feed, both of which stimulate uterine contractions.

- Fever is a warning sign of infection. Tell the nurse or doctor immediately if you suspect you may be running a temperature.

- Pain on urination can be a sign of bladder or kidney infection. In addition to taking whatever antibiotics your physician prescribes, you can hasten recovery by drinking plenty of water.

- If you had developed preeclampsia, you may need to continue on medication and have your blood pressure closely monitored for about 24 hours after delivery. During that time, you must stay in bed. Do not eat or drink anything unless your doctor says it is all right.

Mothers of multiples who deliver by cesarean section should also take note of the following:

- During the first days after delivery, the incision usually does hurt, but no more so than if you had given birth to a singleton. Pain medication is provided and should be adequate to keep discomfort easily within tolerable levels—at or below a score of

3 on a pain rating scale of 0 to 10. Tell your doctor if you think you need more pain medication—or less. "After my first child was born by emergency C-section, I was given a morphine drip for the pain. But that made me feel so out of it that I couldn't help take care of my newborn," says Judy Levy. "That's why, in recovering from the planned C-section with the twins, I took only Tylenol and Motrin. To me, being slightly uncomfortable was a price worth paying in order to be alert and involved with my babies."

- About 12 hours after delivery, your obstetrician may encourage you to get out of bed and move around. To minimize discomfort, brace the incision site with your hands and try to maintain good posture. Do not attempt to leave your bed unaided before getting your doctor's approval.

- The staples used to close the skin are typically removed three to five days postoperatively for a low transverse incision, or within five to seven days for a vertical incision. In the meantime, your incision site must be examined regularly for signs of infection, such as redness, increased tenderness, or discharge. Notify the medical staff if you notice any such symptoms. Be particularly vigilant about this if you're significantly overweight; obese women are three times more likely to develop an infection after a cesarean delivery.

Being discharged from the hospital does not mean that the postpartum recovery period is over. Once you're home, you must be careful not to overdo it—particularly if you had a cesarean section. That's no easy assignment when you've got twins or supertwins to take care of, so line up plenty of help in advance (see Chapter 11 for tips), and be sure to follow these suggestions:

- Get as much rest as possible. This is a critical element of the recovery process, particularly in the first two weeks after delivery. Though uninterrupted slumber may be hard to come by, do make a point of sitting down and putting your feet up at every opportunity. Catch a nap whenever you can—and turn off the phone first so you won't be interrupted by well-meant but ill-timed calls of congratulations.

- Resume physical activity gradually. Check with your physician for recommended limitations on lifting, stair-climbing, and housecleaning. Refrain from driving a car for a week to 10 days after delivery, if so instructed. And don't plan on rushing back to work too soon. "After the birth of my older daughter, I tried to do way too much, way too fast—taking care of chores around the house, handling much of the baby care on my own, and going back to law school after only one week. I was constantly exhausted, and it seemed like forever until my body felt good again," says Judy Levy. "I didn't want to make the same mistakes after the twins were born. This time, I did a minimum of housework, lined up lots of child-care helpers, and took a longer maternity leave. All that made quite a difference in how I felt, physically as well as emotionally."

Now that you know better what to expect during labor and delivery, try to relax in these last weeks of your pregnancy. Heather Nicholas shares her healthy philosophy: "There's so much unwarranted fear and negativity about labor. Sure, the pain can be bad, but childbirth is a beautiful experience too. Remember that it's such a short event compared to the many months of pregnancy. And it's a blink of the eye in comparison to the wonderful years to follow, as you watch your babies grow—from tiny newborns, to adorable toddlers, to active school-agers, and all the way up to adulthood." Rather than dwelling on whatever worries you may have about giving birth, focus on the excitement of the present and on all the joys the future will bring.

Chapter 9

Your Babies' Hospital Experience: The Nursery and the NICU

From conception, your multiples have been physically linked to you. Your every breath, heartbeat, meal, and movement have been shared, in a way, by them. But at the moment of birth, your babies begin an independent existence. For each, the first experiences in the outside world depend on his or her own state of health.

At the moment of delivery, each of your babies comes under the care of an individual health care team, which includes a neonatologist or pediatrician, a labor and delivery nurse, and perhaps others. The team's first action is to clear the infant's airway. The baby is then placed on a radiant warmer, a small open crib with an overhead heat source, which provides the warmth a newborn needs while allowing the doctors and nurses full visual and physical access. Once under the warmer, the baby is completely dried to reduce heat loss.

Doctors use a rating scale called the Apgar score to assess how well each of your newborns is adapting to life outside the womb. This scale helps to quantify a baby's condition at birth and the need for additional medical intervention. The rating is done at 1 minute, 5 minutes, and sometimes again at 10 minutes after birth.

There are five components to the Apgar score: heart rate, respirations, muscle tone, reflex irritability, and color. Each component is given a value of 0, 1, or 2, depending on the condition of the baby. These figures are then added to give the total score, on a scale of 0 to 10. If the initial score is less than 7, it indicates that the baby is in distress and needs immediate medical treatment. For instance, the doctor gives resuscitative assistance to any baby who is not breathing on his own and/or whose heart rate is less than 80 to 100 beats per minute. Table 9.1 shows what each score means.

Apgar Scores

Component	0	1	2
Heart rate	Absent	Slow; less than 100 beats/minute	More than 100 beats/minute
Respirations	Absent	Weak	Good, strong cry
Muscle tone	Limp	Some bending	Active motion
Reflex irritability	No response	Grimace	Cough or sneeze
Color	Blue or pale	Body pink, extremities blue	Completely pink

Table 9.1

In between the one-minute and five-minute Apgar scores, or shortly thereafter, the health care teams perform routine newborn care for each baby. This includes the following:

- Weighing the baby.
- Measuring head circumference and overall length.
- Taking footprints.
- Placing identifying wristbands on the mother and the infants.
- Administering erythromycin ointment or silver nitrate eyedrops to prevent eye infections.
- Giving an injection of vitamin K to prevent bleeding in the first hours and days of life. Vitamin K, which is necessary for the synthesis of blood-clotting factors, is produced by the intestinal flora. Because the intestinal tract is sterile at birth, a newborn lacks this vitamin. The injection provides an adequate supply until the baby can begin to produce his own.

- Taking a small sample of blood via a heel stick, or pinprick in the heel. The blood is sent to a laboratory to be checked for a variety of rare but serious diseases, including phenylketonuria and hypothyroidism. You and your pediatrician are notified if there are any problems. The blood may be taken soon after birth or at some later point, but it is required by law prior to discharge from the hospital. If the test is done before your babies are 24 hours old, it must be repeated in two or three days, either in the hospital or, if your babies have been discharged, at your pediatrician's office.

THE WELL-BABY EXPERIENCE

DR. LUKE: If all your babies are fine, they are soon handed over to you and your partner for some first snuggles—and first feedings. The issue of feeding is so important that we've devoted a full chapter to it. Please take time to read Chapter 10 *before* your multiples are born, so you can make an informed and careful decision about whether to feed by breast, bottle, or both.

If you have any problems during those first feedings, ask a nurse or the hospital's lactation consultant for help. They should be able to answer all your questions and offer suggestions and support. They can also assist you in finding feeding positions that don't place pressure on your incision, if you had a cesarean delivery.

ROOMING-IN WITH MULTIPLES

Rooming-in refers to the practice of keeping a mother and her baby—or babies, in your case—together during their hospital stay. Part of the trend in obstetrics to make all aspects of childbirth as natural as possible, it is now the norm at most hospitals around the country. The practice has a number of advantages. Studies have shown that mothers who share a hospital room with their newborns are more successful at breast-feeding and more sensitive to their infants' needs. Rooming-in also gives you confidence in your caretaking abilities as you learn routine baby-care skills like bathing and diapering through hands-on experience and under the supervision of nurses. You benefit physically too, since recovery is hastened when a mother gets up and moves around soon after delivery.

Typically the babies sleep in small separate cribs in the mother's room, but you may have other ideas. "The nurses were going to put Benjamin and Madeleine into separate bassinets, but my husband said, 'No, they've been snuggled up to each other until now. They'd probably be happier sleeping together.' So the twins shared a bassinet while they roomed in with me," says Heather Nicholas, mother of boy/girl twins.

There may even be space for your husband. "Tim was able to sleep in my room, along with the babies and me, the whole time I was in the hospital," says Stacy Moore, mother of fraternal twin boys. "It was a wonderful experience for us all to be together as a family right from the beginning."

The major potential disadvantage of rooming-in includes lack of sleep for Mom. Remember that you always have the option of sending one or all of your babies to the nursery for a while. "After my singleton daughter was born, I wouldn't let the nurses take her away from me even for a few minutes. With the twins, though, I let up a bit. They were born at ten o'clock in the morning, and by three o'clock the following morning, I really needed to rest, so I asked the nurses to take care of the babies for a few hours," says Judy Levy, mother of fraternal twin girls. "Later I realized that this had set a healthy precedent, because it let me feel that it was okay to accept assistance. Once I was home, then, it was easier to say yes to friends who offered to help."

Many twins, if born healthy and mature, go home just a few days after delivery with their mothers. When will that be? While the exact timing of discharge depends on your medical condition, laws mandate that health insurance companies pay for a minimum hospital stay of 48 hours after a vaginal delivery and 96 hours after a cesarean. Says Amy Maly, mother of identical twin girls, "We were extremely grateful that both our babies were able to be discharged from the hospital with me two days after they were born. We had been working toward that goal throughout the pregnancy and felt so fortunate that all had gone well. It was a wonderful homecoming."

If you too are taking your multiples home shortly after their birth, you can skip the rest of this chapter. But if one or more of your babies needs special care, you'll want to read on to learn how to navigate through the neonatal intensive care unit. This truly will help you meet the challenges that lie ahead, as one reader of the first edition of this book explains: "The information [in this chapter] prepared me to handle the interventions that were necessary; gave me enough knowledge to ask the right questions; and helped me to accept without shock and fear the special needs of my newborns in the NICU. If it weren't for this book, I would have been a basket case!"

What's What and Who's Who in the NICU

Even when born with a good birthweight and at a favorable gestational age, supertwins generally do stay in the NICU for a few days, just for observation. If you're expecting triplets or quadruplets, it's prudent to prepare yourself emotionally for this eventuality.

"The books I read while pregnant seemed to assume that multiple-birth babies would have to spend time in the NICU, yet I was in total denial about that. I planned to bring all my babies home from the hospital with me—but that's not how it ended up," says Ginny Seyler, mother of triplets. "In retrospect, I think the best approach is to maintain a positive and hopeful attitude during your pregnancy, but to keep your mind open to the possibility that some NICU time may be required. That way, if it happens, it won't be quite so much of a shock."

If your multiples are born prematurely or have other medical problems, they are stabilized in the delivery room and then transferred in a portable incubator to the NICU, where medical care continues. Within the first few hours after birth, each baby receives a full physical examination. Samples of urine and stool are collected for analysis. Blood samples are drawn to determine each infant's blood type and Rh group, and to obtain data on levels of oxygen, carbon dioxide, glucose, and other essential factors. All of this information is used to evaluate the condition of your babies, and to plan for their care.

DR. LUKE: Some preemies need to stay in the NICU for just a few days, others for a few weeks, and others much longer. Regardless of whether they are singletons, twins, triplets, or quads, premature babies are just that—premature—which means they may not be ready to face the challenges of life outside the womb. In order to do so, they must receive a lot of intensive and specialized care.

This can leave parents feeling powerless, alone, and afraid. You may even feel reluctant to continue reading this chapter. Please understand, we are not sharing this information in order to frighten you. On the contrary, knowing the basics about the NICU will help you have a more confident and capable voice in your babies' care. To start, familiarize yourself with the following descriptions of the NICU equipment and personnel, and how each contributes to the care of your multiples.

COMMON NICU EQUIPMENT
Body Temperature Equipment

A premature infant cannot regulate her body temperature very well, so in the NICU she is placed under an open radiant warmer that provides the heat she needs while also allowing doctors and nurses easy access should she require immediate assistance. Once stabilized, a preemie may be placed inside an incubator or isolette, which can be opened from the front or accessed via portholes. A temperature probe taped to the baby's skin provides feedback to the thermostat, which in turn controls heat output to provide a constant level of warmth.

Premature babies typically spend their first days or weeks of life alone in their isolettes. But a new double incubator, with enough room and temperature monitors for two, is now being tested. Early data indicate that twins who are allowed to snuggle and soothe each other in the NICU may gain weight faster and head home earlier.

Oxygen, Breathing, and Heart Rate Monitors

Infants at risk for apnea are placed on a cardiorespiratory monitor that monitors their heart and breathing rates. In addition, they may be put on a pulse oximeter, which measures the amount of oxygen in the blood via a monitor attached to the hand or foot. These machines have built-in alarms that sound when the heart rate, breathing rate, or level of oxygen falls below specified levels. The alarms are designed to buzz when these levels are still well within the safe range, so that the baby can be stabilized before a serious situation develops.

A transcutaneous monitor is another method of measuring the amount of oxygen and carbon dioxide in the bloodstream. It is placed on the baby's skin, and oxygen diffuses from the capillaries to the probe, resulting in a numerical value that is electronically calculated and displayed. This monitor allows the health care team to adjust respirator settings and oxygen levels without needing to draw blood as frequently.

Blood Pressure Monitor

Just as your blood pressure is taken by inflating a cuff around your arm, an infant's blood pressure can be measured the same way. The monitor automatically inflates at preset intervals and displays the blood pressure reading. Blood pressure can also be read via an umbilical arterial line.

Umbilical Lines

Each baby's umbilical cord contains two arteries and one vein. Normally the doctor ties off these blood vessels at birth. But when an infant is born prematurely, the doctor may instead thread the arteries with an umbilical arterial catheter. This can then be used to draw blood samples, give fluids and medications, and measure blood pressure.

Respiratory Equipment

Preemies often need oxygen in higher concentrations than the 21 percent level available in room air. Supplemental oxygen can be given in several ways. For a baby who has no difficulty breathing, oxygen may be given inside an oxyhood (a plastic box or hood placed over the baby's head) or a clear tent. Oxygen can also be delivered directly into the incubator or isolette, or via small nasal tubing.

When additional assistance is needed, oxygen may be delivered via continuous positive airway pressure, or CPAP (pronounced "see-pap"). A machine provides a steady supply of air and oxygen under pressure, thereby keeping the lungs from collapsing and reducing the amount of effort required to draw a breath. CPAP can be delivered via a mask that fits over the nose. If a baby has been intubated—meaning a tube has been threaded down the trachea, or windpipe, and into the lungs—CPAP can be used to deliver supplemental oxygen directly into the lungs. For a preemie unable to breathe on her own, a ventilator or respirator is used to deliver a controlled mixture of air and oxygen, under pressure, at a regulated number of breaths per minute.

Feeding Methods

Many babies born before 34 weeks' gestation cannot suck effectively. These preemies are fed by gavage, a method in which a thin flexible tube called a nasogastric tube is inserted through the nose or mouth and threaded into the stomach. A vial of formula or breast milk is attached to the end of the tube, and gravity causes the milk to flow down into the baby's stomach. Babies fed this way are carefully monitored for distention of the abdomen, spitting up, and the amount of milk remaining in the stomach (called residuals) before the next feeding is given.

If your preemies cannot yet begin gavage feedings, they may be fed intravenously with a special formula containing all essential nutrients. This is known as parenteral nutrition or hyperalimentation. A baby may receive some of his feedings by gavage and others by parenteral nutrition.

The decision on when to start nipple feedings or "nippling"—whether at the breast or the bottle—is based on the baby's developmental maturity and health status. Factors that are considered include the ability to coordinate breathing and swallowing, breathing rate, and growth pattern.

THE MEDICAL STAFF

Neonatologist

A neonatologist is a physician who specializes in the development, care, and diseases of newborns. The field of neonatology was first officially recognized by the American Academy of Pediatrics in 1975. A neonatologist has completed medical school, three years of pediatric residency training, and three more years of specialized training in the care of high-risk newborns.

At a Level III hospital (the type of facility equipped to handle the sickest and smallest babies, as described in Chapter 2), the neonatologists take primary responsibility for the care of your premature multiples. They are usually present at the birth and lead the health care teams that resuscitate the babies in the delivery room, if necessary. Once your multiples are transferred to the NICU, the neonatologists direct the treatment of any medical problems, adjust feedings, and coordinate on a daily basis the efforts of all other health care professionals involved with your babies.

Pediatrician

The pediatrician specializes in the development, care, and diseases of children after completing medical school and at least a three-year residency training program in pediatrics. If a pregnancy lasts a minimum of 35 weeks, and if the babies weigh at least 5 pounds at birth, it is generally a pediatrician who handles the care of the infants, regardless of the level of the hospital. When babies are premature and/or of low birthweight, however, the pediatrician plays a secondary role during their NICU stay. The neonatologists should keep your pediatrician informed of any developments so that once the babies come home from the hospital, your pediatrician is prepared to take charge of their care.

Pediatric Neurologist

Also a pediatrician, this doctor has advanced training and experience in the diagnosis and treatment of diseases of the nervous system as they pertain to infants and children. He or she may be called in as a consultant when a baby has a sleeping or feeding problem, a metabolic disorder, poor muscle tone, partial paralysis, seizures, a breathing disorder, or a brain hemorrhage. The neurologist assesses the infant's motor strength, body and extremity movement, reflexes, and coordination of sucking and swallowing, and advises on the appropriate treatment.

Pediatric Ophthalmologist

An eye specialist, this physician has undergone advanced training in the diagnosis and treatment of vision disorders in infants and children. Your babies may have several eye exams by a pediatric ophthalmologist while in the NICU, particularly if they are hospitalized for an extended period of time. Because as many as one-third of preemies (particularly those with a birthweight of less than 2 pounds) develop vision problems, these eye examinations are extremely important. Your babies will probably have follow-up visits with this specialist after they are discharged from the hospital.

Radiologist

The radiologist administers and interprets the radiographic (X-ray) and ultrasonographic tests used to diagnose various medical conditions. Some of these procedures are performed routinely to detect any problems so that treatment can begin as early as possible. For example, an ultrasound of the brain is typically performed on all babies born before 34 weeks' gestation to check for brain hemorrhages. An ultrasonogram is also one of the first tests ordered if a physical problem is suspected, since it is noninvasive and does not involve the use of radiation.

Interns and Residents

Medical school graduates who are enrolled in a residency program are called residents, except during the first year of their program, when they are called interns. The requirements, duration, and responsibilities of each type of residency program vary, depending on the specialty. The majority of residents working in the NICU are doing a pediatric residency, but you may also encounter residents from obstetrics, family practice, surgery, or internal medicine. Since they perform many of the procedures in the NICU, these are the doctors you are likely to see most often.

THE NURSING STAFF

Neonatal Nurses

Most neonatal nurses are registered nurses (RNs) with intensive care experience and special training in the care of preemies and other newborns with medical problems. Typically one nurse per shift is assigned as the primary care provider for a particular patient until discharge, handling about 90 percent of the care for that baby. The neonatal nurses are the health professionals with whom NICU parents interact most often, and from whom you can learn the special parenting skills you need to care for your babies with confidence.

Certified Registered Nurses

RNs who have passed national specialty examinations in NICU nursing, critical care nursing, or mother-baby nursing are known as certified registered nurses. This level of training is required in some NICUs; in other cases, nurses opt to take these challenging exams from a personal sense of commitment to their specialty.

Nurse Practitioners

Nurse practitioners are registered nurses who have completed advanced education and training. Their ranks include neonatal nurse practitioners (NNPs), pediatric nurse practitioners (PNPs), and advanced registered nurse practitioners (ARNPs). Nurse practitioners work under the direction of a neonatologist and can provide some of the more advanced aspects of your babies' care.

Clinical Nurse Specialist

An RN with a master's degree, the clinical nurse specialist is a resource person for the nursing staff. He or she provides staff education, conducts nursing research, develops programs, and directs patient care.

Case Manager

Typically a case manager is a nurse who works with the NICU health care team to coordinate care, ensuring that everything necessary is completed to prepare for discharge.

ADDITIONAL HEALTH CARE TEAM MEMBERS

Physical Therapist/Occupational Therapist

The PT or OT works with premature babies who need help with their neuromuscular development, performing special exercises and other therapies. Depending on your babies' long-term health status, a PT or OT may be very involved in their follow-up developmental care.

Developmental Specialist

Usually a nurse, physical therapist, or occupational therapist with advanced training and expertise in infant development, the developmental specialist evaluates some or all of the infants in the NICU. He or she can offer specific suggestions to parents, such as how to improve feedings and how to pick up on the babies' behavioral cues.

Audiologist

This medical professional is trained to detect, diagnose, and treat patients with impaired hearing. An audiologist may be called in as a consultant if any of your babies develop certain complications that could affect hearing. Your multiples are also likely to see an audiologist as part of their follow-up examinations after they are discharged from the NICU.

Neonatal Dietitian

A dietitian with special training in the nutritional needs of newborns, this person helps to formulate diets tailored to the changing needs of your babies, based on each one's medical condition, laboratory test results, and rate of growth.

Respiratory Therapist

Trained to assemble, calibrate, and monitor the respiratory equipment used in the NICU, this therapist sets up the equipment, changes the tubing daily, and monitors the air and oxygen flow-through.

Pharmacist

The hospital pharmacist works closely with the neonatologist and other members of the health care team to provide whatever medications each of your babies may need, in the appropriate form and dosage.

Technicians

These health care team members perform behind-the-scenes tests such as X-rays, ultrasounds, and blood and urine analyses to diagnose and monitor problems. Technicians provide important data to guide doctors' decisions about patient care.

PARENT SUPPORT STAFF

Social Worker

The social worker's role is to provide information, counseling, and emotional support to NICU parents and families. She or he can help you deal with any personal, medical, or financial problems related to your pregnancy and your babies' birth and acts as a liaison between you and the health care team.

Lactation Consultant

Typically a nurse with expertise in breast-feeding, the lactation consultant can arrange for you to rent or buy a breast pump and instruct you in its use and in how to safely store and transport your expressed milk to provide nourishment for your hospitalized babies. She also helps you solve any nursing problems that may arise and offers encouragement over the course of your multiples' hospital stay.

Medical Complications of Prematurity

In general, the shorter a pregnancy, the more severe the newborn babies' health problems are likely to be. Gestational age at birth doesn't tell the whole story, however. In fact, it is not uncommon among multiples for one baby's health status to be significantly worse than that of his wombmates.

Triplet mom Ginny Seyler explains, "Heather and Brian had no serious problems at all. They were 'feeders and growers,' which meant they were basically fine but needed to get bigger and stronger. But Dillon didn't do as well as the other two babies, primarily because his lungs were underdeveloped. He was on a respirator for a day and needed several transfusions. He was just a very fragile little being for a long time."

Below is a brief discussion of the medical problems that are most common among premature and/or low-birthweight babies:

JAUNDICE

Jaundice is caused by the buildup of bilirubin, a greenish-yellow pigment formed during the normal breakdown of red blood cells. The liver removes bilirubin from the bloodstream, and during pregnancy, the placenta and the mother's liver removed bilirubin from the fetus. During the transition period immediately after birth, however, until the baby's own liver takes over, bilirubin may build up in the blood. This causes the skin to take on a yellowish tinge, a condition called physiologic jaundice.

Nearly half of all full-term newborns and 80 percent or more of premature infants develop physiologic jaundice. Bilirubin levels usually peak within the first week, then fall to minimal levels in the second week. With appropriate feedings, ample water, and exposure to sunshine, mild physiologic jaundice usually does not require any special treatment.

An infant with bilirubin levels that are higher than normal, or whose levels are rising faster than normal, has a condition known as hyperbilirubinemia, which can be toxic to the baby's developing nervous system. In severe cases, a blood transfusion may be required. But usually hyperbilirubinemia can be successfully treated with phototherapy: the use of light waves to break down bilirubin into components that the baby can eliminate in the urine. A baby receiving phototherapy is undressed to expose as much skin surface as possible, then placed for a set period of time under a bank of lights called bili-lights. During this time, the baby's eyes are covered with protective pads or soft goggles. Because babies who receive phototherapy often have more frequent and looser bowel movements, additional fluids are given.

BODY TEMPERATURE PROBLEMS

Body heat is generated primarily by shivering, something newborns cannot do. Instead, babies have a special type of heat-generating body fat called brown fat, which is located around the shoulders and base of the neck and over the heart and kidneys. The inadequate stores of brown fat in premature infants, particularly those born before 30 weeks' gestation, are quickly used up. At that point, preemies must produce heat metabolically. This siphons off their supplies of oxygen and glucose, which in turn leads to weight loss, low blood sugar, and breathing difficulties.

Maintaining body temperature is a vital component of newborn care from the moment of birth and throughout the hospital stay. That's why temperature monitors are used along with radiant warmers and temperature-controlled incubators or isolettes. Whenever a premature baby is taken out of the isolette, he is wrapped in blankets and wears a stocking cap to prevent heat loss from the head.

HEART PROBLEMS

Before birth, a baby's blood flows through the ductus arteriosus, a short vessel connecting the pulmonary artery to the aorta. At the time of delivery, when the umbilical cord is cut, blood flows through the baby's lungs to receive oxygen. This causes a pressure change in the pulmonary artery as the lungs expand and the ductus arteriosus closes to prevent the mixing of oxygenated and nonoxygenated blood.

When an infant is born prematurely, however, the fetal connection between the aorta and the pulmonary artery may not close properly. This condition, called patent ductus arteriosus (PDA), is the most common heart problem associated with prematurity. The diagnosis of PDA is made by the neonatologist, often in conjunction with a pediatric cardiologist. Treatment may include increasing the amount of supplemental oxygen the baby is receiving, administering medications, or surgically closing the ductus.

PDA is also a factor in the breathing problems of prematurity.

BREATHING PROBLEMS

Throughout pregnancy, an unborn baby receives oxygen through the placenta as blood bypasses the fetal lungs and instead flows through the ductus arteriosus. During labor, uterine contractions squeeze a baby's chest, clearing fluid from the lungs as he passes through the birth canal. At the moment of birth, physical and chemical signals trigger the intake of the baby's first breath, filling his lungs with air. With each additional breath, some of the air remains in the lungs to keep them partially open. The lungs of a healthy full-term infant contain a fatty substance called surfactant that keeps the lungs' moist air sacs from collapsing. With the lungs thus partially expanded, breathing becomes easier with each subsequent breath.

A premature newborn, though, lacks sufficient surfactant to keep the lungs open. Pressure then forces blood back through the ductus arteriosus, maintaining the fetal circulation. When this occurs, nonoxygenated blood circulates throughout the body, and the baby becomes oxygen-deprived. Without adequate surfactant, each breath is as difficult as the first, because with each inhalation the baby must completely fill his lungs. His breathing becomes rapid and labored, his chest retracts (sucks in deeply), and he grunts as he tries to close off the back of his throat to prevent air from leaving the lungs. With each breath, additional lung tissue collapses, less oxygen enters the bloodstream, and breathing becomes progressively more difficult.

This is known as respiratory distress syndrome (RDS)—perhaps the most common complication of prematurity. As the baby's condition worsens, breathing becomes irregular and there may be periods of apnea, when breathing stops completely. Inadequate oxygen supply to the lungs further aggravates the situation, slowing down the production of new surfactant and hastening the destruction of lung tissue.

Artificial surfactant is now used to combat this problem. Made from the lungs of pigs or cows or synthetically manufactured, it is placed directly into the lungs of a premature infant immediately after delivery, via an endotracheal tube. The artificial surfactant drains into the baby's alveoli, coating them and keeping them from collapsing. Although artificial surfactant does not prevent RDS, it does decrease the severity of this complication.

Over time, the baby's lungs begin to produce surfactant naturally. Until that occurs, the premature baby needs respiratory therapy. For this, various levels of oxygen and air can be delivered through an oxyhood, face mask, nasal tubing, or endotracheal tube inserted through the mouth and into the trachea (as discussed in the section on respiratory equipment).

Although respiratory therapy can get a premature baby past the critical early period of RDS, it can also cause some damage to the delicate lung tissue, a complication called bronchopulmonary dysplasia (BPD) or chronic lung disease (CLD). The damaged tissue forms scars that further impair air exchange. Until the lungs can heal and grow sufficiently, the baby remains dependent on respiratory therapy.

Infants who have had BPD are also more susceptible to colds, pneumonia, and other respiratory illnesses. The good news is that most children born prematurely outgrow their respiratory problems by school age.

NEUROLOGIC PROBLEMS
The nervous system of the premature baby is still developing and thus is vulnerable to conditions outside the womb. Changes in pressure during a vaginal delivery, fluctuations in blood sugar levels and oxygen levels, hyperbilirubinemia, and the presence of infection can all cause some degree of brain injury.

The fragile blood vessels in a preemie's brain may rupture and bleed, an event known as intraventricular hemorrhage (IVH). This happens most commonly within the first week after birth. The smaller and more premature a baby is, the greater his chances of a hemorrhage. At highest risk are those born weighing less than 1,500 grams (about 3 lb., 5 oz.). IVH is categorized by four grades of severity:

- *Grade I:* The mildest hemorrhage, this involves a small amount of blood in the lining of the ventricle (one of the four hollow spaces in the brain).
- *Grade II:* A small amount of blood enters the ventricles but does not cause them to enlarge.
- *Grade III:* A greater amount of blood enters the brain ventricles, causing them to enlarge temporarily and blocking the flow of spinal fluid into and out of the ventricles.
- *Grade IV:* The most severe type of hemorrhage, this involves bleeding into the brain tissue itself.

Symptoms of IVH include seizures, an enlarged head, breathing problems, vomiting, irritability, and an abnormal neurological exam. Ultrasound is typically used to diagnose IVH, although a spinal tap to detect blood in the spinal fluid may also be necessary. Once diagnosed, a hemorrhage is closely monitored. Treatment may include medication to decrease the size of the enlarged ventricle and to inhibit production of cerebrospinal fluid, thereby decreasing pressure on the brain. In severe cases, surgery is required.

IVH can lead to developmental disabilities or delays, seizure disorders, and vision or hearing loss. While the long-term consequences depend on a variety of factors, including the severity of the hemorrhage, most babies do not experience major handicaps.

VISION PROBLEMS

The most common eye problem associated with preterm birth is called retinopathy of prematurity (ROP), sometimes known as retrolental fibroplasia. It occurs when the blood vessels of the retina grow abnormally, triggering bleeding into the eye structure and causing scar tissue to form. This scar tissue may then block the lens of the eye, causing vision loss. It also may shrink, thereby tearing or detaching the retina.

Doctors are not sure exactly what causes ROP. The condition occurs most often among very small premature babies who are born weighing less than 1,000 grams (about 2 lb., 3 oz.), and among those born prior to 28 weeks' gestation. ROP is classified by stages, with Stage 1 being the mildest and Stage 5 being the most severe.

Fortunately, most cases of ROP are relatively mild and clear up without treatment. However, parents should be aware that premature babies, especially those who had ROP, are at a greater risk for developing strabismus (crossed eyes) and amblyopia (lazy eye) during early childhood. For this reason, annual eye exams are very important.

For more severe cases of ROP, treatment options include cryotherapy to freeze the abnormal blood vessels, which then shrink to allow new blood vessels to grow normally. Some cases may require surgery to reattach the retina. To minimize the risk of permanent, extensive loss of vision, early treatment is the best option.

Hearing Problems

Various medical conditions can contribute to hearing loss among newborns. These include intraventricular hemorrhage, severe jaundice, bacterial meningitis, and cranial or facial abnormalities. If hearing loss is detected, intervention should begin in infancy in order to minimize impairment of speech and language development.

Infections

Because preemies have immature immune systems, they are more prone to developing various infections. These include sepsis (bacteria in the bloodstream), pneumonia (infection in the lungs), and meningitis (infection of the spinal cord and layers around the brain).

Some infections are contracted at birth as the baby passes through the birth canal. Others are the result of premature rupture of the membranes prior to delivery, when the mother has had symptoms of infection such as a high fever and tenderness of the kidneys or uterus. These babies may be immediately treated with antibiotics, even before laboratory results confirm the diagnosis.

An infection picked up from the hospital environment is termed a nosocomial infection. Even though hospital personnel and visitors scrub hands and put on hospital gowns and masks before touching a patient, no one is germ-free. And even though hospital equipment is sterilized, it is not possible to eliminate all bacteria in the environment. Infectious agents can enter a preemie's body through a variety of sites, including a surgical incision, an intravenous line, a catheter, or a respirator. The smaller and more premature the baby, and the more medical and surgical intervention she requires, the greater her risk of infection.

Feeding Problems

Like the other organ systems of the premature baby, the digestive system is not developed enough to handle its role in life outside the womb—digesting food. Circulation to the digestive tract may be lower than normal because the baby's body is diverting blood to the more essential organs (the brain, lungs, heart, and kidneys). If anything were to be given by mouth to a very premature or very sick infant, it would be poorly digested and would trigger additional problems. For instance, oral feedings could increase the risk of necrotizing enterocolitis (NEC), in which poor circulation and infection contribute to the death of parts of the digestive tract.

Preemies also may be unable to suck effectively because this reflex generally does not develop until around the 34th week of pregnancy. The effort involved in sucking can, for a preemie, use up more calories than the feeding provides.

For these reasons, many premature babies are initially nourished intravenously. The very first feedings consist of sterile sugar water, given for calories and fluids. The amount given is carefully calculated based on how much the baby is urinating and on the concentration of the urine. Gradually other nutrients are added to the intravenous formula—sodium, potassium, calcium, protein, fat, vitamins—each of which has a vital role in growth and development. In fact, a premature infant's need for various nutrients exceeds that of his full-term nursery mates because of his lower nutrient stores, more rapid growth, and the stress of any complications he may be experiencing. To achieve just the right combination of nutrients, feedings are adjusted daily based on the baby's clinical symptoms and blood levels.

As the premature baby develops, he makes a transition from intravenous to gavage feedings—receiving nourishment via a small, flexible tube inserted through the nose or mouth and into the stomach. First gavage feedings consist of sugar water, then progress to more enriched formulas.

Breast milk can be given by gavage, and in some NICUs, as many as 95 percent of babies are fed breast milk. Breast milk may be fortified with additional calcium, or it may be concentrated through a process called lacto-engineering, which increases the amount of fat and decreases the amount of fluid. The purpose is to promote maximum growth for the baby.

Before a premature infant can be breast-fed or bottle-fed, he must be able to suck, swallow, and breathe—all in the right sequence—without choking, turning blue, or showing a drop in heart rate. He also must be gaining weight and be medically stable. The transition from gavage feeding to "nippling" may be done gradually, with the number of nipple feedings increasing each day until gavage is no longer needed at all. If all goes well, this may be achieved around the time the preemie reaches what would have been the 35th week of pregnancy.

Parenting Your Hospitalized Babies

TAMARA: "Push!" my doctor commanded. But I didn't want to push. I didn't want my twins to be born, not yet. "It's too soon, they're too little," I cried to my husband, Bill.

There was no stopping the labor. Nine weeks premature, my 3-pound son announced his arrival in the world with a barely audible cry. The nurse placed him on my abdomen, but I, shocked by the sight of this minuscule infant, could not react. Three minutes later, my 2-pound daughter was born, blue and still and unable to breathe. "Intubate!" I heard someone command sharply.

As soon as they were stabilized, my babies were rushed by ambulance to a NICU miles away. I did not see them again for two days, until I was discharged.

Those 48 hours were agony. Foremost was fear—that both babies would die, that one would die, most likely my daughter, so small and dependent on a respirator. I had heard that some parents are too afraid to bond with a baby whose survival is uncertain, and I wondered if that coldness born of terror would seize me. Or what if the twins were physically or mentally impaired, as preemies sometimes are? Was I selfless enough to care for disabled children?

Self-centered as it sounds, I also felt cheated. Out of a third trimester filled with good wishes from friends and encouraging smiles from strangers. Out of a labor marked by excited anticipation. Out of the ecstasy a woman feels when first she holds her Apgar-perfect newborn in her arms. I had lost all that, and gained . . . what? A jumbled memory of two tiny infants I had scarcely seen and never held. A few precious Polaroid pictures my husband had hastily snapped. A smudged set of footprints a kind-hearted nurse had made on a scrap of paper.

Discharged at last, I was in a near-panic of impatience as Bill drove me straight to the other hospital to visit my babies. Stepping into the NICU, I was instantly overwhelmed by the sounds and sights: the buzzing alarms, the bustling nurses, the bright lights, and in every isolette, an unbelievably tiny baby.

Bill guided me toward one particular incubator and lifted the lid. "Samantha, Mommy's here," I whispered in a voice choked with tears. My miniature daughter turned her head, opened her eyes—and captured my heart. In an instant, I knew, no matter how fleeting our future together, I would treasure this child and her twin brother forever.

But the ordeal was far from over. Samantha came off the respirator, relapsed, and went back on. James had a small brain hemorrhage. Samantha's jaundice worsened. James's eyesight was threatened by retinopathy of prematurity. My babies' hold on life and health seemed perilously precarious.

Precarious too was my sense of myself as a mother. Surely I was less important to my children than were the doctors and nurses who guarded their lives. I couldn't breast-feed them, since they were too weak to suck. I couldn't hold them for long, since their body temperature was unstable outside the isolettes. Through the portholes, I tentatively stroked their bodies, fearful of dislodging the many tubes and wires. It was not what I had ever imagined motherhood to be.

Gradually, though, I adapted to this peculiar form of parenting. I learned to swaddle a baby without disturbing the cardiorespiratory monitor or temperature probe. I learned to hold the vial of the gavage tube high so that no air bubbles formed. In the NICU all day, every day, I rocked James for hours, then put him back in his isolette and walked to the next room to sing to Samantha. But each night in bed, I was tormented by the fear that the twins might never get well and come home, never sleep in their new cribs, never go to school, never become the nice normal children I had dreamed they would be.

The NICU staff knew not to promise parents a happy ending. But after two weeks, they were cautiously optimistic. Samantha was breathing well; James's IVH had cleared without intervention, and his eyes seemed better. Both babies, it appeared, had escaped the most devastating complications of prematurity. With encouragement from the nurses, I bought several preemie-size terrycloth suits. Seeing my twins dressed for the first time in something other than hospital-issue undershirts, the fear in my heart was at last outweighed by joyous hope.

A few weeks later, Bill and I brought our babies home.

DR. LUKE: Nothing can quite prepare a person for the emotional upheaval of being a NICU mom or dad, but it helps to know that you are not alone. It's also encouraging to realize that there is much you can do to take an active role in your babies' care during their hospital stay.

To start, vow that every time you visit the NICU, you will safeguard your multiples by following all recommended procedures for preventing infection. Before entering the unit, scrub your hands and forearms thoroughly for several minutes and put a sterile gown over your street clothes. Also, don't try to bend the rules about visitors. Many NICUs grant access only to parents and perhaps grandparents. Visits by the babies' older siblings may be permitted provided that the children wear surgical masks and gowns, though policies vary greatly. Most important, remember that no one who has been exposed to or is experiencing an infectious disease should ever enter the NICU—not even the parents—until given a clean bill of health.

There's much more you can do as well. Some of our Multiples Clinic patients and other mothers and fathers of twins and supertwins have described their NICU experiences. Their suggestions and insights can help you *feel* better—and can even help your babies *get* better.

How you may feel: *"I'm so lonely. I haven't been able to see my babies since they were born, and I miss them terribly."*

Of course you are lonely! Your babies have been with you every moment for many months, and now there is a huge void in your heart. If you are in the same hospital as your multiples, ask politely but firmly to see them as soon as possible. Amid all the activity of a busy labor and delivery unit, the staff may have forgotten to arrange this. "I didn't get to see my twins for 11 hours after delivery because they had been whisked away to the NICU. I knew that I had given birth, but it almost seemed as if I hadn't, since there was no tangible evidence of my babies' existence," says Marcy Bugajski, mother of fraternal twin boys. "Finally, long after midnight, a nurse came into my room and asked if I had held my babies yet. When I told her I didn't even have a picture of them, she was appalled. Immediately she helped me into a wheelchair and wheeled me down to the NICU."

If your multiples require major interventions such as a respirator, you may feel nervous about seeing them for the first time. Try not to delay. The longer you wait, the more time you have to imagine that your worst fantasies are true. Seeing your babies, on the other hand, gives you a chance to note all their positive features—this one's strength and alertness, that one's cowlick just like Grandpa's. Marcy adds, "I cried when I first saw my babies. They seemed so small, and they had these big tubes running down their throats from the ventilators. Yet at the same time, I was happy because they were alive. I couldn't believe that Dave and I had actually produced such beautiful little beings."

Your multiples may have to be transported to another hospital if the one where you gave birth has no NICU, or if the NICU is filled to capacity or has an outbreak of infection. Should this occur, ask to be transferred yourself to the same hospital where they are going, so you can finish your postpartum recovery in close proximity to your babies.

If a transfer is not possible, stay in touch by phoning the NICU often for updates. Don't worry about "bothering" the staff—they welcome calls from parents. Send your husband to the NICU to visit the babies, and have him call you on a cellular phone to deliver a detailed, moment-by-moment description of what's going on with each baby. Make sure he gets some photos and footprints to bring back to you.

How you may feel: *"I can't bear the thought of going home from the hospital without my babies."*

Admittedly, this is a very painful experience. "Other couples were walking out of the hospital carrying carefully swaddled bundles, but I had to leave with empty arms. I felt like I was leaving a part of myself behind," says Marcy Bugajski.

There is a thin silver lining: Unlike most parents of newborns, you can get some uninterrupted sleep at night. Don't deny yourself this small advantage. Helen Armer, mother of triplets, explains, "My babies needed to stay in the hospital to be treated for jaundice. The nurses told me it was a blessing in disguise, and it turns out they were right. I was worn down physically from the pregnancy, and I really needed that week to recover while the babies were hospitalized. Emotionally it wasn't too bad because I knew they were not very sick."

Make it a policy to visit the NICU often. You'll naturally want to be with your multiples as much as possible—and they'll benefit from your presence. In fact, studies show that premature infants who are touched or talked to daily experience more rapid weight gain and better brain development. "While my triplets were in the NICU, there wasn't any question about where I would be and what I would be doing. Every morning, I got up, went to the hospital, and stayed all day. I felt an urgent need to be there, helping to take care of them and following each baby's every little step forward or backward," Ginny Seyler says.

Of course, it's important to spend some time away from the NICU too. A nonstop bedside vigil is exhausting. Realize that if your babies were at home, you wouldn't be sitting next to their cribs day and night. You need to take a breather sometimes, so go out to dinner or see a movie. If you're worried that the hospital staff won't be able to reach you, carry a pager or cell phone.

How you may feel: *"I don't feel like a 'real' parent because I'm not the one taking care of my babies."*

Though your initial emotion may be one of powerlessness, you need to trust your ability to begin parenting. Learn to perform as many basic baby-care tasks as possible. Sure, those preemie diapers seem awfully small, but you can change them exactly as you would any diaper. The nurses are happy to have you help at bath time too.

Even before your babies are ready to "nipple" at the breast or bottle, you can participate in gavage feedings. Cradle one of your infants in one arm, and use the other hand to raise the vial of formula above the level of the baby's nose. "It was a sweet feeling to hold a baby who was getting formula through a nasogastric tube and to know that he was 'eating,'" says quad mom Anne Seifert.

Karen Danke, mother of fraternal twin boys, adds, "When your multiples are in the NICU, it's important to be very involved with their care. Not only does this make you feel more like a parent, it's good training for when the babies are discharged and you have to manage on your own. They're so tiny—Jacob weighed only 3 lb., 14 oz., when he came home, for example—that it's intimidating to take care of them unless you've been practicing under the watchful eye of the hospital staff."

Many NICUs place multiple-birth siblings in separate rooms to minimize the risk that a feeding or treatment intended for "Baby A Jones" will inadvertently be given to "Baby B Jones." Ask the nurse to arrange a few minutes of togetherness time for you, your husband, and all your babies. This simple pleasure can go a long way toward making you feel like "real" parents of multiples.

How you may feel: *"The doctors and nurses are much more important to my babies' well-being than I am."*

Karen Danke admits, "I was afraid the babies would think the doctors and nurses were their parents, instead of Chris and me. But that didn't happen. Right from day one, they definitely recognized our voices because they had been able to hear us during those last months of the pregnancy." Karen's right: Studies confirm that newborns recognize their mother's voice, and often their father's as well.

Recognize too that there are things you and you alone can do for your babies. Most important is to hold them. "At first, I was afraid to touch my twins for fear of hurting them. But the doctor assured me that a parent's loving touch was very therapeutic in a way no technology could provide," says Lydia Greenwood, mother of boy/girl twins. With the help of a nurse to manage the tubes and wires, sit back and try to relax. Make sure to keep your baby well swaddled, and do not remove her stocking cap for more than a moment or two. If an alarm sounds, don't lose your cool. "It was frightening at first when an alarm would go off while I was holding one of the quads," says Anne Seifert. "But pretty soon I got to know which button was which, and then I didn't panic anymore. I knew the nurse would come right over and reattach the loose electrode or fix whatever problem there was."

You may also be encouraged to practice a therapeutic-touch technique called kangaroo care, which involves holding a baby skin-to-skin against your chest. Studies show that this practice helps premature infants to regulate their breathing and body temperature and also promotes parent-infant bonding. Here's how it's done: The baby, dressed only in a diaper, is carefully brought up underneath Mom's or Dad's shirt to be snuggled against the parent's chest. Your body heat keeps the baby warm as you stroke his skin and whisper softly to him.

Anne Seifert explains, "By the end of the second week, I was able to begin kangaroo care. The staff put a little drape around the isolette so no one could see, and I opened my loose top and slipped the baby in against my chest. All of my quads really responded to that, opening their little eyes and nuzzling close. I loved it too." There are certain guidelines for this type of care. Typically a baby must be in stable health, require no more than 50 percent supplemental oxygen, and have no central lines or drainage tubes that could become dislodged. Ask your health care team if kangaroo care is an option for you and your multiples.

Another way in which you and only you can contribute to your babies' well-being is by providing them with the best possible source of nourishment—your breast milk. Preemies in particular can benefit from the protection against infection and the greater digestibility that mother's milk provides. Ginny Seyler says, "While my triplets were in the NICU, I pumped my breasts every four hours and gave it to the nurses, who fed it to the babies through nasogastric tubes. It was very gratifying for me to be able to make this important contribution to their care." (For full information on breast-feeding, see Chapter 10.)

How you may feel: *"I don't know what's going on with my babies because I can't understand what the doctors say."*

"Physicians sometimes tend to talk above the average person's level of understanding. This can be intimidating, so you just nod and go along with whatever they are saying, even if you don't have a clue what it means," says Benita Moreno, mother of fraternal twin boys. "I learned that it's important not to be afraid to interrupt the doctor and say, 'I don't understand what you mean. Please explain it again in simpler terms.'"

Of course, while it's fine to ask questions, you do need to accept that answers may not always be immediately forthcoming. Test results take time, diagnoses are not always clear-cut, no one can predict the future—and sometimes there simply are no answers. Your best bet is to write down your questions, identify each of your babies' health care teams, and then direct your queries to them. Refrain from interrogating every doctor who walks by, even those who are not involved in your babies' care, in the hope of getting "better" answers.

Develop a mutually respectful relationship with each of your multiples' primary care nurses. They can keep you up-to-date about feedings, sleep patterns, and response to treatments. Nurses are also skilled at translating the stream of technical terms you may be hearing from the neonatologists and other health care team members. Remember, the neonatal nurses are taking care of your children 24 hours a day. If you wake up in the middle of the night and want a status report, you can phone the NICU and talk to the nurse in charge of each of your babies. These women and men are extraordinarily devoted and skilled caretakers, accustomed to handling not only the needs of physically fragile newborns, but also the needs of emotionally fragile parents.

Familiarize yourself with the common NICU terminology presented in this chapter. You'll feel more confident once words such as gavage, supplemental oxygen, and phototherapy become an established part of your vocabulary. And because the NICU staff refer to their little patients' weight and size in grams and centimeters, you may want to keep at hand the conversion charts shown in Tables 9.2, 9.3, 9.4, and 9.5. With practice, you will soon be adept at thinking in metric terms rather than in pounds, ounces, and inches.

Conversion of Grams to Pounds and Ounces

	0 g	100 g	200 g	300 g	400 g	500 g	600 g	700 g	800 g	900 g
0 kg	0	3.5 oz.	7.0 oz.	10.6 oz.	14.1 oz.	1 lb., 1.6 oz.	1 lb., 5.2 oz.	1 lb., 8 oz.	1 lb., 12 oz.	2 lb.
1 kg	2 lb., 3.3 oz.	2 lb., 6.8 oz.	2 lb., 10.3 oz.	2 lb., 13.9 oz.	3 lb., 1.4 oz.	3 lb., 5 oz.	3 lb., 8.4 oz.	3 lb., 12 oz.	3 lb., 15.5 oz.	4 lb., 3 oz.
2 kg	4 lb., 6.5 oz.	4 lb., 10 oz.	4 lb., 13.6 oz.	5 lb., 1.1 oz.	5 lb., 4.7 oz.	5 lb., 8.2 oz.	5 lb., 11.7 oz.	5 lb., 15.2 oz.	6 lb., 2.8 oz.	6 lb., 6.3 oz.
3 kg	6 lb., 9.8 oz.	6 lb., 13.3 oz.	7 lb., 0.9 oz.	7 lb., 4.4 oz.	7 lb., 8 oz.	7 lb., 11.4 oz.	7 lb., 15 oz.	8 lb., 2.5 oz.	8 lb., 6 oz.	8 lb., 9.6 oz.
4 kg	8 lb., 13 oz.	9 lb., 0.6 oz.	9 lb., 4.2 oz.	9 lb., 7.7 oz.	9 lb., 11.2 oz.	9 lb., 15 oz.	10 lb., 2.3 oz.	10 lb., 5.8 oz.	10 lb., 9.3 oz.	10 lb., 12.8 oz.

Table 9.2

Conversion of Pounds and Ounces to Grams

Lb.	Oz. 0	1	2	3	4	5	6	7	8	9	10	11	12	13	14	15
1	454	482	510	538	568	596	624	653	681	709	737	765	795	823	851	880
2	908	936	966	994	1,022	1,050	1,078	1,107	1,135	1,163	1,191	1,219	1,249	1,277	1,305	1,334
3	1,362	1,390	1,418	1,446	1,476	1,504	1,533	1,561	1,589	1,617	1,645	1,673	1,703	1,731	1,759	1,786
4	1,814	1,843	1,871	1,900	1,928	1,956	1,984	2,013	2,041	2,070	2,098	2,126	2,155	2,183	2,211	2,240
5	2,268	2,296	2,325	2,353	2,381	2,410	2,438	2,466	2,495	2,523	2,551	2,580	2,608	2,637	2,665	2,693
6	2,722	2,750	2,778	2,807	2,835	2,863	2,892	2,920	2,948	2,977	3,005	3,033	3,062	3,090	3,118	3,147
7	3,175	3,203	3,232	3,260	3,289	3,317	3,345	3,374	3,402	3,430	3,459	3,487	3,515	3,544	3,572	3,600
8	3,629	3,657	3,685	3,714	3,742	3,770	3,799	3,827	3,856	3,884	3,912	3,941	3,969	3,997	4,026	4,054
9	4,082	4,111	4,139	4,167	4,196	4,224	4,252	4,281	4,309	4,337	4,366	4,394	4,423	4,451	4,479	4,508
10	4,536	4,564	4,593	4,621	4,649	4,678	4,706	4,734	4,763	4,791	4,819	4,848	4,876	4,904	4,933	4,961

Table 9.3

Conversion of Centimeters to Inches

Centimeters	Inches	Centimeters	Inches
1	0.39	45	17.72
2	0.79	50	19.69
3	1.18	55	21.65
4	1.57	60	23.62
5	1.97	65	25.59
10	3.94	70	27.56
15	5.91	75	29.53
20	7.87	80	31.50
25	9.84	85	33.46
30	11.81	90	35.43
35	13.78	95	37.40
40	15.75	100	39.37

Table 9.4

Conversion of Inches to Centimeters

Inches	Centimeters	Inches	Centimeters
10	25.4	17.5	44.4
10.5	26.7	18	45.7
11	27.9	18.5	47.0
11.5	29.2	19	48.3
12	30.5	19.5	49.5
12.5	31.8	20	50.8
13	33	20.5	52.1
13.5	34.3	21	53.3
14	35.6	21.5	54.6
14.5	36.8	22	55.9
15	38.1	22.5	57.2
15.5	39.4	23	58.4
16	40.6	23.5	59.7
16.5	41.9	24	61
17	43.2	24.5	62.2

Inches	Centimeters	Inches	Centimeters
25	63.5	28	71.2
25.5	64.8	28.5	72.5
26	66.1	29	73.8
26.5	67.4	29.5	75.1
27	68.7	30	76.4
27.5	69.9	30.5	77.6

Table 9.5

How you may feel: *"The NICU is so institutional. I'm heartbroken that my babies must spend their first weeks there instead of in the lovely nursery at home."*

Even though your multiples are not yet ready for that beautiful bedroom you've prepared, you can make their current environment cozier. Ask the nurse for guidelines on what's okay to bring into the NICU. Most hospitals allow parents to decorate the outside of the isolettes with family photos or simple black-and-white drawings, for instance, provided there is sufficient open space to observe the baby. A small mobile hanging above the incubator is also a nice touch. If you want to place a toy inside the isolette, choose one that can be sterilized, such as a soft plastic plaything. Skip any furry or stuffed toys that may harbor bacteria.

To help your multiples look less like patients and more like the adorable little people they are, bring in some cute preemie clothing. Wardrobe items for the tiniest babies are available at Babies "R" Us, BabyGap, and JCPenney. You can also mail-order clothes through Preemie Store and More: 1682 Roxanna Lane, New Brighton, MN 55112. Telephone 800–676–8469; Web site www.preemiestore.com.

How you may feel: *"I am wracked with guilt over the outcome of my pregnancy. I must have done something horribly wrong, and now my poor babies are paying the price."*

Please stop beating yourself up. Chances are that you did everything in your power to give your babies the healthiest start in life, and it's not your fault if things didn't turn out ideally.

And even if there were actions you regret, it does your babies no good (and does you much harm) to mull over the entire pregnancy and berate yourself for every steak left unfinished and every extra stairway climbed.

"I felt terribly guilty after the boys were born at 34 weeks, because I blamed myself for their prematurity. I kept thinking, 'I should have listened to my doctor and quit work when she told me to. This is all my fault.' That feeling lasted for a long time," admits Benita Moreno. "But finally I realized that I had to let go of the guilt and move on. I had done the best I could, and some things were simply beyond my control."

How you may feel: *"My friends don't know whether to offer congratulations or condolences. I feel so alone, like no one understands what I'm going through."*

It's natural to feel isolated from family and friends who have never experienced the NICU firsthand. Particularly tough to take right now is the company of pals who have recently had healthy babies, because they are fretting about diaper rash and spit-up, while you are worrying about brain hemorrhages and collapsed lungs. "My advice is to ignore any insensitive comments," says Ginny Seyler. "People don't understand how much it hurts you to hear remarks like, 'Gosh, they are so tiny!'"

You want your own parents to visit the NICU with you, but you're afraid of how they'll react? You need to trust your instincts—but don't sell your folks short, either. "My in-laws are elderly, so I wasn't sure whether or not to encourage them when they asked if they were allowed in the NICU. It could be quite a shock for them to see a room full of tiny, sick babies," says Lydia Greenwood. "But when I voiced my concerns, my mother-in-law drew herself up and said, 'Of course we want to see our new grandchildren.' And they handled it beautifully, holding the twins without fretting about the many tubes and monitors. After their visit, I felt cheered."

The best moral support, though, probably comes from other mothers and fathers whose babies have graduated from the NICU. Many hospitals offer support groups where you can hook up with such parents. You can also contact your local Mothers of Multiples Club, which may provide a "big sister" service to link current NICU moms with those who've had similar experiences.

If, despite these measures, you continue to feel extremely isolated or depressed, it would be wise to consult a mental health professional who is experienced at dealing with these types of family issues.

How you may feel: *"I'm overwhelmed at the thought of having to care for disabled children."*

There is a common saying in the NICU—"Babies often take two steps forward and one step back"—so try not to get discouraged. Ginny Seyler suggests, "It's important to understand that hospitalized infants have their good days and their bad days. To stay sane, you have to take one day at a time and try to focus on their overall progress."

You may want to keep a daily log of each baby's weight, feedings, sleep patterns, and health status. When you feel dispirited, leaf back through its pages. You will probably see how far your babies have come since the first day they entered the NICU.

If your multiples do develop problems that have long-term consequences, remember that help is available. You will be referred to specialists who can provide appropriate treatment or assistance. The outlook for today's preemies is brighter than ever before.

How you may feel: *"I live with a constant sense of terror that one or more of my babies won't survive."*

Try to cultivate an attitude of cautious optimism. Your babies may surprise you. "Despite my fears, my 3½-pounder did much better than I expected, considering that he weighed 2 pounds less than his brother," says Marcy Bugajski. "The doctor said it was due to the fact that little Ben was used to fighting for everything *in utero*, because big Alex had always gotten the lion's share of the nourishment."

Hospital support groups and social workers can be immensely helpful in handling your fears, particularly if they can hook you up with NICU graduates and their parents. To see a robust toddler who once lay where your babies are now can provide a powerful surge of confidence.

How you may feel: *"But what if the worst does happen? How will we cope?"*

The loss of a baby is a terrible tragedy; the loss of two or more is undeniably harder to bear. However, outsiders do not always understand the terribly complex mix of conflicting emotions faced by parents who must grieve the death of one baby while celebrating the birth of the other (or others). Too often, sadness is compounded when family and friends are less sympathetic because the parents "still have one baby to love." A professional grief counselor experienced in working with parents of multiples may be able to provide more understanding. It can also be very helpful to connect with other parents who've experienced the loss of one or more of their multiples. Here are some contacts:

- Center for Loss in Multiple Birth (CLIMB). Support by and for parents and bereaved families; quarterly newsletter; relevant articles; samples of birth and memorial announcements. PO Box 91377, Anchorage, AK 99509. Telephone 907–222–5321; e-mail newsletter@climb-support.org; Web site www.climb-support.org.
- National Organization of Mothers of Twins Clubs (NOMOTC). Bereavement support coordinator corresponds with families. PO Box 438, Thompsons Station, TN 37179-0438. Telephone 615–595–0936 or 877–540–2200; e-mail info@nomotc.org; Web site www.nomotc.org.

- Triplet Connection. Networking information for bereaved higher-order multiple families. PO Box 99571, Stockton, CA 95209. Telephone 209–474–0885; e-mail janet@tripletconnection.org; Web site www.tripletconnection.org.
- Parents of Multiples Forever. Personal stories and memorial site; Web site www.erichad.com/pom/.
- Angels Forever. Parental support, on-line chats, links; Web site www.angels4ever.com; click on "Multiples Angels Network."
- Loss in Multiple Birth Outreach (LIMBO). Personal stories, on-line chats; Web site www.geocities.com/heartland/lake/5142/index.html.

Parents who've faced the loss of a multiple say that it is comforting to have photographs, a lock of hair, and footprints or handprints of the baby who died. Such mementos will also be important to the surviving child or children later in life, as they offer a means of connecting with their sibling.

It may help to find a meaningful way to honor a baby who was lost. Many hospitals arrange memorial services or candle-lighting ceremonies. Some parents hold a private gathering for close family and friends, and devise a personal tribute to the lost twin, such as asking participants to release one helium balloon into the sky while hanging on to a second balloon. Other parents prefer to plant a tree in memory of the baby, or to wear a ring engraved with the child's name. Writing about your feelings can help too.

For some parents, the greatest comfort comes from cherishing their own personal memories of their child, no matter how brief the life may have been. Karen Danke, who lost a set of boy/girl twins the year before giving birth to her fraternal twin boys, shares her experience: "In my first pregnancy, I went for an ultrasound at 20 weeks, and the doctor realized that one of the babies had died already. The following week, I went into labor and delivered the twins. My little girl, the doctors estimated, had died about a month earlier. Though my son was born alive, there was no way to save him. The hospital staff encouraged us to hold our son and take his picture. At first, we didn't want to, but later we were glad we did. We counted his tiny little fingers and toes, and we named him—Kenneth Peter. Later, the nurses gave us both babies' receiving blankets and preemie outfits. We will always cherish those little treasures."

DR. LUKE: The death of a child touches us like nothing else, and the memory of that brief life stays in our hearts forever. In some ways, we grieve longer over the loss of a baby because we are also grieving for all the hopes and dreams that were never realized, and all the experiences and achievements that can never be.

Yet children always teach us lessons about ourselves, and the lessons learned from the children who have been in our lives for the shortest of times can be uniquely poignant. We need to honor those children by keeping our hearts open and free from bitterness, so that their memory can remind us every day of just how precious life is.

When Can Your Babies Go Home?

Discharge day is what most NICU parents dream of, pray for, and work toward hardest. Yet it's not always easy to predict just when that day will come. Barring serious complications, parents are often told to expect that their preemies will be ready to face the world outside the hospital about the time they should have been facing the world outside the womb—in other words, close to their original due date. Many preemies, though, are ready to leave even sooner. In general, here's what each baby must achieve in order to be discharged:

- All medical problems have been resolved or are under control.
- The baby practices "demand feeding"—deciding for herself when and how much to eat, and doing so about every two to three hours.
- The infant has shown steady, progressive weight gain over a period of several days to a week.
- A minimum weight (typically about 4 pounds) has been reached.
- The baby can maintain body temperature in an open crib when covered only with a diaper, T-shirt, and blanket.
- There is good respiratory control, with no episodes of apnea.

In some cases, babies take a half-step toward home by being transferred out of the NICU and into what's called a special-care nursery or "low-maintenance room." This facility, while not equipped to handle the most serious neonatal needs, can provide a level of care more sophisticated than that of the typical nursery in a labor and delivery unit. Anne Seifert explains, "All four of our babies were in the NICU at the University of Michigan, which is a 90-minute drive from our house. After two weeks, though, they were strong enough to be transferred to the special-care nursery in a smaller hospital closer to home. That was much more convenient."

One increasingly common practice is to send home a baby who has a particular special need, but is otherwise ready for discharge, with equipment such as a respiratory support system or an apnea monitor. The infant is closely supervised by a visiting nurse or other health care professional, and parents are carefully instructed in the use of the equipment. Karen Danke says, "After 17 days in the NICU, Zachary came home from the hospital on supplemental oxygen, which he used during feedings. Without it, he didn't have the energy to eat enough, although other than that, he was fine."

Frequently one multiple may be discharged before his siblings, particularly if the babies had different birthweights or different health problems. "Heather came home after six weeks in the NICU, and Brian came home after seven weeks, but little Dillon was in the hospital for three months," Ginny Seyler recalls.

Work out the logistics so that you can continue to visit any babies that remain in the hospital. "Ed and I were concerned that we wouldn't be able to spend as much time visiting Holly after Alexander came home from the NICU," says Lydia Greenwood. "But soon we developed a system. Ed stopped to see her on his way to work each morning, while I stayed home all day with Alexander. Then Ed took care of our baby boy in the evening, while I went to the hospital to be with our daughter. That lasted for 11 days, until finally Holly came home too."

Though you may feel conflicted about leaving one or more babies behind, try to look on the bright side: You have the chance to get used to taking care of just one infant at a time before facing the challenge of caring for them all at once. And sooner or later the day will come when you have all your multiples gathered around you—home at last.

Chapter 10

Feeding the Masses...Including the Busy New Mom

Certain baby-care skills can be acquired on an as-needed basis. You can muddle through the early days, learning as you go along and improving over time. After all, your babies are no worse off if your first attempts at diapering or dressing are amateurish.

But when it comes to feeding your multiples, it's essential to get off to a good start. That's why you should look over this chapter *before* your babies are born. You have an important decision to make—breast, bottle, or both?—and you need to consider these options calmly and carefully. If you wait until delivery day, with all its hustle and bustle, you may get shunted toward a course of action you will later find disappointing.

No matter how you choose to nourish your babies, though, understand that feedings are bound to be a bit crazy at first. And like so many other aspects of parenting multiples, the more babies you have, the more hectic mealtimes may be.

Anne Seifert, mother of quadruplets, knows this from personal experience. "Mason came home from the NICU first, at eight weeks. My husband or I fed him every three hours, and that seemed pretty easy. When Sarah came home two days later, things got a little more complicated. But still, between Mark and me, we managed," says Anne. "Then Lindsey was discharged from the hospital. Was she colicky! It was nerve-wracking to try to feed and care for three 5-pound babies while one was screaming nonstop. Thank goodness, switching her formula eased her stomach distress. Finally little Andrew came home at nine and a half weeks. Because he was still tiny, he had to eat every two hours. Each feeding took 45 minutes, and still he got more milk on him than in him. The only way to handle it was to have Mark devote himself full-time to feeding and taking care of Andrew, while I took care of the other three babies."

To ensure that those early feedings go as smoothly as possible, gather your information and make your decision ahead of time. Then prepare whatever supplies you will need—whether a breast pump, nursing bras and breast pads, or bottles and formula, or all of the above. Finally find an experienced mother of multiples who supports your decision and can troubleshoot with you should any difficulties arise.

Yes, You Can Nurse All Those Babies

TAMARA: Shortly after the ambulances had whisked my premature twins from the community hospital where they were born to a major medical center 30 miles away, my obstetrician came into my hospital room. Patting my hand, he said he'd called the NICU and was told that my babies were doing relatively well. Then he checked me over and assured me that my own physical recovery seemed to be on track.

As he headed for the door, he remarked, "Oh, I almost forgot to mention that I ordered the medication to dry up your breast milk. I imagine you aren't planning on nursing, are you? Breast-feeding two can be tough, especially since no one knows how long your babies will be in the hospital. . . ."

The doctor's voice trailed off as he noticed the look of horror on my face. "You didn't give me that medicine already, did you?" I cried.

"No, no," he quickly answered. "And of course I won't, if you don't want it."

"I *don't* want it. What I want is a breast pump. I am determined to nurse my babies someday, so I'd better start building up my milk supply now."

And pump I did, for weeks. No, it wasn't the intimate bonding experience I had expected to have with my babies. In fact, sometimes I felt as physically attached to that pump as I was emotionally attached to my twins! I even had a dream in which I defended my breast pump (with maternal ferocity) against pirates who were attacking my ship. Yet upon waking, I knew what the dream meant: My breast milk was a lifeline that I—and *only* I—could throw to my babies, via nasogastric tubes, as they faced their sink-or-swim struggles in the NICU. Considering how much of their care I was forced to entrust to others, providing this unique form of nourishment helped me feel more like a real mother.

By the time my twins came home from the hospital, they had become champion nursers. And to me, breast-feeding had come to feel so natural that I continued until the twins were 14 months old. I weaned them on their due date—what would have been their first birthday if they'd gone full term. When we went to the Premature Baby Follow-up Clinic later that month, the pediatrician congratulated me on being "the mother of preemie twins who had nursed the longest." In light of the guilt I had felt over their too early birth, her praise gave me a sweet sense of satisfaction.

DR. LUKE: One major difficulty for women who want to breast-feed is finding help and support—a role model who can offer practical advice on how to get started and how to resolve any problems. When it comes to child care, we automatically turn to our own mothers, and in most instances, they can provide sensible guidance based on personal experience. But a generation ago, when many of our own mothers were giving birth, the myriad benefits of breast milk were not commonly recognized, and therefore breast-feeding was not as widely encouraged as it is today.

That frustration is magnified with a multiple pregnancy. Patients at the Multiples Clinic tell me how often they hear discouraging comments like, "With twins to take care of, you won't have time to breast-feed," or, "Mothers of triplets or quads can't possibly make enough milk to nourish their babies properly." Even some health care professionals don't always encourage mothers of multiples to breast-feed, particularly in cases where the babies will be staying in the hospital for a while.

This lack of support is most unfortunate, especially since it is based on incorrect information. The fact is that most mothers of multiples *can* breast-feed quite successfully—as a number of my patients have proven.

Strangely enough, discouragement also occasionally comes from people who supposedly support breast-feeding yet strongly disparage any plans to supplement nursing with formula. The attitude seems to be, "If you're willing to put that 'fake stuff' into your babies' bodies sometimes, why bother to breast-feed at all?" Yet for many mothers of twins and especially supertwins, supplementing is an excellent option because it gives the babies the advantages of breast milk while affording the parents additional flexibility.

Whether you choose to breast-feed exclusively or to supplement your nursing with bottles of formula, your babies stand to benefit greatly by receiving your breast milk. Here's why:

- Breast milk is the ideal food for infants. It contains all the needed nutrients in exactly the right proportions.
- Breast milk contains unique antibodies that protect your babies against infection. These antibodies can't be manufactured any other way. Studies show that infants who are breast-fed have fewer gastrointestinal infections, respiratory infections,

middle-ear infections, and food allergies. They develop fewer cases of pneumonia and meningitis.

- The risk of sudden infant death syndrome (SIDS) is lower among breast-fed infants.
- Benefits last way beyond weaning. People who were breast-fed are less likely later in life to be obese or to develop intestinal disease or cancer.
- Breast milk may increase intelligence. Recent research reveals that premature infants who were tube-fed with breast milk scored an average of eight points higher on IQ tests given at age eight than did formula-fed preemies. Because all the children were fed through nasogastric tubes, scientists conclude that the results are the effect of the milk alone, and not the nurturing bond that nursing provides.

There are health advantages for the nursing mother as well. Consider this:

- Nursing helps you regain your figure faster by stimulating the uterus to contract—a real plus after your abdomen has been stretched by two, three, or four babies.
- Breast-feeding allows you to lose pregnancy pounds without dieting. Producing milk for just a single baby uses up 500 calories a day, so if you're nursing multiples, your milk production could use up as many as 1,000 to 2,000 calories a day.
- Women who have breast-fed are at lower risk for developing breast cancer and ovarian cancer.

Diet Tips for Nursing Moms of Multiples

Months before you find yourself in the delivery room looking into your newborns' eyes for the first time, Mother Nature starts preparing your body to feed your babies. Nutrient reserves are built up in anticipation of the day your babies will begin their lives outside the womb and take their first meal at your breast.

During pregnancy, you gain a certain amount of fat (as discussed in Chapter 3), particularly around your shoulder blades, thighs, and upper arms. The purpose of this fat is twofold. First, it's a ready reserve of concentrated calories for the last months of pregnancy, when you may not be able to eat enough to meet the nutritional demands of your growing babies. Second, this fat acts as a caloric warehouse, ready to be mobilized when required for milk production.

Fat reserves alone, however, can't handle the long-term demands placed on your body when you are nursing. For that, you need to eat right. Dietary guidelines for breast-feeding women are set with two goals in mind:

- To allow healthy, full-term babies to double their birthweight within four to six months. This requires that the mother produce a sufficient amount of milk. Generally that's not a problem because the driving force behind breast milk production is supply and demand. In other words, the more you feed your babies, the more milk you produce.
- To keep nursing mothers in good health. Meeting this goal can be more of a challenge. The nutrient content of breast milk is amazingly constant, whether the mother is underweight or overweight, anemic or well nourished—which means that if your diet is inadequate, your *own* health will suffer.

The Food and Nutrition Board of the National Academy of Sciences has established recommended dietary allowances (RDAs) for women breast-feeding a single baby. These recommendations indicate that a nursing mother's calorie requirements increase about 500 calories per day, or 23 percent above nonpregnant levels. In addition, the need for certain nutrients (folic acid, riboflavin, thiamin; vitamins A, C, and D; and the minerals calcium, phosphorus, and zinc) increases by 50 percent or more. Other nutrient requirements (such as for niacin; vitamins B_6, B_{12}, and E; and the minerals iodine, iron, magnesium, and selenium) also increase, but by a lesser percentage.

DR. LUKE: Just as there are no current national dietary guidelines for women *pregnant* with multiples, there are as yet no official dietary guidelines for women *breast-feeding* multiples. Extrapolating from the RDAs for nursing mothers of singletons, however, I have made some educated estimates about the nutritional needs of women who are exclusively nursing twins, triplets, or quadruplets. If you're supplementing with bottles, these calorie counts can be adjusted downward, depending on how much formula your babies receive each day. For instance, if each of your quadruplets gets half her feedings at the breast and the other half from formula, you can follow the guidelines for nursing twins.

Estimated Dietary Requirements:
Nonpregnant Woman Versus
Woman Breast-Feeding Twins or Supertwins

Nutrient	Nonpregnant Woman	Breast-Feeding			
		Singleton	Twins	Triplets	Quads
Calories (kcal)	2,200	2,700	3,200	3,700	4,200
Protein (grams) 20% of calories	110	135	160	185	210
Carbohydrate (grams) 40% of calories	220	270	320	370	420
Fat (grams) 40% of calories	98	120	142	165	187

Table 10.1

If it's confusing to keep track of all these numbers, simplify matters by thinking of your nutritional needs in a familiar way—by calorie count. Compared to a prepregnancy diet, here are the higher calorie counts that nursing women need if their babies are exclusively breast-fed. (Again, remember that calorie counts go down when breast-feeding is supplemented with formula.)

- To nurse a singleton: an extra 500 to 600 calories a day
- To nurse twins: an extra 1,000 to 1,200 calories a day
- To nurse triplets: an extra 1,500 to 1,800 calories a day
- To nurse quadruplets: an extra 2,000 to 2,400 calories a day

If you've always been a weight-conscious calorie-counter, these numbers may seem shockingly high. But in order to breast-feed successfully, you do need to eat—a lot!

Some moms learn this the hard way. "After the girls were born, I just wasn't as hungry as I had been during the pregnancy. I felt less motivated to eat too—and I had less time for it, busy as I was taking care of the babies," says Amy Maly, mother of identical twin girls. "In hindsight, though, I realize that by not eating enough, I sabotaged my efforts at breast-feeding. Not only was I worried about producing too little milk, but I also felt drained and exhausted."

DR. LUKE: Where should all those additional calories come from? As a nursing mother of multiples, you need to eat the same foods as any other woman who is breast-feeding, but you should eat more often and have larger portions.

Remember, you need almost as many calories to breast-feed as you did when you were pregnant. Yet while the calorie counts are close, their food sources should be somewhat different when you are breast-feeding. Back in Chapters 3 and 4, where we discussed what to eat while pregnant, the emphasis was on getting adequate calories, protein, and iron, with a focus on meats and a well-balanced diet overall. Although your caloric needs have changed by only about 300 calories, the focus now is on getting enough calories and calcium, with *more dairy* and *less meat*, while still maintaining a balanced diet.

You also need extra fluids. Nursing moms are often very thirsty, even more so than during pregnancy. Drinking plenty of water, milk, and juice throughout the day helps to maintain your breast-milk supply.

Nutrient needs vary depending on how much milk you produce—and that of course is determined by how many babies you have and whether you are supplementing with formula. The menu guidelines given in Table 10.2 are based on your estimated nutrient needs if you are exclusively breast-feeding your multiples. (Adjust the numbers downward if your babies also receive formula.) To make your menu planning easier, I've translated data like "milligrams of vitamins" and "grams of protein" into the more familiar terms of "servings per day."

Comparison of Menu Guidelines for Mothers of Multiples:
Preconception, Pregnancy, and Breast-Feeding

	Nonpregnant	Singleton		Twins		Triplets		Quadruplets	
		Pregnancy	Breast-Feeding	Pregnancy	Breast-Feeding	Pregnancy	Breast-Feeding	Pregnancy	Breast-Feeding
Calories per day	2,200 kcal	2,500 kcal	2,700 kcal	3,500 kcal	3,200 kcal	4,000 kcal	3,700 kcal	4,500 kcal	4,200 kcal
Protein 20% of calories	110 g	126 g	135 g	176 g	160 g	200 g	185 g	225 g	210 g
Carbohydrate 40% of calories	220 g	248 g	270 g	350 g	320 g	400 g	370 g	450 g	420 g
Fat 40% of calories	98 g	112 g	120 g	155 g	142 g	178 g	164 g	200 g	187 g
Food Group *Serving Sizes*									
Dairy 8 oz. milk, cottage cheese or ice cream, or 1 oz. hard cheese	4	6	8	8	10	10	12	12	14
Meat, fish, poultry 3 oz.	2	2	2	3	2	3	2	4	3

		Nonpregnant	Singleton		Twins		Triplets		Quadruplets	
			Pregnancy	Breast-Feeding	Pregnancy	Breast-Feeding	Pregnancy	Breast-Feeding	Pregnancy	Breast-Feeding
Eggs	1 fresh	-	1	1	2	2	2	2	2	2
Vegetables	½ cup cooked or 1 cup fresh	4	4	4	4	4	5	5	6	6
Fruits	½ cup or 1 fresh	4	4	4	7	5	8	5	8	5
Grains, bread	1 oz., ¾ cup cooked, or 1 slice	8	8	8	10	10	12	12	12	12
Fats, oils, nuts	1 tsp. oil 1 tsp. butter 1 oz. nuts	4	5	5	6	5	7	5	8	6

Table 10.2

DR. LUKE: Even expressed in terms of servings per day, these numbers may still seem overwhelming, so I've taken a sample menu and modified it for nursing mothers of multiples. Table 10.3 shows how the amount of food and serving sizes would need to change from pregnancy to breast-feeding for mothers of twins, triplets, and quadruplets.

Within three to six months after delivery, you should be fairly close to your prepregnancy weight. If you're not and you want to continue to lose, decrease the amount of fat in your diet and reduce portion sizes for all the various foods *except dairy*. For additional information on postpregnancy nutrition, consult another of our books, *Program Your Baby's Health: The Pregnancy Diet for Your Child's Lifelong Well-Being*. Also, I invite you to get personalized nutrition counseling through my Web site, www.drbarbaraluke.com.

Sample Menu for Mothers of Multiples: Pregnancy Versus Breast-Feeding

Meal	Menu Suggestion	Twins		Triplets		Quads	
		Pregnancy	Nursing	Pregnancy	Nursing	Pregnancy	Nursing
Breakfast	Scrambled eggs	2 eggs	2 eggs	2 eggs	2 eggs	2 eggs	2 eggs
	Canadian bacon	1 oz.	—	1 oz.	1 oz.	1 oz.	1 oz.
	Whole-wheat toast	2 slices	2 slices	3 slices	3 slices	3 slices	3 slices
	Cheddar cheese	1 oz.	1½ oz.	1½ oz.	2 oz.	2 oz.	2 oz.
	Sliced bananas	1 banana	1 banana	1 banana	1 banana	1 banana	1 banana
	Decaffeinated coffee	optional	optional	optional	optional	optional	optional
Midmorning	Whole-wheat toast	2 slices	2 slices	2 slices	2 slices	2 slices	2 slices
	Peanut butter	2 tbsp.	—	2 tbsp.	—	2 tbsp.	2 tbsp.
	Cheese	—	1 oz.	1 oz.	1½ oz.	2 oz.	2 oz.
	Apple slices	1 apple	1 apple	1 apple	1 apple	1 apple	1 apple
	Milk	1 cup	1½ cups	1½ cups	2 cups	2 cups	2 cups

Meal	Menu Suggestion	Twins		Triplets		Quads	
		Pregnancy	Nursing	Pregnancy	Nursing	Pregnancy	Nursing
Lunch	Tuna	2 oz.	2 oz.	2 oz.	2 oz.	3 oz.	3 oz.
	Swiss cheese	—	—	½ oz.	1 oz.	1 oz.	1 oz.
	Toasted rye	2 slices	2 slices	2 slices	2 slices	2 slices	2 slices
	Lettuce/tomato salad	1 small	1 small	1 small	1 small	1 medium	1 medium
	Potato salad	½ cup	½ cup	½ cup	½ cup	½ cup	½ cup
	Ice cream	1 cup	1 cup	1 cup	1 cup	1 cup	1½ cups
	Milk	1 cup	1½ cups	1½ cups	1½ cups	2 cups	2 cups
	Orange sections	—	—	1 orange	—	1 orange	—
Midafternoon	Ritz crackers	4 crackers	4 crackers	8 crackers	8 crackers	8 crackers	8 crackers
	Liver pâté	1 oz.	—	1 oz.	—	1 oz.	—
	Cottage cheese	—	½ cup	—	½ cup	—	1 cup
	Fresh grapes	½ cup	½ cup	½ cup	½ cup	½ cup	½ cup
Dinner	Broiled steak	5 oz.	4 oz.	5 oz.	4 oz.	6 oz.	4 oz.
	Baked potato	1 small	1 small	1 small	1 small	1 medium	1 medium
	Sour cream	1 tbsp.	1 tbsp.	2 tbsp.	2 tbsp.	3 tbsp.	2 tbsp.
	Caesar salad	1 small	1 small	1 medium	1 medium	1 medium	1 medium
	Dinner roll	1 roll	1 roll	1 roll	1 roll	1 roll	1 roll
	Milk	1 cup	1 cup	1 cup	1 cup	1 cup	1½ cups
	Tapioca pudding	1 cup	1 cup	1 cup	1 cup	1 cup	1 cup
	Sliced strawberries	½ cup	—	½ cup	—	½ cup	½ cup
After dinner	Ice cream	1 cup	1 cup	1 cup	1 cup	1 cup	1 cup
Bedtime	Cereal	¾ cup	¾ cup	¾ cup	¾ cup	¾ cup	¾ cup
	Milk	1 cup	1 cup	1 cup	1 cup	1 cup	1 cup
	Fruit	½ cup	½ cup	½ cup	½ cup	½ cup	½ cup

Table 10.3

Fourth Trimester: Emphasis on Calcium, Omega-3 Fatty Acids, Zinc, and Iodine

Chapter 4 includes a discussion on the three trimesters of pregnancy, and the nutrients that are most vital during each time period. The postpartum period is sometimes referred to as the "fourth trimester," and it too involves unique nutritional needs:

- Calcium requirements increase by 50 percent or more when you are nursing—and the more babies you're feeding, the more calcium you need. If your diet doesn't supply enough, this mineral will be drawn from your own bones, making them weaker. Good sources include dairy foods such as milk, cheese, and yogurt; sardines and salmon with bones; eggs; tofu; peanuts; spinach, beans, and potatoes.
- Omega-3 fatty acids are important now because, while the quantity of fat in your breast milk remains fairly constant no matter what you eat, the type of fat in your milk depends on your diet. In order for your breast milk to be rich in the omega-3 fatty acids your babies need for proper visual and neurologic development, your diet also must be rich in these fatty acids. Be sure your diet includes ample amounts of fish, plus oils such as canola, safflower, flaxseed, and olive. Omega 3–enriched eggs are another good choice.
- Zinc is a critical component of many enzymes throughout the body. It benefits your babies by promoting their neurologic development. In order for your breast milk to provide the zinc your multiples need, your diet should include beef, pork, lamb, poultry, seafood, and eggs. Zinc is also provided by vegetable sources such as whole-grain breads and cereals, beans, and nuts; however, the fiber in these foods results in less absorption.
- Iodine is essential for the production of thyroxine by the thyroid gland. This hormone regulates the rate of oxidation within cells, and in so doing, influences many aspects of your babies' health: body temperature control; metabolism of all nutrients; functioning of the nervous system and muscle tissue; and physical and mental development. Your breast milk will be rich in iodine if your diet includes fish and seafood, milk, enriched breads, and iodized salt.

With two or more babies to take care of, you have precious little time for meal-planning. To make the task easier, refer to the following suggestions. (An asterisk indicates that the recipe appears at the back of this book.)

BREAKFAST

*Autumn Pancakes

French Toast with Applesauce

Grilled Ham and Cheese Sandwich

Oatmeal with Dried Cherries

*Pumpkin Waffles

Whole-Wheat Toast with Peanut Butter

LUNCH OR DINNER

Baked Manicotti

Cheeseburgers

Cheese Lasagna

Chicken Pot Pie

*Citrus Salmon

*Linguine with Clams and Dried Tomatoes

London Broil

*Mini–Meat Loaves

New England Clam Chowder

Pork Roast

Pot Roast

*Salmon Burgers

Spaghetti and Meatballs

Tuna Salad

*Vegetarian Lasagna

SNACKS

Apple Slices and Peanut Butter

*Basic Fruit Smoothie

*Basic Vegetable Smoothie

Deviled Eggs with Toast

Fruit Salad with Cheese and Crackers

Oatmeal-Walnut Cookies with Yogurt

Shrimp Cocktail

ARE ALL YOUR BABIES GETTING ENOUGH TO EAT?

Back in the days when wetnurses were common, one woman would sometimes breast-feed as many as six children at once! Clearly, the female body is capable of nourishing more than one baby at a time. But because there are cases in which an infant does not get enough milk from nursing, you will of course want to be certain that your breast-fed babies are receiving the nourishment they need to thrive.

The quantity of breast milk or formula your multiples need for proper growth and development depends on their state of health, activity level, and metabolism. Most babies require 120 to 150 calories per kilogram of body weight, or about 55 to 68 calories per pound of body weight, in a 24-hour period. Both breast milk and infant formula contain about 20 calories per ounce. That means a 5-pound baby generally needs about 14 to 17 ounces per day; a 7-pound baby needs about 20 to 24 ounces per day; and a 10-pound baby needs about 28 to 34 ounces per day.

There's no way to measure in ounces the amount of breast milk your babies are taking in, unless you're pumping your breasts and feeding it to them with a bottle. But you can feel confident that your babies' intake is adequate if these other signs are present:

- Each baby soaks at least six diapers a day.
- Each baby has at least one bowel movement in a 24-hour period.
- The babies each gain ½ to 1 ounce per day, on average, during the first two to three months after they come home from the hospital.

If any of your babies does *not* meet these criteria, be sure to alert your pediatrician without delay. There are a variety of factors that can undermine your milk production, and it's important that these be identified and remedied promptly:

- Fatigue, illness, stress, anger, or depression can sap the energy your body needs to produce an adequate supply of milk. They can also interfere with the let-down reflex, the normal hormonal mechanism by which milk is released from the milk-producing glands and moved into the milk ducts. If let-down is inhibited, your babies won't be able to draw the milk from your breasts, no matter how plentiful the supply is. To resolve these problems, try lining up some help at home (see Chapter 11 for tips) and spending a day or two in bed, devoting yourself entirely to resting and nursing.
- Dieting seriously curtails milk production. If you've been skimping on meals, review Tables 10.1 and 10.2 on recommended calorie counts and servings per day for nursing mothers of multiples.
- Excessive alcohol intake interferes with the let-down reflex, making it hard for your babies to get the milk out of your breasts. An occasional alcoholic beverage is okay, but you would be wise to limit your intake to no more than a drink or two per week.
- Inadequate stimulation of the breasts can impede milk production, so be sure to empty at least one breast at each feeding. If your babies are not strong sucklers, you may need to use a breast pump after feedings to empty your breasts. This sends your body a message to boost milk production.

The Mechanics of Breast-Feeding Multiples

With twins, the simplest way to divide your milk is to offer each baby one breast per feeding. For triplets or quads, devise a rotation system that allows each baby equal time at the breast.

Do be sure to alternate which side each baby suckles from. If you assign the same breast to the same infant every time, it limits her visual stimulation. It can also lead to lopsided breasts and a diminished milk supply on one side if one baby has a smaller appetite. Furthermore, a baby may grow accustomed to "her" breast and refuse to nurse on the other. That can be a painful problem if you develop a clogged duct on one side and need the help of two or more babies to release the milk, or if one infant is unable to nurse for a few days, or if one child weans himself earlier.

Full-term newborns usually nurse 10 to 12 times in 24 hours. Preemies may need to eat more often until they reach full-term size; your pediatrician can advise you on this. In any event, don't plan on feedings occurring like clockwork. Your babies will let you know when they're hungry—and this won't always happen at strictly regular intervals.

Simultaneous breast-feeding of multiples using the combination hold

How long will each feeding last? That too may vary from baby to baby, from day to day, even from feeding to feeding. Typically a baby will suck eagerly, swallowing quickly, for the first 8 to 10 minutes of a feeding. Initially she receives the "foremilk," or the milk that has collected in the breast since the last time you nursed. Foremilk is relatively thin and lower in fat.

Then, as milk flow slows and her tummy starts to fill, the baby may start to doze or appear to lose interest. Take that as a sign that it's time to burp her, then put her back on the breast for some additional, more leisurely sucking. Now the baby is receiving the richer "hindmilk," which is higher in fat. Because hindmilk more effectively promotes the baby's weight gain, it's important that feedings last long enough to fully satisfy her hunger. Again, follow each baby's lead in determining how long a given feeding should last.

Does it sound like you'll be nursing around the clock? You're not alone in feeling that way. "At first, it seemed I spent every waking hour feeding babies—and almost all my hours were waking ones," says Lisa McDonough, a mother of boy/girl twins and two older children. No wonder: One study reports that it takes 10 to 15 hours daily to feed newborn twins separately. With triplets or quads, of course, the time demands of nursing are even more daunting. But you can cut down significantly on the hours spent feeding if you learn to nurse two babies simultaneously.

First, get your shirt and bra out of the way, and have pillows strategically placed to support your arms and back. Then choose one of three positions:

- Both babies in the traditional cradle hold, bodies crisscrossed in front of you
- Both in the football hold, legs tucked behind you
- The combination hold, with one baby cradled and one held football-style

Arrange pillows to support your arms and the babies' bodies. Or buy a special cushion designed for tandem nursing, such as the NurseEz twin nursing pillow from Twin Connection (telephone 800–526–2594; Web site www.nurturingmothersboutique.com).

TAMARA: My twins were so little that they didn't have much muscle tone those first months. Try to pick up a floppy baby with one arm while your other arm is busy holding another infant to your breast, and you'll see why I considered this business of moving the second baby into position to be the trickiest part of simultaneous nursing. It was no big deal, of course, if someone else was on hand to help me. But it took a lot of trial and error before I finally figured out how to manage it on my own.

Here's my method, using the combination hold. I sat on the sofa with James cradled in my left arm, my left elbow supported by the armrest. Samantha lay lengthwise on a pillow next to my right thigh, her head near my knee and her feet pointing toward my hips. Once James had latched onto my left breast, I encircled Samantha *and her pillow* with my right arm and pulled them onto my lap. Then with my right hand, I raised her head to my right breast, letting the pillow support her body.

If You Need Help

If you have questions or problems with breast-feeding, help is readily available from the following organizations:

- International Lactation Consultant Association: 1500 Sunday Drive, Suite 102, Raleigh, NC 27607. Telephone 919–861–5577; e-mail info@ilca.org; Web site www.ilca.org.
- La Leche League International: 1400 N. Meacham Road, Schaumburg, IL 60173-4808. Telephone 800–LA–LECHE or 847–519–7730; Web site www.lalecheleague.org. La Leche also publishes two books, *The Womanly Art of Breastfeeding* and *Breastfeeding Your Premature Baby*.
- Lactation Education Resources: 3621 Lido Place, Fairfax, VA 22031. Telephone 703–691–2069; e-mail LERonline@yahoo.com; Web site www.LERon-line.com.

- U.S. Breastfeeding Committee: 1500 Sunday Drive, Suite 102, Raleigh, NC 27607. Telephone 919–787–5181; e-mail info@usbreastfeeding.org; Web site www.usbreastfeeding.org.

GETTING PRIMED TO PUMP

"Toward the end of my pregnancy, my brother, who is a family physician, offered to lend me the top-of-the-line electric breast pump he keeps on hand in case one of his patients should need it. Though at first I couldn't imagine ever using such a device, I took it just to be polite," says Lydia Greenwood, mother of boy/girl twins. "But it turned out to be a real boon to my breast-feeding efforts, particularly after I went back to work. Pumping during the day allowed me to keep up my milk supply, so I was able to nurse my babies a lot longer than I had ever thought would be possible."

There are a number of situations in which a breast pump can come in handy. One such circumstance is when babies are in the hospital. For premature newborns in the NICU, the effort involved in sucking from the breast or bottle can use up more calories than a feeding provides. That's why preemies are often fed through a nasogastric tube that runs from the nose directly down into the stomach. If you pump, your breast milk rather than formula can be given to your babies through this tube. Ginny Seyler says, "While my triplets were in the NICU, I pumped my breasts every four hours and gave it to the nurses, who fed it to the babies through nasogastric tubes. I wanted to be sure my babies got the benefits of breast milk, even though they were too little to suck."

Later, as your babies gain strength, they will begin to "nipple," or drink from a tiny bottle with a special soft rubber nipple. Again, if you pump, breast milk rather than formula can be used for these feedings. (Don't be upset if the NICU staff suggests fortifying your milk. Although mother's milk is inarguably superior to formula, certain babies do best when breast milk is enhanced by specific extra nutrients.)

It's true that pumping lacks the emotional satisfaction nursing brings. But bear in mind that your milk is a precious gift *you alone* can provide for your hospitalized babies. For many women with babies in the NICU, this is a gratifying confirmation of motherhood. Plus, putting up with the hassle of pumping now will enable you to enjoy all the closeness and naturalness of nursing later, when your babies are stronger.

Usually the hospital staff is very supportive of a mother's pumping—but sometimes encouragement is not forthcoming. "I was determined to breast-feed, but there was little support for that at the NICU. The staff seemed surprised that I even wanted to try. They brought me a pump, but no one showed me how to use it. I watched a video on nursing, but still couldn't figure out how to get the boys to latch on properly. I pumped for six weeks and gave the breast milk to the boys in bottles. But it was so disappointing not to be able to really nurse that I eventually switched to formula," says Benita Moreno, mother of fraternal twin boys. "In hindsight, I wish I had called La Leche. I think a lactation consultant could have helped me work through the problems."

Pumping is also a convenient way to meet your babies' nutritional needs when you cannot be with them around the clock. Suppose you're ready to return to work but want to continue nursing. You can pump during the workday, refrigerate your milk, and have your caregiver feed it to your babies the following day, from bottles. Or suppose you want to get out of the house for the evening and have a much-deserved date with your husband. Again, the milk you pumped earlier can be fed to your babies in your absence. (Even if you don't plan to reserve your milk for your babies to drink later, you may at times need to pump. Three to four hours after your last nursing session, your breasts will grow uncomfortably full unless you relieve the engorgement by pumping.)

There may also be times when you are temporarily unable to breast-feed but want to maintain your milk supply in anticipation of resuming nursing as soon as possible. For instance, if you are sick and require medication that your doctor feels could pass through to your milk, you can pump and discard that milk until you've completed your course of medication.

You may occasionally develop a plugged duct that refuses to be dislodged despite all your babies' best sucking efforts. In that case, the stronger suction of the pump can bring speedy relief.

Quickest, easiest, and most efficient are the electric breast pumps. They are expensive to buy—several hundred dollars or more—but can be rented at reasonable rates from hospitals, pharmacies, or La Leche groups. Manually operated pumps are much cheaper, but are generally more difficult to use and less effective at emptying the breast. Your doctor or a breast-feeding support group can recommend the best pump and instruct you in its use.

STORING BREAST MILK SAFELY

Before you begin to pump, wash your hands. Follow the pump manufacturer's instructions for cleaning the breast shield and tubing, and for sterilizing the container used to collect the milk.

Have on hand the special plastic bags designed for storing breast milk; these bags, which are available at pharmacies, do not interfere with the infection-fighting properties of your milk. Do not use regular plastic bags or other containers that haven't been sterilized. Label each bag with the date and time you filled it so you can use the oldest milk first. Limit the amount of milk in a bag to about 4 ounces.

Refrigerate breast milk as soon as possible after pumping. Breast milk can be safely stored in the refrigerator for 48 hours, in a refrigerator freezer for two weeks, or in a separate-door freezer for several months. Thaw milk by placing the container in a bowl of room-temperature water. Don't heat it on the stove or in the microwave; high temperatures reduce breast milk's nutritional content and present a risk of scalding. Once thawed, milk can be stored in the refrigerator for up to eight hours; it should never be refrozen.

If you're transporting breast milk to the NICU, pack it in ice for the journey. Be sure each bag is labeled with your babies' names and hospital identification numbers. You may also want to pump your breasts at the hospital each day so your babies will get some fresh milk, which is somewhat higher in nutrients and infection-fighting antibodies than milk that has been frozen.

Supplementing: The Best of Both Worlds?

Some people argue that combining breast-feeding and bottle-feeding involves all the hassles of both methods and only half the benefits of either. But many nursing mothers of multiples find that supplementing their nursing with formula eases their load. Lydia Greenwood says, "Much as I enjoyed nursing, it was a relief to be able to have someone else feed the twins so I could sleep an extra hour or get out of the house occasionally. Supplementing was also a boon in public places. I could nurse one twin discreetly (for me, there was nothing discreet about simultaneous breast-feeding) while my husband gave a bottle to the other."

Particularly in families with older children, supplementing often makes sense. "I felt disappointed about how little I was able to mother my two-year-old while I was pregnant with the twins. Because I wasn't supposed to overexert myself physically, I couldn't pick her up or play actively. Then, after the twins were born, nursing exclusively proved to be so time-consuming that there wasn't much time left for their big sister," says one mother of twins. "So after about two months, I started to supplement my breast-feeding with one bottle in the evening. This way, someone else could feed the babies while I read to my toddler or gave her a bath."

For most nursing mothers of triplets or quadruplets, supplementing with formula has great appeal. For one thing, it affords the babies the benefits of breast milk while alleviating any doubts as to whether or not everyone is receiving enough nourishment. What's more, it allows Mom to share the feeding workload with Dad or another helper—a very welcome option, considering how time-consuming it can be to feed supertwins.

Working mothers, too, often opt to supplement. "For the first three months, Benjamin and Madeleine were breast-fed exclusively. But then it was time for me to return to my job as an occupational therapist," says Heather Nicholas. "I started nursing in the mornings and evenings only, and they got formula during the day. This was a lot less hassle than it would have been to pump my milk at work. It was a good balance—so good, in fact, that I nursed until the twins were eight months old."

A word to the wise: If you think you'll want to supplement eventually, it's best to introduce one daily bottle by age three to four weeks, if not sooner. If you wait too long, one or more of your multiples may refuse the rubber nipple completely. For the first bottle-feedings, you might pump or express some breast milk and mix that with formula, to allow your babies to adjust gradually to the difference in taste. Also, ask your partner or assistant to hold the babies during those initial offerings of the bottle. Otherwise, knowing that Mommy's breasts are nearby, your multiples may reject their bottles and hold out for "the real thing."

Bottle-Feeding Basics

Have you decided to supplement your nursing with an occasional bottle, or to forgo breast-feeding altogether in favor of formula? Then you'll need to know the basics of bottle-feeding. Any good manual on infant care can provide detailed instructions. But there are some additional points that parents of multiples should be aware of.

While no infant formula can claim to convey all the advantages of breast milk, the brands available today are nutritious and easy to prepare, and you needn't doubt that your babies can thrive on them. Most formulas are derived from cow's milk. If any of your multiples has allergies or a sensitive stomach, however, that baby may do better on a soy-based or protein-hydrolysate formula. If this is the case, ask your pediatrician if it's all right to simplify your life by putting all your multiples on that type of formula.

Most infant formulas come in three ways. Ready-to-pour is the most convenient but also the most expensive. Liquid formula concentrate is cheaper yet must be mixed with sterilized water, and any unused portion has to be promptly refrigerated. Least expensive is powdered formula. The opened can of powder does not require refrigeration, but it too must be combined with sterilized water—and mixed well to prevent clumps.

Formula should be gently warmed before being given to your babies. Never heat bottles in the microwave oven; too many babies have had their mouths badly scalded this way. Instead, warm the bottles by placing them in a bowl of hot tap water for a few minutes. Before serving, test the temperature on the inside of your wrist to make sure it is warm enough but not hot.

One other note of caution: Never put your babies to bed with bottles. If milk is allowed to pool in their mouths as they sleep, serious tooth decay can result. There is also the danger of choking, should a baby bite through the rubber nipple while you are not there to immediately handle the emergency.

TIME-SAVING TIPS ABOUT BOTTLES

With two or more babies to feed, you'll want to make mealtimes as easy as possible. Take a tip from Kelly Kassab, an experienced mother of multiples: "Each evening, I cleaned the bottles and nipples, sterilized the water, mixed the formula, and poured it into enough bottles to get us through the next 24 hours. Then whenever the girls were hungry, all I had to do was warm up two bottles."

Another time-saving tactic is to feed your multiples simultaneously. This is simple if other people are on hand to give bottles to the other babies. But what if you're alone? Propping bottles is not recommended. Along with the nourishment a feeding provides, babies also need the emotional and physical closeness that comes from being held or touched as they eat. (If you feel you must prop bottles on occasion, be sure not to leave the babies unsupervised. A baby who begins to choke must be attended to at once.)

Here are several positions that allow you to feed two babies at the same time:

- Sit on the floor with your back against the wall. Open your legs in a V and place the babies between your knees, their heads supported by a pillow and their feet pointing toward you. Use your thighs as armrests while you hold the bottles in either hand, stroking the babies' cheeks with a free finger and gazing into their eyes.
- Sit in a comfortable armchair so you can prop your left elbow on the armrest. Support the babies' weight in your lap while supporting both their heads with your left arm and hand. Lean one baby's bottle against your chest or in the crook of your right arm, and hold the other bottle in your right hand.
- Cradle one baby, curling your left arm around her to support her head while your left hand holds her bottle. Lay the other baby with his head in your lap, and hold his bottle with your right hand.
- Lean back in an armchair and put both babies in a semiseated position on your lap, their backs and heads supported by your chest and arms. Hold one bottle in each hand.

What if several babies are screaming with hunger, yet you can't manage to feed simultaneously? Give the fussiest baby half a feeding to calm him, then feed the others, and then finish up with the first. To keep track of how much each child eats and avoid inadvertent bottle swaps between babies, use color-coded bottles.

All About Burping

Whether your babies get breast milk or formula, you won't want to neglect an essential element of every feeding: the burp. An infant whose tummy is uncomfortably full of gas won't be able to take in the milk she needs to thrive. So be sure to burp your multiples once or twice during each feeding, and again at the end.

If the traditional over-the-shoulder hold doesn't elicit the desired release of gas, try a different position. "Holly always belched whenever I patted her back, no matter how I held her. But her twin brother, Alexander, was trickier," says Lydia Greenwood. "Finally I found two positions that usually worked. I could lay him tummy side down across my lap and very gently move my knees up and down against his stomach. Or I could sit him in my lap, with one hand supporting his chest and head, and the other rubbing his back. One or the other technique usually brought up a very satisfying burp."

And satisfaction—for you and for all your babies—is what successful feeding is all about.

Chapter 11

Survival Tips for Those Crazy First Months at Home

Ruth Markowitz looked around the nursery and broke into a cold sweat. There was the changing table, but she scarcely knew how to fasten a diaper. There was the infant bathtub, but she panicked at the thought of holding a wet, wiggling baby. There was the crib, where newborn Nicola was screaming with hunger. And there was the *other* crib, where Evan was mingling his cries with those of his twin. "I was petrified," confesses Ruth. "How would I manage to feed, carry, clean, and soothe two babies at once? I was afraid to touch them."

There's a word for what Ruth was feeling: twinshock. If you've just brought home two babies, you probably feel it too.

Of course, the impact increases exponentially for parents in the throes of tripletshock and quadshock. Just ask Anne Seifert, the mother of quadruplets: "During the pregnancy, I hadn't let myself worry about how I'd manage to take care of four babies at once, because I didn't want the stress to trigger contractions. Once the quads were born, though, the reality hit. I had several sweaty panic attacks just thinking about the challenges to come."

To get past the anxiety and take pleasure in your babies, you need more than a pep talk. You need specific strategies for coping.

How to Recruit Help

DR. LUKE: After talking with hundreds of mothers of multiples, I'm utterly convinced of one basic truth: You will need help, especially during those first hectic weeks after the babies come home. And the more babies you've got, the more assistance you'll require. One Australian study, for instance, showed that it takes 197 hours per week to care for infant triplets and do household chores—yet there are only 168 hours in a week!

Help is particularly vital if you've had little previous experience in taking care of an infant. For instance, Stacy Moore said to me, "Before my twins were born, I had changed maybe two diapers in my entire life. The first time I saw a newborn's bowel movement, I looked at that sticky black meconium in horror and thought, 'Is this what baby poop always looks like?' It was intimidating to have to learn everything from scratch."

There's nothing self-indulgent about seeking help; it's truly in your babies' best interests. If you try to do everything yourself, you'll quickly sink into such extreme exhaustion that you won't be able to take good care of your multiples. So consider the alternatives, such as those outlined in this chapter, and select the ones that seem best suited to your situation.

Hire a pro.
If you can afford it, a baby nurse is an excellent option—particularly one who specializes in multiples. (Despite the title, this person is usually an experienced caregiver, not a registered nurse.) Locate a qualified baby nurse through word of mouth, or find a baby-nurse placement agency in the yellow pages under "Child Care." Reserve at least several months in advance.

While details of the arrangement vary from agency to agency, you can probably count on certain basics. The typical baby nurse lives in your home for as long as you request, whether a couple of weeks or many months. Some work 12-hour shifts; others work around the clock except for a few hours off during the day. If you're breast-feeding, she gets up at night to help. Otherwise, she manages night feedings herself so you can sleep. She takes care of the babies, their laundry and room, but does not shop or clean house.

One mother of boy/girl twins hired a nurse who stayed three months. Says she, "The baby nurse taught me to breast-feed, give baths, even recognize thrush. And she took care of me as I recovered from my C-section." To ensure a positive experience, meet with the nurse or agency director beforehand to clarify duties, hours, and payment.

Even experienced moms often regard professional help as a necessity when they're trying to meet the needs of their older children as well as newborn multiples. "For the first six weeks after the triplets were born, I had some help during the day, but I was on my own every night. My husband couldn't get any time off work, and I also had to take care of our three-year-old daughter. On average, I was getting two hours of sleep a night. It was really tough," admits Helen Armer. "Then I hired an overnight nanny for eight weeks. Each weekday evening, she came at 11 P.M. and stayed till 7 A.M., handling all the triplets' needs during that time. I couldn't sleep the entire eight hours, of course. I stayed up till midnight paying bills or doing laundry, then woke up at 6 A.M. to get my daughter ready for nursery school. But at least I was able to rest for six hours, five nights a week."

Such help doesn't come cheap, unfortunately. Depending on the area of the country in which you live, you can expect to pay $15 to $25 or more per hour, in addition to an agency finder's fee. "The nanny cost me a lot of money," says Helen, "but it was worth it. I'm not sure I would have survived without her!"

If live-in or overnight help isn't financially feasible, have a daytime babysitter with you for much of the day, or arrange her schedule to overlap your babies' fussiest time. Through your local Mothers of Multiples Club, you may find a levelheaded teenager or twenty-something sitter who has twin or triplet siblings herself and is experienced at handling more than one baby at a time. Even more economical is a "mother's helper," typically a preteen. She's not mature enough to be left alone in the house with the babies of course, but she can help you feed and change your newborns and entertain them while you take a shower or relax with a cup of tea.

But do beware of the "sitter plays/Mom cleans" trap. Says Lydia Greenwood, the mother of boy/girl twins, "I found myself scrubbing floors one afternoon, while my hired help played peekaboo with Alexander and Holly. *That* didn't seem quite fair! So I negotiated a change in the sitter's duties to include kitchen cleanup, vacuuming, and clutter control—giving me more free time to enjoy my twins." If such an arrangement doesn't sit well with your sitter, have a cleaning service or housekeeper take up the slack.

And don't let yourself feel even the slightest bit guilty about it. "Since I don't work outside the home, at first I felt sheepish about spending my husband's hard-earned paycheck on a housekeeper," says one mother of twins and an older child. "But I stopped feeling guilty when my husband pointed out that my 'job responsibilities' had virtually tripled overnight, and it was okay to 'outsource' some of my duties."

Invite relatives to stay for a week, a month, or longer.

You may prefer that your mother or mother-in-law stay with you those first weeks, as Ruth Markowitz did. "At first, I left the child care in their experienced hands, but once they showed me what to do, I realized it wasn't that hard," she recalls.

Afraid it's an imposition to take so much of someone's time? Instead of asking a favor, offer a job. "My twins were born in late spring, which was great timing. My college-age sister needed a summer job, and I needed around-the-clock assistance. She lived with us for two months and helped take care of the babies, and I paid her as much as she would have made at any other job," says Lydia Greenwood. "I was so sorry to see her go in the fall—not only because she had made life immeasurably easier, but also because we had grown much closer emotionally. Although she has many nieces and nephews now, I know my twins hold a special place in her heart."

Let friends lend a helping hand.

When a pal offers to help, give her a specific assignment or let her choose from a list you've prepared. For example, she can:

- Feed one baby a bottle or amuse her while she waits her turn at the breast.
- Dress one infant while you bathe another.
- Take the babies for a walk while you nap.
- Accompany you to the pediatrician.
- Fold laundry or wash dishes while you chat.
- Bring a bag of groceries or replenish your stock of diapers and wipes.
- Drive your older child to the playground or preschool so that you can concentrate on the babies.
- Drop off a frozen meal or prepare dinner. Best are the "one-handed meals"—hamburgers, salads, casseroles, things that don't require a knife—so each parent can hold a fussy baby while eating.

Hang on to your sense of humor when asking for help. For instance, Ginny and David Seyler's answering machine bears this message: "Hi. We can't come to the phone right now. But if you'd like to come over and diaper a baby or two or three, feel free! Otherwise, leave a message."

If you feel shy about asking over and over for assistance, just ask once, as Judy Levy did when her twin daughters were born. "I told a friend that even though many people had offered to help, I was embarrassed to follow through. She made a list of the names and phone numbers of everyone who had volunteered, and established a schedule whereby a different person dropped off a meal each Wednesday and Sunday. With the leftovers, we only had to cook once or twice a week. That was the greatest!"

You have three or four babies? You'll need more than dinner delivery. Again, try to find a friend willing to take charge of coordinating the volunteers. "My friend Janice would work everything out for the week, then call me and say, 'Get your calendar and write all this down. Sue is coming Monday to help with laundry, Mary will be there Tuesday to clean the house, Jane will bring groceries on Wednesday,' and so on and so on," explains quad mom Anne

Seifert. "It was hard to open my house to all these people, but I thank God for them. No way could I have managed everything myself."

Seek out other unpaid volunteers.

Call your local college and ask if any student might be interested in a hands-on research project on twins or supertwins. Find out if the high school would allow a student who assists you to earn extra credit for a child-care or cooking class. A Girl Scout or church youth group member might run errands, while an elderly neighbor could play surrogate grandparent.

Make sure your husband is a full partner.

"Tim took two weeks off work after the twins were born, and that was the most helpful thing for me," says Stacy Moore. "We learned together how to take care of the babies, encouraging each other and saying, 'Yeah, that looks right!' whenever we mastered a new skill."

Urge Daddy to take as much time off from work as possible in those first challenging weeks after the babies come home. He can assist with feedings and baths, change diapers, clean up spit-up, empty the diaper pail, and soothe a crying baby or two. If he doesn't know how to do basic baby-care tasks, teach him. Chances are he's already used to doing the vacuuming, cooking, and food shopping, since you were cautioned against overexerting yourself during the pregnancy—so let him continue with these jobs now.

Nocturnal duties also can be shared. If you're bottle-feeding, you might take turns on the night shift, assigning one parent to handle all infant care while the other sleeps through, then switching roles the next night. "At first, Mark and I would both get up to take care of the quads, but that meant neither of us got any decent sleep at all," says Anne Seifert. "Then we started switching off, letting one person sleep for six hours while the other handled all the babies' needs. It was still tough, but far more manageable."

Another option is to split the night shift. "After my sister went back to college, I quickly exhausted myself handling all the twins' nighttime needs alone. So I told my husband he had to help!" says Lydia Greenwood. "Ed came up with a great system. In the evenings, we shared baby-care duties until we went to bed at 10 P.M. It was my job to wake up and handle any baby care that needed to be done between bedtime and 4 A.M. Any cries that came after that, Ed answered until he left for work in the morning. Typically this meant that I nursed the twins at 2 A.M., Ed gave them bottles at 6 A.M., and then I nursed again at 9 A.M. Once we hit upon this schedule, my fatigue eased dramatically."

Even if you're exclusively breast-feeding, your partner can still share the load. Let him be the one to get up when a hungry baby howls. He can bring the child to your bed and help snuggle her up to your breast, so you can continue to doze as she nurses. When she's done, he can burp her, change her if necessary, and settle her back to sleep—then repeat the process when the next baby needs to be fed. Just be sure you both agree on Dad's responsibilities before going to bed, because 2 A.M. is not the best time to argue it out.

Sanity-Saving Schedules

If your babies were hospitalized after birth, they may already be used to a schedule. Ask the staff to outline it for you before the babies are discharged. "Once the twins came home, I just stuck with the same routine the nurses had them on," says one mother of identical twin boys born 13 weeks premature.

But for most parents, life with newborn multiples seems at first to have no rhythm—no pattern to when the babies sleep or eat, and no way to predict the course of the day. This can be frustrating. You finally think you have five minutes to jump into the shower, but then one baby or another suddenly wakes up from his nap. You struggle to get everyone bundled up and into the stroller, only to be forced to cut the walk short when someone starts screaming with hunger before you've gone a block.

The solution is to ease your babies toward similar schedules. During the day, when one baby is hungry, feed the others too. Do the same at night, even if it means waking a sleeping baby or two in order to feed them with or immediately after the first.

But what about those oft-heard recommendations to feed on demand rather than on a schedule? While it's true that feeding on demand is generally a good thing, it's simply not always realistic with multiples, particularly for nighttime feedings. If you allow twins total control over the schedule, you may find yourself feeding the first one at 1 A.M. and the second at 2:30 A.M.—which means that by 4 A.M., the first one will be hungry again. You'll never get more than an hour of uninterrupted sleep. And with triplets or quads, you'll be dragging yourself out of bed every half hour.

Once your babies reach the age of three months, however, one if not both may be ready to sleep five or six hours at a stretch. At that point, experiment for a few nights to see what happens if you don't wake that second baby along with the first. If she screams to be fed 20 minutes after you've returned her sister to bed, go back to feeding them together for a few more weeks. But if you're lucky, baby number two will sleep through the night—and you'll be halfway home to a full night's sleep yourself.

Speaking of sleep, you'll want to coax your babies toward similar snoozing schedules, during the day as well as at night. When one is ready to nap, try to settle the whole crew in their cribs. The reward: You gain a few free hours to yourself, which can make a huge difference in your ability to cope with the many demands of caring for multiples.

Do the same in the evening by getting your multiples ready for bed at the same time. A pleasant bedtime ritual encourages babies to settle down more easily. "To help get our infant twins on the same schedule, we established a nightly routine of bath-bottle-bed. The girls were down by 8 P.M. every evening, giving my husband and me some adult time," notes Kelly Kassab, mother of twin girls and another child.

If you have trouble synchronizing your multiples, try keeping a daily log. It helps you spot the regularities and similarities in your babies' schedules, so you can build on these emerging patterns. It also comes in handy when you're trying to remember whether it was Kaitlyn or Kira who had that bath or BM an hour ago. Record the time and the number of minutes each child nurses or ounces of formula consumed; when each nap starts and ends; how many wet and dirty diapers each baby produces; when each baby is bathed; and when vitamins or other medications are given. Also leave space to jot down your multiples' milestones, as well as any questions you may have for the pediatrician.

TAMARA: As I studied my twins' daily logs, I realized both babies typically napped for two hours in the morning, but James fell asleep around 11 and Samantha closer to noon. I postponed his nap by actively entertaining him for half an hour, and moved hers up to 11:30 by cutting short the midmorning games and rocking her instead. Within a week, they were accustomed to falling asleep at about the same time—most mornings anyway.

It was such a luxury to have that hour to myself when both babies were napping. Usually I'd nap too. But if I was feeling relatively frisky, I could use that precious time to check in at the office, call a friend, clean the house, or just relax with a magazine.

For easier comparison, I used a side-by-side format for my twins' log, a sample of which appears here. You can adjust it as needed for the number of babies in your family.

A DAY IN THE LIFE: KEEPING A LOG
Establishing a routine is half the task when it comes to parenting twins or supertwins. To record your children's daily habits, first devise a master sheet covering a 24-hour period. Start and end the page at whatever time you consider the "start" of the day. For easy comparison, use paper large enough to accommodate side by side the information for all your babies. Table 11.1 shows a partial-day sample that you can adapt to suit your own situation.

Date: June 8

James					Samantha			
Time	Feed	Diaper	Sleep	Bath	Feed	Diaper	Sleep	Bath
5 A.M.	Formula, 7 oz.	Wet	Up 5:10 Down 5:45	—	Formula, 6 oz.	BM	Up 5:10	—
6 A.M.	—	—	—	—	—	—	Down 6:15	—
7 A.M.	—	—	—	—	—	—	—	
8 A.M.	Nurse, 15 mins.	BM	Up 8:10	—	Nurse, 25 mins.	Wet	Up 8:10	—
9 A.M.	—	—	—	Tub	—	—	—	Sponge
10 A.M.	Nurse, 20 mins.	—	Down 10:50	—	Formula, 8 oz.	—	—	—
11 A.M.	—	—	—	—	—	BM	—	—
Noon	—	—	—	—	—	—	Down 12:05	—

Notes:	Ask doctor about spitting up		Diaper rash improving
Meds:	Vitamins		Vitamins, diaper ointment
News:	James found his fingers!		Samantha's first smile!

Table 11.1

Savvy Sleep Strategies

If you're going to get your multiples on the same general schedule, it makes sense to work toward a routine that's as convenient as possible for you. That means one in which the babies are most eager to play during the day and most inclined to sleep at night.

The difference this will make in your own sense of well-being cannot be overemphasized. "At first, when the twins were up at all hours of the night, I was so sleep-deprived that I felt weepy much of the time. That was weird, because normally I'm a happy person," admits Amy Maly, mother of identical twin girls. "This lasted about five or six weeks, until the twins were sleeping better at night—which of course meant I was sleeping better too. Getting a decent amount of rest made me feel human and happy again."

Unfortunately, infants are not born with an instinctive sense of day versus night. Instead of automatically coordinating their body rhythms to those of the sun and stars, you may find that your multiples often reverse those cycles—snoozing most of the day away and then shining with energy when the moon beams.

Such an out-of-sync schedule can be a pain. It's frustrating to hang around the house all day while one or more babies indulge in interminable naps. Worse, their animated nighttime antics leave you exhausted, since midnight demands for attention interfere with your own shut-eye.

Fortunately, you can address this problem. By helping your babies differentiate between day and night, you give them a good start toward sleeping through the night (a milestone typically reached around age three to four months). The key: Within a week of birth, most infants begin to have one long stretch of sleep that lasts from three to five hours—and your task is to make sure that, for all your babies, this long rest period occurs at night.

Show that daytime is playtime.

In order to consolidate their sleep into nighttime, your babies must also consolidate their wakefulness into daytime. So keep your multiples active when the sun's up. Establish a rise-and-shine routine for morning. As you lift your babies from their cribs, greet them with a big smile and a cheerful "Good morning, darlings!" With excitement in your voice, tell your babies of your plans for the day. Make a show of raising the window shades and turning on their music box.

Make daytime feedings fun. Beginning with breakfast and continuing with each feeding throughout the day, your multiples' meals should be social occasions. Sing or talk to them as they nurse. Gaze into their eyes and exclaim how happy you are to hold them.

After a feeding, don't just plunk them all in their cribs. Entertain them instead with a game of "This Little Piggy," a waltz around the room, or a guided tour of their new home. Need to shower? Line up the bouncy seats in the bathroom, and let your multiples interact with each other while they absorb the sights and sounds of the running water and your hair dryer.

Make naps distinct from nighttime slumber.

You don't want to go overboard in your efforts to keep your multiples awake during the day of course. They do need to nap. Your job is simply to teach them that daytime sleep is different from—and briefer than—nighttime slumber.

To start, keep the nursery well lit at naptime. Light is the major clue that tells us when we're supposed to be awake. With the window shades up and curtains open, those sunbeams can remind your babies that siestas ought not to last all afternoon.

Don't be too insistent about hushing household noises. By imposing a ban on noise, you encourage infants to sleep for hours on end during the day—the opposite of your true goal. What's more, you force everyone else in the house to tiptoe. Babies learn to sleep under whatever conditions they are introduced to from the beginning. Go ahead, turn on the CD player, run the vacuum, leave the phone on the hook, let siblings play in the next room.

Cut short naps that last too long. To weary parents of multiples desperate for a few hours of peace, the idea that their infants might nap too long seems ludicrous. But it isn't—not when prolonged napping interferes with the babies' ability to sleep well at night. A good rule of thumb is to limit daytime naps to no more than three hours at a stretch. This helps your children learn to save their longest sleep period for nighttime. So try not to groan when one baby, waking from her nap, startles her sisters into wakefulness too.

What if one of your babies continues to nap past that three-hour mark? Try picking him up and patting his back, changing his diaper or stripping off his clothes, rubbing under his chin or tickling his toes. If you simply cannot rouse him no matter what you do, he's probably in a deep-sleep stage. Wait 15 minutes to give him time to cycle into a lighter sleep stage, then try again to wake him.

Let evening be transition time.

Just as your babies learn that their morning routine means "get up and go," so can they learn that the evening routine is prelude to an extended rest. Be careful not to begin bedtime preparations too soon, however. The earlier in the evening you tuck them in, the earlier they're likely to awaken.

A vital step is to establish a soothing bedtime ritual. Human circadian rhythms operate on a 25-hour day. To click back to a 24-hour schedule, adults watch the clock. But your babies can't tell time. For them, a nightly ritual signals that it's time to wind down. Change each one into pajamas, as a sign that the day is done. Help them grow sleepy by rocking, reading aloud, and singing a soothing song.

Ready the nursery for nighttime too. Let your infants watch as you pull down the window shades and draw the curtains. Turn off all lights except for a nightlight; remember, darkness is a cue for sleep. Now is the time to keep the house fairly quiet. Set the stereo on low, and save noisy chores for morning.

Before the final tucking in, make sure each baby is comfortable. During the day, it doesn't matter much if some slight discomfort wakes a baby—and his wails then wake the others—since siestas shouldn't be overlong anyway. But before laying your multiples down at night, try to ensure that they're cozy enough to sleep a good while.

Change any diaper that is wet or soiled. If you use cloth diapers, make sure there's no Velcro closure scratching a tiny waist. For disposables, be certain the tabs aren't stuck to anyone's skin, that the corners of the tabs aren't poking a tummy, and that the edges aren't digging into a delicate thigh.

Next do climate control. Check each baby's hands. If they feel cold, chase away the chill with an extra quilt. Is the back of anyone's neck damp? That baby is too warm; take off a layer of clothing.

A sudden belch can startle a baby out of slumber, so be sure to burp everyone after feeding. And be on the lookout for other discomforts that could cut short sleep. Might a hand or foot get stuck between the mattress and crib slats? Cushiony crib bumpers can prevent this. Has the neck or crotch of the biggest baby's pajamas grown too tight? Time for a larger size.

Keep nighttime calm and quiet.

When your multiples are newborns, their stomachs hold only enough to satisfy them for three to four hours (or even less if they were low birthweight). They'll need to be fed at least once each night for several months. You should not attempt to prevent those normal hunger-induced awakenings. But you can help your babies understand that a nighttime feeding is not an invitation to party.

Feed the babies in their bedroom. Infants learn to associate the nursery with sleep. If you take them to the living room to nurse, they may be so excited by this "new" environment that they won't be able to drop off again when the meal's over.

Don't turn on the lights. You don't need 100-watt illumination in order to offer a breast or bottle. The soft glow of a nightlight or filtered rays from the hallway will suffice. This semi-darkness cues the babies that the sandman will come again soon.

Keep things quiet. If you turn on the TV or CD player for entertainment while you nurse, your babies will be entertained too—and they won't want to settle back to bed once their tummies are full. Think twice about serenading your little one with lullabies; instead, save your songs for daytime. And take a tip from Lydia Greenwood: "I don't even talk to my twins much during nighttime feedings. I figure we have plenty of time to chat during the day."

Skip the fun and games too—2 A.M. is not the time to indulge in a round of "Pop Goes the

Weasel." If a nighttime feeding takes more than 20 minutes per baby, handling or burping is excessive. If a diaper is wet or soiled, change it, but without any fanfare. You're not being cold or cruel; you're simply letting your multiples know that at this time of night grown-ups are very boring. Don't feel guilty. You'll more than make up for any missed fun the next morning.

TAMARA: Premature babies often have unique sleep patterns and problems, as I found out in the weeks after my twins came home from the hospital. Like every parent, I had looked forward to saying, "The baby slept through the night!" But preemies usually take longer to achieve this magical milestone, in part due to the corrected age phenomenon. While most full-term babies are developmentally capable of sleeping through the night by about three to four months of age, preemies are unlikely to be ready until they are five, six, or even seven months old—in other words, about three to four months after their original due date.

Another way in which prematurity affects sleep has to do with nutritional needs. Premature infants need to eat more often. When my twins were discharged from the NICU, they weighed just over 4 pounds. No way could their tiny tummies hold enough milk to carry them through for four hours, so I was given strict instructions to feed them every two hours. Not until your babies' weight has climbed to about 9 pounds will your pediatrician give you the go-ahead to stretch feedings to every three to four hours. Until that happens, expect catnaps to be the order of business.

Preemies are particularly prone to mixing up their days and nights. This stems from the fact that in the hospital, certain routine procedures such as bathing are often performed on the late-night shift. By the time your babies come home, they may be used to snoozing the day away and splashing around at midnight. You'll have to work harder to reverse this pattern.

You also may have to put some extra effort into helping your premature twins or supertwins adjust to a dark, quiet nursery. The first evening my son was home from the hospital, after all the well-wishers had departed, I sat with him in the nursery and quietly rocked him as I watched the sunlight gradually fade. It dawned on me then that little James had never before experienced darkness or silence. The neonatal intensive care unit had been a brightly lit ward filled with beeping vital-signs monitors, ringing phones, and constant conversation between parents and staff.

If your preemies seem fretful in the unfamiliar quietude of home, try leaving a light on in the nursery. Near the cribs, place a radio, ticking clock, or tape player with a recording of hospital sounds. Then over the next week or so, gradually dim the light and turn down the sound, until your babies adapt to a more tranquil way of life.

Do Multiples Need Mountains of Equipment?

Twins, triplets, or quads will need more equipment and supplies than a singleton of course—but not necessarily two, three, or four times as much stuff. Here are tips on what to buy and how to save:

Each Baby Needs His Own . . .

- **Car seat:** Choose seats narrow enough to fit side by side in your car. Many parents prefer infant car seats (where the base stays belted inside the car and the seat lifts out) because this makes it possible to carry twins together for short distances, putting the seats on the ground in order to open doors. The babies can snooze undisturbed as you move them around, and stairs aren't the problem they'd be for a stroller.
- **Crib:** Two babies may be able to share a single crib for the first three months or so, but then it gets overcrowded. Be sure your cribs meet current federal safety standards; furniture manufactured before 1976 often does not.
- **Stroller seat:** Before you buy, assess what kind of use you expect the stroller to get. Each style has its own advantages and disadvantages. A tandem-style twin stroller has two forward-facing seats and fits easily through doorways, but it can be heavy. A face-to-face stroller lets twins share toys on a center tray, but it may not collapse for easy storage. Side-by-side strollers often are lightweight and collapsible, but may not fit through doorways and aisles. Umbrella side-by-side models are narrower and lightweight, but they may not provide the back support and full recline that newborns need. If possible, select a style with individually reclining seats. For triplets or quads, choices are more limited; go with whatever seems sturdiest.
- **Infant seat:** Separate seats are easier to carry and move around than double or triple styles. Bouncers provide extra fun.
- **High chair:** A one-handed tray release mechanism is essential, since you may have more babies than hands. Extra-large trays make handy play tables when multiples are being kept conveniently immobilized. But before you buy, make sure they won't crowd your kitchen.

DUPLICATES ARE NICE BUT NOT ESSENTIAL

- **Swing:** Motorized styles are quieter than manual cranks. Gliders take up less space, but some babies seem to prefer the motion of the swing.
- **Front pack or sling:** One front pack and a single stroller make it easier to maneuver twins through a crowd. Two packs let each parent carry a load while keeping hands free. A double front pack may seem smart, but the twins' combined weight may prove too cumbersome.

ONE WILL DO

- **Playpen or play yard:** Choose an extra-large model.
- **Rocking chair:** Make sure it's wide enough for you to cuddle at least two babies at a time.
- **Diaper bag:** Go for jumbo, with a shoulder strap. Or try a diaper backpack; it holds lots and leaves your hands free. (One mom of twins swears by the backpack she ordered through the Eagle Creek catalog.)
- **Infant bathtub:** You can bathe only one baby at a time.

FIND DEALS, SAVE DOLLARS

- Borrow furniture, clothes, and equipment, or buy it "gently used" at tag sales, consignment shops, or Mothers of Twins Club sales.
- When buying new, ask the store for a discount on items purchased in duplicate.
- To cut down on your initial expenditure, delay purchases of equipment that won't be needed immediately, such as the high chairs and playpen. Even that second crib can wait a few months if necessary.
- Comparison shop. Store-brand disposable diapers can save you money; powdered formula is cheaper than ready-to-feed. Find out if a local price club sells baby food in bulk.
- Through doctors' offices and magazines, some manufacturers distribute postcards inviting you to join their mailing lists to receive coupons and special offers. Or call the companies direct and request extra discount coupons. Also watch for baby-product coupon swaps held by local Mothers of Twins Clubs.
- If you're using cloth diapers, find a diaper service that charges a flat fee for delivery, with only a modest increase for additional diapers.

- Each baby will need her own snowsuit, jacket, shoes, and sun hat. But everyone can share play clothes and pajamas.
- Most in-home caregivers charge only slightly more (not twice as much) for twins. Many day-care centers offer a sibling discount.
- Your pediatrician may give you a two-for-one break on fees. It never hurts to ask.

STRETCH YOUR LIVING SPACE

- Even a small nursery can accommodate multiples. To create a play area in the center of the room, arrange twins' cribs in an L in the corner. If you have triplets, arrange cribs in a U shape along three walls.
- To increase closet capacity, install a second rod two feet below the first, and hang a shoe bag inside the door to store booties, bonnets, and pacifiers.
- Sling saddlebags over the changing table to hold diapers, wipes, and ointment, leaving drawers free for clothes and blankets.
- Use shelves rather than toy boxes to keep playthings organized without sacrificing floor space.
- Raise the rod in your coat closet, and use the space beneath to store the stroller.
- If having two or more high chairs in the kitchen leaves no room for grown-ups to eat, install a wall-mounted table that flips up and out of the way when not in use.

Stress-Busters for Busy Parents

TAMARA: What kept me from stressing out completely was learning to catnap whenever and wherever opportunity presented itself. If I'd driven the twins to the pediatrician or the park, for instance, they were both sure to fall asleep on the way home. I knew from experience that if I tried to move them into the house, one or both would wake up, and I'd lose any chance of catching 40 winks for myself.

Instead, I'd park in my driveway, turn off the engine, crank back the driver's seat, and snooze right there until one baby or the other woke up. My neighbors thought it was funny, but I didn't care. I logged a lot of shut-eye this way, and felt better for it.

I shared this tip at one Mother of Twins Club meeting, and soon everyone was piping up with stress-reducing suggestions of their own. Below are some smart ones to try:

Save steps.

The less you have to run around the house, the more energy you'll have for playing with your babies. Spread the baby equipment throughout the house—infant seats in the family room, swings in the dining room, playpen in the den—so your multiples are readily accommodated no matter what room you're in. Store some diapers, wipes, and clean clothes downstairs. That way, you don't have to run up to the nursery every time one baby or another needs changing. "I keep spit-up cloths in every room, handy for emergencies. My home isn't House Beautiful, but I have what I need where I need it," says Lisa McDonough, mother of boy/girl twins and two older children.

To spare yourself those 2 A.M. treks to the kitchen, put several bottles of sterilized water and a can of powdered formula in the nursery before you go to bed. If you use ready-to-serve formula, which must be kept refrigerated once it's opened, invest in several bottle warmers. These keep bottles cold, then quickly warm bottles up when the babies are ready to eat.

Home delivery can be a boon. Shop for baby clothes, toys, and child-proofing supplies by catalog or on-line. Find a pharmacy that delivers formula, diapers, and other supplies.

Avoid interruptions.

On your phone answering machine, record your newborns' vital statistics, or progress reports as they grow. Program the machine to answer automatically when you're resting or feeding or bathing the babies. Use a nursery monitor during the babies' naps so you can work undisturbed anywhere in the house, without constant hikes to the nursery to check on the children.

Eliminate unnecessary tasks.

There's no rule that says you must give each baby a full tub bath daily. You can alternate days as long as the diaper area, hands, and face are wiped clean. Once the babies can handle the big bathtub, bathe one right after the other; don't bother to change the water unless it's really dirty. When your multiples can sit with complete steadiness, bathe them all together.

Don't let germ patrol drive you to distraction.

Of course you'll do your best to avoid illness—washing your hands often, disinfecting toys, and asking friends with sick tots to stay away until they're well. But unless your babies have compromised immune systems, there's no point in making yourself crazy. Lisa McDonough reports, "At first, I was fastidious about using separate spoons and bowls for each twin, but meals took forever, dirty dishes were everywhere, and I'd mix up the spoons anyway. Then my pediatrician pointed out that the twins were in such constant close proximity that they were bound to catch each other's colds. So when the twins seemed healthy and I was crunched for time, I made do with a single spoon and bowl. Mealtimes were a lot simpler."

Get out of the house.

"For the first five weeks after my twin girls were born, I didn't get out of the house with the babies for anything other than doctor appointments," Judy Levy moans. She's not exaggerating:

One study from England showed that mothers of young twins leave the house far less often than do mothers of singletons. This isolation compounds the emotional strains of parenting multiples. Make a point of getting out for fresh air and a change of scenery as often as possible.

True, it's not easy to get two or more babies fed, changed, dressed, and alert enough to enjoy the wide world simultaneously. Yet once outings become part of the pattern of the day, the effort involved eases significantly. It needn't be an elaborate adventure. A walk in the park, a visit with a neighbor, or a stroll through the mall can lift spirits. "After being stuck in the house for days, a trip to the dry cleaner's seems exotic," says Lydia Greenwood.

Key to cutting down on prep time is a well-stocked diaper bag. Prepare a checklist: two diapers per baby, plus wipes, ointment, and changing pad; a clean outfit, bib, and blanket for each baby; spit-up cloths and bottles; pacifiers, teethers, and small toys; your wallet and keys; and whatever else you need. Lydia adds, "I restock my bag each evening. It still takes hours to get out the door the next morning, but at least the packing is done."

Figure out what time of day works best for an excursion, given your babies' schedules. "At first, I made myself frantic trying to get errands done in the morning—an impossibility, considering my twins' eating and napping routines," says Lydia Greenwood. "Once I started scheduling their doctor's appointments and play dates for afternoons only, outings got much easier."

A note of caution: You never want to leave one baby alone in the stroller or car while you go back inside to finish dressing another. Get everyone completely ready to roll, then quickly settle them into their stroller or car seats.

Safeguarding Your Babies' Health

DR. LUKE: After all you went through to ensure that your babies would arrive in this world as healthy as possible, you certainly don't want to risk any accidents now that they're here. While the task of keeping two or more babies safe and sound may seem daunting at first, with some forethought and basic training, you'll rise to the challenge.

I do urge you to take a class in infant first aid and CPR. I hope you never need to use these skills, but it's wise to be prepared for an emergency. Also be sure to post the phone number of the local poison control center next to each telephone in your home.

SKILLS YOU NEED TO LEARN

Any good manual on baby care will describe these essential skills in detail. Whether you're taking care of one baby or four, the basics remain the same. You do have one advantage, however, over all those singleton families—as a parent of multiples, you'll more quickly gain the practice you need to perform all these tasks expertly. Check out the instructions on how to:

- Feed your babies
- Bathe your babies
- Diaper your babies
- Recognize and treat diaper rash
- Recognize and treat cradle cap
- Use a bulb syringe to clear a baby's stuffy nose
- Take a baby's temperature, rectally or with an ear thermometer
- Give a baby medicine, orally or rectally

THE WELL-STOCKED MEDICINE CABINET

When a baby (or two or three) spikes a fever, it's a bad feeling to discover that your medicine cabinet is bare. Use this checklist to shop ahead, and you'll be ready whenever supplies are needed:

- Rectal thermometers—one per baby, labeled with each child's name—or an ear thermometer
- Calibrated medicine dropper or syringe for measuring dosage (do *not* use kitchen spoons; they vary greatly in size and may result in giving too much or too little medicine)
- Bulb syringes for suctioning mucus from tiny stuffed-up noses
- Tweezers for removing splinters and ticks
- Sterile bandages in various sizes and shapes
- Gauze pads and adhesive tape
- Infant Tylenol (acetaminophen) or other liquid aspirin substitute (never give "baby aspirin" or any other type of aspirin to a child. It can lead to Reye's syndrome, a potentially fatal neurological disease)
- Pedialyte or other rehydration liquid, to avoid dehydration from diarrhea
- Liquefied charcoal and syrup of ipecac, to induce vomiting (if recommended by your local poison control center)
- Diaper ointment or cream for diaper rash
- Antiseptic ointment, cream, or spray for minor cuts or scrapes
- Calamine lotion or 0.5 percent hydrocortisone cream for insect bites and itchy rashes

- Sunscreen (sunscreen is recommended for babies over six months old. Prior to that, be especially careful to avoid excessive sun exposure)

BEFORE YOU CALL THE PEDIATRICIAN

Of course, you should call the doctor anytime a baby seems to have a medical problem. But in order for the pediatrician to advise you, she'll need certain information. Before you pick up the phone, jot down the following:

- Each baby's symptoms and when they began
- Each baby's temperature, and when and how (rectally or by ear) it was taken
- When, what, and how much each baby ate last
- If and when your babies were exposed to a sick person

BABY-PROOFING BASICS TIMES TWO (OR MORE)

"As soon as my twins became mobile, I realized how quickly one could crawl toward danger while I was busy chasing, changing, or feeding the other," says Lydia Greenwood. "Basic baby-proofing clearly wasn't enough in our household. We needed that extra measure of thoroughness I call twin-proofing." To make your home safe for your multiples, follow these room-by-room guidelines:

Living Room

Put breakables up high or out of sight. Store out of reach any small items that might present a choking hazard—chess pieces, small knickknacks, coin collections. Shorten window cords from blinds or draperies by tying them with secure knots or using wraparound cord shorteners. Replace glass tabletops with Plexiglas. Place a gate at the *top and bottom* of stairs.

Dining Room

Use place mats rather than a tablecloth; with their combined strength, your tots could easily yank on the corner of a tablecloth and pull a hot casserole down onto themselves. When setting the table, lay out knives for the adults only after all the babies are safely strapped into their high chairs. Put locks on china cabinets to keep little ones away from breakables like goblets and candlesticks. Bolt cabinets and bookshelves to the wall so they don't topple over if a child tries to climb them. Install a latch to keep swinging doors open so they don't pinch tiny fingers. Never leave a half-finished glass of an alcoholic beverage where your children can reach it. Just a few swallows can be toxic.

Kitchen

Store all toxic products—polishes, drain cleaner, scouring powder—in the highest cupboards. Install baby-proof latches on any cabinet that holds breakable items. Keep electric appliances (mixer, blender, food processor, carving knife, waffle iron, toaster, microwave oven) out of reach. Never leave knives in the dishwasher where curious crawlers could easily reach them. Always put pots on back burners. Install stove knob covers to keep kids from turning on burners. Store unused plastic trash bin liners out of reach. Before discarding any plastic bag, fold it lengthwise and tie tight knots in the center. Keep the garbage can inside a latched cabinet, place the trash bin on a high counter, or use a garbage pail with a locking mechanism similar to that on a diaper pail. Otherwise, your tots may paw through the garbage, encountering sharp cans or choking hazards like chicken bones.

Nursery

Once your babies can stand, move their crib mattresses to the lowest position to thwart attempts to climb out. Remove from the walls any pictures within reach of the cribs; you don't want the children to cut themselves on the glass or sharp corners. For electrical outlets, install covers that automatically snap closed to conceal the outlet opening whenever the plug is removed, or use box-shaped covers that fit over outlet plates to prevent your children from removing the plug from the outlet. Tack down cords to all lamps, air conditioners, and other appliances; chewing on cords can lead to disfiguring or even life-threatening burns. Be sure the toy chest has holes for ventilation, in case the kids climb inside, and hinges that hold the cover securely in any position to prevent the lid from slamming on a small hand or head. Don't place a toy box—or anything else—beneath a window where it could be used as a stepladder to climb out. Install window guards on all windows above the first floor.

Bathroom

Empty the tub immediately when bath time is over. *Never* leave any of the children alone in a bathtub, even for an instant. Turn the thermostat on the hot water heater down to 120 degrees so your babies won't scald themselves if they turn on the faucet. Pad the sharp spout of the tub with a soft spout cover. Put a nonskid mat on the bottom of the tub. Keep all electrical appliances such as hair dryers and curling irons unplugged and out of reach. Install a latch on the toilet lid. Keep all medications in a locked box. Lock up all toxic products, including perfumes, mouthwash, aftershave, cosmetics, cleansers, and disinfectants.

> **TAMARA:** If you're still feeling overwhelmed by all the time and energy required to take care of your multiples, don't despair. You're not alone. In that first chaotic year after my

twins were born, a triumphant day was one in which I accomplished *anything* beyond the all-consuming baby-care essentials. Often, even a single load of laundry was more than I could manage.

Trust me—things do get easier with time as you and your babies settle into a manageable routine. In the meanwhile, don't worry about those days when nothing gets done. If you've made time to cherish your babies and give them good care, you've done all you really need to do.

Chapter 12

Becoming One Big Happy Family

Every pregnant woman imagines that magical moment: Seconds after birth, her baby (or babies!) will be placed in her arms, and she'll be immediately overwhelmed by love. This ideal has been promoted for nearly three decades, since early research on parent-infant bonding sparked a revolution that gave fathers access to the maternity ward and mothers more control over labor.

Sounds wonderful to fall instantly, effortlessly, in love with your newborns? Sure. The problem is that parents of singletons and multiples alike have come to *expect* that enchanted moment—yet studies show that only about 25 percent actually experience it.

The reasons are myriad. Some mothers are simply too exhausted to feel anything more profound than relief that the ordeal of labor is over. For others, disappointment may cloud that first encounter. Perhaps you and your husband had always longed for a daughter but wound up with a trio of boys. Or perhaps you had hoped to experience natural childbirth but, like 50 percent of mothers of twins and nearly all mothers of supertwins, ended up having a cesarean section.

"I expected the textbook bonding experience—go to the hospital, have the babies, breast-feed the twins right on the delivery table, and bond with both at that very instant," says Amy Maly, mother of identical twin girls. "But that just didn't happen. I wanted to deliver vaginally, but I wound up with a C-section. Because I wasn't able to see the twins as they were delivered, I had this weird sense of alienation—'Gosh, did those babies really come out of *me*?' Afterward I was too groggy from the anesthesia to be able to nurse well. Then I was afraid that I had missed the golden opportunity and that we'd never really bond quite right."

Bonding with All Those Babies

DR. LUKE: In the days following delivery, many of our patients at the Multiples Clinic express concerns similar to Amy's. Fortunately, such worries are usually dispelled fairly quickly as the parents' love for their babies blossoms.

Research has shown that parent-infant bonding is an ongoing process that evolves over time. It is not a bolt-from-the-blue moment that must occur at the moment of birth in order for the relationship to thrive. It is more like falling in love—that first rush is like a crush, but true intimacy develops over the months as you get to know each other.

It's important to accept this fact because with multiples, the bonding issue can be extra complicated. Who ever expects to fall in love with two, three, or four people at the same time? Yet this is precisely the challenge that parents of multiples must confront. No wonder that bonding with twins, triplets, or quadruplets may take longer than with a singleton. Here's why:

Time limitations interfere with enjoyment.

An Israeli study showed that mothers of twins spend 35 to 39 percent of their time on infant-related tasks, whereas mothers of one baby spend only 22 to 29 percent. This means that parents of multiples have less time for playing, snuggling, talking, and especially the one-on-one interacting so essential to the bonding process.

"I didn't bond with my triplets nearly as quickly as I did with my first child," admits Helen Armer. "It was mainly the fatigue. In the beginning, I had enough to do just taking care of their basic needs. I sometimes joked, 'All I can do is feed, burp, and change each baby, then plunk it back in the crib'—but it wasn't really funny. There was no time to play." For Helen, the situation eased and affection grew once she and her triplets were getting more sleep at night, leaving everyone with more energy for daytime fun.

To maximize your pleasure in parenthood, tune in to your babies' quiet alert periods, when infants are at their most engaging. Take note of how your babies respond to you by following your movements with their eyes, molding their body to yours, and exploring your skin with their hands. Stick out your tongue or open your mouth, then wait patiently; within a minute, one or more of your babies may imitate you. Talk to your little ones too, using a soft high-pitched tone. Infants won't understand the words, but they'll recognize a loving tone.

One-on-one time is difficult to come by.

Ginny Seyler, another mother of triplets, says, "I worried about how I would be able to make my babies understand that I loved each and every one of them. How do you look into the eyes of three babies at a time? How do you hold them all when they all need cuddling at once?"

The answer to that dilemma is to seize every opportunity to give each child your undivided attention. Diaper changes and baths are, of necessity, performed on one baby at a time—so make the most of those chances to talk and play one on one. Even during simultaneous feedings, you can have a moment "alone" with one infant simply by making eye contact and smiling. Perhaps exempt one or two daily feedings from the simultaneous system, setting aside the extra time needed to gaze into just one little face for the full feeding. Use a front pack or sling around the house (not just on excursions out), and alternate which baby you carry in it. This allows you to stay physically close and helps you learn to read each baby's unique signals. As you become more adept at interpreting and responding to their needs, your babies will cry less—leaving more opportunities for pleasant interaction with each one.

And don't forget that although multiples may not always get quite as much parental attention as singletons do, they enjoy a unique benefit—the warm relationship they share with their wombmates. Anne Seifert says, "I can't always give my quadruplets as many hugs and kisses as I'd like to. I can hold two at a time, but I can't hold all four. Yet it's comforting to see how much affection they get from one another. They love to laugh together, play together, and snuggle up close together. They're the best of friends now, and I hope they always will be."

Mothers and fathers may get caught up in "unit bonding."
Parents may feel attached to their multiples as a matched set rather than as separate individuals. One warning sign of "unit bonding" is when parents insist on always dressing their babies identically. While there's no harm in coordinating the babies' outfits on occasion, do beware of overdoing it. If you find yourself changing all the kids' clothes every time one soils her suit, you're probably overinvested in the idea of presenting your multiples to the world as a team.

What to do with all those matching outfits your babies received as gifts? "At our baby shower, it was fun to open two of this, two of that. But there's no law saying we have to dress the boys in those identical outfits on the same day," says Stacy Moore, mother of fraternal twin boys. "If Brandon wears his bunny overalls on Monday, I'll wait till Thursday to have Steven wear his. Those matching gifts get used and are very much appreciated—they just don't get used at the same time."

Studies suggest that unit bonding is more problematic with identicals than with fraternals, since parents may have trouble telling the babies apart. So make an effort to prevent identity mix-ups. You might leave on the babies' hospital bracelets for the first week or two, until you identify some distinguishing features. Does this child have a longer face? Does that one have a small birthmark or a distinctive hair swirl? "It was impossible to tell my babies apart until I noticed that their eyes were a slightly different color," says one mother of identical twin boys. Once you've figured out how to tell the babies apart, clue in friends and relatives.

Consider too whether it's in your babies' best interests to have matching names. Though one U.S. study found that 40 percent of parents choose alliterative or rhyming names for their multiples, it may be easier for everyone to regard your children as individuals if their names are quite distinct. Too late now because the babies are already born and named? Stay open to the possibility that in the future it may prove expedient to begin referring to Camille and Lucille as Cammy and Lucy, or to stretch Donny and Danny to Donald and Daniel. Whatever monikers are chosen, consciously call your babies by name rather than referring to them as "the twins" or "the quads."

Bonding with each baby as an individual is also enhanced when you make the effort to appreciate each baby's unique qualities. Notice each child's preferences for certain activities, sounds, or textures. Try to determine which baby is most energetic, which loves to be tickled on the toes, and which one can yell the loudest. But don't feel guilty if such recognition takes time. "At first I felt overwhelmed by the challenge of bonding with two babies at once, and disappointed that I wasn't able to point out lots of distinctions between my twins," says Judy Levy, mother of fraternal twin girls and an older daughter. "But then I realized that all I really needed to do in the beginning was to give them love and tenderness. Their personalities would emerge over time."

Favoritism may come into play.

Most parents expect to love their children equally, so you may be shocked to find yourself drawn more to a particular baby. Perhaps one of your multiples has a temperament that fits more easily with yours. Maybe she's prettier, or easier to soothe, or developmentally more advanced. With boy/girl twins, you might prefer the child of the sex you'd hoped for. If one twin is hospitalized longer, you might feel closer to the baby who's already at home—or to the "poor little angel" who's still in the NICU. One mother of twins even confessed that because she had wanted just one child, it took months to overcome her resentment of the second-born "unplanned" twin.

Whatever triggers favoritism, take steps to overcome it. If one child has a difficult temperament, focus on his positive traits. Accept that developmentally multiples are not clones; one may be crawling while the others are still learning to sit. Visit your hospitalized baby every day, even if it means leaving the at-home infants with a sitter. Even if you don't love all the babies equally at first, if you treat them fairly and lovingly, genuine affection will follow.

Infertility treatments can complicate bonding.

Because parents of multiples are often infertility patients, they may experience unique emotional concerns about bonding if the babies were conceived using donor sperm or donor eggs. "For more than a decade, I tried various infertility treatments, including Pergonal and *in vitro* fertilization, but never managed to carry a pregnancy past seven weeks. Finally, when I was 42, my fertility specialist suggested using donor eggs from a younger woman, which could be fertilized with my husband's sperm. That's when I conceived quadruplets," says Sarah Turner.

Given that the quads were not genetically related to Sarah, her doctor suggested that she talk to a counselor about any conflicting emotions she might have. "That would be good advice for anyone concerned about bonding," says Sarah, "but honestly, I haven't had the slightest bit of trouble falling in love with these babies. With all I went through to bring them into this world, I feel like a full-fledged, bona fide mother."

Developmental delays may lead to disappointment.

Another common hindrance to bonding stems from the fact that many multiples are born prematurely. Parents who expect their children to keep pace developmentally with their peers may feel cheated when their babies fail to smile, sit, or walk on schedule.

To get past this disappointment, understand that it's normal during pregnancy for expectant parents to develop a mental picture of their babies. One early task of parenting is to resolve the discrepancy between this idealized image and the real infants. When newborns have medical problems, this task is harder. Parents must mourn the loss of the dreamed-of infants—a process that may take weeks—before they can bond with the living children.

For this reason, it is essential that you think of your preemies in terms of their corrected age, or the age they would be now had they been born at full term. Sure, your girlfriend's six-week-old singleton is already bestowing those heart-melting first smiles on Mommy. You'll see first smiles too—but probably not for about six weeks after your babies' original due date.

TAMARA: The deepest shock I ever felt was at first sight of my premature twins. My son's head was no larger than a lemon; red, wrinkled flesh draped his bony 3-pound frame. My daughter lay still and unbreathing, her skin a sickening blue. My heart, overwhelmed with anguish, had little room to register love.

Separation intensified my pain. My twins were rushed to a major medical center miles away, while I stayed behind for two days at the hospital where I'd given birth. I felt desperately lonely. The Twin Tigers (as I had called them when they were snug inside me) were gone. Yet the James and Samantha who had replaced them—babies I'd scarcely seen and never held—seemed far less real.

That started to change when I was discharged. I spent endless hours each day in the NICU, scurrying between the twins' separate rooms. But I had only a shaky sense of motherhood. Surely I was less vital to my children's well-being than were the doctors and nurses who had been charged with their care. My overriding emotion was not love, but fear that my babies would die.

The turning point came two weeks later. I was holding my son when a nurse walked into his room unannounced and said, "Samantha wants to meet James." She placed my daughter (who had been momentarily freed from the many monitors that connected her to her isolette) into my empty arm. For the first time, I saw my twins together. Suddenly I knew they would live. My dread turned to hope, my disappointment to joy, my loneliness to an overwhelming love. I felt like a real mother at last.

In the months that followed my twins' homecoming, my adoration for them grew ever deeper. Yet occasionally I'd wonder: "Is there some part of a mother's heart that can be given only in those euphoric postpartum moments? Would I have loved my twins even more if I had not had to endure those days of separation and uncertainty?"

The answer came two years later, when I delivered my third child, a healthy 7½-pounder. Little Jack and I had a heavenly first embrace just moments after he was born, and my passion for him is profound—yet no more profound than my passion for the twins. Though James and Samantha and I were denied a blissful experience at their birth, ours is a comradeship shared only by those who face disaster together and triumph. And I believe that, having known the fear of losing my twins, I can now offer *all* my children even more patience, compassion, and love than I might otherwise have found in my heart.

How to Help a Big Brother or Sister Adjust

For an older sibling, the arrival of twins, triplets, or quads can be traumatic. Not one baby but several have displaced him as the center of his parents' universe. Eager to admire the infants, visiting relatives and friends—to say nothing of strangers on the street—often ignore him. And just when he finally has Mommy to himself for a moment, some baby or another cries to be fed or changed.

When one baby is born, the father usually compensates the older sibling for the mother's lack of time and attention. But with multiples, Dad is needed to help with the newborns, so the older child may end up feeling abandoned. Helen and Tom Armer can relate to that. Says Helen, "Caroline had just turned three when the triplets were born, and she was pretty jealous at first. She wanted a lot more attention from Mom and Dad than we were able to give her, and that led to all kinds of tantrums."

Parents naturally may wind up feeling guilty for causing an older child pain. Those guilt feelings may arrive at the same moment your multiples do. Judy Levy confesses, "When I delivered my twins, I was put in the same recovery bay on the maternity ward where I had been when my first child was born two years earlier. When they handed me the twins, I kept flashing back to Rianna's birth. I felt so guilty and I wondered, 'How can I love these little newborns and still keep loving my first baby?'"

For other parents, guilt grows along with their awareness of the demands of caring for multiples. One mother of twins recalls, "About three weeks after the babies were born, I was nursing them as my 18-month-old daughter stood next to me. She started to sob, and soon her tears were soaking the edge of my nursing pillow. I promised her I would play soon, but she couldn't understand why Mommy wouldn't play *now*. It broke my heart to think she was being gypped."

To minimize such problems, take steps to ease a sibling's adjustment to her expanded family. Some ideas to try:

- The first time your older child meets the multiples, have a gift for her on hand "from the babies." Thereafter, let her open any gifts that well-wishers may bring for the newborns. Says Judy, "Two-year-old Rianna didn't care what was in the box. She just liked the thrill of the unwrapping."
- Spend time alone with your firstborn every day—reading, playing, talking together, or whatever your child enjoys most. Build this ritual into your routine. Helen explains, "Now that the triplets are here, my three-year-old daughter and I cherish our private morning time together, eating breakfast, packing her lunchbox, and then driving to her preschool."
- If a big brother or sister enjoys fetching diapers or holding bottles for the babies, express your thanks enthusiastically. But don't make it seem as though he or she must accept this responsibility in order to stay in your good graces.
- Read storybooks about sibling rivalry to your older child to encourage him to express his resentment. Share your own frustration—"Boy, these babies cry a lot, don't they?"—to show that you understand his feelings.
- Explain that you are so busy because two or more babies take extra time, not because multiples are "special." Ask friends not to tell the older child that she's special because she has twin or triplet siblings. She needs to be appreciated for her own unique qualities.
- Let your older child share play sessions or outings with just one of the multiples at a time, so he can form his own one-on-one relationship with each new sibling.
- Remind visitors to talk to the older child. "We have a rule that anyone who comes to the house has to play with Rianna before they even are allowed to see the babies," Judy Levy reports.
- On outings, attach a sign to the stroller that says, "The babies won't mind if you greet their older brother first." Or let your toddler and one twin sit in the stroller, while the other twin rides in a front pack or sling. This makes the babies' twinship less obvious.

- If a passerby remarks on the babies' big blue eyes, for example, you can say, "Yes, they have beautiful eyes just like their big sister."
- Make sure your firstborn has an exciting, enjoyable life outside the home. Says Helen, "Caroline felt less neglected once she started nursery school. It gave her friends and activities of her own—a world apart from the triplets."

If You're Feeling Blue

"After my babies were born, my emotions were all mixed up. I was thrilled to be a mother, but I often felt weepy too. I'd start to cry if anyone even looked at me cross-eyed," says Meredith Alcott, mother of identical twin girls. "Thank goodness, within a few weeks I started to feel like myself again."

Meredith is far from alone. Postpartum mood disorders affect as many as 50 to 80 percent of mothers in the United States. The mildest form is known as the new-baby blues—or among mothers of multiples, the new-babies blues. That let-down, quick-to-cry feeling usually begins within a few days of delivery, and typically abates within several weeks.

Most new moms can feel better fast by doing one simple thing—spending a few minutes each day mothering *themselves*. Yes, it's hard to find a free moment, but you need nurturing too. Set aside time every day to read a novel, phone a friend, play an instrument, chat on-line, or indulge in some other relaxing activity. To ease that "chained to the nursery" feeling, hire a babysitter every week or two, and treat yourself to a professional manicure or massage, a lunch date with a friend, or a movie matinee. The sooner such activities are worked into your regular routine, the sooner you'll start feeling more like yourself.

Another excellent option is to exercise, because the hormones released during a workout provide a mood boost. If you can't find time to hit the gym, bundle the babies in their stroller and take a brisk walk. Do some simple stretches and sit-ups while the babies nap. Or put the babies in their bouncy seats in the TV room, and let them watch while you work out to an aerobics video.

Regular workouts also help to strengthen and tone your muscles so you can reclaim your figure faster—and that makes you feel better emotionally as well as physically. It's important, though, to have realistic goals and expectations. Because you had a multiple pregnancy, your abdominal muscles have been stretched far more than if you had given birth to just one baby. It may take six months to a year for your body to get back into shape. Meanwhile, focus on the fun of exercising again, and on the miracle of the beautiful babies your wonderful body produced.

In some cases, postpartum mood disorders are more severe than simple new-baby blues. From 10 to 20 percent of new mothers suffer from postpartum depression (PPD), symptoms of which are similar to those of clinical depression. If you experience several of the following symptoms for more than two weeks, you may have PPD:

- Uncontrollable weeping
- Despondency or hopelessness
- Feelings of inadequacy
- Loss of interest in activities that used to be enjoyable
- Inability to concentrate
- Memory problems
- Food cravings or loss of appetite
- Sleep troubles

There is no clear-cut answer as to why postpartum women sometimes get depressed, but the most likely explanation involves a mix of physiological, genetic, and lifestyle factors. Scientific evidence suggests the following:

- Hormone levels, particularly of estrogen and progesterone, shift dramatically after childbirth. These hormones are known to affect mood.
- Thyroid levels also drop significantly in the postpartum period. Low thyroid levels are associated with symptoms of depression.
- Genetics play a part. A family history of mood disorders increases a woman's odds of developing PPD.
- Personal history is also a risk factor. If you had PPD following an earlier pregnancy, you have a 30 to 50 percent chance of experiencing it after subsequent pregnancies.
- Diet has a role. A recent study from the National Institutes of Health suggests that women who consume less omega-3 fatty acids are at higher risk for PPD. The omega-3s are crucial ingredients in the biochemical processes that produce brain neurotransmitters such as serotonin and dopamine, which affect mood.
- Women who lack social support are more likely to develop PPD.
- Marital conflict and financial problems contribute to depression.

Are new mothers of multiples more susceptible to postpartum mood disorders? Perhaps so. The hormonal shifts that follow a multiple pregnancy may be more dramatic than those of mothers of singletons. One recent Swedish study found that the more complications a woman experienced during pregnancy, the more likely she was to develop PPD—and mothers of multiples are more prone to pregnancy complications. Likewise, some research suggests an association between cesarean deliveries and a higher incidence of PPD—and again, moms of twins and supertwins are more likely to have had a C-section. All these factors may be compounded by the more extreme physical, emotional, and financial demands involved in taking care of two or more newborns.

Unfortunately, too many moms suffer in silence. Says one mother of twins, "I had expected motherhood to be the most fulfilling experience of my life. But less than a week after the twins were born, I found myself feeling either sad or mad most of the time. I was so ashamed that I couldn't bring myself to talk to anyone about it." Even when a woman does broach the subject with family or friends, she may be told, "Snap out of it. You're a mother now, and you're responsible for these babies."

Yet if you are suffering from PPD, it is very important to get help. If you're reluctant to seek help for your own sake, do it for your babies' sake: Studies show that maternal depression early in an infant's life can have significant negative effects on his psychological, social, and intellectual development.

The most serious form of postpartum mood disorder is called postpartum psychosis. Here, the distinguishing symptom is a break with reality—the woman loses the ability to distinguish what is real from what is not, and so can be a threat to herself and her babies. Immediate treatment is necessary, usually involving hospitalization and antipsychotic medications. Fortunately, this condition is rare.

The vast majority of women with PPD can be helped far more easily. Treatment typically includes short-term psychotherapy, and/or one of the newer antidepressants such as Prozac, Zoloft, Celexa, or Wellbutrin. Help is also available from the following groups:

- Postpartum Support International; Web site www.postpartum.net.
- Center for Postpartum Health: 20700 Ventura Boulevard, #203, Woodland Hills, CA 91364. Telephone 818–887–1312; Web site www.postpartumhealth.com.
- Postpartum Health Alliance: PO Box 503396, San Diego, CA 92150. Telephone 619–685–7458; e-mail info@postpartumhealthalliance.org; Web site www.postpartumhealthalliance.org.

When should you seek treatment? If your baby blues haven't eased within three weeks of delivery, speak to your doctor. You've been through a lot in order to bring these babies into the world, and you deserve to enjoy them to the fullest.

Married . . . with Multiples

TAMARA: One evening a few months after the twins came home, I was having dinner with my husband and my sister. As I chattered on and on about the babies—how much they had grown, how adorable they were, how intensely in love I was with both of them— Bill was uncharacteristically quiet. Suddenly he excused himself from the table, said he wanted to take a walk, and left the house.

I looked at my sister in surprise. "What's with him?" I asked. My sister gave me a long look and then said simply, "I think he misses his wife."

Many men are dismayed to find that with the birth of an infant, they are forced to relinquish the number one spot in their wife's life. This feeling is multiplied when two or more babies simultaneously join the family, because it leaves the husband as low man on a *very* tall totem pole.

The intense physical connection you felt to your babies during the pregnancy is transformed, after they're born, into a powerful emotional bond—a bond that may, to some degree, exclude the father. It's as if sometimes a mother draws a circle around herself and the babies, leaving the father out.

Feeling neglected, he may withdraw to spend more time at work or with friends, or he may pick fights at home just to feel less invisible. He may even suffer the prick of a double-edged sword: He's jealous of the babies for captivating all your attention, and jealous of you for being the babies' favorite.

Caught up as you are in the all-consuming thrill of multiple motherhood (not to mention the time-consuming task of taking care of twins or supertwins), you may not recognize your partner's pain. But that's a risky oversight. If you and your husband let your relationship slide, you'll lose the thrill of being lovers.

For a marriage to stay strong after two, three, or four new members suddenly join the family, the partners have to devote some time to nurturing and nourishing their relationship. That's not to say you need to escape for a two-week cruise together. With newborn multiples to take care of, a getaway is probably not an option—but neither is it necessary, psychologists believe. Studies show that one big romantic blitz does less to reduce marital stress than do small loving moments together, repeated day after day. So carve out a few minutes to reconnect.

Encourage your partner to take paternity leave.

The more time he can take off work, the more involved he'll feel with the babies, and the more he'll enjoy them. The bonus: He'll also have more in common with you. But be sure not to hover over him with instructions on how to handle the babies. Treat him like a competent equal.

Make contact during the day.

When you're apart, try to phone, fax, or e-mail each other at least once daily. Don't just say, "Please pick up some diapers on the way home from work." Give each message some affectionate content, like, "I'm so glad I am married to you." When your husband walks into the house, give him a hug *before* you thrust a crying baby or two into his arms. He wants to feel like a partner in love, not just a partner in parenthood.

Share a meal.

Sit down to one intimate meal together each day, even if it's just a bowl of cereal before the babies wake up. Spend at least part of that time talking about something other than your multiples. As you eat, intertwine your feet with his under the table, or hum a few bars of "your song."

Compliment each other.

"Lydia and I are facing a lot of challenges right now. Not only do we have the kids to take care of, but she's trying to start up a home-based business, and I've just taken a new job," says Ed Greenwood, father of boy/girl twins. "Whenever I feel stressed out, she reminds me of all we've accomplished already, and I do the same for her. When we confirm our confidence in each other, the demands of our lives seem less daunting."

Reconnect as lovers.

First, ask your doctor when it's okay to resume having sex. In general, physicians recommend that women wait four to six weeks after delivery, so the cervix can close and vaginal tissues can heal. If you had a cesarean section, your physical recovery may take a little longer.

For many women, though, the bigger issue is emotional readiness. You're tired and stressed out; you're worried that lovemaking may hurt; and you're getting as much skin-to-skin contact as you can handle just from rocking, soothing, and feeding all those babies. Your husband, on the other hand, is probably eager to resume an active sex life.

Try to be open to feelings of romance. Instead of fretting about colic while you wash your hair, let your mind linger on the memory of the last time your husband and you shared a long, slow kiss. A fantasy that provides a 60-second sabbatical from the demands of parenting can refresh your romantic spirit and rekindle your desire.

TAMARA: My husband, Bill, and I have always had a really good relationship. But I'll admit that the first year after the twins' birth was a challenging time in our marriage. I kept thinking, "What's wrong here? I'm sure other couples could handle this better than we're doing."

Then I went to a meeting of the Mothers of Twins Club, and I was shocked to learn how many of the members' marriages had split up in the first few years after their twins or supertwins were born. But at the same time, it was encouraging to hear from numerous other moms that the task of parenting multiples gets much easier over time, if you can stick together through the initial adjustment.

When I got home that night, I sat down at the dining room table with Bill, and we talked for hours and hours. We agreed to remind ourselves and each other every day that we were in love, that we adored our children, and that *together* we could get through the toughest of times.

We have. Our twins as well as our singleton "baby" are all healthy, happy school-age kids now. Bill and I are heading toward our 20th wedding anniversary. This marriage—and this family—are stronger than ever.

DR. LUKE: Some years ago, I was involved in a field study on the childhood growth of twins at the annual Twins Days Festival in Twinsburg, Ohio. Over the course of the study, which lasted several years, we weighed and measured nearly 1,000 twin children. We also interviewed their parents regarding the pregnancy as well as each child's birthweight and health during infancy. The results of our research showed that children are amazingly resilient. Most multiples grew to be within the normal range for weight and height, even if they had been born prematurely and/or at a low birthweight.

But what was even more striking was the resilience and strength of the mothers. They were the most organized, calm, unflappable women I had ever met. Because the festival takes place the first weekend in August, it's typically hot and muggy—the perfect setup for irritable kids and aggravated parents. Yet despite the hassles of helping kids take off their shoes to be weighed and measured, and answering our many questions—all while soothing whining children who were overheated, overstimulated, and overtired—never once did a mother lose her temper. Nor did anyone forget the details of her children's arrival in this world, down to the exact minute of birth, birthweight, and birth length.

The fathers, likewise, were the most knowledgeable and easygoing dads I had ever seen. Never once did a man turn to his wife and insist, "*You* help the kids with their shoes," or bark at a child who was being uncooperative. Often they remembered, in almost as much detail as the moms, the specifics of their children's birth. It was obvious how proud these couples were of their kids, and how confident and relaxed they were in their roles as parents.

Of course, there were single-parent families present. During the interviews, some of them confided that the stress—of infertility treatments, or of months-long vigils in the

NICU, or of having a houseful of colicky newborns—had torn their marriages apart. Yet in some ways these single parents seemed to have an even closer bond with their children.

Although I had never met any of these mothers or fathers before the interviews, my heart went out to each of them as they told me their unique stories. I was particularly touched by those who had had complicated pregnancies and coped courageously with weeks of bedrest, difficult deliveries, or months of visiting their multiples in the NICU. These parents seemed to know their children better than most do, because they had endured so much to get to this stage. They remembered every little victory and loved their children all the more for being survivors.

Because my work with the University Consortium on Multiple Births is primarily in the field of obstetrics, I rarely get to see this metamorphosis—this transformation from anxious parents-to-be coping with a challenging pregnancy to confident, well-adjusted, loving mothers and fathers. The experience was both heartening and humbling.

Parenthood is one of life's most profound and rewarding adventures, and as parents of multiples, you will experience it even more intensely. Couples open to this opportunity for personal growth will find their marriages immeasurably enriched.

Given how rapidly your family has expanded, it may take some time to see yourselves as "one big happy family." But when you do, the feeling will be like nothing you've experienced before. For as often as you are overwhelmed by the demands of having multiples, you and your partner will be more often overwhelmed with joy—with wonderment at your babies' beauty, with pride as you watch them grow, and with profound gratitude at having been multiply blessed.

Best Recipes for
Moms-to-Be of Multiples

One of the most common questions asked by expectant mothers of multiples is, "What should I eat to make sure I'm getting all the calories and nutrients my unborn babies need?" To answer that question as thoroughly as possible, this revised edition of *When You're Expecting Twins, Triplets, and Quads* has been expanded to include 50 recipes. Each has been designed by Dr. Barbara Luke to provide excellent nutrition, delicious flavor, and easy preparation.

To help you meet your daily goal for calorie intake, all recipes include a per-serving calorie count. Also listed are the amounts of protein, carbohydrate, and fat, as well as fiber, calcium, and iron, per serving.

You'll notice that many of the recipes include egg whites rather than whole eggs, and low-fat versions of dairy products like milk, cheese, yogurt, and mayonnaise. The point is not to cut calories. Rather, such ingredients allow for a higher proportion of protein for the calories provided, while reducing saturated fats and cholesterol, and utilizing healthier monounsaturated and polyunsaturated fats.

In addition, for easy reference, each recipe receives two ratings. First is the Blue-Ribbon Rating, which shows the number of specific nutrients each serving provides at 20 percent or more of the recommended dietary allowance (RDA) for pregnancy. You can also refer to the chart on page 310, "Summary of Nutrient Content of Recipes," to find out which recipes provide the specific nutrients you may be looking for (again, at 20 percent or more of the RDA) to round out the day's diet. For instance, if you know you need more calcium today, check the chart to find out which specific recipes—16 of them, in this case—can provide you with a healthy calcium boost.

The second rating for each recipe is the All-Star Rating. This shows the number of Top 25 Food All-Stars (as described in Chapter 4) that are included in the recipe. Many of the common Food All-Stars—eggs, milk, vegetables, meat—can be readily found in most cookbook recipes. Other All-Stars—pumpkin, legumes, nuts, tofu—appear less frequently in typical cookbooks. That's why so many of the original recipes included in this section contain these often-overlooked nutritional powerhouses.

Bon appétit!

Index to Recipes

Summary of Nutrient Content of Recipes

	Protein	Antioxidant Vitamins A, C, or E	B-Vitamins	Calcium	Iron	Other Minerals	Fiber
Beef Entrées							
Beef Stew	✓	✓	✓			✓	✓
Mini–Meat Loaves	✓		✓			✓	
Spicy Beef	✓	✓	✓			✓	✓
Pork Entrées							
French Toast with Ham and Cheese			✓	✓		✓	✓
Ham and Pumpkin Quiche	✓	✓	✓	✓		✓	
Pasta with Peas and Ham	✓	✓	✓	✓		✓	
Pork and Cashew Bok Choy		✓	✓			✓	
Pork with Apple Stuffing	✓		✓			✓	✓
Spicy Pork with Peanut Sauce	✓		✓			✓	

	Protein	Antioxidant Vitamins A, C, or E	B-Vitamins	Calcium	Iron	Other Minerals	Fiber
Poultry Entrées							
Cashew Chicken	✓	✓	✓			✓	
Chicken and Dumplings	✓	✓	✓	✓		✓	
Chicken and Sweet Potatoes	✓	✓	✓			✓	✓
Chicken and Wild Rice Casserole	✓	✓	✓	✓		✓	
Chicken-Barley Soup	✓	✓	✓			✓	✓
Golden Chicken Salad	✓	✓					
Greek Lemon Chicken	✓	✓	✓			✓	✓
Pasta with Chicken and Peanut Sauce	✓	✓	✓			✓	
Seasoned Baked Chicken	✓	✓	✓			✓	✓

(continued)

	Protein	Antioxidant Vitamins A, C, or E	B-Vitamins	Calcium	Iron	Other Minerals	Fiber
Seafood Entrées							
Citrus Salmon	✓		✓			✓	
Linguine with Clams and Dried Tomatoes		✓	✓			✓	
Salmon Burgers	✓	✓	✓	✓		✓	
Shrimp and Scallop Grill	✓	✓	✓		✓	✓	
Vegetarian Entrées							
Asparagus Quiche	✓	✓	✓	✓		✓	
Autumn Pancakes		✓	✓	✓		✓	
Ginger Stir-Fry	✓	✓	✓			✓	
Greek Spinach and Cheese Pie	✓	✓	✓			✓	✓
Lentil Soup	✓	✓	✓		✓	✓	✓
Mediterranean Sauté	✓		✓			✓	✓
Oatmeal-Walnut Pancakes	✓	✓	✓	✓		✓	✓

	Protein	Antioxidant Vitamins A, C, or E	B-Vitamins	Calcium	Iron	Other Minerals	Fiber
Pasta with Green Sauce	✓	✓		✓	✓		✓
Powerhouse Granola		✓	✓			✓	✓
Pumpkin Waffles		✓	✓				✓
Ratatouille		✓	✓			✓	✓
Salsa Frittata	✓	✓	✓	✓	✓		
Spinach and Pumpkin Casserole	✓	✓	✓	✓		✓	✓
Vegetarian Lasagna	✓	✓	✓			✓	✓
Vegetarian Stroganoff	✓	✓	✓			✓	✓
Wild Rice Omelet	✓	✓	✓		✓	✓	✓

Side Dishes and Snacks

	Protein	Antioxidant Vitamins A, C, or E	B-Vitamins	Calcium	Iron	Other Minerals	Fiber
Chickpea Salad		✓	✓			✓	✓
Harvest Muffins		✓				✓	
Pumpkin Custard	✓	✓	✓	✓			✓

(continued)

	Protein	Antioxidant Vitamins A, C, or E	B-Vitamins	Calcium	Iron	Other Minerals	Fiber
Pumpkin-Fruit Muffins		✓					
Pumpkin Loaf		✓	✓			✓	✓
Sunrise Bread Pudding		✓	✓			✓	✓
Tabbouleh		✓	✓			✓	✓
Weekend Hash Browns	✓	✓		✓		✓	
Yogurt Guacamole			✓			✓	✓

Smoothies

	Protein	Antioxidant Vitamins A, C, or E	B-Vitamins	Calcium	Iron	Other Minerals	Fiber
Basic Fruit Smoothie	✓	✓	✓	✓		✓	
Basic Vegetable Smoothie	✓	✓	✓	✓		✓	
Ginger Smoothie		✓					

Beef Entrées

Beef Stew

3 tablespoons olive oil

1½ pounds lean stew beef, trimmed and
    cut into bite-size pieces

1 medium onion, cut into 1-inch pieces

2 tablespoons all-purpose flour

1 garlic clove, chopped

½ teaspoon paprika

½ teaspoon ground black pepper

¼ teaspoon dried thyme

3 cups beef broth

2 medium carrots, cut into 1-inch pieces

2 cups celery, cut into 1-inch pieces

8 ounces potatoes, peeled and
    cut into 1-inch cubes

1½ cups green peas

In a large Dutch oven, heat the oil; add the beef and cook for 2 to 4 minutes, stirring, until the meat is browned. Stir in the onion, flour, garlic, and seasonings. Add the broth and bring to a boil. Reduce the heat, cover, and cook for about 1½ hours, or until the meat is tender. Add the carrots, celery, potatoes, and peas. Cook until the vegetables are tender, about 15 minutes. Makes 6 servings.

All Star Ratings: 2 Stars ★		*Nutrient Content Per Serving*	
Beef	Peas	Calories	329 kcal
		Protein	28 g
Blue Ribbon Rating: 12 Ribbons 🎖		Carbohydrate	19 g
Fiber	Thiamin	Fat	15 g
Niacin	Vitamin A	Fiber	4.1 g
Phosphorus	Vitamin B$_6$	Calcium	75 mg
Protein	Vitamin B$_{12}$	Iron	4 mg
Riboflavin	Vitamin C		
Selenium	Vitamin K		

Mini–Meat Loaves

2 pounds extra-lean ground beef

¾ cups spaghetti sauce

1 cup seasoned bread crumbs

½ cup chopped fresh parsley

½ cup chopped celery

4 large egg whites, beaten

1 envelope dried onion soup mix

12 ounces nonfat evaporated milk

Preheat the oven to 375°F. In a large bowl, combine all the ingredients. Divide the mixture into two small loaf pans. Bake, uncovered, for 45 to 60 minutes, or until a meat thermometer inserted into the center of a loaf reaches 180°F. Pour off the grease; let stand for 10 minutes before serving. Makes 2 mini-loaves, or 8 servings.

All Star Ratings: 4 Stars ★		Nutrient Content Per Serving	
Beef	Milk	Calories	390 kcal
Egg whites	Tomato (sauce)	Protein	30 g
		Carbohydrate	21 g
Blue Ribbon Rating: 8 Ribbons 🎖		Fat	20 g
Magnesium	Selenium	Fiber	1.7 g
Niacin	Vitamin B$_6$	Calcium	180 mg
Phosphorus	Vitamin K	Iron	3.3 mg
Protein	Zinc		

Spicy Beef

12 ounces boneless beef sirloin steak

¼ cup hot bean sauce or hot bean paste
(available in the ethnic foods section of
the grocery store)

¼ cup dry white wine

2 tablespoons soy sauce

½ teaspoon ground black pepper

½ teaspoon cornstarch

1 teaspoon chili oil

1 tablespoon canola oil

2 medium carrots, bias sliced

1 garlic clove, minced

1½ cups snow peas

6 ounces fresh mushrooms, thinly sliced

2 cups hot cooked rice

2 green onions, cut into slivers

Trim the fat from the beef. Thinly slice across the grain into bite-size strips. (For easier slicing, partially freeze the beef first.) Set aside. For the sauce, in a small bowl, stir together the bean sauce or paste, wine, soy sauce, black pepper, cornstarch, and chili oil. Set aside. Pour the canola oil into a wok or large skillet. (Add more oil as necessary during cooking.) Preheat over medium-high heat. In the hot oil, stir-fry the carrots and garlic for 2 minutes. Add the snow peas; stir-fry for 2 minutes. Add the mushrooms; stir-fry for 1 to 2 minutes, or until the vegetables are crisp-tender. Remove the vegetables from the wok. Add the beef to the wok. Stir-fry for 2 to 3 minutes or to the desired doneness. Push the beef from the center of the wok. Stir the sauce. Add the sauce to the center of the wok. Cook and stir until thickened and bubbly. Return the cooked vegetables to the wok. Stir all the ingredients together to coat with the sauce. Cook and stir for 1 minute more, or until heated through. Serve immediately with the rice. Garnish with the green onions. Makes 6 servings.

All Star Ratings: 2 Stars ★		Nutrient Content Per Serving	
Beef	Snow peas	Calories	468 kcal
		Protein	26 g
Blue Ribbon Rating: 15 Ribbons		Carbohydrate	49 g
Fiber	Thiamin	Fat	18 g
Folate	Vitamin A	Fiber	4.1 g
Magnesium	Vitamin B₆	Calcium	59 mg
Niacin	Vitamin B₁₂	Iron	4.5 mg
Phosphorus	Vitamin C		
Protein	Vitamin K		
Riboflavin	Zinc		
Selenium			

Pork Entrées

French Toast with Ham and Cheese

2 large egg whites	2 slices lean boiled ham
¼ cup skim milk	2 slices Muenster cheese
½ teaspoon ground cinnamon	1 teaspoon butter
4 slices cinnamon-raisin bread	1 cup chunky applesauce

In a small bowl, whisk together the egg whites, milk, and cinnamon. Make two sandwiches with the bread, ham, and cheese. Add the sandwiches to the egg mixture, turning to soak thoroughly. In a small skillet, melt the butter. Add the soaked sandwiches, cooking until the undersides are browned and the cheese is melted, 5 to 7 minutes. Turn the sandwiches and cook for 5 to 7 minutes on the other side, or until browned. Serve topped with the applesauce. Makes 2 servings.

All Star Ratings: 5 Stars ★		*Nutrient Content Per Serving*	
Apples	Ham	Calories	580 kcal
Cheese	Milk	Protein	26 g
Eggs		Carbohydrate	100 g
		Fat	11 g
Blue Ribbon Rating: 11 Ribbons 🎗		Fiber	10.8 g
Calcium	Riboflavin	Calcium	252 mg
Fiber	Selenium	Iron	5.5 mg
Folate	Thiamin		
Magnesium	Vitamin B$_{12}$		
Niacin	Zinc		
Phosphorus			

Ham and Pumpkin Quiche

15 ounces canned pumpkin

4 ounces extra-lean ham (5% fat), chopped

½ cup finely chopped onion

1 cup sliced fresh mushrooms

4 large egg whites

12 ounces nonfat evaporated milk

½ cup grated Parmesan cheese

2 tablespoons all-purpose flour

1 unbaked 10-inch pie shell

Preheat the oven to 375°F. In a medium bowl, combine the pumpkin, ham, onion, mushrooms, and egg whites; mix well. Gradually add the milk, stirring until well blended. Toss the cheese with the flour; fold into the pumpkin mixture. Pour into the pie shell; bake for 60 minutes, or until a knife inserted in the center comes out clean. Makes 6 servings.

All Star Ratings: 4 Stars ★		Nutrient Content Per Serving	
Cheese	Ham	Calories	303 kcal
Eggs	Pumpkin	Protein	17 g
		Carbohydrate	31 g
Blue Ribbon Rating: 10 Ribbons		Fat	12 g
Calcium	Selenium	Fiber	3.6 g
Magnesium	Thiamin	Calcium	339 mg
Phosphorus	Vitamin A	Iron	2.6 mg
Protein	Vitamin B₁₂		
Riboflavin	Vitamin K		

Pasta with Peas and Ham

1 tablespoon whipped butter

2 tablespoons all-purpose flour

2 teaspoons brown mustard

2½ cups skim milk

1 cup shredded Colby cheese

1 cup shredded Monterey Jack cheese

8 ounces uncooked enriched macaroni

8 ounces lean boiled ham, cut into
    bite-size pieces

1 pound canned sweet peas

½ cup seasoned bread crumbs

Preheat the oven to 375°F. In a large saucepan, melt the butter; add the flour and mustard, mixing well. Add the milk, and stir until the sauce is smooth and slightly thickened. In a small bowl, toss together the shredded cheeses. Set aside ½ cup of the cheese mixture. To the saucepan, add the remaining 1½ cups cheese and heat until melted, stirring occasionally. Cover and remove from the heat. Cook the macaroni according to the package directions; drain. In a 2-quart casserole, combine the sauce with the macaroni, ham, and peas. Sprinkle the remaining cheese and the bread crumbs on top. Bake, uncovered, for 20 to 25 minutes, or until browned and bubbly. Makes 8 servings.

All Star Ratings: 4 Stars ★		*Nutrient Content Per Serving*	
Cheese	Milk	Calories	355 kcal
Ham	Peas	Protein	22 g
		Carbohydrate	35 g
Blue Ribbon Rating: 10 Ribbons		Fat	14 g
Calcium	Riboflavin	Fiber	2.9 g
Folate	Selenium	Calcium	318 mg
Niacin	Thiamin	Iron	2.9 mg
Phosphorus	Vitamin A		
Protein	Vitamin B$_{12}$		

Pork and Cashew Bok Choy

12 ounces lean boneless pork

4 tablespoons soy sauce

2 teaspoons peeled, grated fresh ginger

2 garlic cloves, minced

½ cup hoisin sauce

½ cup water

1 tablespoon cornstarch

1 teaspoon sugar

1 tablespoon canola oil

2 medium onions, cut into thin wedges

1 Chinese cabbage (bok choy), cut
    diagonally into 1-inch pieces

4 cups hot cooked rice

¼ cup dry-roasted cashews

Trim the fat from the pork. Thinly slice across the grain into bite-size strips. (For easier slicing, partially freeze the pork first.) In a medium bowl, stir together the pork, 2 tablespoons of the soy sauce, the ginger, and garlic. Cover and refrigerate for 1 to 2 hours. For the sauce, in a small bowl, stir together the hoisin sauce, water, remaining soy sauce, cornstarch, and sugar. Set aside. Pour the canola oil into a wok or large skillet. (Add more oil as necessary during cooking.) Preheat the wok over medium-high heat. Stir-fry the onions and cabbage in the hot oil for 1 minute. Remove the vegetables from the wok. Add the pork mixture to the hot wok. Stir-fry for 2 to 3 minutes, or until no pink remains. Push the pork from the center of the wok. Stir the sauce. Add the sauce to the center of the wok. Cook and stir until the sauce is thickened and bubbly. Return the cooked vegetables to the wok. Stir all the ingredients together to coat with the sauce. Cover and cook for 1 minute more, or until heated through. Serve immediately with the rice. Sprinkle with the cashews. Makes 6 servings.

All Star Ratings: 3 Stars ★		Nutrient Content Per Serving	
Cabbage	Pork	Calories	554 kcal
Cashews		Protein	30 g
		Carbohydrate	61 g
Blue Ribbon Rating: 12 Ribbons		Fat	20 g
Folate	Thiamin	Fiber	3.6 g
Magnesium	Vitamin A	Calcium	113 mg
Niacin	Vitamin B$_6$	Iron	4.1 mg
Phosphorus	Vitamin B$_{12}$		
Riboflavin	Vitamin C		
Selenium	Zinc		

Pork with Apple Stuffing

4 boneless pork loin chops, 1 inch thick
  (approximately 4 ounces each)
1 teaspoon salt
1 tablespoon butter
1 medium celery stalk, diced
1 large onion, diced
2 large Golden Delicious apples, peeled,
  cored, and diced

4 slices firm white bread, cut into ½-inch
  pieces
½ cup apple juice
1 teaspoon poultry seasoning
1 large egg
¼ cup raisins

Preheat the oven to 325°F. Slice each pork chop nearly through to create a pocket in the center. Sprinkle the pork chops with the salt. Place in a roasting pan and roast for 30 minutes. Meanwhile, in a large saucepan, melt the butter over medium heat. Add the celery and onion and cook until tender, about 10 minutes, stirring often. Add the apples and cook for 6 to 8 minutes more, until softened. Remove from the heat; stir in the bread pieces, apple juice, poultry seasoning, egg, and raisins. After the pork chops have cooked for 30 minutes, remove from the oven. Spoon the stuffing into the center of each chop. Place the remaining stuffing in a greased 1½-quart casserole. Return the pork chops and stuffing to the oven. Cook for 30 minutes more, or until a meat thermometer inserted in the thickest part of a chop reaches 155°F. (If the stuffing browns too quickly, cover it loosely with foil.) Let the chops stand for 5 minutes; the internal temperature of the meat will rise to 160°F upon standing. Makes 4 servings.

All Star Ratings: 3 Stars ★		*Nutrient Content Per Serving*	
Apples	Pork	Calories	536 kcal
Egg		Protein	36 g
		Carbohydrate	48 g
Blue Ribbon Rating: 12 Ribbons 🎗		Fat	21 g
Fiber	Selenium	Fiber	5.6 g
Folate	Thiamin	Calcium	119 mg
Niacin	Vitamin B$_6$	Iron	3.5 mg
Phosphorus	Vitamin B$_{12}$		
Protein	Vitamin K		
Riboflavin	Zinc		

Spicy Pork with Peanut Sauce

8 ounces uncooked enriched linguine

4 boneless pork loin chops, 1 inch thick
(approximately 4 ounces each)

¼ teaspoon ground black pepper

½ teaspoon salt

4 green onions, cut into 1-inch
diagonal slices

1 tablespoon peeled, minced fresh ginger

3 garlic cloves, crushed with a garlic press

3 tablespoons creamy peanut butter

1 tablespoon soy sauce

½ teaspoon ground red pepper

¾ cups water

Cook the linguine according to the package directions. Drain, cover, and keep warm. Sprinkle the pork chops with the pepper and ¼ teaspoon of the salt. Heat a large skillet over medium-high heat until hot. Add the pork chops and cook for 4 minutes; turn the chops over and cook 4 minutes longer. Transfer the pork to a platter; cover with foil to keep warm. To the same skillet, add the green onions and the remaining ¼ teaspoon salt. Cook over medium heat for 4 minutes, stirring frequently. Stir in the ginger and garlic; cook for 1 minute. Return the pork to the skillet. In a small bowl, stir the peanut butter, soy sauce, ground red pepper, and water until blended. Pour the peanut-butter mixture into the same skillet; heat to boiling over medium-high heat. Reduce the heat to low; simmer for 1 minute. Serve with the peanut sauce poured over the chops. Makes 4 servings.

All Star Ratings: 2 Stars ★		*Nutrient Content Per Serving*	
Peanut butter	Pork	Calories	481 kcal
		Protein	43 g
Blue Ribbon Rating: 12 Ribbons		Carbohydrate	47 g
Folate	Selenium	Fat	12 g
Magnesium	Thiamin	Fiber	2.7 g
Niacin	Vitamin B$_6$	Calcium	39 mg
Phosphorus	Vitamin B$_{12}$	Iron	4.5 mg
Protein	Vitamin K		
Riboflavin	Zinc		

Poultry Entrées

Cashew Chicken

½ cup chicken broth

3 tablespoons oyster sauce (such as Kame)

1½ tablespoons cornstarch

1½ tablespoons honey

1 tablespoon soy sauce

2 teaspoons white wine vinegar

2 tablespoons oil

1 cup chopped green onions

1 small onion, cut into 8 wedges

½ cup diagonally sliced carrots

1 cup snow peas

1 pound boneless, skinless chicken breasts, cut into 1½-inch pieces

¼ cup canned pineapple chunks in juice, drained

¼ cup cashews

6 cups hot cooked rice

Combine the first 6 ingredients in a small bowl; set aside. Heat 1 tablespoon of the oil in a stir-fry pan or wok over medium-high heat. Add ½ cup of the green onions and the onion wedges; stir-fry for 1 minute. Add the carrots; stir-fry for 2 minutes. Add the snow peas; stir-fry for 2 minutes. Remove the vegetables from the pan; keep warm. Heat the remaining 1 tablespoon oil in the pan over medium-high heat. Add the chicken; stir-fry for 5 minutes. Add the broth mixture, cooked vegetables, the pineapple, and cashews; bring to a boil and cook for 1 minute, or until thick. Stir in the remaining ½ cup green onions. Serve with the rice. Makes 6 servings.

All Star Ratings: 3 Stars ★		Nutrient Content Per Serving	
Cashews	Peas	Calories	391 kcal
Chicken		Protein	22 g
		Carbohydrate	52 g
Blue Ribbon Rating: 10 Ribbons 🎗		Fat	10 g
Folate	Selenium	Fiber	10 g
Magnesium	Vitamin A	Calcium	47 mg
Niacin	Vitamin B$_6$	Iron	2.6 mg
Phosphorus	Vitamin C		
Protein	Vitamin K		

Chicken and Dumplings

1 tablespoon safflower or olive oil
1 pound cooked, diced chicken
1 cup chopped onions
1 cup chopped carrots
1 cup chopped celery
1 cup chicken broth

1½ cups reduced-fat all-purpose
  baking mix
½ cup cornmeal
¾ cup skim milk
¼ cup sliced green onions
½ cup shredded Parmesan cheese

In a large skillet or Dutch oven, heat the oil and sauté the cooked chicken pieces until golden. Add the onions, carrots, celery, and chicken broth. Bring to a boil; reduce the heat. Cover and simmer for 5 minutes, stirring occasionally. In a medium bowl, combine the baking mix, cornmeal, milk, and green onions. Mix until a soft dough forms; drop by rounded spoonfuls onto the chicken mixture. Cook, uncovered, for 10 minutes. Sprinkle with the cheese. Cover and cook for an additional few minutes, or until the cheese has melted. Makes 4 servings.

All Star Ratings: 3 Stars ★		*Nutrient Content Per Serving*	
Cheese	Milk	Calories	513 kcal
Chicken		Protein	38 g
		Carbohydrate	47 g
Blue Ribbon Rating: 13 Ribbons		Fat	18 g
Calcium	Thiamin	Fiber	2.6 g
Magnesium	Vitamin B$_6$	Calcium	305 mg
Niacin	Vitamin B$_{12}$	Iron	2.6 mg
Phosphorus	Vitamin E		
Protein	Vitamin K		
Riboflavin	Zinc		
Selenium			

Chicken and Sweet Potatoes

4 boneless, skinless chicken breast halves
    (approximately 1 pound)
Garlic powder to taste
Salt and ground black pepper to taste
½ cup all-purpose flour
1 tablespoon olive or canola oil
1 cup peeled, cubed sweet potatoes

1 cup chopped onions
1 cup chopped green bell peppers
1 cup chopped celery
½ cup golden raisins
¾ cup chicken broth
¾ cup apple cider

Rinse and pat dry the chicken. Cut the chicken into ½-inch pieces. Sprinkle with garlic powder, salt, and pepper. Dip the chicken into the flour to coat well. In a large skillet or Dutch oven, heat the oil and brown the chicken on all sides until golden. Remove the chicken and set aside. Add the sweet potatoes, onions, bell peppers, celery, and raisins; sauté until the onions are tender. Stir in the chicken broth and apple cider. Add the browned chicken and bring to a boil. Reduce the heat, cover, and simmer for 25 to 30 minutes, or until the chicken is cooked and the potatoes are tender. Makes 4 servings.

All Star Ratings: 2 Stars ★		Nutrient Content Per Serving	
Chicken	Sweet potatoes	Calories	535 kcal
		Protein	26 g
Blue Ribbon Rating: 13 Ribbons 🎗		Carbohydrate	56 g
Biotin	Riboflavin	Fat	21 g
Fiber	Selenium	Fiber	6.1 g
Folate	Thiamin	Calcium	118 mg
Magnesium	Vitamin B$_6$	Iron	3.2 mg
Niacin	Vitamin C		
Phosphorus	Vitamin K		
Protein			

Chicken and Wild Rice Casserole

1 6.2-ounce package fast-cooking long-
    grain and wild rice mix

1 pound chicken breasts, roasted and cut
    into bite-size pieces

1 10.75-ounce can condensed cream of
    chicken soup

½ cup skim milk

1 cup sliced fresh mushrooms

1 cup frozen green peas

1 cup shredded Muenster cheese

Preheat the oven to 350°F. Prepare the rice according to package directions, omitting the butter. Add the chicken, soup, milk, mushrooms, and peas; mix well. Pour into a 2-quart casserole.
Bake, covered, for 30 minutes. Uncover; sprinkle with the cheese. Bake, uncovered, for an additional 5 to 10 minutes, or until the cheese is melted. Makes 4 servings.

All Star Ratings: 4 stars ★		*Nutrient Content Per Serving*	
Cheese	Milk	Calories	470 kcal
Chicken	Peas	Protein	40 g
		Carbohydrate	37 g
Blue Ribbon Rating: 13 Ribbons		Fat	17 g
Calcium	Selenium	Fiber	3.2 g
Magnesium	Vitamin A	Calcium	243 mg
Niacin	Vitamin B_6	Iron	2.7 mg
Phosphorus	Vitamin B_{12}		
Protein	Zinc		
Riboflavin			

Chicken-Barley Soup

½ cup lentils

2 tablespoons salted margarine or butter

1 cup chopped onions

1 garlic clove, minced

6 cups chicken broth

¼ teaspoon crushed dried rosemary

¼ teaspoon ground black pepper

1½ cups cooked, diced chicken

½ cup finely chopped fresh parsley

½ cup green peas

1½ cups sliced carrots

½ cup uncooked quick-cooking barley

Rinse and drain the lentils; set aside. Melt the margarine or butter in a large saucepan or Dutch oven. Sauté the onions and garlic until tender but not brown. Stir in the chicken broth, rosemary, pepper, and lentils; bring to a boil. Reduce the heat and simmer, covered, for 20 minutes. Stir in the chicken, parsley, peas, carrots, and barley. Simmer, covered, for about 20 minutes more, or until the carrots are just tender. Makes 6 servings.

All Star Ratings: 3 Stars ★		Nutrient Content Per Serving	
Chicken	Peas	Calories	397 kcal
Lentils		Protein	35 g
		Carbohydrate	41 g
Blue Ribbon Rating: 13 Ribbons		Fat	11 g
Fiber	Thiamin	Fiber	12.5 g
Magnesium	Vitamin A	Calcium	80 mg
Niacin	Vitamin B₆	Iron	4.9 mg
Phosphorus	Vitamin B₁₂		
Protein	Vitamin C		
Riboflavin	Vitamin K		
Selenium			

Golden Chicken Salad

1 cup canned pumpkin

½ cup fat-free mayonnaise

1 teaspoon lemon juice

1 teaspoon salt

¼ teaspoon ground black pepper

3 cups cooked, chopped chicken

2 ounces chopped almonds

Combine the pumpkin, mayonnaise, lemon juice, salt, and pepper; mix well. Add the chicken and almonds; mix lightly; chill. Makes 4 servings.

All Star Ratings: 3 Stars ★		*Nutrient Content Per Serving*	
Almonds	Pumpkin	Calories	288 kcal
Chicken		Protein	21 g
		Carbohydrate	10 g
Blue Ribbon Rating: 3 Ribbons		Fat	17 g
Protein	Vitamin K	Fiber	3 g
Vitamin A		Calcium	69 mg
		Iron	2.7 mg

Greek Lemon Chicken

3 pounds bone-in chicken parts
½ cup Roditis wine (Greek white wine)
½ cup olive oil
¼ cup lemon juice
2 tablespoons dried oregano
1 teaspoon dried thyme
1 teaspoon dried basil
1 teaspoon salt
½ teaspoon ground black pepper
1 14-ounce can artichoke hearts, drained
1 lemon, sliced
3 cups hot cooked white rice

Rinse the chicken and pat dry with paper towels. In a large baking dish, combine the wine, olive oil, lemon juice, and seasonings. Add the chicken; cover and marinate for at least 3 hours, or overnight. Preheat the oven to 350°F. Add the artichoke hearts and lemon slices. Bake for 1 hour, basting occasionally. Serve over the rice. Makes 6 servings.

All Star Ratings: 1 Star ★		Nutrient Content Per Serving	
Chicken		Calories	426 kcal
		Protein	53 g
Blue Ribbon Rating: 14 Ribbons 🎖		Carbohydrate	31 g
Fiber	Selenium	Fat	10 g
Folate	Thiamin	Fiber	4.7 g
Magnesium	Vitamin B$_6$	Calcium	100 mg
Niacin	Vitamin B$_{12}$	Iron	4.9 mg
Phosphorus	Vitamin C		
Protein	Vitamin E		
Riboflavin	Zinc		

Pasta with Chicken and Peanut Sauce

8 ounces uncooked enriched pasta

2 cups chicken broth

2 tablespoons soy sauce

1 tablespoon cornstarch

¼ cup creamy peanut butter

1 tablespoon canola oil

½ cup thinly sliced onions

2 garlic cloves, minced

4 boneless, skinless chicken breast halves
(approximately 1 pound), cut into
1-inch pieces

2 green onions, sliced

¼ cup chopped peanuts

Cook the pasta according to the package directions. Drain; keep warm; set aside. In a medium mixing bowl, stir together the chicken broth, soy sauce, and cornstarch. Stir in the peanut butter until smooth. Set the sauce aside. In a wok or large skillet, heat the canola oil over medium-high heat. Add the onions and garlic to the hot oil; stir-fry for 2 to 3 minutes. Remove the onion mixture from the skillet. Add the chicken to the wok. Stir-fry for about 3 minutes, or until the chicken is no longer pink. Push the chicken from the center of the wok. Stir the sauce; add to the center of the wok. Cook and stir for 4 minutes, or until thickened and bubbly. Return the onion mixture to the skillet; stir all the ingredients together. Arrange the pasta on individual plates or a large platter. Spoon the chicken mixture over the pasta. Sprinkle with the green onions and peanuts. Makes 4 servings.

All Star Ratings: 3 Stars ★		*Nutrient Content Per Serving*	
Chicken	Peanuts	Calories	561 kcal
Peanut butter		Protein	33 g
		Carbohydrate	54 g
Blue Ribbon Rating: 13 Ribbons		Fat	24 g
Folate	Thiamin	Fiber	3.8 g
Magnesium	Vitamin B$_6$	Calcium	50 mg
Niacin	Vitamin B$_{12}$	Iron	4 mg
Phosphorus	Vitamin E		
Protein	Vitamin K		
Riboflavin	Zinc		
Selenium			

Seasoned Baked Chicken

1 cup plain bread crumbs

1 envelope dried onion soup mix

½ teaspoon ground black pepper

½ teaspoon ground red pepper

4 boneless, skinless chicken breast halves
  (approximately 1 pound)

½ cup light mayonnaise

2 cups diced carrots

2 baking potatoes, peeled and quartered

Preheat the oven to 425°F. Combine the bread crumbs, onion soup mix, and seasonings. Coat the chicken breast halves with the mayonnaise, then coat in the bread crumb mixture. Place in a baking dish; add the carrots and potatoes. Bake for 20 to 30 minutes, or until the potatoes are tender and the chicken is cooked through. Makes 4 servings.

All Star Ratings: 1 Star ★		*Nutrient Content Per Serving*	
Chicken		Calories	563 kcal
		Protein	43 g
Blue Ribbon Rating: 13 Ribbons		Carbohydrate	60 g
Fiber	Thiamin	Fat	16 g
Magnesium	Vitamin A	Fiber	6.4 g
Niacin	Vitamin B$_6$	Calcium	99 mg
Phosphorus	Vitamin B$_{12}$	Iron	4.5 mg
Protein	Vitamin C		
Riboflavin	Vitamin K		
Selenium			

Seafood Entrées

Citrus Salmon

1 6.2-ounce package fast-cooking long-grain and wild rice mix

3 tablespoons orange marmalade

1 teaspoon ground cumin

1 teaspoon ground coriander

¾ teaspoon salt

¾ teaspoon grated fresh lemon peel

¼ teaspoon ground black pepper

4 salmon fillets, ¾ inch thick (approximately 6 ounces each), skin removed

Lemon wedges

Preheat the grill. Cook the rice according to the package directions. Cover and keep warm. In a small bowl, mix the marmalade, cumin, coriander, salt, lemon peel, pepper, and 1 teaspoon very hot water until blended. With tweezers, remove any bones from the salmon. Brush the marmalade mixture all over the salmon pieces. Place the salmon on the grill over medium heat and cook for 4 minutes. With a wide metal spatula, carefully turn the salmon over; cook for 4 to 5 minutes more, until the salmon turns opaque throughout and flakes easily when tested with a fork. Serve over the hot rice. Garnish with lemon wedges. Makes 4 servings.

All Star Ratings: 1 Star ★		*Nutrient Content Per Serving*	
Salmon		Calories	350 kcal
		Protein	32 g
Blue Ribbon Rating: 8 Ribbons		Carbohydrate	43 g
Magnesium	Selenium	Fat	5 g
Niacin	Thiamin	Fiber	1.2 g
Phosphorus	Vitamin B$_6$	Calcium	45 mg
Protein	Vitamin B$_{12}$	Iron	1.9 mg

Linguine with Clams and Dried Tomatoes

8 ounces uncooked linguine, fettuccine, or
    spaghetti
1 pound canned minced clams
2 tablespoons olive oil
2 garlic cloves, minced

½ cup dry white wine
½ cup oil-packed dried tomatoes, drained
    and cut into strips
½ cup grated Parmesan cheese

Cook the pasta according to the package directions. Drain; keep warm; set aside. For the sauce, drain the clams, reserving the liquid; set the clams aside. In a medium saucepan, heat the olive oil; stir in the garlic. Stir in the reserved clam liquid and the wine. Bring to a boil. Simmer for 10 minutes, or until the sauce is reduced to about 1 cup. Stir in the clams and tomatoes; heat through. Arrange the pasta on individual plates or a large platter. Spoon the sauce over the pasta. Sprinkle with the cheese. Makes 4 servings.

All Star Ratings: 3 Stars ★		*Nutrient Content Per Serving*	
Cheese	Tomatoes	Calories	420 kcal
Clams		Protein	30 g
		Carbohydrate	49 g
Blue Ribbon Rating: 7 Ribbons		Fat	13 g
Folate	Selenium	Fiber	2.2 g
Niacin	Thiamin	Calcium	194 mg
Phosphorus	Vitamin C	Iron	4.3 mg
Riboflavin			

Salmon Burgers

1 pound canned red or pink salmon, drained and flaked

1 green onion, sliced

3 tablespoons prepared white horseradish

¼ cup seasoned bread crumbs

2 tablespoons chopped fresh parsley

1 tablespoon soy sauce

¼ teaspoon ground black pepper

1 tablespoon olive oil

8 ounces enriched orzo, cooked

In a medium bowl, with a fork, lightly mix all the ingredients except the olive oil and orzo. Shape the mixture into four 3-inch round patties. Heat the olive oil in a skillet over medium heat until hot. Add the salmon cakes, and cook for about 5 minutes per side, or until golden and hot. Serve over the warm orzo. Makes 4 servings.

All Star Ratings: 1 Stars ★		*Nutient Content Per Serving*	
Salmon		Calories	465 kcal
		Protein	28 g
Blue Ribbon Rating: 12 Ribbons		Carbohydrate	49 g
Calcium	Selenium	Fat	17 g
Magnesium	Thiamin	Fiber	2.2 g
Niacin	Vitamin B$_{12}$	Calcium	287 mg
Phosphorus	Vitamin D	Iron	2.5 mg
Protein	Vitamin E		
Riboflavin	Vitamin K		

Shrimp and Scallop Grill

1 tablespoon brown sugar

1 tablespoon soy sauce

1 tablespoon vegetable oil

2 teaspoons Chinese five-spice powder

¼ teaspoon ground black pepper

1 pound large shrimp, shelled and deveined

8 ounces sea scallops

2 large onions, each cut into 6 chunks

2 green bell peppers, each cut into
   6 chunks

12 cherry tomatoes

4 cups hot cooked white rice

Preheat the grill. In a large bowl, mix the brown sugar, soy sauce, vegetable oil, Chinese five-spice powder, and pepper; add the shrimp and scallops, tossing to coat. Onto 6 long metal skewers, alternately thread the shrimp, onions, scallops, bell peppers, and cherry tomatoes. Place the skewers on the grill over medium heat. Grill for 10 to 12 minutes, until the shrimp and scallops turn opaque throughout, turning the skewers occasionally and brushing the shrimp and scallops with any remaining spice mixture halfway through cooking. Serve over the rice. Makes 6 servings.

All-Star Rating: 3 Stars ★		*Nutrient Content per Serving*	
Scallops	Tomatoes	Calories	419 kcal
Shrimp		Protein	37 g
		Carbohydrate	48 g
Blue-Ribbon Rating: 13 Ribbons 🎗		Fat	8 g
Folate	Vitamin A	Fiber	2.3 g
Iron	Vitamin B$_{12}$	Calcium	105 mg
Magnesium	Vitamin C	Iron	5.7 mg
Niacin	Vitamin D		
Phosphorus	Vitamin E		
Protein	Vitamin K		
Selenium			

Vegetarian Entrées

Asparagus Quiche

1 pound fresh asparagus, trimmed and cut
    into ¾-inch pieces
1 unbaked 10-inch pie shell
2 large eggs or 4 large egg whites
2 cups skim milk

⅛ teaspoon ground black pepper
Pinch of ground nutmeg
1 cup coarsely shredded low-fat Swiss
    cheese

Preheat the oven to 425°F. In a 2-quart saucepan, boil 4 cups water. Add the asparagus and cook for 6 to 8 minutes, until tender. Drain the asparagus and rinse with cold running water. Drain again and set aside. Line the pie shell with foil and fill with pie weights or uncooked rice. Bake the pie shell for 10 minutes; remove the foil with the weights, and bake for 7 to 10 minutes more, until the crust is golden. Reduce the oven temperature to 350°F. Meanwhile, in a medium bowl, with a wire whisk or fork, mix the eggs, milk, pepper, and nutmeg until well blended. Sprinkle the asparagus and cheese into the pie shell. Pour the liquid mixture over the asparagus and cheese. Place a sheet of foil underneath the pie plate to catch any drips during baking. Bake the quiche for 40 to 45 minutes, until a knife inserted in the center comes out clean. Makes 6 servings.

All-Star Rating: 4 Stars ★		Nutrient Content per Serving	
Asparagus	Eggs	Calories	355 kcal
Cheese	Milk	Protein	24 g
		Carbohydrate	26 g
Blue-Ribbon Rating: 13 Ribbons		Fat	17 g
Calcium	Vitamin A	Fiber	1.8 g
Folate	Vitamin B₁₂	Calcium	455 mg
Magnesium	Vitamin C	Iron	2.1 mg
Protein	Vitamin E		
Riboflavin	Vitamin K		
Selenium	Zinc		
Thiamin			

Autumn Pancakes

2 tablespoons canola oil

2 cups all-purpose flour

1 tablespoon baking powder

1 teaspoon salt

1½ cups low-fat (1%) milk

½ cup canned pumpkin-pie mix

2 large egg whites

Preheat a lightly oiled griddle to 375°F. In a large bowl, combine the flour, baking powder, and salt. In another bowl, combine the milk, pumpkin-pie mix, and egg whites; add to the dry ingredients, stirring until just moistened. For each pancake, pour ¼ cup batter onto the hot griddle. Spread the batter into a 4-inch circle before it sets. Cook until the surface bubbles and appears dry; turn and continue cooking for 2 to 3 minutes. Serve with butter and maple syrup. Makes 15 pancakes, or 5 servings.

All-Star Rating: 3 Stars ★		*Nutrient Content per Serving*	
Eggs	Pumpkin	Calories	294 kcal
Milk		Protein	9 g
		Carbohydrate	49 g
Blue-Ribbon Rating: 7 Ribbons 🎖		Fat	7 g
Calcium	Selenium	Fiber	3.6 g
Folate	Thiamin	Calcium	312 mg
Niacin	Vitamin A	Iron	2.7 mg
Phosphorus			

Ginger Stir-Fry

1 cup vegetable broth
¼ cup dry white wine
2 tablespoons soy sauce
2 tablespoons cornstarch
1 tablespoon canola oil
2 teaspoons peeled, grated fresh ginger
1½ cups sliced zucchini
1 pound fresh asparagus, cut into 1-inch
   pieces, or 1 10-ounce package frozen cut
   asparagus, thawed and well drained

2 green onions, sliced
1 10½-ounce package extra-firm tofu
   (fresh bean curd), cut into ½-inch cubes
1 ounce pine nuts or chopped almonds,
   toasted
2 cups hot cooked brown rice

For the sauce, in a small bowl, stir together the broth, wine, soy sauce, and cornstarch. Set aside. Pour the canola oil into a wok or large skillet; preheat over medium-high heat. Stir-fry the ginger in the hot oil for 15 seconds. Add the zucchini and fresh asparagus (if using); stir-fry for 3 minutes. Add the green onions and thawed asparagus (if using); stir-fry for 1½ minutes more, or until the asparagus is crisp-tender. Remove the vegetables from the wok. Add the tofu to the hot wok. Stir-fry for 2 to 3 minutes, or until lightly browned. Remove from the wok. Add the sauce to the hot wok. Cook and stir until thickened and bubbly. Return the vegetables and tofu to the wok. Stir all the ingredients together for 1 minute more, or until heated through. Stir in the nuts. Serve over the rice. Makes 4 servings.

All-Star Rating: 3 Stars ★		Nutrient Content per Serving	
Asparagus	Tofu	Calories	352 kcal
Nuts		Protein	16 g
		Carbohydrate	51 g
Blue-Ribbon Rating: 11 Ribbons		Fat	9 g
Folate	Selenium	Fiber	4.7 g
Magnesium	Thiamin	Calcium	97 mg
Niacin	Vitamin C	Iron	3.5 mg
Phosphorus	Vitamin E		
Protein	Vitamin K		
Riboflavin			

Greek Spinach and Cheese Pie

¼ cup olive oil

2 pounds fresh spinach (approximately 3
    10-ounce bags)

1 large onion, finely chopped

4 large eggs

8 ounces feta cheese, crumbled

8 ounces part-skim-milk ricotta cheese

¼ cup chopped fresh parsley

17 sheets phyllo pastry (thawed, if frozen)

3 tablespoons butter, melted

In a skillet, heat the oil. Sauté the spinach and onion until the onion is clear and tender; remove from the heat. In a medium bowl, beat the eggs. Stir in the feta and ricotta cheeses, parsley, and onion-spinach mixture. Lightly grease a 13 × 9-inch baking pan. Lay 1 sheet of phyllo in the pan; brush with the butter. Layer 8 more sheets of phyllo, one at a time, brushing each with the melted butter. Cover evenly with the spinach mixture. Top with the 8 remaining sheets of phyllo, one at a time, brushing each with the melted butter. Refrigerate for 30 minutes. Preheat the oven to 350°F. Bake the pie for 35 to 40 minutes, or until golden brown. Cut into 12 pieces, each about 3 × 4 inches. Makes 6 servings.

All-Star Rating: 4 Stars ★		*Nutrient Content per Serving*	
Eggs	Ricotta cheese	Calories	303 kcal
Feta cheese	Spinach	Protein	18 g
		Carbohydrate	6 g
Blue-Ribbon Rating: 15 Ribbons 🎗		Fat	23 g
Calcium	Selenium	Fiber	14 g
Fiber	Vitamin A	Calcium	430 mg
Iodine	Vitamin B$_6$	Iron	11.3 mg
Iron	Vitamin B$_{12}$		
Magnesium	Vitamin C		
Phosphorus	Vitamin E		
Protein	Zinc		
Riboflavin			

Lentil Soup

1 pound lentils

1 cup chopped celery

1 medium onion, chopped

2 garlic cloves, finely chopped

½ cup olive oil

1 6-ounce can tomato paste

1 tablespoon chopped fresh parsley

1 teaspoon salt

Ground black pepper to taste

1 bay leaf

2 tablespoons white vinegar

Rinse and soak the lentils in warm water for 2 hours; drain. To a large saucepan, add 8 cups water, the lentils, celery, onion, and garlic. Bring to a boil, cover, and simmer for 30 minutes. Add the olive oil, tomato paste, parsley, salt, pepper, and bay leaf. Simmer for 20 minutes, or until the lentils are tender. Remove the bay leaf and discard. Add the vinegar before serving. Makes 6 servings.

All-Star Rating: 2 Stars ★		*Nutrient Content per Serving*	
Lentils	Tomato paste	Calories	450 kcal
		Protein	23 g
		Carbohydrate	51 g
Blue-Ribbon Rating: 12 Ribbons		Fat	19 g
Fiber	Thiamin	Fiber	25 g
Folate	Vitamin B$_6$	Calcium	72 mg
Iron	Vitamin C	Iron	7.7 mg
Magnesium	Vitamin E		
Phosphorus	Vitamin K		
Protein	Zinc		

Mediterranean Sauté

1 tablespoon butter

1 tablespoon olive oil

1 garlic clove, finely chopped

1 cup chopped celery

¼ teaspoon fennel seed

6 green onions, chopped

½ cup golden raisins

1 cup uncooked quick-cooking barley

1 15-ounce can garbanzo beans, rinsed and drained

2 cups vegetable broth

1 cup chopped fresh parsley

½ cup chopped walnuts

Heat the butter and oil in a large skillet. Add the garlic and cook until golden brown. Add the celery, fennel seed, and green onions. Cover and cook over medium heat until the vegetables are tender. Add the remaining ingredients except the parsley and walnuts. Bring to a boil; cover and reduce the heat. Cook for 10 minutes, or until the barley is tender. Stir in the parsley and walnuts. Makes 4 servings.

All-Star Rating: 3 Stars ★		*Nutrient Content per Serving*	
Barley	Walnuts	Calories	503 kcal
Garbanzo beans		Protein	14 g
		Carbohydrate	77 g
Blue-Ribbon Rating: 6 Ribbons 🎗		Fat	16 g
Fiber	Protein	Fiber	15.1 g
Folate	Selenium	Calcium	106 mg
Magnesium	Vitamin K	Iron	3.5 mg

Oatmeal-Walnut Pancakes

2½ cups skim milk
1 cup rolled oats
1 cup all-purpose flour
½ cup whole-wheat flour
¼ cup toasted wheat germ
2 ounces ground almonds
¼ cup firmly packed brown sugar

2 teaspoons baking powder
1 teaspoon baking soda
1 teaspoon ground cinnamon
½ teaspoon salt
4 large egg whites, beaten
2 teaspoons flaxseed oil

Combine the milk and oats in a small bowl. Let stand for 30 minutes to soften the oats. In a large bowl, stir together all remaining dry ingredients. To the dry mixture, add the oat mixture and eggs; stir gently until blended. Brush a large skillet with the oil; heat over medium heat. Using ¼ cup batter for each pancake, pour the batter onto the skillet; cook until the underside is browned; flip. Transfer to a platter and keep warm. Repeat with the remaining batter, brushing the skillet with more oil as necessary. Serve hot with applesauce. Makes 12 pancakes, or 4 servings.

All-Star Rating: 5 Stars ★		Nutrient Content per Serving	
Almonds	Oats	Calories	525 kcal
Eggs	Wheat germ	Protein	22 g
Milk		Carbohydrate	72 g
		Fat	16 g
Blue-Ribbon Rating: 12 Ribbons		Fiber	6 g
Calcium	Riboflavin	Calcium	422 mg
Fiber	Selenium	Iron	4.4 mg
Magnesium	Thiamin		
Niacin	Vitamin B₁₂		
Phosphorus	Vitamin E		
Protein	Zinc		

Pasta with Green Sauce

1 cup frozen chopped spinach

1 cup vegetable broth

½ cup part-skim-milk ricotta cheese

¼ cup chopped fresh parsley

¼ cup grated Parmesan cheese

1 garlic clove, chopped

1 pound uncooked enriched linguine

2 ounces pine nuts

Mix all the ingredients except the pasta and nuts together in a food processor or blender until well blended. Cook the pasta according to the package directions; drain well. Pour the sauce over the pasta; toss to coat. Garnish with pine nuts. Makes 4 servings.

All-Star Rating: 4 Stars ★		Nutrient Content per Serving	
Parmesan cheese	Ricotta cheese	Calories	530 kcal
Pine nuts	Spinach	Protein	26 g
		Carbohydrate	70 g
Blue-Ribbon Rating: 6 Ribbons		Fat	16 g
Calcium	Protein	Fiber	4.5 g
Fiber	Vitamin A	Calcium	254 mg
Iron	Vitamin K	Iron	6 mg

Powerhouse Granola

3 cups rolled oats

½ cup wheat germ

½ cup chopped almonds

2 tablespoons ground flaxseed

1 12-ounce can apple juice concentrate, thawed

¼ cup firmly packed brown sugar

½ cup chopped dried apricots

½ cup chopped dried apples

1 cup dried cherries

Preheat the oven to 300°F. In a large bowl, combine the oats, wheat germ, almonds, and flaxseed. In a small bowl, combine the apple juice concentrate and brown sugar. Add the juice mixture to the oat mixture and mix thoroughly. Spread on a baking sheet and bake, stirring occasionally, for 40 to 50 minutes, or until golden brown. Stir in the apricots, apples, and cherries. Bake for 5 minutes more. Let cool; store in an airtight container. Makes 8 cups, or 8 servings.

All-Star Rating: 5 Stars ★		Nutrient Content per Serving	
Almonds	Oats	Calories	417 kcal
Apples	Wheat germ	Protein	10 g
Cherries		Carbohydrate	72 g
		Fat	11 g
Blue-Ribbon Rating: 6 Ribbons 🎖		Fiber	7.1 g
Fiber	Thiamin	Calcium	72 mg
Magnesium	Vitamin E	Iron	3.4 mg
Phosphorus	Zinc		

Pumpkin Waffles

2 cups sifted cake flour

4 teaspoons baking powder

1 teaspoon salt

6 large egg whites

1½ cups low-fat (1%) milk

1 cup canned pumpkin-pie mix

½ cup finely chopped pecans

Preheat a waffle iron. Into a large bowl, sift the flour, baking powder, and salt. In a medium bowl, beat the egg whites; add the milk, pumpkin-pie mix, and nuts; mix well. Pour the pumpkin mixture into the bowl with the flour mixture; stir gently until all the ingredients are blended. Lightly oil the waffle iron, or spray with nonstick cooking spray. Pour 1 cup batter onto the waffle iron. Cook for 3 to 5 minutes, or until the waffles are golden brown and steam no longer rises from the waffle iron. Repeat with the remaining batter. Makes 18 waffles, or 6 servings.

All-Star Rating: 4 Stars ★		Nutrient Content per Serving	
Eggs	Pecans	Calories	287 kcal
Milk	Pumpkin	Protein	10 g
		Carbohydrate	46 g
Blue-Ribbon Rating: 5 Ribbons		Fat	7 g
Folate	Thiamin	Fiber	5.2 g
Fiber	Vitamin A	Calcium	152 mg
Riboflavin		Iron	3.4 mg

Ratatouille

4 tablespoons olive oil

1 medium eggplant (approximately 1 pound), peeled and cut into 1-inch cubes

1 zucchini (approximately 1 pound), cut into 1-inch cubes

1½ cups sliced onions

3 garlic cloves, chopped

2 red bell peppers, cut into bite-size pieces

Salt and ground black pepper to taste

1½ cups peeled, chopped tomatoes

3 sprigs fresh thyme

1 bay leaf

¼ cup chopped fresh basil

4 cups hot cooked saffron rice

In a large saucepan, heat 2 tablespoons of the oil. Add the eggplant and zucchini, and sauté over medium heat until tender. Remove the vegetables to a bowl; set aside. In the same saucepan, heat the remaining 2 tablespoons oil. Add the onions and sauté until tender. Add the garlic and bell peppers; cook until tender. Season with salt and pepper. Add the tomatoes, thyme, and bay leaf. Reduce the heat to low, cover, and cook for 5 minutes. Add the eggplant and zucchini; cook for 20 minutes more. Stir in the basil. Remove the bay leaf and discard. Serve over the saffron rice. Makes 4 servings.

All-Star Rating: 1 Star ★		Nutrient Content per Serving	
Tomatoes		Calories	430 kcal
		Protein	9 g
		Carbohydrate	68 g
Blue-Ribbon Rating: 10 Ribbons		Fat	15 g
Fiber	Thiamin	Fiber	8 g
Folate	Vitamin A	Calcium	103 mg
Magnesium	Vitamin B₆	Iron	3.8 mg
Niacin	Vitamin C		
Selenium	Vitamin E		

Salsa Frittata

1 teaspoon olive oil

1 pound sweet potatoes or yams, peeled
   and cut into ½-inch cubes

3 large eggs or 6 large egg whites

1 jar medium-hot salsa (approximately 12
   ounces)

½ teaspoon salt

¼ teaspoon ground black pepper

1 cup shredded sharp Cheddar cheese

1 medium tomato, diced

Preheat the oven to 425°F. In a large skillet with an oven-safe handle (or cover the handle with heavy-duty foil for baking in the oven later), heat the olive oil over medium-high heat. Add the sweet potatoes and cook, covered, until they are tender and golden brown, about 10 minutes, stirring occasionally. Meanwhile, in a medium bowl, with a wire whisk or fork, beat the eggs with ¼ cup of the salsa (chopped, if necessary), the salt, and the pepper. Stir in the cheese; set aside. Stir the diced tomato into the remaining salsa. Stir the egg mixture into the sweet potatoes in the skillet. Cover and cook over medium heat, without stirring, for 3 minutes, or until the egg mixture begins to set around the edges. Remove the cover and place the skillet in the oven. Bake for 4 to 6 minutes, until the frittata is set. To serve, invert the frittata onto a cutting board. Cut into wedges and top with the salsa mixture. Makes 4 servings.

All-Star Rating: 4 Stars ★		Nutrient Content per Serving	
Cheese	Sweet potatoes or yams	Calories	415 kcal
Eggs	Tomato	Protein	21 g
		Carbohydrate	44 g
Blue-Ribbon Rating: 9 Ribbons 🎗		Fat	17 g
Calcium	Vitamin A	Fiber	2.3 g
Phosphorus	Vitamin B₁₂	Calcium	246 mg
Protein	Vitamin C	Iron	2.6 mg
Riboflavin	Vitamin E		
Selenium			

Spinach and Pumpkin Casserole

½ cup fat-free mayonnaise
½ cup all-purpose flour
1½ cups low-fat (1%) milk
8 large egg whites
1 cup canned pumpkin

1 10-ounce package frozen chopped
spinach, cooked and drained
6 slices white or whole-wheat toast,
cut into cubes
1½ cups shredded sharp Cheddar cheese

Preheat the oven to 350°F. In a medium saucepan, combine the mayonnaise and flour; mix well. Add the milk and egg whites; cook over low heat, stirring constantly, until thickened. Stir in the pumpkin and spinach. In the bottom of a 12 × 8-inch baking dish, layer the toast cubes. Top with half the cheese and half the pumpkin mixture; repeat. Bake for 45 to 50 minutes, or until thoroughly heated. Makes 4 servings.

All-Star Rating: 5 Stars ★		*Nutrient Content per Serving*	
Cheese	Milk	Calories	455 kcal
Eggs	Pumpkin	Protein	28 g
	Spinach	Carbohydrate	49 g
		Fat	16 g
Blue-Ribbon Rating: 12 Ribbons		Fiber	5.2 g
Calcium	Selenium	Calcium	586 mg
Fiber	Thiamin	Iron	4.1 mg
Folate	Vitamin A		
Magnesium	Vitamin B_{12}		
Protein	Vitamin E		
Riboflavin	Vitamin K		

Vegetarian Lasagna

1 tablespoon olive oil

½ cup chopped onions

½ cup chopped green bell peppers

½ cup chopped celery

1 teaspoon crushed garlic

2 15-ounce cans tomato sauce

¼ cup chopped fresh cilantro

1 12-ounce package low-fat (1%) cottage cheese

1 8-ounce package reduced-fat cream cheese (Neufchâtel), softened

½ cup nonfat sour cream

9 packaged enriched lasagna noodles, cooked and drained

Preheat the oven to 350°F. In a large skillet, heat the oil and sauté the onions, bell peppers, celery, and garlic; cook until tender. Add the tomato sauce and cilantro; heat well. In a medium bowl, combine the cottage cheese, cream cheese, and sour cream. Grease a 13 × 9-inch baking dish with butter or margarine. Arrange 3 lasagna noodles on the bottom of the dish. Top with one-third of the sauce and one-third of the cheese mixture. Repeat the layers twice, topping with the cheese mixture. Bake, uncovered, for 40 to 45 minutes. Let stand for 10 minutes before cutting. Makes 8 servings.

All-Star Rating: 2 Stars ★		*Nutrient Content per Serving*	
Cheese	Tomato sauce	Calories	442 kcal
		Protein	21 g
		Carbohydrate	59 g
Blue-Ribbon Rating: 8 Ribbons 🎖		Fat	13 g
Niacin	Thiamin	Fiber	3 g
Protein	Vitamin A	Calcium	122 mg
Riboflavin	Vitamin B$_{12}$	Iron	3.8 mg
Selenium	Vitamin C		

Vegetarian Stroganoff

10 ounces uncooked enriched spinach fettuccine

1 tablespoon butter

1 tablespoon olive oil

2 pounds fresh mushrooms, sliced

1 cup chopped onions

1 garlic clove, finely chopped

¼ cup all-purpose flour

2 cups vegetable broth

¼ cup tomato paste

1 cup nonfat sour cream

½ cup chopped walnuts

Cook the fettuccine according to the package directions; drain and keep warm. In a large saucepan, melt the butter and olive oil. Sauté the mushrooms, onions, and garlic until tender. Mix in the flour, vegetable broth, and tomato paste, stirring constantly until the mixture comes to a boil. Reduce the heat and stir in the sour cream and walnuts. Cook, without boiling, until thoroughly heated. Pour the sauce over the hot fettuccine. Makes 4 servings.

All-Star Rating: 3 Stars ★		*Nutrient Content per Serving*	
Spinach (pasta)	Walnuts	Calories	500 kcal
Tomato paste		Protein	21 g
		Carbohydrate	65 g
Blue-Ribbon Rating: 10 Ribbons 🎖		Fat	20 g
Fiber	Riboflavin	Fiber	6.7 g
Folate	Thiamin	Calcium	127 mg
Niacin	Vitamin A	Iron	3.9 mg
Phosphorus	Vitamin B$_6$		
Protein	Vitamin D		

Wild Rice Omelet

¾ cup All-Whites (pasteurized liquid egg whites)

1 green onion, sliced

1 ounce skim milk

Salt and ground black pepper to taste

1 teaspoon butter

½ cup cooked long-grain and wild rice

¼ cup shredded Muenster cheese

1 tomato, sliced

¼ cup chopped walnuts

Combine the egg whites, green onion, milk, salt, and pepper in a medium bowl. Melt the butter in a medium skillet. Pour in the egg mixture and cook over medium-low heat until the omelet is set. Lift the edges with a spatula to allow the uncooked egg mixture to flow underneath. Place the rice and cheese on half of the omelet and fold the other half over the filling. Continue cooking until the cheese has melted. Garnish with the tomato slices and chopped walnuts. Makes 1 serving.

All-Star Rating: 5 Stars ★		Nutrient Content per Serving	
Cheese	Tomato	Calories	450 kcal
Eggs	Walnuts	Protein	23 g
Milk		Carbohydrate	51 g
		Fat	19 g
Blue-Ribbon Rating: 12 Ribbons 🎗		Fiber	25 g
Fiber	Thiamin	Calcium	72 mg
Folate	Vitamin B$_6$	Iron	7.7 mg
Iron	Vitamin C		
Magnesium	Vitamin E		
Phosphorus	Vitamin K		
Protein	Zinc		

Side Dishes and Snacks

Chickpea Salad

2 cups canned chickpeas, rinsed and
    drained
½ cup chopped onions
¼ cup chopped fresh parsley
3 tablespoons lemon juice

2 tablespoons olive oil
1 teaspoon Dijon mustard
1 medium carrot, chopped
4 cups shredded romaine lettuce
½ cup chopped almonds

Stir all the ingredients together except for the lettuce and almonds. Serve over the shredded lettuce. Garnish with the chopped almonds. Makes 4 servings.

All-Star Rating: 2 Stars ★		*Nutrient Content per Serving*	
Chickpeas	Almonds	Calories	282 kcal
		Protein	11 g
		Carbohydrate	27 g
Blue-Ribbon Rating: 7 Ribbons		Fat	15 g
Fiber	Vitamin C	Fiber	8.7 g
Folate	Vitamin E	Calcium	115 mg
Magnesium	Vitamin K	Iron	2.7 mg
Vitamin A			

Harvest Muffins

1 cup canned pumpkin-pie mix	¾ cup firmly packed brown sugar
1 cup low-fat (1%) milk	2 cups all-purpose flour
¼ cup butter, melted	1 tablespoon baking powder
¼ cup honey	¼ teaspoon salt
1 tablespoon vanilla extract	1 cup chopped walnuts
2 large egg whites	½ cup raisins

Preheat the oven to 400°F. Line a muffin tin with 12 paper liners. In a medium bowl, combine the pumpkin-pie mix, milk, butter, honey, vanilla, egg whites, and brown sugar; mix well. Into a large bowl, sift together the flour, baking powder, and salt. Add the pumpkin mixture to the flour mixture, stirring gently until just blended. Stir in the nuts and raisins. Spoon the batter into the muffin tin, filling each cup about half full. Bake for 15 to 20 minutes, or until a toothpick inserted in the center comes out clean. Makes 1 dozen muffins.

All-Star Rating: 4 Stars ★		*Nutrient Content per Serving*	
Eggs	Pumpkin	Calories	278 kcal
Milk	Walnuts	Protein	5 g
		Carbohydrate	44 g
Blue-Ribbon Rating: 2 Ribbons 🏵		Fat	9 g
Phosphorus	Vitamin A	Fiber	3 g
		Calcium	144 mg
		Iron	1.8 mg

Pumpkin Custard

4 large egg whites, lightly beaten
1 pound canned pumpkin-pie mix
½ teaspoon salt

12 ounces nonfat evaporated milk
¼ cup chopped almonds

Preheat the oven to 350°F. In a large bowl, mix the egg whites, pumpkin-pie mix, salt, and evaporated milk. Pour into 8 greased 6-ounce custard cups. Set the custard cups in a shallow pan; fill the pan with hot water. Bake for 45 to 50 minutes, or until a knife inserted in the center of the custard comes out clean. Chill. Top with the chopped almonds. Makes 4 servings.

All-Star Rating: 4 Stars ★		*Nutrient Content per Serving*	
Almonds	Milk	Calories	248 kcal
Eggs	Pumpkin	Protein	13 g
		Carbohydrate	42 g
Blue-Ribbon Rating: 7 Ribbons		Fat	4 g
Calcium	Riboflavin	Fiber	10 g
Fiber	Vitamin A	Calcium	337 mg
Phosphorus	Vitamin D	Iron	1.7 mg
Protein			

Pumpkin-Fruit Muffins

1 cup uncooked old-fashioned rolled oats

½ cup skim milk

2½ cups all-purpose flour

1 cup firmly packed brown sugar

1 tablespoon baking powder

½ teaspoon baking soda

½ teaspoon ground cinnamon

2 cups canned pumpkin

½ cup raisins

2 large eggs

¼ cup flaxseed oil

1 teaspoon vanilla extract

Preheat the oven to 350°F. Line a muffin tin with 12 paper liners. Combine the oats and milk; mix well. Set aside. In a large bowl, combine the flour, brown sugar, baking powder, baking soda, and cinnamon; mix well. Stir in the pumpkin, raisins, oat mixture, eggs, flaxseed oil, and vanilla; mix just until the dry ingredients are moistened. Pour into the muffin tin. Bake for 20 to 30 minutes, or until the muffins are golden and a toothpick inserted in the center comes out clean. Makes 12 muffins.

All-Star Rating: 4 Stars ★		*Nutrient Content per Serving*	
Eggs	Oatmeal	Calories	310 kcal
Milk	Pumpkin	Protein	6 g
		Carbohydrate	52 g
Blue-Ribbon Rating: 2 Ribbons		Fat	7 g
Vitamin A	Vitamin E	Fiber	1.6 g
		Calcium	40 mg
		Iron	1.7 mg

Pumpkin Loaf

2 cups all-purpose flour

2 cups whole-wheat flour

4 teaspoons baking powder

1 teaspoon baking soda

2 teaspoons salt

2 cups canned pumpkin-pie mix

¼ cup firmly packed brown sugar

1 cup milk

8 large egg whites

½ cup canola oil

2 cups chopped walnuts or pecans

Preheat the oven to 350°F. Grease two 9 × 5-inch loaf pans. Into a large bowl, sift together the white flour, wheat flour, baking powder, baking soda, and salt. In another large bowl, combine the pumpkin-pie mix, brown sugar, milk, egg whites, and oil. Add the pumpkin mixture to the flour mixture; stir gently just until the dry ingredients are moistened. Stir in the nuts. Pour the batter into the loaf pans. Bake for 60 to 65 minutes, or until a toothpick inserted in the center comes out clean. Let cool for 10 minutes; remove from the pans. Makes 2 loaves, or 12 servings.

All-Star Rating: 4 Stars ★		*Nutrient Content per Serving*	
Eggs	Nuts	Calories	324 kcal
Milk	Pumpkin	Protein	7 g
		Carbohydrate	38 g
Blue-Ribbon Rating: 7 Ribbons		Fat	17 g
Fiber	Thiamin	Fiber	6.3 g
Magnesium	Vitamin A	Calcium	120 mg
Phosphorus	Vitamin E	Iron	2.1 mg
Selenium			

Sunrise Bread Pudding

1½ cups canned pumpkin-pie mix
½ cup low-fat (1%) milk
4 large egg whites

8 slices raisin bread, cubed
1 teaspoon ground cinnamon
½ teaspoon ground nutmeg

Preheat the oven to 325°F. In a large bowl, combine the pumpkin-pie mix, milk, and egg whites; stir in the bread and spices. Spoon into a 1-quart casserole. Bake for 50 minutes, or until a knife inserted in the pumpkin mixture comes out clean. Makes 4 servings.

All-Star Rating: 3 Stars ★		*Nutrient Content per Serving*	
Eggs	Pumpkin	Calories	277 kcal
Milk		Protein	10 g
		Carbohydrate	56 g
Blue-Ribbon Rating: 5 Ribbons		Fat	3 g
Fiber	Selenium	Fiber	10.6 g
Folate	Vitamin A		
Riboflavin			

Tabbouleh

4 cups boiling water	¼ cup olive oil
1 cup uncooked fine bulgur	¼ cup lemon juice
1 cup finely minced fresh parsley	1 teaspoon salt
½ cup finely minced fresh mint leaves	Ground black pepper to taste
1 large tomato, chopped	1 head romaine lettuce

In a large pot, pour the boiling water over the bulgur and let stand for 2 hours. Drain and squeeze out the excess water; place in a large bowl. Stir in all the other ingredients except the lettuce; let stand for 1 hour before serving. Divide the lettuce among 4 plates; top with the tabbouleh. Makes 4 large salads.

All-Star Rating: 2 Stars ★		*Nutrient Content per Serving*	
Bulgur	Tomato	Calories	275 kcal
		Protein	7 g
Blue-Ribbon Rating: 7 Ribbons		Carbohydrate	34 g
Fiber	Vitamin C	Fat	14 g
Folate	Vitamin E	Fiber	9.3 g
Magnesium	Vitamin K	Calcium	83 mg
Vitamin A		Iron	3.3 mg

Weekend Hash Browns

1 tablespoon safflower oil

2 cups frozen shredded hash brown
   potatoes, thawed

¾ cup sliced green onions

4 slices white or whole-wheat toast, cut into
   small cubes

2 large eggs plus 6 large egg whites, beaten

1 cup shredded Muenster cheese

Salt and ground black pepper to taste

In a large skillet, heat the oil; add the hash browns and ½ cup of the green onions. Cook, stirring occasionally, until the potatoes are a deep golden brown. Add the toast cubes, eggs and egg whites, cheese, salt, and pepper. Cook until the eggs are set. Garnish with the remaining ¼ cup green onions. Makes 4 servings.

All-Star Rating: 2 Stars ★		Nutrient Content per Serving	
Cheese	Eggs	Calories	352 kcal
		Protein	20 g
Blue-Ribbon Rating: 9 Ribbons		Carbohydrate	33 g
Calcium	Vitamin B_{12}	Fat	15 g
Phosphorus	Vitamin C	Fiber	3.3 g
Protein	Vitamin E	Calcium	270 mg
Riboflavin	Vitamin K	Iron	2.9 mg
Selenium			

Yogurt Guacamole

3 ripe avocados (approximately 1½ pounds)
2 garlic cloves, finely chopped
2 tablespoons lemon juice
1½ cups plain low-fat yogurt
2 tablespoons medium-hot salsa

¼ teaspoon ground cumin
¼ cup chopped fresh cilantro
Salt and ground black pepper to taste
6 pita breads, split

In a large bowl, mash the avocados. Stir in the remaining ingredients except the pita breads. Serve on the pita breads. Makes 6 servings.

All-Star Rating: 3 Stars ★		Nutrient Content per Serving	
Avocados	Yogurt	Calories	244 kcal
Tomatoes (salsa)		Protein	10 g
		Carbohydrate	42 g
Blue-Ribbon Rating: 5 Ribbons 🎗		Fat	6 g
Fiber	Selenium	Fiber	7.4 g
Magnesium	Thiamin	Calcium	131 mg
Phosphorus		Iron	2.2 mg

Smoothies

Basic Fruit Smoothie

2 ounces Silken tofu, soft (approximately ½ cup)

1 cup plain or vanilla nonfat yogurt

½ cup cut-up fresh or frozen fruit

½ cup fruit juice

1 tablespoon lemon or lime juice

2 All-Whites (pasteurized liquid egg whites)

2 tablespoons nonfat dry milk solids

1 tablespoon flaxseed oil

4 ice cubes, crushed

Put all the ingredients in a blender. Process until smooth and blended. Makes 1 large smoothie.

All-Star Rating: 5 Stars ★		*Nutrient Content per Serving*	
Eggs	Tofu	Calories	414 kcal
Fruit	Yogurt	Protein	26 g
Milk		Carbohydrate	44 g
		Fat	15 g
Blue-Ribbon Rating: 10 Ribbons 🎗		Fiber	2 g
Calcium	Selenium	Calcium	582 mg
Magnesium	Vitamin B$_{12}$	Iron	1.5 mg
Phosphorus	Vitamin C		
Protein	Vitamin E		
Riboflavin	Zinc		

Note: With each Basic Fruit Smoothie, you can meet your daily requirement of:

1 serving of meat or meat equivalents	2 ounces tofu + 2 egg whites
2 servings of dairy	1 cup yogurt + 2 tablespoons nonfat dry milk
2 servings of fruit	½ cup fresh or frozen + ½ cup juice
1 serving of fat	1 tablespoon flaxseed oil

Variations on the Basic Fruit Smoothie

Fruit

Apples

Applesauce

Apricots

Bananas

Blackberries

Blueberries

Cherries

Cranberries

Dates, rehydrated

Mangoes

Oranges

Papayas

Peaches

Pears

Pineapple

Prunes, rehydrated

Strawberries

Fruit Juice

Apple

Cranberry

Grape

Guava nectar

Orange

Pear nectar

Pineapple

Optional Nutrient Boosters

Brewer's yeast, 1 teaspoon

Old-fashioned rolled oats, 1 tablespoon

Wheat germ, 1 tablespoon

Optional Flavorings

Almond extract

Carob powder

Cinnamon

Cloves

Coffee or tea, brewed

Ginger, freshly grated

Honey

Mint or peppermint extract

Maple syrup

Nutmeg

Vanilla extract

Basic Vegetable Smoothie

2 ounces Silken tofu, soft (approximately
  ½ cup)
1 cup plain low-fat yogurt
½ cup cut-up vegetables
½ cup vegetable juice
1 tablespoon lemon or lime juice
2 All-Whites (pasteurized liquid egg whites)

2 tablespoons nonfat dry milk solids
1 tablespoon flaxseed oil
Seasoning (optional, add 1 or more):
  balsamic vinegar, celery salt, onion salt,
  Tabasco sauce
4 ice cubes, crushed

Put all the ingredients in a blender. Process until smooth and blended. Makes 1 large smoothie.

All-Star Rating: 5 Stars ★		*Nutrient Content per Serving*	
Eggs	Vegetables	Calories	416 kcal
Milk	Yogurt	Protein	28 g
Tofu		Carbohydrate	35 g
		Fat	19 g
Blue-Ribbon Rating: 14 Ribbons 🎗		Fiber	2.3 g
Calcium	Thiamin	Calcium	648 mg
Folate	Vitamin A	Iron	1.9 mg
Magnesium	Vitamin B_6		
Phosphorus	Vitamin B_{12}		
Protein	Vitamin C		
Riboflavin	Vitamin E		
Selenium	Zinc		

Note: With each Basic Vegetable Smoothie, you can meet your daily requirement of:

1 serving of meat or meat equivalents   2 ounces tofu + 2 egg whites ·
2 servings of dairy   ½ cup yogurt + 2 tablespoons nonfat dry milk
2 servings of vegetables   ½ cup fresh + ½ cup juice
1 serving of fat   1 tablespoon flaxseed oil

Ginger Smoothie

2 ounces Silken tofu, soft (approximately ½ cup)

½ cup lemon sorbet

½ cup ginger ale

1 teaspoon peeled, grated fresh ginger

1 tablespoon honey

1 tablespoon lemon juice

Put all the ingredients in a blender. Process until smooth and blended. Makes 1 large smoothie.

All-Star Rating: 1 Star ★		*Nutrient Content per Serving*	
Tofu		Calories	270 kcal
		Protein	4 g
Blue-Ribbon Rating: 1 Star		Carbohydrate	61 g
Vitamin C		Fat	2 g
		Fiber	0.4 g
		Calcium	91 mg
		Iron	1.2 mg

Note: Ginger Smoothie is excellent for easing nausea.

Appendix B

Resources for Parents of Multiples

Bedrest and High-Risk Pregnancy

Sidelines High Risk Pregnancy Support: PO Box 1808, Laguna Beach, CA 92652. Telephone 888–447–4754; e-mail sidelines@sidelines.org; Web site www.sidelines.org. *Support group for women with high-risk pregnancies.*

Breast-Feeding

International Lactation Consultant Association: 1500 Sunday Drive, Suite 102, Raleigh, NC 27607. Telephone 919–861–5577; e-mail info@ilca.org; Web site www.ilca.org. *Education resources and referrals to consultants in your area.*

La Leche League International: 1400 North Meacham Road, Schaumburg, IL 60173-4808. Telephone 800–LA–LECHE or 847–519–7730; Web site www.lalecheleague.org. *Breast-feeding information for parents; referrals to local support groups. Books include* The Womanly Art of Breastfeeding *and* Breastfeeding Your Premature Baby.

Lactation Education Resources: 3621 Lido Place, Fairfax, VA 22031. Telephone 703–691–2069; e-mail LERonline@yahoo.com; Web site www.LERon-line.com. *Educational materials.*

U.S. Breast-Feeding Committee: 1500 Sunday Drive, Suite 102, Raleigh, NC 27607. Telephone 919–787–5181; e-mail info@usbreastfeeding.org; Web site www.usbreastfeeding.org.

Childbirth Preparation

American Academy of Husband-Coached Childbirth (aka The Bradley Method): PO Box 5524, Sherman Oaks, CA 91413-5224. Telephone 800–4–A–BIRTH; Web site www.bradleybirth.com.

International Childbirth Education Association: PO Box 20048, Minneapolis, MN 55420. Telephone 952–854–8660; Web site www.icea.org.

Lamaze International (aka American Society for Psychoprophylaxis in Obstetrics): 2025 M Street NW, Suite 800, Washington, DC 20036-3309. Telephone 800–368–4404; Web site www.lamaze.org.

Diet and Pregnancy

American Dietetic Association Nutrition Hotline: 216 West Jackson Boulevard, Chicago, IL 60606-6995. Telephone 800–366–1655, ext. 5000; Web site www.eatright.org. *Referrals to dietitians in your area.*

Barbara Luke, Sc.D., M.P.H., R.D.: Web site www.drbarbaraluke.com. *Personalized nutrition counseling.*

Program Your Baby's Health: The Pregnancy Diet for Your Child's Lifelong Well-Being, by Barbara Luke, Sc.D., M.P.H., R.D., and Tamara Eberlein. Ballantine Books, New York, 2001.

Women, Infants, and Children Supplemental Food Stamp Program (WIC): Web site www.fns.usda.gov/wic.

Grief and Bereavement

Angels Forever: Web site www.angels4ever.com (click on "Multiples Angels Network icon"). *Parental support, on-line chats, links.*

Center for Loss in Multiple Birth (CLIMB): PO Box 91377, Anchorage, AK 99509. Telephone 907–222–5321; e-mail newsletter@climb-support.org; Web site www.climb-support.org. *Support by and for parents and bereaved families; quarterly newsletter; relevant articles; samples of birth and memorial announcements.*

Loss in Multiple Birth Outreach (LIMBO): Web site www.geocities.com/heartland/lake/5142/index.html. *Personal stories; on-line chat.*

National Organization of Mothers of Twins Clubs (NOMOTC): PO Box 438, Thompsons Station, TN 37179-0438. Telephone 615–595–0936 or 877–540–2200; e-mail info@nomotc.org; Web site www.nomotc.org. *Bereavement support coordinator corresponds with families.*

Parents of Multiples Forever: Web site www.erichad.com/pom/. *Personal stories and memorial site.*

Triplet Connection: PO Box 99571, Stockton, CA 95209. Telephone 209–474–0885; e-mail janet@tripletconnection.org; Web site www.tripletconnection.org. *Networking information for bereaved higher-order multiple families.*

Health Information

National Healthy Mothers, Healthy Babies Coalition: 121 North Washington Street, Suite 300, Alexandria, VA 22314. Telephone 703–836–6110; Web site www.hmhb.org.

National Perinatal Association: 3500 East Fletcher Avenue, Suite 205, Tampa, FL 33613-4712. Telephone 888–971–3295; e-mail npa@nationalperinatal.org; Web site: www.nationalperinatal.org.

National Women's Health Information Center: 8550 Arlington Boulevard, Suite 300, Fairfax, VA 22031. Telephone 800–994–WOMAN; Web site www.4women.org.

Medical Organizations

American Board of Medical Specialties: 1007 Church Street, Suite 404, Evanston, IL 60201-5913. Telephone 866–ASK–ABMS; Web site www.abms.org. *Verification of an individual doctor's status as a board-certified specialist.*

American College of Obstetricians and Gynecologists: 409 12th Street, SW, PO Box 96920, Washington, DC 20090-6920. Telephone 800–673–8444; Web site www.acog.org. *Referrals to maternal-fetal medicine specialists in your area.*

Multiple Birth Organizations

Center for the Study of Multiple Birth: 333 East Superior, Suite 464, Chicago, IL 60611. Telephone 312–266–9093. *Research, publications.*

International Society for Twin Studies: Louisville Twin Study, Child Development Unit, Department of Pediatrics, University of Louisville, Louisville, KY 40292. Telephone 502–588–5134; Web site www.ists.qimr.edu.au.

Mothers of Supertwins (MOST): PO Box 951, Brentwood, NY 11717-0627. Telephone 631–859–1110; Web site www.mostonline.org. *Information and referrals to local chapters.*

National Organization of Mothers of Twins Clubs (NOMOTC): PO Box 438, Thompsons Station, TN 37179-0438. Telephone 615–595–0936 or 877–540–2200; e-mail info@nomotc.org; Web site www.nomotc.org. *Information and referrals to local chapters.*

Triplet Connection: PO Box 99571, Stockton, CA 95209. Telephone 209–474–0885; e-mail janet@tripletconnection.org; Web site www.tripletconnection.org. *Resources, information, and support for families of supertwins.*

Twins magazine: 11211 East Arapahoe Road, Suite 101, Centennial, CO 80112-3851. Telephone 888–558–9467. *Six issues, $25.95.*

Twin Services: PO Box 10066, Berkeley, CA 94709. Telephone 510–524–0863; Web site www.twinservices.org. *Publications, counseling.*

Nutritional Supplements

Mead Johnson & Company: PO Box 3204, Evansville, IN 47731-3204. Telephone 800–247–7893; e-mail askmeadjohnson@bms.com; Web site www.meadjohnson.com.

Ross Products/Abbott Laboratories: 625 Cleveland Avenue, Columbus, OH 43215-1724. Telephone 800–986–8510; Web site www.ross.com.

Sandoz Nutrition (available through McKesson Corporation): Telephone 800–446–6380; Web site www.mckesson.com.

Postpartum Depression

Center for Postpartum Health: 20700 Ventura Boulevard, Suite 203, Woodland Hills, CA 91364. Telephone 818–887–1312; Web site www.postpartumhealth.com.

Postpartum Health Alliance: PO Box 503396, San Diego, CA 92150. Telephone 619–685–7458; e-mail info@postpartumhealthalliance.org; Web site www.postpartumhealthalliance.org.

Postpartum Support International: Web site www.postpartum.net.

Products

Affiliated Genetics: PO Box 58535, Salt Lake City, UT 84158. Telephone 800–362–5559; Web site www.affiliatedgenetics.com. *Provides cheek-swab, mail-order genetic test used to determine twin type ($120 plus $10 handling for twins; $60 more for each additional multiple).*

More Than One: 941 Matthews-Mint Hill Road, Suite M, Matthews, NC 28105. Telephone 800–388–TWIN; e-mail morthan1@aol.com; Web site www.morethan1.com. *Mail-order products for multiples.*

Preemie Store and More: 1682 Roxanna Lane, New Brighton, MN 55112. Telephone 800–676–8469; e-mail pat@preemie-clothes.com; Web site www.preemiestore.com. *Clothing and products for premature infants.*

Prenatal Cradle: PO Box 443, Hamburg, MI 48139. Telephone 800–607–3572; e-mail prenatalcradle@prenatalcradle.com; Web site www.prenatalcradle.com. *Supportive undergarment for pregnancy.*

Twin Connection: Telephone 800–526–2594; Web site www.nurturingmothersboutique.com (click on "Twin Connection" icon). *Mail-order products for multiples, including the NurseEz twin nursing pillow; breast-feeding supplies; preemie clothes.*

Glossary

abruptio placenta Condition in which the placenta begins to separate from the uterus before or during birth.

AGA *See* appropriate for gestational age.

alpha-fetoprotein A type of protein produced by an unborn baby or its yolk sac; a test of the mother's blood done at 15 to 18 weeks' gestation can suggest that more than one fetus is present, or that the fetus has an abnormality.

amino acids The structural components of protein.

amniocentesis A test done between 15 and 20 weeks' gestation to screen for certain genetic disorders; performed by inserting a needle through the mother's abdomen into the womb to withdraw a sample of amniotic fluid.

amnion The membrane closest to the unborn babies.

amniotic fluid The fluid within the uterus surrounding the unborn babies.

amniotic sac The fluid-filled, membranous sac within which the unborn baby grows, cushioned from shocks from the outside environment and kept at an even temperature; also called bag of waters.

analgesia Medication that provides pain relief without total loss of sensation.

anemia *See* iron-deficiency anemia.

anesthesia Medication that provides pain relief by loss of sensation.

anthropometric measures The clinical assessments of body weight and measurements of upper-arm circumference, midthigh circumference, and skinfold thickness at various sites; used as indicators of nutritional status.

Apgar score A score given at one, five, and ten minutes after birth, summarizing a newborn's physical condition.

apnea The cessation of breathing for 15 to 20 seconds.

appropriate for gestational age (AGA) A newborn who weighs between the 10th and 90th percentiles for gestational age.

ART *See* assisted reproductive technologies.

assisted reproductive technologies (ART) The collective term for medications and therapies used to treat infertility.

bag of waters *See* amniotic sac.

betamethasone (Celestone) A steroid drug given to the mother by injection to speed maturation of the unborn babies' lungs.

bili-lights A bank of lights used for phototherapy in the treatment of hyperbilirubinemia.

biophysical profile A test combining information from the nonstress test with that of ultrasound; an assessment of the unborn babies' heart rates, breathing patterns, body movements, and muscle tone, and the amount of amniotic fluid surrounding each baby.

bloody show The blood-tinged mucous plug that is released when the cervix begins to dilate.

BPD *See* bronchopulmonary dysplasia.

Braxton-Hicks contractions Irregular contractions occurring throughout pregnancy that do not lead to effacement or dilation of the cervix.

breech presentation The position of a fetus who is lying with his feet or buttocks closest to the cervix.

bronchopulmonary dysplasia (BPD) Damage to an infant's lungs caused by the use of a respirator.

cardiorespiratory monitor A piece of equipment that monitors a baby's heart and breathing rates.

catecholamines Hormones produced by the body during periods of stress.

Celestone *See* betamethasone.

cerclage A procedure to treat an incompetent cervix that involves stitching the cervix closed.

cervix The opening at the bottom of the uterus that thins out (effaces) and opens (dilates) during labor and delivery.

chloasma An area of darkened pigmentation over the nose and cheeks that frequently appears during pregnancy.

chorion The membrane closest to the placenta.

chorionic villus sampling (CVS) A test of part of the chorion, performed at 10 to 12 weeks' gestation, to screen for a variety of potential congenital conditions.

chromosomes The genetic material contained in the mother's egg and the father's sperm that combines during fertilization.

chronic lung disease *See* bronchopulmonary dysplasia.

conception The fertilization of a woman's egg by a man's sperm.

contraction stress test A prenatal test in which a small amount of oxytocin is given to initiate uterine contractions, in order to evaluate how well the babies respond physically to the potential demands of labor.

corrected age The age a premature infant would have been if he had been born on his due date; for example, on his first birthday, a baby born two months premature has a corrected age of ten months.

crib death *See* sudden infant death syndrome.

CVS *See* chorionic villus sampling.

diamniotic Two amniotic placental membranes.

dichorionic Two chorionic placental membranes.

dilation The progressive opening of the cervix during labor, measured in centimeters from zero (not dilated) to 10 (fully dilated).

dizygotic Twins that develop from two separate zygotes; also known as fraternal twins.

Doppler flow study Prenatal evaluation of the blood flow to the placenta.

ductus arteriosus A short vessel connecting the pulmonary artery to the aorta.

ectopic pregnancy The implantation of an embryo in tissues other than the uterus, usually in the fallopian tube.

effacement The progressive thinning out of the cervix during labor.

electronic fetal monitoring Measurement of the fetal heart rates with external monitors before and during labor.

embryo The term for the developing baby prior to the third month of gestation.

endometrium The outer layer of the tissue lining the uterus.

episiotomy An incision made at delivery to widen the vaginal opening and prevent tearing as the baby emerges.

essential amino acids The components of proteins that cannot be produced by the body and must be supplied in the diet.

essential fatty acids The components of fats that cannot be produced by the body and must be supplied in the diet.

external version A procedure in which a physician or nurse presses on a pregnant woman's abdomen in an attempt to change the position of a fetus who is breech or transverse.

fertilization When the mother's egg and the father's sperm unite; also known as conception.

fetus The term for the unborn child from the end of the embryonic period until delivery.

fraternal Twins or supertwins that developed from separate zygotes.

full term Delivery between 38 and 42 weeks' gestation, as calculated from the last menstrual period.

fundal height The distance from the fundus to the pelvic bone.

fundus The top of the uterus.

gavage feeding Infant feeding via a thin, flexible tube passed through either the nose or the mouth and into the stomach.

gestational age An unborn baby's age in weeks, as calculated from the mother's last menstrual period.

gestational age at birth The length of the pregnancy, as calculated from the mother's last menstrual period to the day of delivery.

gestational diabetes The development of diabetes during pregnancy.

HCG *See* human chorionic gonadotropin.

hematocrit The percentage of red blood cells in the blood.

hemoglobin The iron-containing component of red blood cells.

higher-order multiples A collective term for three or more babies resulting from one pregnancy; also called supertwins; includes triplets, quadruplets, quintuplets, sextuplets, septuplets, and so on.

home uterine activity monitor (HUAM) An electronic device worn around the waist that measures the frequency and intensity of uterine contractions.

HUAM *See* home uterine activity monitor.

human chorionic gonadotropin (HCG) A hormone produced by the chorion; it can be measured soon after conception to confirm a pregnancy.

hyperalimentation *See* parenteral nutrition.

hyperbilirubinemia Excessively high levels of bilirubin in the blood during the newborn period.

hypoglycemia Abnormally low blood sugar levels.

identical Twins or supertwins that developed from a single zygote; also known as monozygotic.

incompetent cervix A cervix that opens spontaneously in early to midpregnancy, potentially resulting in a miscarriage or early preterm birth.

Indomethacin *See* tocolytics.

intrauterine growth retardation (IUGR) Birthweight of less than the 10th percentile for gestational age.

intraventricular hemorrhage Bleeding into the ventricles of the brain.

in utero Occurring in the uterus, before birth.

iron-deficiency anemia Abnormally low levels of red blood cells, which carry oxygen to the tissues.

IUGR *See* intrauterine growth retardation.

jaundice *See* physiologic jaundice.

kangaroo care The practice of having a parent hold a premature baby skin to skin against the chest, shown in studies to help the infant regulate his breathing and body temperature and to promote parent-infant bonding.

ketones A by-product of the breakdown of fat for energy.

kilogram (kg) Unit of weight of the metric system, equivalent to 1,000 grams, or 2.2 pounds.

labor The process by which the cervix thins and opens to allow the babies to pass from the uterus through the vagina and be born.

large for gestational age (LGA) Birthweight above the 90th percentile for gestational age.

LBW *See* low birthweight.

let-down reflex The flow of milk into the ducts and collection areas behind the nipples, felt as a tingling sensation by the nursing mother.

LGA *See* large for gestational age.

lightening When the baby closest to the cervix settles deeper into the pelvis before delivery.

linea nigra A line of darkened pigment from the navel to the pubic bone that occurs in some women during pregnancy.

low birthweight (LBW) A birthweight of less than 2,500 grams, or 5½ pounds.

magnesium sulfate Medication used in treating preeclampsia and preterm labor.

MBR *See* multiple birth ratio.

monoamniotic A single inner placental membrane, indicating identical twins.

monochorionic A single outer placental membrane surrounding the fetuses, indicating identical twins.

monozygotic Twins or supertwins that developed from a single zygote, which divided an extra time to result in two or more equal and matching embryos.

multiple birth ratio (MBR) The number of multiple births per 1,000 total live births.

NEC *See* necrotizing enterocolitis.

necrotizing enterocolitis (NEC) A potential complication of prematurity that involves a gangrenelike condition of portions of the gastrointestinal tract.

neonatal intensive care unit (NICU) A specialized nursery staffed and equipped to care for seriously ill newborns.

NICU *See* neonatal intensive care unit.

nifedipine *See* tocolytics.

nonstress test An evaluation of fetal movements and fetal heart rate using an electronic fetal monitor.

nosocomial infection An infection picked up from the hospital environment.

nutritional supplements Specially formulated foods, usually in beverage form, that contain extra calories and/or protein.

OGTT *See* oral glucose tolerance test.

oral glucose tolerance test (OGTT) A test, often given prenatally, that involves ingesting a high-carbohydrate beverage and then having blood drawn at set intervals to determine blood glucose levels.

ovulation The release of a mature egg from the ovaries.

oxy-hood A plastic box or hood placed over the baby's head to deliver supplemental oxygen.

oxytocin (Pitocin) A hormone that stimulates uterine contractions and the let-down reflex in breast-feeding women.

Pap smear A procedure that involves scraping a few cells from the cervix and examining them under a microscope to detect any abnormal changes.

parenteral nutrition A special formula for premature infants, given intravenously, that contains all essential nutrients; also called hyperalimentation.

patent ductus arteriosis (PDA) Condition in which the fetal connection between the aorta and the pulmonary artery fails to close after birth.

PDA *See* patent ductus arteriosis.

pelvic examination An internal examination performed manually to evaluate the cervix and uterus; may also involve using a vaginal probe for vaginal ultrasound.

perineum The area between the opening of the vagina and the rectum.

phototherapy A treatment for hyperbilirubinemia that uses light waves to break down bilirubin so that it can be excreted in the urine.

physiologic jaundice A buildup of bilirubin in the blood during the newborn period, causing the skin to become yellow.

Pitocin *See* oxytocin.

placenta The outer layer of the fertilized egg; it develops into the vascular organ lining the uterus to supply the baby with nutrients and oxygen before birth.

placenta previa A condition in which the placenta lies partially or completely over the cervix, resulting in bleeding as the cervix dilates during labor and delivery.

pneumonia Infection in the lungs.

polyhydramnios An excessive amount of amniotic fluid.

postpartum depression (PPD) A temporary feeling of depression after delivery, resulting from hormonal shifts and other factors.

PPD *See* postpartum depression.

PPROM *See* preterm premature rupture of membranes.

preeclampsia A pregnancy complication in which there is protein in the urine, rapid weight gain, rise in blood pressure, and swelling from fluid retention; formerly called toxemia.

premature birth Birth prior to 37 full weeks of pregnancy.

preterm birth Birth prior to 37 full weeks of pregnancy.

preterm labor Labor that begins prior to 37 full weeks of pregnancy.

preterm premature rupture of membranes (PPROM) Breaking of the membranes surrounding the fetus prior to 37 weeks' gestation.

radiant warmer A small open crib with an overhead heat source.

RDS *See* respiratory distress syndrome.

reduction *See* selective multifetal reduction.

respiratory distress syndrome (RDS) A common complication of prematurity in which lung tissue collapses on itself owing to lack of surfactant, the soaplike substance that helps to keep the lungs inflated.

retinopathy of prematurity (ROP) An eye complication of some premature babies in which blood vessels of the eye grow abnormally; also called retrolental fibroplasia.

retrolental fibroplasia *See* retinopathy of prematurity.

Rh factor A protein in red blood cells that can lead to complications if present in the blood of the unborn babies (Rh-positive) but not in the mother (Rh-negative).

ritodrine *See* tocolytics.

ROP *See* retinopathy of prematurity.

rupture of membranes Breaking of the membranes surrounding the fetus, often at the onset of labor.

selective multifetal reduction A procedure by which one or more fetuses of a multiple gestation are selectively aborted in an attempt to improve the chances of a good pregnancy outcome for the remaining fetuses.

sepsis Bacteria in the bloodstream.

SGA *See* small for gestational age.

SIDS *See* sudden infant death syndrome.

singleton A baby conceived and born alone.

small for gestational age (SGA) A newborn whose birthweight is below the 10th percentile for gestational age.

sonogram *See* ultrasound.

sudden infant death syndrome (SIDS) The death, during sleep and from unknown causes, of an infant who had appeared to be healthy; also called crib death.

supertwins A collective term for three or more babies resulting from one pregnancy; also called higher-order multiples; includes triplets, quadruplets, quintuplets, sextuplets, septuplets, and so on.

surfactant A fatty substance formed in the lungs that keeps the small air sacs, or alveoli, from collapsing.

terbutaline *See* tocolytics.

tocolytics Drugs used to attempt to halt preterm labor.

TOLAC *See* trial of labor after cesarean.

toxemia *See* preeclampsia.

transition The end of the first stage of labor, when the cervix dilates from 8 to 10 centimeters.

transverse presentation The position of a fetus who is lying sideways in the uterus.

trial of labor An attempt to deliver vaginally in the presence of certain factors that could ultimately necessitate a cesarean delivery.

trial of labor after cesarean (TOLAC) An attempt to deliver vaginally after a previous cesarean birth.

trimester One of the three periods of pregnancy, each lasting about three months.

twin type The identical or fraternal status of twins or supertwins.

ultrasound Technology that bounces sound waves off the unborn babies and the surrounding fluid and membranes, then projects the resulting images onto a video screen; also called a sonogram.

umbilical arterial catheter A catheter threaded into a premature baby's umbilical artery in order to draw blood samples, give fluids and medications, and measure blood pressure.

urinary tract infection (UTI) Infection of the bladder or other structure of the urinary tract.

UTI *See* urinary tract infection.

vaginal birth after cesarean (VBAC) A vaginal delivery that follows a previous cesarean birth.

VBAC *See* vaginal birth after cesarean.

vertex presentation The position of a fetus who is lying head-down in the uterus.

vital signs Pulse, temperature, and blood pressure.

zygote The term for the fertilized egg prior to 12 weeks' gestation.

Bibliography

Alcohol and Smoking During Pregnancy

Ahluwalia, I. B., R. Merritt, L. F. Beck, and M. Rogers. 2001. "Multiple Lifestyle and Psychosocial Risks and Delivery of Small for Gestational Age Infants." *Obstetrics and Gynecology* 97:649–56.

Drews, C. D., C. C. Murphy, M. Yeargin-Allsopp, and P. Decoufle. 1996. "The Relationship Between Idiopathic Mental Retardation and Maternal Smoking During Pregnancy." *Pediatrics* 97:547–53.

Landgren, M., B. Kjellman, and C. Gillberg. 1998. "Attention Deficit Disorder with Developmental Coordination Disorders." *Archives of Disease in Childhood* 79:207–12.

Lorente, C., S. Cordier, J. Goujard, S. Aymé, F. Bianchi, E. Calzolari, H.E.K. De Walle, and R. Knill-Jones. 2000. "Tobacco and Alcohol Use During Pregnancy and Risk of Oral Clefts." *American Journal of Public Health* 90:415–19.

McDonald, S. D., S. L. Perkins, C. A. Jodouin, and M. C. Walker. 2002. "Folate Levels in Pregnant Women Who Smoke: An Important Gene/Environment Interaction." *American Journal of Obstetrics and Gynecology* 187:620–25.

Martin, J. A., B. E. Hamilton, S. J. Ventura, F. Menacker, and M. M. Park. 2002. "Births: Final Data for 2000." *National Vital Statistics Reports*, vol. 50, no. 5. National Center for Health Statistics: Hyattsville, MD.

Pollack, H., P. M. Lantz, and J. G. Frohna. 2000. "Maternal Smoking and Adverse Birth Outcomes Among Singletons and Twins." *American Journal of Public Health* 90:395–400.

Sørensen, H. T., B. Nørgård, L. Pedersen, H. Larsen, and S. P. Johnsen. 2002. "Maternal Smoking and Risk of Hypertrophic Infantile Pyloric Stenosis: 10 Year Population Based Cohort Study." *British Medical Journal* 325:1011–12.

Tarter, J. G., A. Khoury, J. R. Barton, D. L. Jacques, and B. M. Sibai. 2002. "Demographic and Obstetric Factors Influencing Pregnancy Outcome in Twin Gestations." *American Journal of Obstetrics and Gynecology* 186:910–12.

Wisborg, K., T. B. Henriksen, and N. J. Secher. 2001. "Maternal Smoking and Gestational Age in Twin Pregnancies." *Acta Obstetricia et Gynecologica Scandinavica* 80:926–30.

Childhood Health of Multiples

Akerman, B. A., and P. A. Thomassen. 1992. "The Fate of 'Small Twins': A Four-Year Follow-up Study of Low-Birthweight and Prematurely Born Twins." *Acta Genet Med Gemellol* 41: 97–104.

Brandes, J. M., A. Scher, J. Itkovits, et al. 1992. "Growth and Development of Children Conceived by In Vitro Fertilization." *Pediatrics* 90:424–29.

Leonard, C. H., R. E. Piecuch, R. A. Ballard, and B.A.B. Cooper. 1994. "Outcome of Very Low Birthweight Infants: Multiple Gestation Versus Singletons." *Pediatrics* 93:611–15.

Luke, B., S. Leurgans, L. G. Keith, and D. Keith. 1995. "The Childhood Growth of Twin Children." *Acta Genet Med Gemellol* 44:169–78.

Petterson, B., K. B. Nelson, L. Watson, and F. Stanley. 1993. "Twins, Triplets, and Cerebral Palsy in Births in Western Australia in the 1980s." *British Medical Journal* 307: 1239–43.

Saunders, K., J. Spensley, J. Munro, and G. Halasz. 1996. "Growth and Physical Outcome of Children Conceived by In Vitro Fertilization." *Pediatrics* 97:688–92.

Wilson, R. S. 1985. "Risk and Resilience in Early Mental Development." *Developmental Psychology* 21:795–805.

Complications

Arias, F. 1994. "Delayed Delivery of Multifetal Pregnancies with Premature Rupture of Membranes in the Second Trimester." *American Journal of Obstetrics and Gynecology* 170:1233–37.

Bajoria, R., J. Wigglesworth, and N. M. Fisk. 1995. "Angioarchitecture of Monochorionic Placentas in Relation to the Twin-Twin Transfusion Syndrome." *American Journal of Obstetrics and Gynecology* 172:856–63.

Berry, S. M., K. S. Puder, S. F. Bottoms, J. E. Uckele, R. Romero, and D. B. Cotton. 1995. "Comparison of Intrauterine Hematologic and Biochemical Values Between Twin Pairs with and Without Stuck Twin Syndrome." *American Journal of Obstetrics and Gynecology* 172:1403–10.

Coonrod, D. V., D. E. Hickok, K. Zhu, T. R. Easterling, and J. R. Daling. 1995. "Risk Factors for Preeclampsia in Twin Pregnancies: A Population-Based Cohort Study." *Obstetrics and Gynecology* 85:645–50.

De Lia, J. E., R. S. Kuhlmann, T. W. Harstad, and D. P. Cruikshank. 1995. "Fetoscopic Laser Ablation of Placental Vessels in Severe Previable Twin-Twin Transfusion Syndrome." *American Journal of Obstetrics and Gynecology* 172:1202–11.

Eberle, A. M., D. Levesque, A. M. Vinzileos, et al. 1993. "Placental Pathology in Discordant Twins." *American Journal of Obstetrics and Gynecology* 169:931–35.

Houlton, M.C.C., M. Marivate, and R. H. Philpott. 1982. "Factors Associated with Preterm Labour and Changes in the Cervix Before Labour in Twin Pregnancy." *British Journal of Obstetrics and Gynaecology* 89:190–94.

Kovacs, B. W., T. H. Kirschbaum, and R. H. Paul. 1989. "Twin Gestations: I. Antenatal Care and Complications." *Obstetrics and Gynecology* 74:313–17.

Mathews, T. J. 2001. "Smoking During Pregnancy in the 1990s." *National Vital Statistics Reports*, vol. 49, no. 7. National Center for Health Statistics: Hyattsville, MD.

Michaels, W. H., F. R. Schreiber, R. J. Padgett, J. Ager, and D. Pieper. 1991. "Ultrasound Surveillance of the Cervix in Twin Gestations: Management of Cervical Incompetency." *Obstetrics and Gynecology* 78:739–44.

Neilson, J. P., D.A.A. Verkuyl, C. A. Crowther, et al. 1988. "Preterm Labor in Twin Pregnancies: Prediction by Cervical Assessment." *Obstetrics and Gynecology* 72:719–23.

Newman, R. B., P. J. Gill, S. Campion, and M. Katz. 1989. "The Influence of Fetal Number on Antepartum Uterine Activity." *Obstetrics and Gynecology* 73:695–99.

Newman, R. B., R. K. Godsey, J. M. Ellings, et al. 1991. "Quantification of Cervical Change: Relationship to Preterm Delivery in the Multifetal Gestation." *American Journal of Obstetrics and Gynecology* 165:264–69.

Sicuranza, G. B., L. Weinstein, D. H. Saltzman, G. Farmakides, and D. Maulik. 1997. "Incidence of Gestational Diabetes in Multifetal Gestations." *Journal of Maternal-Fetal Investigation* 7:115–17.

Wolf, E. J., A. Mallozzi, J. F. Rodis, W. A. Campbell, and A. M. Vintzileos. 1992. "The Principal Pregnancy Complications Resulting in Preterm Birth in Singleton and Twin Gestations." *Journal of Maternal-Fetal Medicine* 1:206–12.

Corticosteroids Administered Prenatally

ACOG Committee Opinion No. 273. May 2003. "Antenatal Corticosteroid Therapy for Fetal Maturation."

Bloom, S. L., J. S. Sheffield, D. D. McIntire, and K. J. Leveno. 2001. "Antenatal Dexamethasone and Decreased Birth Weight." *Obstetrics and Gynecology* 97:485–90.

Elliott, J. P., and T. G. Radin. 1995. "The Effect of Corticosteroid Administration on Uterine Activity and Preterm Labor in High-Order Multiple Gestations." *Obstetrics and Gynecology* 85:250–54.

Hashimoto, L. N., R. W. Hornung, C. J. Lindsell, D. E. Brewer, and E. F. Donavan. 2002. "Effects of Antenatal Glucocorticoids on Outcomes of Very Low Birth Weight Multifetal Gestations." *American Journal of Obstetrics and Gynecology* 187:804–10.

National Institutes of Health Consensus Development Panel. 2001. "Antenatal Corticosteroids Revisited: Repeat Courses—National Institutes of Health Consensus Development Conference Statement, August 17–18, 2000." *Obstetrics and Gynecology* 98:144–50.

Schaap, A. H., H. Wolf, H. W. Bruinse, H. Smolders-De Haas, I. Van Ertbruggen, and P. E. Treffers. 2001. "Effects of Antenatal Corticosteroid Administration on Mortality and Long-Term Morbidity in Early, Preterm, Growth-Restricted Infants." *Obstetrics and Gynecology* 97:954–60.

Thorp, J. A., P. G. Jones, E. Knox, and R. H. Clark. 2002a. "Does Antenatal Corticosteroid Therapy Affect Birth Weight and Head Circumference?" *Obstetrics and Gynecology* 99:101–8.

Thorp, J. A., P. G. Jones, J. L. Peabody, E. Knox, and R. H. Clark. 2002b. "Effect of Antenatal and Postnatal Corticosteroid Therapy on Weight Gain and Head Circumference Growth in the Nursery." *Obstetrics and Gynecology* 99:109–15.

Walfisch, A., M. Hallak, and M. Mazor. 2001. "Multiple Courses of Antenatal Steroids: Risks and Benefits." *Obstetrics and Gynecology* 98:491–97.

Costs of Multiple Births

Callahan, T. L., J. E. Hall, S. L. Ettner, et al. 1994. "The Economic Impact of Multiple-Gestation Pregnancies and the Contribution of Assisted-Reproduction Techniques to Their Incidence." *New England Journal of Medicine* 331:244–49.

Chelmow, D., A. S. Penzias, G. Kaufman, and C. Cetrulo. 1995. "Costs of Triplet Pregnancy." *American Journal of Obstetrics and Gynecology* 172:677–82.

Goldfarb, J. M., C. Austin, H. Lisbona, B. Peskin, and M. Clapp. 1996. "Cost-Effectiveness of In Vitro Fertilization." *Obstetrics and Gynecology* 87:18–21.

Luke, B., H. R. Bigger, S. Leurgans, and D. Sietsema. 1996. "The Cost of Prematurity: A Case-Control Study of Twins Versus Singletons." *American Journal of Public Health* 86: 809–14.

Neuman, P. J., S. D. Gharib, and M. C. Weinstein. 1994. "The Cost of a Successful Delivery with In Vitro Fertilization." *New England Journal of Medicine* 331:239–43.

Exercise, Work, and Physical Activity During Pregnancy

American College of Obstetrics and Gynecologists, Opinion No. 267. 2002. "Exercise During Pregnancy and the Postpartum Period." *Obstetrics and Gynecology* 99:171–73.

Luke, B., M. Avni, L. Min, and R. Misiunas. 1999. "Work and Pregnancy: The Role of Fatigue and the 'Second Shift' on Antenatal Morbidity." *American Journal of Obstetrics and Gynecology* 181:1172–79.

Magann, E. F., S. F. Evans, B. Weitz, and J. Newnham. 2002. "Antepartum, Intrapartum, and Neonatal Significance of Exercise on Healthy Low-Risk Pregnant Working Women." *Obstetrics and Gynecology* 99:466–72.

Walker, S. P., M. Permezel, S. P. Brennecke, A. M. Ugoni, and J. R. Higgins. 2001. "Blood Pressure in Late Pregnancy and Work Outside the Home." *Obstetrics and Gynecology* 97: 361–65.

Home Uterine Activity Monitoring

Colton, T., H. L. Kayne, Y. Zhang, and T. Heeren. 1995. "A Meta-analysis of Home Uterine Activity Monitoring." *American Journal of Obstetrics and Gynecology* 173:1499–505.

Hill, W. C., A. D. Fleming, R. W. Martin, et al. 1990. "Home Uterine Monitoring Is Associated with a Reduction in Preterm Birth." *Obstetrics and Gynecology* 76:13S–18S.

Iams, J. D., F. F. Johnson, R. W. O'Shaughnessy, and L. C. West. 1987. "A Prospective Random Trial of Home Uterine Activity Monitoring in Pregnancies at Increased Risk of Preterm Labor" (pt. I). *American Journal of Obstetrics and Gynecology* 157:638–43.

Iams, J. D., F. F. Johnson, and R. W. O'Shaughnessy. 1988. "A Prospective Random Trial of Home Uterine Activity Monitoring in Pregnancies at Increased Risk of Preterm Labor" (pt. II). *American Journal of Obstetrics and Gynecology* 159:595–603.

Knuppel, R. A., M. F. Lake, D. L. Watson, et al. 1990. "Preventing Preterm Birth in Twin Gestation: Home Uterine Activity Monitoring and Perinatal Nursing Support." *Obstetrics and Gynecology* 76:24S–27S.

Merkatz, R. B., and I. R. Merkatz. 1991. "The Contributions of the Nurse and the Machine in Home Uterine Monitoring Systems." *American Journal of Obstetrics and Gynecology* 164: 1159–62.

Mou, S. M., S. G. Sunderji, S. Gall, et al. 1991. "Multicenter Randomized Clinical Trial of Home Uterine Activity Monitoring for Detection of Preterm Labor." *American Journal of Obstetrics and Gynecology* 165:858–66.

U.S. Preventive Services Task Force. 1993. "Home Uterine Activity Monitoring for Preterm Labor." *Journal of the American Medical Association* 270:369–70.

Wapner, R. J., D. B. Cotton, R. Artal, R. J. Librizzi, and M. G. Ross. 1995. "A Randomized Multicenter Trial Assessing a Home Uterine Activity Monitoring Device in the Absence of Daily Nursing Contact." *American Journal of Obstetrics and Gynecology* 172:1026–34.

Watson, D. L., R. A. Welch, F. G. Mariona, et al. 1990. "Management of Preterm Labor Patients at Home: Does Daily Uterine Activity Monitoring and Nursing Support Make a Difference?" *Obstetrics and Gynecology* 76:32S–35S.

Incidence of Multiple Births

Jewell, S. E., and R. Yip. 1995. "Increasing Trends in Plural Births in the United States." *Obstetrics and Gynecology* 85:229–32.

Kiely, J. L., J. C. Kleinman, and M. Kiely. 1992. "Triplets and Higher-Order Multiple Births." *American Journal of Diseases of Children* 146:862–68.

Luke, B. 1994. "The Changing Pattern of Multiple Births in the United States: Maternal and Infant Characteristics, 1973 and 1990." *Obstetrics and Gynecology* 84:101–6.

Martin, J. A., and S. M. Taffel. 1995. "Current and Future Impact of Rising Multiple Birth Ratios on Low Birthweight." *Statistical Bulletin* (April–June): 10–18.

Martin, J. A., M. F. MacDorman, and T. J. Mathews. 1997. "Triplet Births: Trends and Outcomes, 1971–1994." DHHS pub. no. (PHS) 97–1933. *Vital and Health Statistics*, series 21, no. 55.

Mushinski, M. 1994. "Trends in Multiple Births." *Statistical Bulletin* (July–September): 28–35.

Taffel, S. M. 1992. "Health and Demographic Characteristics of Twin Births: United States, 1988." DHHS pub. no. (PHS) 92–1928. *Vital and Health Statistics*, series 21, no. 50.

Wilcox, L. S., J. L. Kiely, C. L. Melvin, and M. C. Martin. 1996. "Assisted Reproductive Technologies: Estimates of Their Contribution to Multiple Births and Newborn Hospital Days in the United States." *Fertility and Sterility* 65:361–66.

Infant Mortality

Buekens, P., and A. Wilcox. 1993. "Why Do Small Twins Have a Lower Mortality Rate Than Small Singletons?" *American Journal of Obstetrics and Gynecology* 168:937–41.

Fowler, M. G., J. C. Kleinman, J. L. Kiely, and S. S. Kessel. 1991. "Double Jeopardy: Twin Infant Mortality in the United States, 1983 and 1984." *American Journal of Obstetrics and Gynecology* 165:15–22.

Franche, Renée-Louis. "Psychologic and Obstetric Predictors of Couples' Grief During Pregnancy After Miscarriage of Perinatal Death." Institute for Work and Health and University of Toronto, Ontario, Canada. 597 vol. 97, no. 4, April 2001, 0029–7844/01/PII S0029–7844 (00) 001199–96.

Joseph, K. S., S. Marcoux, A. Ohlsson, M. S. Kramer, A. C. Allen, S. Liu, K. Demissie, R. Sauve, and R. Liston. 2002. "Preterm Birth, Stillbirth and Infant Mortality Among Triplet Births in Canada, 1985–96." *Paediatric and Perinatal Epidemiology* 16:141–48.

Kaufman, G. E., F. D. Malone, K. B. Harvey-Wilkes, D. Chelmow, A. S. Penzias, and M. E. D'Alton. 1998. "Neonatal Morbidity and Mortality Associated with Triplet Pregnancy." *Obstetrics and Gynecology* 91:342–48.

Kiely, J. L. 1990. "The Epidemiology of Perinatal Mortality in Multiple Births." *Bulletin of the New York Academy of Medicine* 66:618–37.

Kiely, J. L. 1991. "Time Trends in Neonatal Mortality Among Twins and Singletons in New York City, 1968–1986." *Acta Genet Med Gemellol* 40:303–9.

Kiely, J. L., J. C. Kleinman, and M. Kiely. 1992. "Triplets and Higher-Order Multiple Births: Time Trends and Infant Mortality." *American Journal of Diseases of Children* 146:862–68.

Kilpatrick, S. J., R. Jackson, and M. S. Croughan-Minihane. 1996. "Perinatal Mortality in Twins and Singletons Matched for Gestational Age at Delivery at Thirty Weeks or More." *Obstetrics and Gynecology* 174:66–71.

Luke, B., and J. Minogue. 1994. "Contribution of Gestational Age and Birthweight to Perinatal Viability in Singletons Versus Twins." *Journal of Maternal-Fetal Medicine* 3:263–74.

Powers, W. F., and J. L. Kiely. 1994. "The Risks Confronting Twins: A National Perspective." *American Journal of Obstetrics and Gynecology* 170:456–61.

Powers, W. F., and N. S. Wampler. 1996. "Further Defining the Risks Confronting Twins." *American Journal of Obstetrics and Gynecology* 175:1522–28.

Zhang, J., W. A. Bowes, T. W. Grey, and M. J. McMahon. 1996. "Twin Delivery and Neonatal and Infant Mortality: A Population-Based Study." *Obstetrics and Gynecology* 88:593–98.

Infertility Treatments and Multiple Pregnancy

Bernasko, J., L. Lynch, R. Lapinski, and R. L. Berkowitz. 1997. "Twin Pregnancies Conceived by Assisted Reproductive Techniques: Maternal and Neonatal Outcomes." *Obstetrics and Gynecology* 89:368–72.

Bonduelle, M., I. Liebaers, V. Deketelaere, M.-P. Derde, M. Camus, P. Devroey, and A. Van Steirteghem. 2002. "Neonatal Data on a Cohort of 2,889 Infants Born After ICSI (1991–1999) and of 2,995 Infants Born After IVF (1983–1999)." *Human Reproduction* 17:671–94.

Centers for Disease Control and Prevention. 2000. "Contribution of Assisted Reproductive Technology and Ovulation-Inducing Drugs to Triplet and Higher-Order Multiple Births—United States, 1980–1997." *Morbidity and Mortality Weekly Report* 49(24):535–38.

Centers for Disease Control and Prevention. 2002. "Use of Assisted Reproductive Technology (ART)–United States, 1996 and 1998." *Morbidity and Mortality Weekly Report* 51(05):97–101.

Källen, B., P. O. Olausson, and K. G. Nygren. 2002. "Neonatal Outcome in Pregnancies from Ovarian Stimulation." *Obstetrics and Gynecology* 100:414–19.

Lambalk, C. B., and M. van Hooff. 2001. "Natural Versus Induced Twinning and Pregnancy Outcome: A Dutch Nationwide Survey of Primiparous Dizygotic Twin Deliveries." *Fertility and Sterility* 75:731–36.

Luke, B., E. Anderson, R. Misiunas, D. Martin, V. H. Gonzalez-Quintero, L. Tolaymat, M. J. O'Sullivan, F. R. Witter, R. B. Newman, M. D'Alton, E. A. Reece, and G.D.V. Hankins. 2001. "Do Outcomes Differ in Spontaneous vs Assisted-Conceived Twins? [abstract]" *American Journal of Obstetrics and Gynecology,* 185:S71.

Luke, B., M. B. Brown, E. Anderson, R. Misiunas, D. Martin, V. H. Gonzalez-Quintero, M. J. O'Sullivan, C. Nugent, C. van de Ven, F. R. Witter, J. Mauldin, R. B. Newman, G.D.V. Hankins, G. Saade, D. Grainger, and G. Macones. 2002. "Risk Factors for Adverse Outcomes in Spontaneous Versus Assisted-Conception Twin Pregnancies [abstract]." *American Journal of Obstetrics and Gynecology* 187:S82.

Skupski, D. W., S. Nelson, A. Kowalik, M. Polaneczky, M. Smith-Levitan, J. M. Hutson, and Z. Rosenwaks. 1996. "Multiple Gestations from In Vitro Fertilization: Successful Implantation Alone Is Not Associated with Subsequent Preeclampsia." *American Journal of Obstetrics and Gynecology* 175:1029–32.

Society for Assisted Reproductive Technology/American Fertility Society. 1993. "Assisted Reproductive Technology in the United States and Canada: 1991 Results from the Society for Assisted Reproductive Technology Generated from the American Fertility Society Registry." *Fertility and Sterility* 59:956–62.

Male Gender

Divon, M. Y., A. Ferber, H. Nisell, and M. Westgren. 2002. "Male Gender Predisposes to Prolongation of Pregnancy." *American Journal of Obstetrics and Gynecology* 187:1081–83.

Steier J. A., M. Ulstein, and O. L. Myking. 2002. "Human Chorionic Gonadotropin and Testosterone in Normal and Preeclamptic Pregnancies in Relation to Fetal Sex." *Obstetrics and Gynecology* 100:552–56.

Management and Outcome of Multiple Births

Albrecht, J. L., and P. G. Tomich. 1996. "The Maternal and Neonatal Outcome of Triplet Gestations." *American Journal of Obstetrics and Gynecology* 174:1551–56.

Bivins, H. A., R. B. Newman, J. M. Ellings, T. C. Hulsey, and A. Keenan. 1993. "Risks of Antepartum Cervical Examination in Multifetal Gestations." *American Journal of Obstetrics and Gynecology* 169:22–25.

Chappell, L. C., P. T. Seed, A. L. Briley, F. J. Kelly, R. Lee, B. J. Hunt, K. Parmar, S. J. Bewley, A. H. Shennan, P. J. Steer, and L. Poston. 1999. "Effect of Antioxidants on the Occurrence of Pre-eclampsia in Women at Increased Risk: A Randomized Trial." *The Lancet* 354:810–16.

Chappell, L. C., P. T. Seed, F. J. Kelly, A. Briley, B. J. Hunt, S. Charnock-Jones, A. Mallet, and L. Poston. 2002. "Vitamin C and E Supplementation in Women at Risk of Preeclampsia Is Associated with Changes in Indices of Oxidative Stress and Placental Function." *American Journal of Obstetrics and Gynecology*, 187:777–84.

Chien, L.-Y., R. Whyte, K. Aziz, P. Thiessen, D. Matthew, and S. K. Lee. 2001. "Improved Outcome of Preterm Infants When Delivered in Tertiary Care Centers." *Obstetrics and Gynecology* 98:247–52.

Collins, M. S., and J. A. Bleyl. 1990. "Seventy-one Quadruplet Pregnancies: Management and Outcome." *American Journal of Obstetrics and Gynecology* 162:1384–92.

Crowther, C. A., D.A.A. Verkuyl, M. F. Ashworth, C. Bannerman, and H. M. Ashurst. 1991. "The Effects of Hospitalization for Bedrest on Duration of Gestation, Fetal Growth, and Neonatal Morbidity in Triplet Pregnancy." *Acta Genet Med Gemellol* 40:63–68.

Eller, D. P., R. B. Newman, J. M. Ellings, et al. 1993. "Modifiable Determinants of Birthweight Variability in Twins." *Journal of Maternal-Fetal Medicine* 2:254–59.

Ellings, J. M., R. B. Newman, T. C. Hulsey, H. A. Bivins, and A. Keenan. 1993. "Reduction in Very Low Birthweight Deliveries and Perinatal Mortality in a Specialized, Multidisciplinary Twin Clinic." *Obstetrics and Gynecology* 81:387–91.

Elliott, J. P., and T. G. Radin. 1992. "Quadruplet Pregnancy: Contemporary Management and Outcome." *Obstetrics and Gynecology* 80:421–24.

Elster, A. D., J. L. Bleyl, and T. E. Craven. 1991. "Birthweight Standards for Triplets Under Modern Obstetric Care in the United States, 1984–1989." *Obstetrics and Gynecology* 77:387–93.

Fishman, A., D. K. Grubb, and B. W. Kovacs. 1993. "Vaginal Delivery of the Nonvertex Second Twin." *American Journal of Obstetrics and Gynecology* 168:861–64.

Friedman, S. A., E. Schiff, L. Kao, J. Kuint, and B. M. Sibai. 1997. "Do Twins Mature Earlier Than Singletons?" *American Journal of Obstetrics and Gynecology* 176:1193–99.

Garcia, F.A.R., H. B. Miller, G. R. Huggins, and T. A. Gordon. 2001. "Effect of Academic Affiliation and Obstetric Volume on Clinical Outcome and Cost of Childbirth." *Obstetrics and Gynecology* 97:567–76.

Gardner, M. O., M. A. Amaya, and J. Sakakini. 1990. "Effects of Prenatal Care on Twin Gestations." *Journal of Reproductive Medicine* 35:519–21.

Gardner, M. O., R. L. Goldenberg, S. P. Cliver, J. M. Tucker, K. G. Nelson, and R. L. Copper. 1995. "The Origin and Outcome of Preterm Twin Pregnancies." *Obstetrics and Gynecology* 85:553–57.

Gonzalez-Quintero, V. H., B. Luke, D. Martin, C. Nugent, R. B. Misiunas, E. Anderson, F. Witter, J. Mauldin, R. Newman, M. D'Alton, G. Hankins, and G. Saade. 2002. "The Hispanic Epidemiologic Paradox: Outcomes in Twin Pregnancies" [abstract]. *American Journal of Obstetrics and Gynecology* 187:S90.

Gonzalez-Quintero, V. H., B. Luke, M. J. O'Sullivan, R. Misiunas, E. Anderson, C. Nugent, F. Witter, J. Mauldin, R. Newman, M. D'Alton, D. Grainger, G. Saade, G. Hankins, and G. Macones. 2003. "Antenatal Factors Associated with Significant Birthweight Discordancy in Twins." *American Journal of Obstetrics and Gynecology* 189:813–17.

Greig, P. C., J.-C. Veille, T. Morgan, and L. Henderson. 1992. "The Effect of Presentation and Mode of Delivery on Neonatal Outcome in the Second Twin." *American Journal of Obstetrics and Gynecology* 167:901–6.

Hediger, M. L., B. Luke, R. Misiunas, D. Martin, M. J. O'Sullivan, F. R. Witter, J. G. Mauldin, R. B. Newman, G.D.V. Hankins, M. D'Alton, and E. A. Reece. 2001. "Fetal Growth Rates and Very Preterm Birth of Twins" [abstract]. *American Journal of Obstetrics and Gynecology* 185:S105.

Jones, J. S., R. B. Newman, and M. C. Miller. 1991. "Cross-Sectional Analysis of Triplet Birthweight." *American Journal of Obstetrics and Gynecology* 164:135–40.

Leveno, K. J., J. G. Quirk, P. J. Whalley, W.N.P. Herbert, and R. Trubey. 1984. "Fetal Lung Maturation in Twin Gestation." *American Journal of Obstetrics and Gynecology* 148:405–11.

Lipitz, S., R. Achiron, Y. Zalel, E. Mendelson, M. Tepperberg, and R. Gamzu. 2002. "Outcome of Pregnancies with Vertical Transmission of Primary Cytomegalovirus Infection." *Obstetrics and Gynecology* 100:428–33.

Luke, B. 1996. "Reducing Fetal Deaths in Multiple Births: Optimal Birthweights and Gestational Ages for Infants of Twin and Triplet Births." *Acta Genet Med Gemellol* 45:333–48.

Luke, B., M. B. Brown, R. Misiunas, E. Anderson, C. Nugent, C. van de Ven, B. Burpee, S. Gogliotti. 2003. "Specialized Prenatal Care and Maternal and Infant Outcomes in Twin Pregnancy." *American Journal of Obstetrics and Gynecology* 189:934–8.

Luke, B., R. Misiunas, E. Anderson, C. Nugent, M. Hediger, B. Burpee, and S. Gogliotti. 2002. "The Effects of a Prenatal Nutrition and Education Program on Neonatal and Early Childhood Outcomes in Twins" [abstract]. *American Journal of Obstetrics and Gynecology* 187:S83.

Luke, B., C. Nugent, C. van de Ven, D. Martin, M. J. O'Sullivan, S. Eardley, F. R. Witter, J. G. Mauldin, and R. B. Newman. 2002. "The Association Between Maternal Factors and Perinatal Outcomes in Triplet Pregnancies." *American Journal of Obstetrics and Gynecology* 187:752–57.

Malone, F. D., S. D. Craigo, D. Chelmow, and M. E. D'Alton. 1996. "Outcome of Twin Gestations Complicated by a Single Anomalous Fetus." *Obstetrics and Gynecology* 88:1–5.

Martin, J. A., B. E. Hamilton, S. J. Ventura, F. Menacker, and M. M. Park. 2002. "Births: Final Data for 2000." *National Vital Statistics Reports,* vol. 50, no. 5. National Center for Health Statistics: Hyattsville, MD.

Mauldin, J. G., R. B. Newman, P. D. Mauldin, M. Myers, and J. M. Ellings. 1998. "Specialized Twin Clinic: Has There Been a Difference in Neonatal Outcomes? [abstract]" *American Journal of Obstetrics and Gynecology* 178 (pt. 2):S80.

Meis, P. J., H. Klebanoff, E. Thom, et al. 2003. "Prevention of Recurrent Preterm Delivery by 17 Alpha-hydroxy-progesterone Caproate." *New England Journal of Medicine* 348:2379–85.

Menard, M. K., R. B. Newman, A. Keenan, and M. Ebeling. 1996. "Prognostic Significance of Prior Preterm Twin Delivery on Subsequent Singleton Pregnancy." *American Journal of Obstetrics and Gynecology* 174:1429–32.

Miller, D. A., P. Mullin, D. Hou, and R. H. Paul. 1996. "Vaginal Birth After Cesarean Section in Twin Gestation." *American Journal of Obstetrics and Gynecology* 175:194–98.

Min, S.-J., B. Luke, B. Gillespie, L. Min, R. B. Newman, J. G. Mauldin, F. R. Witter, F. A. Salman, and M. J. O'Sullivan. 2000. "Birthweight References for Twins." *American Journal of Obstetrics and Gynecology* 182:1250–57.

Min, S.-J., B. Luke, R. Misiunas, E. Anderson, C. Nugent, C. van de Ven, D. Martin, M. J. O'Sullivan, S. Eardley, F. R. Witter, J. G. Mauldin, and R. B. Newman. 2002. "Birthweight References for Triplets" [abstract]. *American Journal of Obstetrics and Gynecology* 187:S82.

Myles, T. D., J. Gooch, and J. Santolaya. 2002. "Obesity as an Independent Risk Factor for Infectious Morbidity in Patients Who Undergo Cesarean Delivery." *Obstetrics and Gynecology* 100:959–64.

Newman, R. B., and J. M. Ellings. 1995. "Antepartum Management of the Multiple Gestation: The Case for Specialized Care." *Seminars in Perinatology* 19:387–403.

Newman, R. B., P. J. Gill, and M. Katz. 1986. "Uterine Activity During Pregnancy in Ambulatory Patients: Comparison of Singleton and Twin Gestations." *American Journal of Obstetrics and Gynecology* 154:530–31.

Newman, R. B., R. K. Godsey, J. M. Ellings, B. A. Campbell, D. P. Eller, and C. Miller. 1991. "Quantification of Cervical Change: Relationship to Preterm Delivery in the Multifetal Gestation." *American Journal of Obstetrics and Gynecology* 165:264–71.

Newman, R. B., C. Hamer, and M. C. Miller. 1989. "Outpatient Triplet Management: A Contemporary Review." *American Journal of Obstetrics and Gynecology* 161:547–55.

Newman, R. B., J. S. Jones, and M. C. Miller. 1991. "Influence of Clinical Variables on Triplet Birthweight." *Acta Genet Med Gemellol* 40:173–79.

Nielsen, H. C., K. Harvey-Wilkes, B. MacKinnon, and S. Hung. 1997. "Neonatal Outcome of Very Premature Infants from Multiple and Singleton Gestations." *American Journal of Obstetrics and Gynecology* 177:653–59.

Palan, P. R., M. S. Mikhail, and S. L. Romney. 2001. "Placental and Serum Levels of Carotenoids in Preeclampsia." *Obstetrics and Gynecology* 98:459–62.

Patolia, D. S., R.L.M. Hilliard, E. C. Toy, and B. Baker. 2001. "Early Feeding After Cesarean: Randomized Trial." *Obstetrics and Gynecology* 98:113–16.

Peaceman, A. M., S. L. Dooley, and R. K. Tamura. 1992. "Antepartum Management of Triplet Gestations." *American Journal of Obstetrics and Gynecology* 167:1117–20.

Pons, J. C., L. Nekhlyudov, N. Dephot, S. Le Moal, and E. Papiernik. 1996. "Management and Outcomes of Sixty-five Quadruplet Pregnancies: Sixteen Years' Experience in France." *Acta Genet Med Gemellol* 45:367–75.

Prins, R. P. 1994. "The Second-Born Twin: Can We Improve Outcomes?" *American Journal of Obstetrics and Gynecology* 170:1649–57.

Ronnenberg, A. G., M. B. Goldman, D. Chen, I. W. Aitken, W. C. Willett, J. Selhub, and X. Xu. 2002. "Preconception Folate and Vitamin B_6 Status and Clinical Spontaneous Abortion in Chinese Women." *Obstetrics and Gynecology* 100:107–13.

Sattar, N., P. Clark, A. Holmes, M.E.J. Lean, I. Walker, and I. A. Greer. 2001. "Antenatal Waist Circumference and Hypertension Risk." *Obstetrics and Gynecology* 97:268–71.

Sattar, N., and I. A. Greer. 2002. "Pregnancy Complications and Maternal Cardiovascular Risk: Opportunities for Intervention and Screening?" *British Medical Journal* 325:157–60.

Seoud, M.A.F., J. P. Toner, C. Kruithoff, and S. J. Muasher. 1992. "Outcome of Twin, Triplet, and Quadruplet In Vitro Fertilization Pregnancies: The Norfolk Experience." *Fertility and Sterility* 57:825–34.

Skentou, C., A. P. Souka, M. S. To, A. W. Liao, and K. H. Nicolaides. 2001. "Prediction of Preterm Delivery in Twins by Cervical Assessment at 23 Weeks." *Ultrasound in Obstetrics and Gynecology* 17:7–10.

Syrop, C. H., and M. W. Varner. 1985. "Triplet Gestation: Maternal and Neonatal Implications." *Acta Genet Med Gemellol* 34:81–88.

Tarter, J. G., A. Khoury, J. R. Barton, D. L. Jacques, and B. M. Sibai. 2002. "Demographic and Obstetric Factors Influencing Pregnancy Outcome in Twin Gestations." *American Journal of Obstetrics and Gynecology* 186:910–12.

Vergani, P., A. Ghidini, G. Bozzo, and M. Sirtori. 1991. "Prenatal Management of Twin Gestation: Experience with a New Protocol." *Journal of Reproductive Medicine* 36:667–71.

Vutyavanich, T., T. Kraisarin, and R.-A. Ruangsri. 2001. "Ginger for Nausea and Vomiting in Pregnancy: Randomized, Double-Masked, Placebo-Controlled Trial." *Obstetrics and Gynecology* 97:577–82.

Wanty, S., B. Luke, M. Avni, B. Gillespie, and B. Lewis. 1998. "Improving Outcomes in Twin Gestations with Nursing and Nutrition Interventions [abstract]." *American Journal of Obstetrics and Gynecology* 178 (pt. 2):S81.

Xiong, X., W. D. Fraser, and N. N. Demianczuk. 2002. "History of Abortion, Preterm, Term Birth, and Risk of Preeclampsia: A Population-Based Study." *American Journal of Obstetrics and Gynecology* 187:1013–18.

Yukobowich, E., E. Y. Anteby, S. M. Cohen, Y. Lavy, M. Granat, and S. Yagel. 2001. "Risk of Fetal Loss in Twin Pregnancies Undergoing Second Trimester Amniocentesis." *Obstetrics and Gynecology* 98:231–34.

Maternal Age

Haebe, J., J. Martin, F. Tekepety, I. Tummon, and K. Sheperd. 2002. "Success of Intrauterine Insemination in Women Aged 40–42 Years." *Fertility and Sterility* 78:29–33.

Paulson, R. J., R. Boostanfar, P. Saadat, P. Mor, D. E. Tourgeman, C. C. Slater, M. M. Francis, and J. K. Jain. 2002. "Pregnancy in the Sixth Decade of Life." *Journal of the American Medical Association* 288:2320–23.

Rolett, A., and J. L. Kiely. 2000. "Maternal Sociodemographic Characteristics as Risk Factors for Preterm Birth in Twins Versus Singletons." *Paediatric and Perinatal Epidemiology* 14:211–18.

Zhang, J., S. Meikle, D. A. Grainger, and A. Trumble. 2002. "Multifetal Pregnancy in Older Women and Perinatal Outcomes." *Fertility and Sterility* 78:562–68.

Maternal Weight Gain in Multiple Births

Brown, J. E., and P. T. Schloesser. 1990. "Prepregnancy Weight Status, Prenatal Weight Gain, and the Outcome of Term Twin Gestations." *American Journal of Obstetrics and Gynecology* 162:182–86.

Casele, H., S. Dooley, and B. Metzger. 1996. "Metabolic Response to Meal Eating and Extended Overnight Fast in Twin Gestation [abstract]." *American Journal of Obstetrics and Gynecology* 174:375.

Dubois, S., C. Dougherty, M.-P. Duquette, J. A. Hanley, and J.-M. Moutquin. 1991. "Twin Pregnancy: The Impact of the Higgins Nutrition Intervention Program on Maternal and Neonatal Outcomes." *American Journal of Clinical Nutrition* 53:1397–1403.

Fenton, T. R., and J. E. Thirsk. 1994. "Twin Pregnancy: The Distribution of Maternal Weight Gain of Non-smoking Normal-Weight Women." *Canadian Journal of Public Health* 85:37–40.

Lantz, M. E., R. A. Chez, A. Rodriguez, and K. B. Porter. 1996. "Maternal Weight Gain Patterns and Birth Weight Outcome in Twin Gestation." *Obstetrics and Gynecology* 87:551–56.

Luke, B., E. Bryan, C. Sweetland, S. Leurgans, and L. Keith. 1995. "Prenatal Weight Gain and the Birthweight of Triplets." *Acta Genet Med Gemellol* 44:93–101.

Luke, B., B. Gillespie, S.-J. Min, M. Avni, F. R. Witter, and M. J. O'Sullivan. 1997. "Critical Periods of Maternal Weight Gain: Effect on Twin Birthweight." *American Journal of Obstetrics and Gynecology* 177:1055–62.

Luke, B., L. Keith, T.R.B. Johnson, and D. Keith. 1991. "Pregravid Weight, Gestational Weight Gain, and Current Weight of Women Delivered of Twins." *Journal of Perinatal Medicine* 19:333–40.

Luke, B., L. Keith, J. A. Lopez-Zeno, F. R. Witter, and E. Saquil. 1993. "A Case-Control Study of Maternal Gestational Weight Gain and Newborn Birthweight and Birth Length in Twin Pregnancies Complicated by Preeclampsia." *Acta Genet Med Gemellol* 42:7–15.

Luke, B., and S. Leurgans. 1996. "Maternal Weight Gains in Ideal Twin Outcomes." *Journal of the American Dietetic Association* 96:178–81.

Luke, B., S.-J. Min, B. Gillespie, et al. 1998. "The Importance of Early Weight Gain on the Intrauterine Growth and Birthweight of Twins." *American Journal of Obstetrics and Gynecology* 179:1155–61.

Luke, B., L. Min, M. L. Hediger, F. R. Witter, R. B. Newman, J. G. Mauldin, and M. J. O'Sullivan. 2003. "Body Mass Index–Specific Weight Gains Associated with Optimal Birthweights in Twin Pregnancies." *Journal of Reproductive Medicine* 48:217–24.

Luke, B., J. Minogue, H. Abbey, L. Keith, F. R. Witter, T. I. Feng, and T.R.B. Johnson. 1992. "The Association Between Maternal Weight Gain and the Birthweight of Twins." *Journal of Maternal-Fetal Medicine* 1:267–76.

Luke, B., J. Minogue, F. R. Witter, L. G. Keith, and T.R.B. Johnson. 1993. "The Ideal Twin Pregnancy: Patterns of Weight Gain, Discordancy, and Length of Gestation." *American Journal of Obstetrics and Gynecology* 169:588–97.

Pederson, A. L., B. Worthington-Roberts, and D. E. Hickok. 1989. "Weight Gain Patterns During Twin Gestation." *Journal of the American Dietetic Association* 89:642–46.

Neonatal and Infant Health of Multiples

Berg, K. A., J. A. Astemborski, J. A. Boughman, and C. Ferencz. 1989. "Congenital Cardiovascular Malformations in Twins and Triplets from a Population-Based Study." *American Journal of Diseases of Children* 143:1461–63.

Fraser, D., R. Picard, E. Picard, and J. R. Leiberman. 1994. "Birthweight Discordance, Intrauterine Growth Retardation and Perinatal Outcomes in Twins." *Journal of Reproductive Medicine* 39:504–8.

Luke, B., E. Anderson, R. Misiunas, C. Nugent, and C. van de Ven. 2002. "A Comparison of Neonatal and Early Childhood Differences in Growth and Development of Twins Versus Triplets" [abstract]. *American Journal of Obstetrics and Gynecology* 187:S83.

Luke, B., M. Hediger, R. Misiunas, E. Anderson, C. Nugent, B. Burpee, and S. Gogliotti. 2002. "Fetal, Neonatal, and Early Childhood Growth and Development of Monochorionic Twins" [abstract]. *American Journal of Obstetrics and Gynecology* 187:S84.

Luke, B., and L. G. Keith. 1992. "The Contribution of Singletons, Twins, and Triplets to Low Birthweight, Infant Mortality, and Handicap in the United States." *Journal of Reproductive Medicine* 37:661–66.

Luke, B., J. Minogue, and F. R. Witter. 1993. "The Role of Fetal Growth Restriction and Gestational Age on Length of Hospital Stay in Twin Infants." *Obstetrics and Gynecology* 81:949–53.

Luke, B., C. Nugent, M. Hediger, R. Misiunas, and E. Anderson. 2002. "Fetal Phenotypes and Neonatal and Early Childhood Outcomes in Twins" [abstract]. *American Journal of Obstetrics and Gynecology* 187:S83.

Stening, W., P. Nitsch, G. Wassmer, and B. Roth. 2002. "Cardiorespiratory Stability of Premature and Term Infants Carried in Infant Slings." *Pediatrics* 110:879–83.

Wolf, E. J., A. M. Vintzileos, T. S. Rosenkrantz, et al. 1992. "A Comparison of Pre-discharge Survival and Morbidity in Singleton and Twin Very Low Birthweight Infants." *Obstetrics and Gynecology* 80:436–39.

Omega-3 Fatty Acids and Antioxidants

Adair, C. D., L. Sanchez-Ramos, D. L. Briones, and P. Ogburn. 1996. "The Effect of High Dietary n-3 Fatty Acid Supplementation on Angiotensin II Pressor Response in Human Pregnancy." *American Journal of Obstetrics and Gynecology* 175:688–91.

Chappell, L. C., P. T. Seed, A. L. Briley, F. J. Kelly, R. Lee, B. J. Hunt, K. Parmar, S. J. Bewley, A. H. Shennan, P. J. Steer, and L. Poston. 1999. "Effect of Antioxidants on the Occurrence of Pre-eclampsia in Women at Increased Risk: A Randomized Trial. *The Lancet* 354:810–16.

Chappell, L. C., P. T. Seed, F. J. Kelly, A. Briley, B. J. Hunt, S. Charnock-Jones, A. Mallet, and L. Poston. 2002. "Vitamin C and E Supplementation in Women at Risk of Preeclampsia Is Associated with Changes in Indices of Oxidative Stress and Placental Function." *American Journal of Obstetrics and Gynecology,* 187:777–84.

Lemay, A., S. Dodin, N. Kadri, H. Jacques, and J.-C. Forest. 2002. "Flaxseed Dietary Supplement Versus Hormone Replacement Therapy in Hypercholesterolemic Menopausal Women." *Obstetrics and Gynecology* 100:495–504.

Olsen, S. F., and N. J. Secher. 2002. "Low Consumption of Seafood in Early Pregnancy as a Risk Factor for Preterm Delivery: Prospective Cohort Study. *British Medical Journal* 324:447–50.

Reece, M. S., J. A. McGregor, K.G.D. Allen, and M. A. Harris. 1997. "Maternal and Perinatal Long-Chain Fatty Acids: Possible Roles in Preterm Birth." *American Journal of Obstetrics and Gynecology* 176:907–14.

Velzing-Aarts, F., F.R.M. van der Klis, F.P.L. van der Dijs, and F.A.J. Muskiet. 1999. "Umbilical Vessels of Preeclamptic Women Have Low Contents of Both n-3 and n-6 Long-Chain Polyunsaturated Fatty Acids." *American Journal of Clinical Nutrition* 69:293–98.

Weisinger, H. S., J. A. Armitage, A. J. Sinclair, A. J. Vingrys, P. L. Burns, and R. S. Weisinger. 2001. "Perinatal Omega-3 Fatty Acid Deficiency Affects Blood Pressure Later in Life." *Nature Medicine* 7:258–59.

Williams, M. A., R. W. Zingheim, I. B. King, and A. M. Zebelman. 1995. "Omega-3 Fatty Acids in Maternal Erythrocytes and Risk of Preeclampsia." *Epidemiology* 6:232–37.

Postpartum Depression

Josefsson, Ann, M.D., Lisbeth Angelsiö, M.D., Göran Berg, M.D., Ph.D., Carl-Magnus Ekström, M.D., Christina Gunnervik, M.D., Conny Nordin, M.D., Ph.D., and Gunilla Sydsjö, Ph.D. 2002. "Obstetric, Somatic, and Demographic Risk Factors for Postpartum Depressive Symptoms." 223 vol. 99, no. 2, February 0029-7844/02. © 2002 by The American College of Obstetricians and Gynecologists. Published by Elsevier Science Inc. PII S0029-7844(01)01722-27.

Selective Multifetal Reduction

Alexander, J. M., K. R. Hammond, and M. P. Steinkampf. 1995. "Multifetal Reduction of High-Order Multiple Pregnancy: Comparison of Obstetrical Outcome with Nonreduced Twin Gestations." *Fertility and Sterility* 64:1201–3.

Berkowitz, R. L., and L. Lynch. 1990. "Selective Reduction: An Unfortunate Misnomer." *American Journal of Obstetrics and Gynecology* 75:873–74.

Berkowitz, R. L., L. Lynch, U. Chitkara, I. A. Wilkins, K. E. Mehalek, and E. Alvarez. 1988. "Selective Reduction of Multifetal Pregnancies in the First Trimester." *New England Journal of Medicine* 318:1043–47.

Berkowitz, R. L., L. Lynch, J. Stone, and M. Alvarez. 1996. "The Current Status of Multi-fetal Pregnancy Reduction." *American Journal of Obstetrics and Gynecology* 174:1265–72.

Bollen, N., M. Camus, H. Tournaye, A. Wisanto, A. C. Van Steirteghem, and P. Devroey. 1993. "Embryo Reduction in Triplet Pregnancies After Assisted Procreation: A Comparative Study." *Fertility and Sterility* 60:504–9.

Boulot, P., B. Hedon, G. Pelliccia, P. Peray, F. Laffargue, and J. L. Viala. 1993. "Effects of Selective Reduction in Triplet Gestation: A Comparative Study of Eighty Cases Managed with and Without This Procedure." *Fertility and Sterility* 60:497–503.

Brandes, J. M., J. Itskovitz, A. Scher, and R. Gershoni-Baruch. 1990. "The Physical and Mental Development of Co-sibs Surviving Selective Reduction of Multifetal Pregnancies." *Human Reproduction* 5:1014–17.

Depp, R., G. A. Macones, M. F. Rosenn, E. Turzo, R. J. Wapner, and V. J. Weinblatt. 1996. "Multifetal Pregnancy Reduction: Evaluation of Fetal Growth in the Remaining Twins." *American Journal of Obstetrics and Gynecology* 174:1233–40.

Evans, M. I., R. L. Berkowitz, R. J. Wapner, et al. 2001. "Improvement in Outcomes of Multifetal Pregnancy Reduction with Increased Experience." *American Journal of Obstetrics and Gynecology* 184:97–103.

Evans, M. I., M. Dommergues, R. J. Wapner, et al. 1993. "Efficacy of Transabdominal Multifetal Pregnancy Reduction: Collaborative Experience Among the World's Largest Centers." *American Journal of Obstetrics and Gynecology* 82:61–66.

Evans, M. I., J. C. Fletcher, I. E. Zador, B. W. Newton, M. H. Quigg, and C. D. Struyk. 1988. "Selective First-Trimester Termination in Octuplet and Quadruplet Pregnancies: Clinical and Ethical Issues." *Obstetrics and Gynecology* 71:289–96.

Groutz, A., I. Yovel, A. Amit, Y. Yaron, F. Azem, and J. B. Lessing. 1996. "Pregnancy Outcome After Multifetal Pregnancy Reduction to Twins Compared to Spontaneously Conceived Twins." *Human Reproduction* 11:1334–36.

Haning, R. V., D. B. Seifer, C. A. Wheeler, G. N. Frishman, H. Silver, and D. J. Pierce. 1996. "Effects of Fetal Number and Multifetal Reduction on Length of In Vitro Fertilization Pregnancies." *Obstetrics and Gynecology* 87:964–68.

Luke, B., E. Anderson, R. Misiunas, D. Martin, V. H. Gonzalez-Quintero, L. Tolaymat, M. J. O'Sullivan, F. R. Witter, R. B. Newman, M. D'Alton, E. A. Reece, and G. D. V. Hankins. 2001. "Do Outcomes Differ in Spontaneous vs Assisted-Conceived Twins?" [abstract]. *American Journal of Obstetrics and Gynecology*, 185:S71.

Luke, B., M. B. Brown, V. H. Gonzalez-Quintero, C. Nugent, F. R. Witter, and R. B. Newman. 2004. "Risk Factors for Adverse Outcomes in Spontaneous VS Assisted–Conception Twin Pregnancies." *Fertility and Sterility* 81:315–19.

Lynch, L., R. L. Berkowitz, J. Stone, M. Alvarez, and R. Lapinski. 1996. "Preterm Delivery After Selective Termination in Twin Pregnancies." *Obstetrics and Gynecology* 87:366–69.

Macones, G. A., G. Schemmer, E. Pritts, B. Weinblatt, and R. J. Wapner. 1993. "Multifetal Reduction of Triplets to Twins Improves Perinatal Outcome." *American Journal of Obstetrics and Gynecology* 169:982–86.

Melgar, C. A., D. L. Rosenfeld, K. Rawlinson, and M. Greenberg. 1991. "Perinatal Outcome After Multifetal Reduction to Twins Compared with Nonreduced Multiple Gestations." *Obstetrics and Gynecology* 78:763–67.

Porreco, R. P., M. S. Burke, and M. L. Hendrix. 1991. "Multifetal Reduction of Triplets and Pregnancy Outcome." *Obstetrics and Gynecology* 78:335–39.

Rebarber, A., C. A. Carreno, H. Lipkind, E. F. Funai, J. Maturi, E. Kuczynski, and C. Lockwood. 2001. "Cervical Length After Multifetal Pregnancy Reduction in Remaining Twin Gestations. *American Journal of Obstetrics and Gynecology* 185:1113–17.

Silver, R. K., B. T. Helfand, T. L. Russell, A. Ragin, J. S. Sholl, and S. N. MacGregor. 1997. "Multifetal Reduction Increases the Risk of Preterm Delivery and Fetal Growth Restriction in Twins: A Case-Control Study." *Fertility and Sterility* 67:30–33.

Smith-Levitan, M., A. Kowalik, J. Birnholz, D. W. Skupski, J. M. Hutson, F. A. Chervenak, and Z. Rosenwaks. 1996. "Selective Reduction of Multifetal Pregnancies to Twins Improves Outcome over Nonreduced Triplet Gestations." *American Journal of Obstetrics and Gynecology* 175:878–82.

Tocolytics

Couser, R. J., R. E. Hoekstra, T. B. Ferrara, G. B. Wright, A. K. Cabalka, and J. E. Connett. 2000. "Neurodevelopmental Follow-up at 36 Months' Corrected Age of Preterm Infants Treated with Prophylactic Indomethacin." *American Journal of Public Health* 154:598–602.

Suarez, R. D., W. A. Grobman, and B. V. Parilla. 2001. "Indomethacin Tocolysis and Intraventricular Hemorrhage." *Obstetrics and Gynecology* 97:921–25.

Suarez, V. R., L. L. Thompson, V. Jain, G. L. Olson, G.D.V. Hankins, M. A. Belfort, and G. R. Saade. 2002. "The Effect of In Utero Exposure to Indomethacin on the Need for Surgical Closure of a Patent Ductus Arteriosus in the Neonate." *American Journal of Obstetrics and Gynecology* 187:886–88.

Ultrasound Determination of Chorionicity

D'Alton, M. E., and D. K. Dudley. 1989. "The Ultrasonographic Prediction of Chorionicity in Twin Gestation." *American Journal of Obstetrics and Gynecology* 160:557–61.

Monteagudo, A., I. E. Timor-Tritsch, and S. Sharma. 1994. "Early and Simple Determination of Chorionic and Amniotic Type in Multifetal Gestations in the First Fourteen Weeks by High-Frequency Transvaginal Ultrasonography." *American Journal of Obstetrics and Gynecology* 170:824–29.

Scardo, J. A., J. M. Ellings, and R. B. Newman. 1995. "Prospective Determination of Chorionicity, Amnionicity, and Zygosity in Twin Gestations." *American Journal of Obstetrics and Gynecology* 173:1376–80.

Sepulveda, W., N. J. Sebire, A. Odibo, A. Psarra, and K. H. Nicolaides. 1996. "Prenatal Determination of Chorionicity in Triplet Pregnancy by Ultrasonographic Examination of the Ipsilon Zone." *Obstetrics and Gynecology* 88:855–58.

Vayssière, C. F., N. Heim, E. P. Camus, Y. E. Hillion, and I. F. Nisand. 1996. "Determination of Chorionicity in Twin Gestations by High-Frequency Abdominal Ultrasonography: Counting the Layers of the Dividing Membrane." *American Journal of Obstetrics and Gynecology* 175:1529–33.

Index

Demerol, 201
denial, 179–80, 187
depression, 181–84
DES, 145
developmental delays, 296
developmental specialists, 34, 225
diabetes, gestational, 146–47
diamniotic, 375
diaper bags, 284, 287
diaper ointment, 288
diaper rash, 288
diapers, 281, 282
diarrhea, 288, 152
dichorionic, 375
dieting, breast-feeding and, 262
dietitians, 35–36, 77, 78, 225
dilation, 156, 196, 375
dining room, baby-proofing of, 289
discomforts of pregnancy, *see* pregnancy discomforts
dizygotic (DZ) twins, 8–9, 11, 375
    see also fraternal twins
DNA-short tandem amplified repeat (DNA-STAR)
    testing, 10
doctors, 31, 37–42
    see also specific types of doctors
donor eggs, 295–96
Doppler, 14
Doppler flow studies, 50, 375
Down syndrome, 46, 48
dried tomatoes and clams, linguine with, 334
drug use, 38
dry skin, 111
ducts, clogged, 262, 266
ductus arteriosus, 228, 375
due date, of multiples, 3, 25–28, 150
Dumplings, Chicken and, 325

ectopic pregnancies, 179, 375
effacement of cervix, 156, 196, 204, 375
Eggland's Best, 79
eggs, 79, 82, 93
electronic fetal monitoring, 199, 200, 375
embryos, 7, 16–18, 375
emotional stages, 177–86
emotions, 177–94
    body image and, 192–94
    of family, 190–91
    of friends and acquaintances, 191–92
    of husbands, 187–89
    insensitive comments and, 191–92, 193
endometrium, 7, 16, 17, 375
epidural block, 201, 205, 206, 210
epidural catheter, 201, 203
episiotomy, 205, 375

equipment for multiples, 283–85
erythromycin, 217
estrogen, 118
evening, as transition, 280–81
exercise:
    after delivery, 299
    while on bedrest, 166–71
    during pregnancy, 134–36
external version, 375

facial abnormalities, 231
family
    childbearing experiences of, 38
    multiple pregnancy and, 190–91
Family and Medical Leave Act (FMLA) of 1993,
    140, 141
family doctors, 29, 30, 33, 37
fast food, 101
fathers, *see* husbands
fats, 73, 74, 78, 227
fatty acids, essential, 74, 375
favoritism, parent-infant bonding and, 295
feeding, 249–70
    on demand, 247, 276
    first, 218
    nipple, 222, 232, 236, 263–65
    of premature infants, 231–32
    on schedule, 276
    see also bottle feeding; breast-feeding
fertility specialists, 30, 37
fertilization, 7, 376
fetal alcohol syndrome (FAS), 114
fetal distress, 208
fetal fibronectin, 47
fetal fibronectin test, 47–48
fetuses, 19–25, 225, 376
    alcohol and, 113–14
    cigarettes and, 115–16
    food plan and, 66
    growth of, 20, 66
    head size of, 116–17, 159
    malnutrition of, 114
    movement of, 14
    oxygen flow to, 131
    varying growth rates of, among multiples,
        147–48
fevers, 213
fiber, 75, 78, 83, 84, 88, 89
first aid, infant, 287
fish, fish oils, 79, 82, 91
flax seed, 79, 91
focus, of pregnant women, 189
folic acid, 78, 83, 84, 87, 116, 253
food groups, 76–80